James Douglas Ogilby

Edible Fishes and Crustaceans of New South Wales

James Douglas Ogilby

Edible Fishes and Crustaceans of New South Wales

ISBN/EAN: 9783337325060

Printed in Europe, USA, Canada, Australia, Japan

Cover: Foto ©Andreas Hilbeck / pixelio.de

More available books at **www.hansebooks.com**

Published by Authority of the New South Wales Commissioners for the World's Columbian Exposition, Chicago, 1893.

Edible Fishes and Crustaceans

OF

NEW SOUTH WALES.

BY

J. DOUGLAS OGILBY.

WITH ILLUSTRATIONS.

SYDNEY: CHARLES POTTER, GOVERNMENT PRINTER.

1893.

[3s.]

INTRODUCTION.

...resent volume must not be considered otherwise than as a... ...ent of a much larger and more important work, which it is ... ...I shall include within its scope the entire fishing industr... ...he Colony, and which it is hoped will be completed within a few years.

For the proper production of a work, dealing exhaustively with the edible fishes of New South Wales, a much longer time would be necessary than was available for the preparation of this volume; and that for several reasons, the chief of which are, that the number of species to be included under that category would have to be raised from 93 as here described to about double that number, and that the life history of almost every species and the distribution of many would have to be worked out by personal observation, which would necessitate a considerable amount of both coastal and inland travel.

The almost total want of reliable evidence on this latter subject, and the apathy and ignorance of those who are brought in daily contact with our food fishes, as forming their means of livelihood, has greatly impeded the author in his endeavor to place before the public as full an account as possible of all such points in connection with the habits of the selected species as would be interesting and useful, and in none has so much difficulty been experienced in obtaining information as in that which concerns the most important function of their lives—the continuation of their species. So little interest has been taken in this subject by those whose means of livelihood depend so closely on it, that there are but few, even of our most abundant fishes, of which the date of spawning is known, while as for the more difficult questions, such as the localities where the ova are deposited, the attachment to foreign substances or the flotation of the ova, and the length of time which elapses before the young fish emerges therefrom, absolutely nothing is known.

With regard to the distribution of the fishes found on our coast New South Wales enjoys a geographical position, which is unique among these colonies, and makes its fish-fauna in some respects even more interesting than that of its neighbors either to the north or the south, for, whereas that of Queensland is enriched by numerous tropical forms, and those of Victoria and Tasmania by the fishes peculiar to the colder waters of the temperate zone, we from our position combine both faunas, many tropical forms, such as *Lutianus* and *Chœrops*, finding their way to the Sydney market from our northern fishing stations, while southern forms, such as *Sebastes* and *Pseudophycis*, occur as far up our coast as the Port Jackson District. The author has had great difficulty in ascertaining even approximately the respective northerly or southerly range of such forms, the absence of local lists and of reliable correspondents proving a serious drawback.

Where only a limited number of species were allowed it became necessary for the author to confine himself to such species as occurred in the Sydney market in greater or less abundance during the preparation of the present work, and, except in the case of our freshwater food fishes which were not obtainable by that means, this arrangement has been strictly adhered to; several well known and excellent fishes have, therefore, been unavoidably omitted, among which may be mentioned the Hairtail (*Trichiurus*), Dory (*Zeus*), River Catfish (*Copidoglanis*), Giant Herrings (*Megalops*, *Chanos*, and *Elops*), Conger (*Conger*), and Silver Eel (*Murænesox*).

The synonymy has also been a source of much trouble and anxiety to the author; it has, nevertheless, been made as full as circumstances permitted, but there was not sufficient time to go thoroughly into the subject, which is rendered doubly difficult by the careless manner in which some Australian writers describe their supposed new species; in the case of large genera many of these descriptions are equally applicable to half a dozen well known species.

J. DOUGLAS OGILBY.

Sydney, July, 1893.

Edible Fishes of New South Wales.

Class.—PISCES.

Fishes are cold-blooded Vertebrate Animals, which are almost exclusively adapted for an aquatic existence; which almost invariably respire by means of specialized organs, known as gills or *branchiæ*, these being persistent throughout life and the functional agents by which the oxygen is dissolved from the surrounding water; which have the limbs for the most part modified into paired fins—the pectorals taking the place of the mammalian arm, the ventrals that of the lower limb—supplemented by unpaired fins—the dorsal, anal, and caudal—situated on the median axis of the body, and chiefly used for the purposes of keeping the body erect and as organs of progression, the latter function being in most fishes wholly confined to the caudal; which have the heart divided into two cavities, one auricle and one ventricle only; and which are scaleless, partially or wholly scaled, or protected by osseous plates.

Fishes are for the most part oviparous; some, however, are ovoviviparous, both methods being not uncommonly present in members of the same family; for instance, our familiar Blenniid genus *Cristiceps* is strictly ovoviviparous, while the equally common allied genus *Petroscirtes* is as strictly oviparous.

Subclass I.—TELEOSTEI.

Skeleton osseous. Brain distinct. Skull possessing cranial bones. Vertebræ completely formed: the vertebral column bony, or with a bony plate posteriorly, diphycercal, or homocercal. Branchiæ free: the water discharged through a single aperture, which is protected by a bony gillcover. Branchiostegal rays present. Heart with a non-contractile bulbus arteriosus, having a pair of proximal valves. Optic nerves decussating. Intestines without spiral valve.

Order I.—*ACANTHOPTERYGII*.

Part of the dorsal, anal, and ventral fins unarticulated, forming spines. Hypopharyngeal bones generally separated. Airbladder, when present, without pneumatic duct in the adult.

In several families of Acanthopterygian Fishes no true spines are present. Among the families which are included in the New South Wales fauna, the *Trichonotidæ* with *Hemerocœtes* and the *Gobiesocidæ* with *Diplocrepis*, both containing small species of no commercial value, may be mentioned as typical of this modification.

Refering to this, Günther (Study of Fishes, p. 374) remarks:—" The Acanthopterygians do not form a perfectly natural group, some heterogeneous elements being mixed up with it; neither are the characters by which it is circumscribed absolutely distinctive. In some forms (certain Blenniids) the structure of the fins is almost the same as in Anacanths." And "the presence or absence of a pneumatic duct"—to the airbladder—"loses much of its value as a taxonomic character, when we consider that probably in all fishes a communication between the pharynx and the airbladder exists at an early stage of development."

Family I.—PERCIDÆ.

Branchiostegals six or seven: pseudobranchiæ generally present (rudimentary in *Lates*). Body oblong or oblong-ovate, rarely elevated or cylindrical. Eyes lateral. Opercles strongly denticulated or spiniferous. Mouth in front of the snout, with lateral cleft, which is horizontal or slightly oblique. Teeth in the jaws villiform, with or without canines: present or absent on the vomer, palatines, and tongue. Dorsal fins generally separated: ventrals thoracic. Scales ctenid or cyclid, small or of moderate size. Lateral line continuous. Airbladder present or absent, simple. Pyloric appendages in small numbers.

Geographical distribution.—Carnivorous fishes, inhabiting chiefly the fresh waters and estuaries of both hemispheres; a few species marine, but never wandering far from land, nor descending beyond a moderate depth.

Genus I.—PERCALATES.

Lates, part. Günther, Ann. Nat. Hist. (3) 1863, xi. p. 114.
Percalates, Rms. & Ogl. Proc. Linn. Soc. N. S. Wales (2), 1887, ii. p. 182.

Branchiostegals six: pseudobranchiæ present. Body oblong-ovate and somewhat compressed. Opercle with two spines: preopercle serrated on the vertical limb, denticulated on the angle and lower limb: preorbital serrated. Villiform teeth on the jaws, vomer, and palatines: tongue smooth. One dorsal fin, deeply notched, with nine spines: the anal with three. Scales moderate, ctenid, absent on the upper surface of the head: bases of the vertical fins scaly. Airbladder large. Pyloric appendages in small numbers.

Geographical distribution.—South-eastern and southern coasts of Australia; northern Tasmania.

PERCALATES COLONORUM.

Lates colonorum, Gnth. Ann. Nat. Hist. (3) 1863, xi. p. 114; Casteln. Proc. Zool. Soc. Vict. 1872, i. p. 43, *and* Proc. Linn. Soc. N. S. Wales, iii. p. 365; McCoy, Prodr. Zool. Vict. dec. ii. pl. 14; Macleay, Catal. Austr. Fish. i. p. 4; Woods, Fisher. N. S. Wales, p. 31, pl. i; Johnston, Proc. Roy. Soc. Tas. 1882, pp. 59, 110.
Dules novem-aculeatus, Steindach. SB. Ak. Wien, 1866, liii. p. 428, pl. ii. fig. 1.
Lates similis, Casteln. Proc. Zool. Soc. Vict. 1872, i. p. 44; Macleay, Catal. Austr. Fish. i. p. 5.
Lates antarcticus, Casteln. Proc. Zool. Soc. Vict. 1872, i. p. 44; Macleay, Catal. Austr. Fish. i. p. 5.
Lates victoriæ, Casteln. Proc. Zool. Soc. Vict. 1872, i. p. 45; Macleay, Catal. Austr. Fish. i. p. 5.
Lates curtus, Casteln. Res. Fish. Austr. p. 5, 1875; Macleay, Catal. Austr. Fish. i. p. 6.
Lates ramsayi, Macleay, Catal. Austr. Fish. i. p. 6, 1881.

Perch.

Plate I.

B. vi. D. 9 (8–10)/10 (9–11). A. 3/7–9. V. 1/5. P. 14–16. C. 17. L. lat. 48–55. L. tr. 8–9/17–21. Cœc. pyl. 10. Vert. 11/14.

Length of head 3·33–4·00, of caudal fin 4·75–5·25, height of body 2·75–3·50 in the total length. Diameter of eye 3·66–4·75 in the length of the head, and 0·75–1·20 in that of the snout: interorbital space slightly convex, from 1·00–1·25 in the diameter of the eye. Nostrils close together, the posterior the larger. Upper profile of head concave, with two longitudinal ridges between the eyes. Lower jaw the longer. Cleft of mouth wide and oblique, the maxilla extending to beneath the middle or somewhat beyond the middle of the orbit. Preorbital denticulated on its lower margin, which is sinuous: vertical limb of preopercle slightly concave and finely serrated: angle and lower limb with a variable number of strong spines, those on the latter directed downwards and generally forwards: opercle with two divergent spines, the lower much the longer and more acute, not seldom subdivided at the tip into two or more points: posttemporal with from four to six strong teeth, which become obsolete with age: clavicular bones with or without serrature. Teeth villiform in the jaws, palatines, and vomer, forming on the latter a subcrescentic band; tongue smooth. The dorsal commences a little behind the base of the pectoral and ends opposite to the middle anal ray; the spinous and rayed portions are subequal in height; the spines are strong, the fourth the longest, four times as long as the first, and from 2·00–2·66 in the length of the head; the length of the base of the rayed dorsal is normally from 1·40–1·60 in that of the spinous; the last spine is one third longer than that which precedes it: the anal commences beneath the third or fourth dorsal ray; the third spine is the longest, 3·00–3·66 in the length of the head, and much shorter than the anterior rays, which are equal in length to those of the dorsal: the ventral reaches almost to the vent; its length is from 1·55–1·70 in that of the head, and the spine is equal to the third or fifth dorsal spines: pectoral small and rounded, reaching to beneath the sixteenth or seventeenth scale of the lateral line, 1·75–2·00 in the length of the head: caudal emarginate, the pedicle much compressed, its least height 2·50–3·00 in the height of the body. Cheeks and opercles, except the outer limb of the preopercle, and a small patch on the temporal region scaly, those behind the inner preopercular margin much the smallest; rest of the head naked. Lateral line slightly sinuous and rising anteriorly, thence almost straight below the spinous dorsal, behind which it descends with a gentle curve to the free tail, along the middle of which it is straight. Airbladder large.

Colors.—Upper surfaces olive green, the head very dark; sides and lower surfaces gray washed with yellow: all the fins dark green.

A few words are necessary here with regard to the forms of the Australian Perch described as new by Castelnau and Macleay, the types of all of which are missing. In 1872 the former created three new species to which he gave the names *Lates similis, L. antarcticus,* and *L. victoriæ*; to these, between the above date and 1881, he added a fourth species, *L. curtus,* from the Richmond River. In 1876 Alleyne and Macleay described, under the name *Pseudolates cavifrons,* a North Australian fish, and in the following year the latter author redescribed the same species as *Lates darwiniensis*; these two names may be at once dismissed from consideration as being mere synonyms of the widely distributed *L. calcarifer,* as an examination of the type specimens at once reveals. Finally in 1881 Macleay described a *L. ramsayi* from a single specimen taken in a freshwater pool near Parramatta, the type of which is also missing. We have, therefore, in the restricted genus *Percalates* no less than five supposititious species, excluding the original *P. colonorum*, all described from a similar and somewhat limited area on what appears to be insufficient grounds; that none of the later writers on Australian fishes (Johnston, Catalogue of Tasmanian Fishes, 1882; McCoy, loc. cit. 1878, and Lucas, Census of Victorian Fishes, 1889), except the author (Catalogue of New South Wales Fishes, 1885), venture an opinion on their specific identity or otherwise, is, it must be conceded, a most unsatisfactory state of affairs, and merits, therefore, a more extended inquiry than is usually necessary in such cases.

In *L. similis* the characters relied on for its separation from the type species are absurdly inadequate; these are the shorter snout, which is "sensibly less than the diameter of the eye"; with the majority of fishes the comparative size of the eye to the head and to the snout varies with the age of the individual, the young fish having that organ much larger proportionately than the adult; as I have shown above the great variation existing between the comparative measurements of the eye and the snout in twenty five specimens of indubitable *P. colonorum* ranging from Adelaide to the Richmond River, it is manifest that the stress laid upon this character is altogether misleading, and must be regarded as valueless; the coarser denticulations of the preopercle are also a sign of immaturity, and as such unreliable; in the large series which has passed through our hands specimens have in rare instances occurred in which the teeth of the lower preopercular limb were directed absolutely downwards; neither this character nor that of the omission of one of the dorsal rays can, therefore, be taken as a valid reason for separating *L. similis* from Günther's well known species.

It is unnecessary to go at any length into the question of the validity of *L. antarcticus*, since, with two exceptions, a comparison of Castelnau's description with that given above will show that no characters are given, which are not equally common to *P. colonorum*. These are the increased number of branchiostegal rays which is stated to be seven in this species as against six which the examination of numerous specimens has shown to be the normal number in *P. colonorum* as here and elsewhere stated, and also recorded by Professor McCoy. I do not, however, attach any importance to this seeming discrepancy, since it is probable that that number is merely copied from the generic description of *Lates* given by Günther (Catalogue of Fishes, i. p. 67) and which is correct of that genus as restricted to the two species *L. niloticus* and *L. calcarifer*; it may be further pointed out that in few, if any, of his other descriptions of new genera or species does Castelnau take any notice of this important point: the second exception, namely the coloration, is not of sufficient importance to justify the retention of *L. antarticus* as a distinct form, and this name also must, therefore, sink into a synonym of the typical species; further on (p. 5) the author will have occasion to refer to a form which, by a casual observer, would at once be set down as distinct, but which, scientifically examined, is easily seen to be no more than a local variety of the common Australian Perch due to the greatly changed conditions under which it exists; this form may possibly be the *L. antarcticus* of Castelnau, though, if so, it is difficult to say why he should especially designate it the "Sea Perch."

Of *L. victoriæ* it is needless to say more than that no rational person is likely to believe that the substitution of a four pointed for a single pointed spine on the opercle is by itself sufficient to constitute a species.

In Castelnau's last form, *L. curtus*, it is only necessary to point out that no reliance can be placed on the depth of the type specimen as indicative of even a variety; the proportion of height to length is given by him as 1 : 3·33, but examples from Port Stephens, Shoalhaven, Shellharbor, and Ulladulla, examined by the writer in preparation of this work, ranged as low as from 1 : 2·75 to 1 : 3·50; this character, therefore, having been proved invalid, and there being no other on which to rely, it follows that *L. curtus* must be merged in *P. colonorum*.

Nothing then remains but to consider the claims of Macleay's *L. ramsayi*, and a very cursory glance at the description suffices to show that no claims to specific recognition can be with justice urged in its behalf. Stress seems to have been laid by its author on the fact of this, to him, unique example having been provided with ten dorsal spines and seven anal rays; variations such as these are, as has been shown above, by no means so uncommon as is generally supposed, though the coincidence of their occurrence in the same individual is no doubt much more rare; in no other character does Macleay's diagnosis differ from that of individual specimens of our common Perch, and it, therefore, with the preceding four, must be relegated to the list of useless synonyms. The fact of its having been taken in a landlocked waterhole doubtless had some effect on its external appearance and thus helped to deceive its describer.

Mention was made above of a variety of the common Perch which differed greatly in outward appearance from the ordinary form; so far these fishes have been sent to the Australian Museum only from the pools in the Snowy River, immediately below the Falls, but without doubt other rivers, both of this and the sister Colony, will, now that notice is drawn to the form, be found to have evolved under similar circumstances a similar variety. The differences, between it and the common market fish, which present themselves at a casual glance are the much more elongated habit, the proportionately longer and more powerful fins, and, though this is a much less important characteristic, the brilliant silvery color of the fish; a moment's thought, however, will suggest that these differences, however important they may at first sight appear, are only to be expected in fishes living under conditions which differ so greatly from those under which the species normally exists, for, being practically forced to inhabit rapidly running waters, subject to sudden, severe, and periodical floods, caused for the most part by the melting of the snow on Kosciusko and the neighboring Ranges, it is patent that their changed surroundings and conditions of life would induce a change in the direction indicated.

To Mr. A. M. N. Rose, of Campbelltown, we are indebted for the knowledge of this well marked form, that gentleman having forwarded at our request two specimens, the first taken at Christmas, the second late in the autumn, to the Australian Museum; neither of these fishes showed the slightest traces of spawning, though, if they breed in the river, it is incredible that the season selected for the deposition of its ova by a fish notoriously fond of warm sheltered spots, should be other than one of the two seasons during which our informant forwarded them. Mr. Rose, however, is of opinion that these fishes do not breed, at least not in the river, and he bases his opinion on the facts, certified to us by him, and through him to us by other residents of the district, that the examples caught vary but little in size, the average length being from fourteen to eighteen inches, that no young fish have ever been observed, that no matter at what season of the year they are captured no milt or roe is present, that they are always in fine condition, and finally that they infinitely excel the estuary Perch in flavor.

The obvious inference is that certain individuals having made their way into the Snowy River at its embouchure into the ocean gradually work upwards and eventually find themselves in the pool below the Falls, and, being unable to proceed, remain there until captured or swept down by flood to the estuary again; these latter, having since their forced return into calmer and warmer waters, grown sybaritic and fat, may possibly be Castelnau's "not very common" *L. antarcticus*, which he describes as "silvery" and "very savory."

With a coast line such as that of New South Wales, extending from lat. 28° 13' S., its northern border at Point Danger, to lat. 37° 30' S. on its southern at Cape Howe, the season or seasons of spawning necessarily vary greatly, but with very few species have such extended observations been recorded as to make the data reliable; it may, however, be taken for granted that the periods as a rule occur earlier in our northern and warmer waters than on our southern seaboard.*

From personal observation of many examples obtained from different localities between Port Stephens and Ulladulla, the Perch spawn during the latter half of June and the earlier half of July only. In the Clarence River District the date, however, is given as July and August.

Their food consists of small fishes and crustaceans, but in one instance seaweeds and corallines alone were detected. As a table fish they are of fair quality; and being voracious they give good sport to river anglers, greedily taking such baits as worms, grubs, prawns, small frogs, &c. It attains to a weight of five pounds at least, and according to Tenison Woods even reaches seven and a half pounds.

The Perch is common in the rivers and estuaries along the entire coast line of the colony at least as far north as the Richmond River, but according to Saville Kent "does not so far appear to have been met with in Queensland waters;" in Victoria it is abundant, the Gippsland Lakes being especial strongholds of the species, while in South Australia it extends at least as far west as the embouchure of the Murray; in Tasmania it appears to be for the most part confined to the "fresh and brackish landlocked waters of the north-east coast" (Johnston), while in a subsequent paper this author states that it is "confined to Anson's River," where it is "abundant all the year round."

Genus II.—ENOPLOSUS.

Enoplosus, Lacépède, Hist. Nat. Poiss. iv. p. 541, 1802; Cuv. & Val. Hist. Nat. Poiss. ii. p. 133, 1828.

Branchiostegals seven: pseudobranchiæ present. Body elevated and strongly compressed. Opercle spineless: preopercle coarsely serrated on both limbs; the produced angle with strong spines: preorbital denticulated. Villiform teeth on the jaws, vomer, palatines, and tongue. Two dorsal fins, the first with eight spines: the anal with three: all the fins, except the caudal, much elongated. Scales moderate, cycloid: bases of the vertical fins scaly. Airbladder large. Pyloric appendages in moderate numbers

Geographical distribution.—South-eastern coasts of Australia.

ENOPLOSUS ARMATUS.

Chætodon armatus, White, Voy. N. S. Wales, pl. xxxix. fig. 1, 1790.
Enoplosus whitii, Lacép. Hist. Nat. Poiss. iv. p. 541.
Enoplosus armatus, Cuv. & Val. Hist. Nat. Poiss. ii. p. 133, pl. xx; Gnth. Catal. Fish. i. p. 81; Casteln. Proc. Zool. Soc. Vict. i. 1872, p. 47; Macleay, Catal. Austr. Fish. i. p. 9; Woods, Fisher. N. S. Wales, p. 32, pl. ii.

---

* This remark is of course intended to apply equally to all our marine or estuarine fishes.

Old Wife.

B. vii. D. S. 1 14–15. A. 3/14–15. V. 1/5. P. 13–14. C. 17. L. lat. 53–60. L. tr. 14/36–40. Cœc. pyl. 15. Vert. 10/17.

Length of head 3·50–4·00, of caudal fin 3·80–4·00, height of body 2·40–2·66 in the total length. Diameter of eye 3·25–3·60 in the length of the head: snout short, its length from 1·10–1·40 in the diameter of the eye: interorbital space flat, with a deep median groove, 1·50–2·00 in the same. Nostrils moderately close together, simple, the anterior round, the posterior oval and slightly the larger. Upper profile of head very concave. Lower jaw the longer. Cleft of mouth small and oblique, the maxilla extending a little beyond the anterior margin of the orbit. Preorbital with five or six strong teeth, the posterior one much the stoutest and pointed directly backwards: preopercle with both limbs strongly serrated, and with the angle much produced, bearing two spines, the upper of which is the strongest, curved, and directed upwards and backwards. Teeth in the jaws villiform with an outer enlarged series anteriorly; those on the vomer in a subtriangular patch; on the palatines in an elevated arcuate band; tongue with a median band. The dorsal commences above the posterior angle of the base of the pectoral and ends above the tenth or eleventh anal ray; the three anterior spines are short and correspond diversely to the last three; the fourth is strong and greatly elevated, its length from one tenth to one third longer than that of the head, and from 1·33–2·00 in that of the first ray which is a little longer than the second, and more than twice as long as the fourth, the third being intermediate, and the remainder short; the length of the base of the first dorsal is from 1·15–1·40 in that of the second: the anal commences beneath the origin of the second dorsal, its spines are strong, the third the longest, from 1·66–2·00 in the length of the head, to which the first ray is equal: the ventral reaches to the third or fourth anal ray, and its length is equal to or as much as one fourth longer than that of the head: pectoral pointed, extending as far back as the ventral, and subequal in length to the head: caudal emarginate with the lobes produced; the least height of its pedicle equal to the distance between the last anal ray and the origin of the caudal. Upper surface of head and preorbital scaleless. Lateral line strongly curved to beneath the middle dorsal rays.

Colors.—Silvery white, with eight blackish vertical bands, the first from immediately behind the occiput passing obliquely forwards and downwards through the eye, and sending two narrow branches along the interorbital space to the snout; the second from in front of the first dorsal to the base of the ventral; the third very broad, beneath the first dorsal, and extending on to that fin; the fourth narrow, beneath the dorsal interspace; the fifth broad, between the soft dorsal and the anal, and continued to the extremities of their elongated rays; the sixth narrow, from behind the dorsal to the last anal rays; the seventh across the caudal pedicle, and the eighth across the base of the caudal fin.

Nothing is known of the breeding habits of the "Old Wife," by which name this species is exclusively known in Port Jackson, although it is excessively common there, frequenting wharves and sheltered places, and probably attaching its ova to the tangle.

Being an excellent little fish for the table it is to be regretted that it does not appear in the market in greater quantities, this being due to its preference for rocky localities, where the seine cannot be used.

E. armatus is abundant in the bays and estuaries of South-eastern Australia from Moreton Bay to Port Phillip, and, though it has not been so far recorded, is probably found in similar spots in northern Tasmania. Its westward range extends at least as far as St. Vincent's Gulf, from which locality Castelnau received specimens from Waterhouse. In addition to the trivial name used here it is known at Melbourne as "Bastard Dory" owing to its shape and the prolongation of the rays of the vertical fins, and "Zebra-fish" from its striped appearance. It attains to a length of nine inches in Port Jackson, but referring to the Melbourne market Castelnau states that "in winter the specimens are small and do not measure more than from four to six inches; but in the warm months (December and January) they are much larger, and some are nearly a foot long." He further remarks that these large examples are generally females with well developed ova; the breeding season, therefore, in the southern Colony would appear to be the latter part of the summer.

Family II.—SERRANIDÆ.

Branchiostegals seven, rarely six or eight : pseudobranchiæ present. Body oblong or ovate. Eyes lateral. Opercles denticulated or spiniferous. Mouth in front of the snout, with lateral cleft, which is slightly oblique. Teeth in the jaws villiform, with or without canines : teeth on the vomer and palatines : absent or present on the tongue. Dorsal fin generally continuous : ventrals thoracic. Scales ctenid, rarely cyclid, small or of moderate size. Lateral line continuous. Airbladder present, simple. Pyloric appendages in small or moderate numbers, or numerous.

Geographical distribution.—Carnivorous fishes of tropical and temperate seas, sometimes ascending rivers.

Genus I.—SERRANUS.

Serranus, sp. Cuvier, Règne Anim.; Cuv. & Val. Hist. Nat. Poiss. ii. p. 210, 1828.

Branchiostegals seven : pseudobranchiæ present. Body oblong. Eyes lateral, of moderate size. Opercle with two or three flat spines : preopercle with its vertical limb more or less serrated, and its horizontal one usually entire. Teeth villiform, with distinct canines present in both jaws : teeth on the vomer and palatines : tongue naked. One dorsal fin with from eight to twelve spines : the anal with three. Scales small, ctenid or cyclid. Pyloric appendages in large, moderate, or small numbers.

The Sea Perches frequent the coasts of all temperate and tropical countries, and sometimes ascend to a great distance up rivers for predatory purposes, one species having been found as high up the Ganges as the confines of Nepal; none, however, so far as has been ascertained spawn in fresh water. About one hundred and fifty species are known, many of which are most handsomely colored. (Gunther, Study of Fishes, p. 381.)

SERRANUS DÆMELI.

Serranus damelii, Gnth. Ann. Nat. Hist. (4) 1876, xvii. p. 391 ; Casteln. Proc. Linn. Soc. N. S. Wales, iii. p. 365 ; Macleay, Proc. Linn. Soc. N. S. Wales, viii. p. 254 ; Woods, Fisher. N. S. Wales, p. 33.

Black Rock-Cod.

Plate II.

B. vii. D. 11/14. A. 3/8. V. 1/5. P. 18. C. 17. L. l. 110-122. L. tr. 23/58-61. Cœc. pyl. num. Vert. 10/14.

Length of head 2·70-3·00, of caudal fin 5·25-5·75, height of body 3·75-4·20 in the total length. Diameter of eye 5·50-7·00 in the length of the head, and 1·00-1·66 in that of the snout, which is obtusely rounded: interorbital space flat, 1·20-1·80 in the diameter of the eye. Upper profile of head slightly convex. Lower jaw the longer. Cleft of mouth large and a little oblique; maxilla remiform, extending to beneath the posterior margin of the eye in immature, to half a diameter behind the eye in adult, examples. Preoperele with a shallow emargination above the angle; the vertical limb finely serrated, the angle more coarsely so: opercle with three strong spines, the middle being the longest. Jaws with a pair—rarely two pairs—of anterior canines; mandible with several series of stout, sharp, cardiform teeth, the inner row being the larger; maxilla with similar but longer teeth in front, and an outer enlarged row laterally, inside of which is a band of minute teeth; vomer with an angular, palatines with a narrow elongate band of small cardiform teeth. Dorsal spines strong, the third or fourth the longest, 3·20-3·66 in the length of the head, the others very gradually decreasing in height to the last; rays subequal, longer than the spines: the anal commences beneath the anterior dorsal ray, and ends a little in front of the termination of that fin; the third spine is a little longer than the second, and is about equal in length to the second dorsal spine; the rays are considerably longer than those of the dorsal, and about twice as long as the third spine: length of the ventral about two thirds of the distance between its origin and the vent, and from 2·25-2·60 in the length of the head: pectorals rounded, their length 1·80-2·00 in the same: caudal rounded, the least height of the pedicle from 2·50-3·00 in the height of the body. Scales minute, ctenid, firmly adherent; the vertical fins with a row between the basal half of the rays; snout, upper half of the preorbital, and the maxilla scaleless. Lateral line following the curvature of the back.

Colors.—Body and fins deep blue black, uniform in the adult: young examples with or without scattered lighter spots on the sides of the head and body, and a black spot crossing the caudal pedicle above: spinous dorsal with a darker, soft dorsal and anal with a lighter submarginal band.

Although well known to be one of the best and highest priced of our edible fishes, and to be present in large numbers along our coastline at least as far south as Jervis Bay, absolutely nothing is known as to its habits during the season of reproduction, nor to the places selected for the deposition of the ova; this, it is most probable, is upon rocky weed-covered ground at a moderate depth. They are only taken by line, and being exceedingly voracious are easily hooked, but from their great strength and the determination with which they fight for their lives very heavy tackle has to be employed for their capture. They affect bold rocky coasts and islands only, and are never found on the sandy beaches.

Fishes, crustaceans, mollusca and radiata, form the greater portion of its food. Examples weighing up to fifteen pounds are excellent for the table, but beyond that weight they grow coarser, the very large examples being almost uneatable.

The Black Rock-Cod, or Black Sea-Perch as it should more properly be termed, is found in numbers along the entire coastline of New South Wales, at least as far south as Jervis Bay, but it has not been recorded from either Victorian or Tasmanian waters. Northwards its range is not so easily determinable, but is probably considerable, as it has been recorded from Normanby Island in the D'Entrecasteaux Group, off the extreme south-eastern shore of New Guinea, where Goldie obtained it in fresh water, presuming that Macleay's identification is correct.

They are abundant at Lord Howe Island where they are much appreciated by the inhabitants on account of their size and excellence.

In the Sydney market it is now rare to see one weighing so much as twenty pounds, but as we proceed northwards the size gradually increases. The district lying between the Macleay and Clarence Rivers has long been known to be a most prolific ground for the pursuit of this species, and at the Solitaries, a group of small islands lying about midway between these points they are reported to have been captured of the weight of a hundred pounds; be this as it may a specimen taken at Lord Howe Island measured forty two inches, and turned the scale at seventy five pounds, while subsequently a mutilated example was brought to the Australian Museum, Sydney, which measured no less than fifty four inches, and would probably, when perfect, have equalled or perhaps exceeded the larger weight.*

Genus II.—PLECTROPOMA.

Plectropoma, Cuvier, Règne. Anim.; Cuv. & Val. Hist. Nat. Poiss. ii. p. 387, 1828.

Branchiostegals seven: pseudobranchiæ present. Body oblong. Opercle with two or three flat spines: preopercle with the vertical limb serrated, the horizontal limb bearing spinous teeth which are directed forwards. Teeth villiform, with canines in both jaws: vomer and palatines toothed: tongue smooth. One dorsal fin, with from seven to thirteen spines: the anal with three. Scales small or of moderate size, ctenoid or cycloid. Pyloric appendages in small numbers.

Geographical distribution.—About thirty species, many of which are brilliantly ornamented, inhabit the seas of tropical and subtropical regions.

PLECTROPOMA ANNULATUM.

Plectropoma annulatum, Gnth. Catal. Fish. i. p. 158, 1859, *and* Brenchl. Cruise of the Curaçoa, p. 415, pl. xxviii. fig. B.; Casteln. Proc. Linn. Soc. N. S. Wales, iii. p. 369.

Banded Sea-Perch.

B. vii. D. 10/18. A. 3/7. V. 1/5. P. 15-16. C. 17. L. lat. 46-48. L. tr. 7/19-21. Vert. 10/17.

Length of head 2·50-2·75, of caudal fin 5·75-6·15, height of body 2·80-3·00 in the total length. Diameter of eye 4·33-4·75 in the length of the head, and equal to or rather more than that of the snout: interorbital

---

* In the *Sydney Morning Herald* Mr. Philip Cohen asserted, and, notwithstanding that we pointed out the vast difference between the two species, reasserted that this fish grows to a weight of three hundred pounds and upwards; any student of zoology can tell that the large fish, to which he refers, is the Giant Perch, *Polyprion prognathus*, more commonly known as *Oligorus gigas*.

space concave, owing to the great projection of the supraorbital margin; its breadth from 1·40–1·66 in the diameter of the eye. A slight concavity on the occiput. Lower jaw the longer. Cleft of mouth wide and oblique; maxilla triangular, extending to between the middle and the posterior third of the orbit. Opercle with three spines, the middle the largest, the upper minute: preopercle rounded, the vertical limb finely serrated; a compressed, frequently bicuspid, spine at the angle; horizontal limb with two spines pointing downwards and forwards: posttemporal and clavicular bones spiniferous. Teeth in the jaws in villiform bands, with two or three pairs of canines anteriorly in each, the outer in the upper jaw being much the strongest; mandible with from one to three pairs of lateral canines; an angular band of minute teeth on the vomer, and a narrow elongate band on the palatines. Dorsal spines strong, the first and last equal in length, the fourth and fifth the longest, 2·25–2·50 in the length of the head; the membrane very deeply notched; dorsal rays not nearly so high as the spines; base of soft dorsal 1·15–1·33 in that of the spinous: the anal commences beneath the first dorsal ray and ends beneath the fourteenth; the second spine is very strong and a little longer than the third, 2·66–2·85 in the length of the head; the rays are slightly longer than the spines, and much longer than those of the dorsal: ventrals small, their length about two thirds of the distance between their origin and the vent, and 2·10–2·50 in that of the head: pectorals rounded and well developed, reaching to above the anal spines, 1·40–1·55 in the same: caudal slightly rounded, the least height of its pedicle about two sevenths of the height of the body. Scales moderate, ctenid, firmly adherent; basal half of all the fins scaly; snout and anterior half of preorbital scaleless. Lateral line approximately following the curvature of the back.

Colors.—Red, deepest above; head with four black bands; the first straight and short, commencing between the posterior margins of the eyes and extending backwards along the occiput; the second slightly curved from the postero-superior angle of the orbit to the hinder edge of the occiput; the third arcuate, from behind the middle of the eye to the origin of the dorsal; the fourth slightly curved crossing the opercle; body with six vertical black bands, the anterior four extending on to the dorsal, and the middle two on to the anal fin.

Though occurring at all seasons of the year in the Sydney market the Banded Sea-Perch appears in larger quantities and more regularly during the warmer months, when they visit Port Jackson and Broken Bay for the purpose of spawning, retiring during the colder months to deeper water. They are essentially rock-fishes, and are almost invariably associated with the Red Rock-Cods (*Scorpæna*), being taken by hook along with them. Their food is similar to that of the last species, and their flesh is firm, flaky, and pleasant.

They attain to a length of eight inches.

PLECTROPOMA NIGRORUBRUM.

Plectropoma nigrorubrum, Cuv. & Val. Hist. Nat. Poiss. ii. p. 402, 1828; Quoy & Gaim. Voy. Astrolabe, Poiss. p. 659, pl. iv. fig. 1; Gnth. Catal. Fish. i. p. 158; Macleay, Catal. Austr. Fish. i. p. 22; Ogilby, Proc. Linn. Soc. N. S. Wales, x. p. 119.

Cuvier's Sea-Perch.

B. vii. D. 10/17–18.   A. 3/8–9.   V. 1/5.   P. 13.   C. 15.   L. lat. 55–58. L. tr. 6/24–25.   Cœc. pyl. 8.

Length of head 2·70–2·80, of caudal fin 5·50–5·75, height of body 3·50–3·66 in the total length.   Diameter of eye 5·40–6·00 in the length of the head, and 1·25–1·40 in that of the snout: interorbital space concave, its breadth 2·33–2·60 in the diameter of the eye.   Nostrils small and moderately distant, the anterior with a low circular rim, which is extended from its inferior margin to and around the upper margin of the hinder nostril. Upper profile of head flat.   Lower jaw the longer.   Cleft of mouth wide and oblique, the maxilla reaching to beneath the hinder margin of the orbit or not quite so far.   Opercle with three spines, the middle one much the longest, the upper short, blunt, and concealed beneath the skin: preopercle rounded, with the vertical limb armed with sharp equal sized denticulations, the angle and lower limb with three, rarely four, strong teeth directed forwards and downwards, the anterior of which is the strongest; posttemporal and clavicular bones spineless.   A broad band of villiform teeth in the jaws, with two or three pairs of small canines anteriorly; one or two pairs of lateral canines in the lower jaw; vomerine teeth in an obtusely angular band; palatines with a narrow curved band.   The dorsal commences above the opercular spine; the first spine is the shortest, less than one third of the fourth or fifth, which are the longest, from 2·75–3·10 in the length of the head; the rays are subequal in height to the spines, and the basal length of the rayed fin is one tenth less than that of the spinous: the anal commences beneath the second or third dorsal ray, and ends beneath the thirteenth or fourteenth; its spines are stronger than those of the dorsal, the second the strongest and a little longer than the third, its length from 3·75–4·00 in that of the head; the rays are fully twice as long as the spines, and much longer than those of the dorsal: ventral pointed, the second ray the longest, three fourths of the distance between its origin and the vent, and from 2·00–2·20 in the length of the head; the spine is short, not half the length of the rays: pectoral pointed, the seventh ray the longest, reaching to the vertical from the vent, and 1·50–1·70 in the same: caudal very slightly rounded, the least height of its pedicle 2·50 in the height of the body.   Soft dorsal with a deep, anal with a low scaly sheath; scales on the head very small.

Colors.—Red, clouded above with dusky brown, below with yellow; body with five dark transverse bands.

This fish is never common in the Sydney market, but occasionally a few are to be seen in company with the next species; the only specimen examined in which the ova were fully developed was caught in the beginning of August.   Their food consists of small fishes, crustaceans, and molluscs, the former predominating in all those which have been examined hitherto. Although this fish has been long known from Port Jackson and King George's Sound I am not aware of its having been recorded from any intermediate locality.

Ten inches is about the maximum size to which the species attains.

PLECTROPOMA OCELLATUM.

Plectropoma cyanostigma, Gnth. Catal. Fish. i. p. 161 (*not Bleeker*).
Plectropoma ocellatum, Gnth. Catal. Fish. i. p. 504, 1859, *and* Brenchl. Cruise of the Curacoa, p. 416, pl. xxix.; Macleay, Catal. Austr. Fish. i. p. 23; Woods, Fisher. N. S. Wales, p. 34.
Plectropoma myriaster, Steindachn. SB. Ak. Wien, 1866, liii. p. 426, pl. i. fig. 3.

Wirrah.

B. vii. D. 13/15.   A. 3/8.   V. 1/5.   P. 19–20.   C. 17.   L. lat. ca. 100.   L. tr. 23–24/58–60.   Cœc. pyl. 9.   Vert. 10/16.

Length of head 2·80–3·00, of caudal fin 5·66–6·00, height of body 3·00–3·66 in the total length. Eye small, situated high up on the head, its diameter 5·50–5·80 in the length of the head, and 1·50 in that of the snout: interorbital space slightly convex, its breadth 1·33–1·66 in the diameter of the eye. Jaws equal. Cleft of mouth wide and oblique, the maxilla almost reaching to beneath the posterior margin of the orbit. Opercle with three spines, the middle being the longest, the lower minute: preopercle rounded, the vertical limb and angle coarsely serrated, the horizontal limb with three strong teeth pointing forwards and downwards, the posterior one being the longest. Jaws with a broad band of villiform teeth, and an outer row of stronger ones, the largest teeth being at the mandibular symphysis; an angular band of small teeth on the vomer, and narrow, elongate bands on the palatines. The dorsal commences above the opercular spines; its spines are strong, the fourth or fifth the longest, rather less than one third of the length of the head; the rayed dorsal is equal to or higher than the spinous, and its outer margin is evenly rounded; the length of its base is 1·75 in that of the spinous portion: the anal commences beneath the third dorsal ray, and does not extend quite so far back as that fin; its outer margin is rounded, and the rays are rather longer than those of the dorsal; the spines are very strong, the second the longest, 3·33–3·75 in the length of the head: ventrals small, their length 1·10–1·25 in the distance between their origin and the vent, and from 2·00–2·20 in the length of the head: pectoral rounded, extending nearly to the vertical from the vent, about 1·75 in the length of the head: caudal rounded, the least height of its pedicle 3·00–3·25 in the height of the body. Scales small, cycloid, firmly adherent, the soft dorsal and anal scaly for the greater part of their height; snout, preorbital, and maxilla scaleless.

Colors.—Rich brown, with a golden tinge on the sides and belly; head and body with numerous small round blue spots, darkest on the head and back; two or three oval blackish spots behind the eye: fins immaculate dark brown.

The Wirrah, by which name it was known to the Aboriginals of Sydney, is a common fish in our markets at all seasons; like its congeners it readily takes a hook. The contents of the stomachs of those examined by us were many and various, including small fishes, crustaceans, molluscs, echinoderms, starfishes, worms, and corallines. As food opinions vary; the late Sir William Macleay considered them to be "tough and flavorless"; Tenison Woods remarks that "the best Wirrah has the flavor and consistency of leather, which no sauce or cooking can change," and in connection with this it may be as well to point out that the fish figured in his work as the "Wirrah" is a *Priacanthus*. We, however, have found that a moderate sized example, of from ten to twelve inches in length, is firm and well flavored when boiled. It is very tenacious of life.

Originally described from specimens of the locality of whose capture was unknown, its habitat has been generally and vaguely put down as "Australian seas." The coast of New South Wales is, however, the only portion of the continent from which we are aware of its having been recorded, and the neighborhood of Port Jackson appears to be the head quarters of the species.

Though the average length of specimens exposed for sale in our markets is from eight to twelve inches, larger ones are not uncommon, the largest measured being just eighteen inches.

Genus III.—LUTIANUS.

Lutjanus, Bloch, Hist. Nat. Poiss. iv. p. 84, 1797.

Branchiostegals seven : pseudobranchiæ present. Body oblong-ovate, compressed. Opercle spiniferous: preopercle serrated, with or without a notch on its vertical margin, intended to receive a knob which is frequently developed on the interopercle. Jaws, vomer, and palatines with villiform teeth: the former with anterior canines, largest in the upper jaw, and a lateral series of strong conical teeth: minute teeth sometimes present on the tongue. One dorsal fin with from nine to thirteen spines: anal with three. Scales ctenid, of moderate size: one or two enlarged rows over the nape: cheeks scaly. Airbladder simple. Pyloric appendages few or absent.

LUTIANUS FULVIFLAMMA.

Sciæna fulviflamma, Forsk. Descr. Anim. p. 45, 1775 ; Gmel. Syst. Nat. p. 1299.
Perca fulviflamma, Bl. Schn. p. 90.
Centropomus hober, Lacép. Hist. Nat. Poiss. iv. p. 255.
Diacope fulviflamma, Cuv. Règne Anim ; Rüpp. Atl. Fisch. p. 72, pl. xix. f. 2, *and* N. W. Fisch. p. 94; Cuv. & Val. Hist. Nat. Poiss. ii. p. 423 ; Klunz. Verh. Ges. Wien, 1870, p. 700.
Mesoprion unimaculatus, Quoy & Gaim. Voy. Freycinet, p. 304, *and* Voy. Astrolabe, p. 665, pl. v. f. 3 ; Cuv. & Val. Hist. Nat. Poiss. p. 441 ; Bleek. Verh. Bat. Gen. xxii. Perc. p. 42.
Mesoprion aurolineatus, Cuv. & Val. Hist. Nat. Poiss. iii. p. 496 ; Day, Fish. Malab. p. 14, pl. iii.
Mesoprion russellii, Bleek. Verh. Bat. Gen. xxii. Perc. p. 41 ; Day, Proc. Zool. Soc. 1867, p. 701.
Lutjanus notatus, Bleek. Ternate, p. 233.
Genyoroge notata, Cantor, Catal. Malay. Fish. p. 12 ; Day, Fish. Malab. p. 8 (*not Cuv. & Val.*).
Mesoprion fulviflamma, Bleek. Amboina, ii. p. 532 ; Gnth. Catal. Fish. i. p. 201 ; Day, Fish. Malab. p. 13 ; Kner, Voy. Novara, Fisch. p. 351.
Lutjanus russellii, Bleek. Atl. Ichthyol. Perc. pl. xxii. f. 2. *and* Lutjani, p. 76.
Lutjanus unimaculatus, Vaillant, Soc. Phil. Paris, May 23rd, 1874.
Lutjanus fulviflamma, Bleek. Halmaheira. p. 55, *and* Lutjani, p. 61 ; Day, Fish. Ind. p. 42, pl. xii. ff. 5, 6.

Black-spotted Sea-Perch.

B. vii. D. 10/14. A. 3/8. V. 1/5. P. 16. C. 17. L. lat. 47-49. L. tr. 10/20. Cœc. pyl. 5.

Length of head 3·33-3·50, of caudal fin 4·25-4·50, height of body 3·40-3·50 in the total length. Diameter of eye 3·66-4·00 in the length of the head, and 1·25 in that of the snout: interorbital space very slightly convex, 1·60-1·90 in the diameter of the eye. Nostrils far apart, simple, oval, subequal ; the anterior pierced in the middle of a shallow circular fossa. Upper profile of head slightly concave. Jaws equal. Cleft of mouth moderate and a little oblique, the maxilla extending to beneath the middle of the orbit. Preopercle denticulated, the teeth on the horizontal limb and angle coarser than those above the notch, which is very shallow : interopercular knob inconspicuous : opercle with two blunt points : posttemporal with a few short blunt teeth. Jaws with a band of villiform teeth, and an outer row of curved cardiform teeth, stronger and more numerous in the lower jaw, in which they grow larger posteriorly ; maxilla with two pairs of anterior canines, the outer one on each side very long and strong; a triangular patch of villiform teeth on the vomer; palatines with broad bands; tongue with a median longitudinal patch narrowing posteriorly. The dorsal commences above the base of the pectoral; the spinous portion is higher than the rayed, and the length of the base of the latter is three fourths of that of the former; the spines are weak, the fourth the longest, three times the length of the first, and from 2·33–2·66 in the length of the head; the last spine is much shorter than the one preceding it: the anal commences beneath the second dorsal ray, the second spine is stronger than, but not so long as, the third, whose height is 3·20 in the length of the head, and two thirds of the anterior rays, which are much longer than those of the dorsal: the ventral does not quite reach to the vent; its outer rays are slightly filamentous, the length of the first 1·66 in that of the head, and the spine is about equal to the seventh dorsal spine: pectoral well developed and pointed, reaching to above or slightly beyond the vent, 1·25–1·40 in the length of the head: caudal slightly emarginate, the least height of its pedicle 2·75 in the height of the body. Cheeks, opercles except the outer margin of the preopercle, and a small stripe on the temporal region scaly; rest of the head naked: soft portion of the vertical fins with a low basal scaly sheath, which in the anal is continued for a short distance between the rays. Lateral line running parallel to the dorsal profile.

Colors.—Olive brown above, the sides rose color, the lower surfaces yellowish-white; a large black oval blotch, covering about eight transverse series of scales on the lateral line beneath the anterior dorsal rays; a black axillary spot; indistinct oblique dusky streaks above and longitudinal yellowish ones below the lateral line: dorsal fin dusky, with a narrow black and chestnut margin; caudal pale brown tinged with red; other fins bright yellow.

Examples of this fish are very rarely seen in the Sydney markets, and then only during the winter months, when a few assignments of fishes occasionally find their way thither from the Richmond and Clarence Districts. They are, however, tolerably abundant on our northern coastline at least as far south as the Bellinger, and are, therefore, entitled to a place here.

L. fulviflamma has a very extensive range having been recorded from the East Coast of Africa and the Seychelles; the Asiatic Coast from the Red Sea to China; the Malay Archipelago; and the northern portion of Australia, extending as has been shown as far south as the Bellinger River on the eastern side of the continent. They attain a length of at least twelve inches.

Genus IV.—GLAUCOSOMA.

Glaucosoma, Schleg. Faun. Japon. Poiss. p. 62, 1843.

Branchiostegals seven, occasionally eight: pseudobranchiæ present. Body oblong-ovate and somewhat compressed. Opercle with one or two inconspicuous flattened points: preopercle finely serrated: clavicle denticulated. Jaws, vomer, and palatines armed with villiform teeth. One dorsal fin with eight spines: the anal with three. Scales moderate, finely ctenid, adherent; the entire head and the bases of the vertical fins scaly.

Geographical distribution.—Australian seas to Japan.

GLAUCOSOMA SCAPULARE.

Glaucosoma scapulare (Ramsay, MS.), Macleay, Catal. Austr. Fish. i. p. 334, 1880; Woods, Fisher. N. S. Wales. p. 34.

Glaucosoma bürgeri, Castcln. Proc. Linn. Soc. N S. Wales, iii. p. 350 (*not* Richardson).

Pearl Perch.
Plate III.

B. vii. D. 8/11. A. 3/9. V. 1/5. P. 16. C. 17. L. lat. 48. L. tr. 12/20.

Length of head 3·25, of caudal fin 4·85, height of body 3·15 in the total length. Diameter of eye 3·80 in the length of the head, and 1·10 in that of the snout: interorbital space convex, 1·33 in the diameter of the eye. Nostrils approximate, vertical, oval, the posterior about twice the size of the anterior. Upper profile of head sinuous. Lower jaw protruding. Cleft of mouth large and oblique, the maxilla, which extends to beyond the posterior margin of the orbit, greatly dilated and with the edges sinuous and the posterior angles rounded. A single flat inconspicuous spine on the opercle: preopercle finely serrated, the denticles at the angle rather coarser: supraclavicle enormously developed, forming a strong ovate bony shield: posttemporal bone concealed. Villiform teeth on the jaws, vomer, and palatines, the outer row in the former greatly enlarged. The dorsal fin commences behind the base of the pectoral and terminates above the third anal ray; the spines are short but strong, the last the longest, little more than half of the second and longest ray, and 3·75 in the length of the head; the bases of the spinous and rayed portions of the fin are subequal: the anal fin commences beneath the fourth dorsal ray; the third spine is the longest, not half the length of the anterior ray, and 4·33 in that of the head: the ventral does not nearly reach to the vent, and its length is 2·20 in the same: the pectoral extends backwards to beneath the eighteenth scale of the lateral line and its length is 1·85 in that of the head: caudal very slightly emarginate, with the angles a little produced and rounded; the least height of the pedicle one third of the height of the body. Head entirely scaly; bases of vertical fins enclosed in a scaly sheath. Lateral line gently curved. Airbladder large.

Colors.—Upper surfaces greenish-brown, with numerous, small, indistinct, darker spots; sides and below silvery: fins immaculate; a small black axillary spot: supraclavicle black.

The Pearl Perch, or Epaulette Fish as it is styled in Queensland, is undoubtedly one of the best food fishes inhabiting the seas of Australia, but it is unfortunately only obtainable in the markets at very rare intervals, for, as the greater number are taken by pleasure parties on deep-water reefs when fishing for Snapper, they do not find their way thither, being too valuable from a gastronomic point of view to be lightly parted with. Under these circumstances it is needless to say that absolutely nothing is known of its habits or economy.

Some confusion exists as to whether the three described species of *Glaucosoma* are one and the same species or not. The genus was first described in the Fauna Japonica (*loc. cit.*) by Schlegel, who, however, neglected to give it a specific name; to remedy this Richardson proposed for the Japanese form the title of *G. bürgeri*, while to West Australian examples he allotted the name of *G. hebraïcum*. Günther considers that these two forms are certainly the same, and it, therefore, remains to be seen whether or not our eastern Australian fish must be included with them. At present we have thought it best to keep them apart, until further evidence, one way or the other, shall be forthcoming.

The Pearl Perch is a fine handsome fish growing to a length of at least two feet.

Family III.—GRYSTIDÆ.

Branchiostegals five, six, or seven: pseudobranchiæ present. Body oblong or elevated. Eyes lateral. Opercles indistinctly serrated, or spiniferous, or entire. Mouth in front of the snout, with lateral cleft which is more or less oblique. Teeth in the jaws villiform or cardiform, without canines: vomerine, palatine, or lingual teeth present or absent. Dorsal fin generally continuous (separated in *Huro* and *Percilia*): ventrals thoracic. Scales minutely ciliated or cycloid, of moderate size, rarely small. Lateral line continuous. Airbladder present, simple. Pyloric appendages in small moderate, or large numbers.

Geographical distribution.—Fresh waters and seas of tropical and temperate regions.

Genus I.—OLIGORUS.

Grystes, part. Cuv. & Val. Hist. Nat. Poiss. iii. p. 58, 1829.
Oligorus, Gnth. Catal. Fish. i. p. 251, 1859.

Branchiostegals seven: pseudobranchiæ little developed. Body oblong and posteriorly compressed. Opercle with two weak points: preopercle smooth, or obtusely denticulated: preorbital, posttemporal, and clavicle entire. Villiform teeth on the jaws, vomer, and palatines: tongue smooth. One dorsal fin with ten to twelve, normally eleven, spines: the anal with three. Scales small and cycloid: the entire head scaly: vertical fins with a deep scaly basal sheath. Airbladder large. Pyloric appendages in small numbers.

Geographical distribution.—Rivers of Australia.

OLIGORUS MACQUARIENSIS.

Grystes macquariensis, Cuv. & Val. Hist. Nat. Poiss. iii. p. 58, 1829; Richards. Voy. Erebus & Terror, Fish. p. 118, pl. liii. ff. 8, 9.
Grystes brisbanii, Less. Voy. Coquille, Zool. ii. p. 227.
Grystes peelii, Mitch. Exped. Austr. p. 39, pl. v. f. 1, 1838.
Oligorus macquariensis, Gnth. Catal. Fish. i. p. 251, *and* Study of Fish. p. 392, f. 164; Casteln. Proc. Zool. Soc. Vict. i. p. 54; Macleay, Catal. Austr. Fish. i. p. 52, *and* Proc. Linn. Soc. N. S. Wales, viii. p. 200; Woods, Fisher. N. S. Wales, p. 102, pl. xli.; McCoy, Prodr. Zool. Vict. dec. ix. pls. 85, 86.
Oligorus mitchelli, Casteln. Proc. Zool. Soc. Vict. ii. p. 150; Macleay, Catal. Austr. Fish. i. p. 53; Woods, Fisher. N. S. Wales, p. 103.
Oligorus gibbiceps, Macleay, Proc. Linn. Soc. N. S. Wales, x. p. 265

Murray Cod.

Plate VIII.

B. vii. D. 10-12/16-14. A. 3/11-13. V. 1/5. P. 19-20. C. 17. L. lat. 75-80. L. tr. 25/45-47. Cæc. pyl. 4.

Length of head 3·33-3·60, of caudal fin 6·00-7·00, height of body 3·75-4·40 in the total length. Eye small, its diameter from 4·33 in immature to 7·00 in adult examples in the length of the head, and 1·33-1·75 in that of the snout, which is rather depressed, broad, and very obtusely rounded: interorbital space slightly convex, its breadth 1·20-1·40 in the diameter of the eye. Nostrils separated by a considerable interval, the anterior provided with a triangular flap, the posterior oval and patent. Upper profile of head concave. Jaws subequal. Cleft of mouth deep and oblique; the maxilla

B

reaches to the hinder margin of the eye or even beyond it. Opercle with two concealed spines, the lower much the longer and more acute. Teeth in the jaws villiform, with the outer series slightly enlarged; vomerine teeth in a triangular, palatine in a lanceolate patch. The dorsal fin commences at a considerable distance behind the base of the pectoral, and extends backwards a little further than the anal; the spines are strong, the fourth, fifth, and sixth subequal and longest, 3·33–3·90 in the length of the head, and much shorter than the rays; the last spine is about equal in height to the second, and five eighths of the longest spine; the base of the rayed dorsal is five sevenths of that of the spinous, and its outer margin, as is also that of the anal, is rounded: the anal fin commences beneath the first or second dorsal ray; the spines are short and stout, the third usually a little longer than the second, its length 4·60–5·00 in that of the head, and 2·00–2·33 in that of the longest ray: ventral small, the outer ray with a short filament, its length from 2·00–2·40 in that of the head, and 2·00–2·25 in the distance between its origin and the vent; the spine is short and weak, equal in length to the last dorsal spine: pectoral short and rounded, its length 2·00–2·33 in that of the head: caudal rounded, the pedicle deep and strong, its least height 2·33–2·50 in the height of the body. Scales small and cycloid, the vertical fins scaly to about half their height.

Colors.—Olive green above, with numerous small darker spots; below white or pale yellow: soft dorsal, anal, and caudal fins with or without pale margins.

Castelnau's *Oligorus mitchelli*, which is said to differ from *O. macquariensis* in having a much broader head, larger eye, the upper jaw longer than the lower, the operculum more rounded, the caudal fin a little longer, and the height of the body much greater, is without doubt identical with the species above described; the size of the eye depends entirely on the age and length of the individual, a specimen six and a half inches in length having the eye as much as four and one third in the length of the head, while in one of twenty inches the proportion is one seventh, as given in the British Museum Catalogue, and in very large and old examples would doubtless be considerably less. With regard to the comparative length of the jaws much variation appears to exist; the authors of the "Histoire Naturelle des Poissons" state that the upper jaw is the longer (*c'est plutôt sa machoire supérieure qui dépasse l'autre*), thus agreeing in this respect with Castelnau; Günther gives the lower jaw as the longer, but in the five specimens examined in the preparation of the above description, the jaws were absolutely equal, while the figure in the study of fishes shows the upper jaw distinctly the longer, and may possibly, therefore, have been drawn from a specimen belonging to Castelnau's supposed form. The length of the caudal fin also varies, not only with the age of the fish, being proportionately shorter in large examples, but also with relation to the conditions surrounding the individual; for instance, those residing in lakes or sluggish creeks and lagunes, would naturally have a less developed caudal fin than those which habitually dwell in swift flowing streams, where a greater expenditure of muscular energy would be necessary to keep them in position against the current. The increased height of the body is obviously due to the condition of the ovaries, but in no case has a specimen come under our notice in which the proportion was so large as four times and a half in the length *without the caudal*, as mentioned by Castelnau, for presumedly the normal proportion; such, indeed, is unusual, even when the caudal fin is included, and only occurs in very young or diseased fishes, or immediately after the deposition of the ova; in a normally developed fifteen inches fish now before us, the height of the body is three and two fifths in the length without the caudal, or almost exactly the same as that given by Castelnau, as distinctive of *O. mitchelli.* These four characters may, therefore, be at once set aside as valueless, while the other two, on which that author relies, namely, the greater breadth of the head, and the more rounded opercle, are of too trivial a nature on which to found even a variety. Fresh water fishes, on account of the diverse character of their surroundings, are much more liable to variation than those which inhabit an element not so subject to sudden changes; greater care should, therefore, be taken in separating on variable characters forms belonging to the selfsame area of distribution. The loss of Castelnau's types of Australian Fishes is most unfortunate, since that erratic scientist's descriptions are frequently remarkable for the ingenuity with which the more important characters are entirely omitted, and trivial or secondary characters brought forward into prominence.

The *Oligorus gibbiceps* of Macleay, the type of which—in the Sydney University Museum—we have been enabled to examine, appears to be merely a stunted Alpine form of *O. macquariensis.*

According to Macleay the Murray cod, or as it might with more regard to correctness be designated the "Cod-Perch," is known to the aborigines of the Murrumbidgee by the name of "Kookoobul," while Tenison Woods mentions that those of the Lower Murray call it "Pundy."

The ova are deposited during the summer months, the statements of trustworthy observers varying between November and January even in the same district. Opinions also vary as to the place selected for the deposition of the ova, one observer reporting that "he has seen the fish, as he believed, actually depositing the spawn, one fish, the female doubtless, moving along the bottom of the water, forming a furrow in the sand with its chin, while another fish (the male) closely followed in its wake;" another observer, however, states that he "never saw the fishes spawning, but had often found what he believed to be the spawn attached to logs, and he affirms that he can discriminate perfectly between the spawn of the Cod and the other Percid Fishes of the Murrumbidgee." (Rep. Roy. Comm.); the latter theory is probably the correct one.

As food this fine species ranks as high as any purely freshwater fish of either hemisphere, medium-sized examples being more delicate than very large ones, which are coarse and tasteless. Their voracity is very great, no living thing, whether beast, bird, reptile, batrachian, fish or crustacean, which it can overpower, coming amiss to it; for this reason, they are very easily captured by almost any bait, care being taken to use sufficiently strong tackle, as the fish is enormously powerful and fights fiercely for liberty.

The true habitat of the Cod is the Murray river and its tributaries, but it is also found in some of the northern coastal rivers of the Colony, though whether introduced thereto or not does not seem to be accurately known; but judging from other Murray Percid fishes whose range is almost or entirely limited to that river system, such as *Ctenolates* and *Macquaria*, it is probable that such is the case, nevertheless the Murray River system, and that of the Richmond and Clarence District approximate so closely at their sources that it is quite possible that during exceptionally heavy floods the fishes of one system may be able to pass over into the other. The same species is also found in the Mary River, Queensland. To other localities it has been introduced with more or less success, as in Lake George, to which it was transplanted by Sir Terence Murray many years ago, where it has increased and thriven well, although some twelve years ago it was threatened with extermination owing to the poisonous water from the Currawang copper mines being allowed to find its way to the lake. That its introduction to the Yarra has not been an unmixed blessing is clear from the following remarks of Prof. McCoy:—"The Cod is now established in the Yarra, but does not thrive, though its voracity has sensibly diminished the numbers of several of the native fishes of that river, particularly the Blackfish (*Gadopsis marmoratus*) and the Yarra Herring or Australian Grayling (*Prototroctes marœna*), which have now disappeared from the lower parts of the Yarra altogether."

This magnificent species attains to a length of nearly five feet, and a weight of upwards of one hundred pounds.

Genus II.—ARRIPIS.

Centropristes, sp. Cuv. & Val. Hist. Nat. Poiss. iii. p. 50, 1829, *and* vii. p. 451; Richards. Voy. Erebus & Terror, Fish. pp. 29, 117.
Arripis, Jenyns, Zool. Beagle, Fish. p. 13, 1842.
Homodon, Brisout de Barneville, Rev. Zool. 1847, p. 133.

Branchiostegals seven: pseudobranchiæ present. Body oblong and but little compressed. Opercle spiniferous: preopercle serrated. Villiform teeth on the jaws, vomer, and palatines: tongue smooth. One dorsal fin with nine flexible spines: the anal with three. Scales moderate, finely ciliated, absent on the upper surface of the head: vertical fins with a basal scaly sheath. Airbladder of moderate size, simple. Pyloric appendages in large or moderate numbers.

Geographical distribution.—Seas of Australia, New Zealand, and the neighboring Islands.

ARRIPIS SALAR.

Centropristes salar, Richards. Trans. Zool. Soc. iii. p. 78, 1849, *and* Voy. Erebus & Terror, Fish. p. 29, pl. xx. ff. 4-6.
Centropristes tasmanicus, Hombr. & Jacq. Voy. Pôle Sud, Poiss. p. 40, pl. iv. fig. 1.
Arripis salar, Gnth. Catal. Fish. i. p. 253, *and* Study of Fish. p. 393, fig. 165; McCoy, Prodr. Zool. Vict. dec. ii. pls. 16, 17; Macleay, Catal. Austr. Fish. i. p. 51; Woods, Fisher. N.S. Wales, p. 35, pl. v.; Sherrin, Handb. N.Z. Fish. p. 50.
Arripis truttaceus, Casteln. Proc. Zool. Soc. Vict. i. p. 52; Johnston, Proc. Roy. Soc. Tas. 1882, pp. 68, 110.

Salmon.
Plate IX.

B. vii. D. 9/15-17. A. 3/10. V. 1/5. P. 16. C. 17. L. lat. 48-52. L. tr. 6/12-13. Cæc. pyl. ca. 75. Vert. 10/15.

Length of head 4·33-4·66, of caudal fin 4·20-4·75, height of body 3·90-4·60 in the total length. Diameter of eye 3·66-4·33 in the length of the head: the length of the snout varies with age from a little more than the diameter of the eye in young to a little less in old examples: interorbital space slightly convex, from 1·00 in young to 2·00 in large examples in the diameter of the eye. Nostrils approximate, separated by a narrow skinny bridge only, the anterior small and elongate-oval, the posterior oval and three times as large. Upper profile of head flat or very slightly concave. Lower jaw the longer. Cleft of mouth oblique and moderately wide, the maxilla reaching to beneath the posterior third of the orbit. Preorbital obsoletely serrated anteriorly: preopercle finely serrated on both limbs: opercle with two small blunt spines. Jaws with a broad band of villiform teeth anteriorly, abruptly narrowing on the sides; vomer with a cordiform patch; bands on the palatines lanceolate. The dorsal commences above the eighth or ninth scale of the lateral line; its spines are feeble, the fourth the longest, its height from 1·75–2·10 in the length of the head, and longer than any of the rays; the length of the base of the spinous dorsal is from 1·60–1·80 in that of the soft: the anal commences beneath the eighth or ninth dorsal ray, and ends on the same plane as the dorsal; the third spine is the longest, from 3·50–4·00 in the length of the head; the outer margin of the rayed portion is emarginate, owing to the elongation of the last rays: in large examples the ventrals extend midway or less than midway to the vent, but in examples under eight inches in length more than midway; their length is from 1·50–1·70 in that of the head: pectorals a little smaller than the ventrals, from 1·60–1·75 in the same: caudal deeply forked, the least height of its pedicle seven ninths of the distance between the last dorsal ray and the origin of the caudal, and 3·25–3·50 in the height of the body. Upper surface of head and the orbital ring naked; a series of five scales on the hinder half of the maxilla; cheek scales in five series; both spinous and soft portions of the dorsal and anal fins with a deep scaly sheath. Lateral line following the curvature of the back during its entire length.

Colors.—Upper surfaces green, the head the darkest: young examples with darker spots: lower surfaces white: fins hyaline.

Common as the Salmon is along the greater part of the coast line of New South Wales, but little is known as to where or when it breeds; as to the latter Tenison Woods remarks:—"It is said to commence to spawn in September on the east coast"; this being taken from Glover's evidence before the Royal Commission which refers to the Twofold Bay District; at Port Macquarie and the Clarence Heads the spawning season is respectively given as November and October. As small fry are frequently washed ashore on the ocean beaches after heavy weather it is possible that the spawn is buried in the sand in suitable places.

During the warmer months of the year Salmon make their appearance along our shores in shoals of marvellous magnitude, and are taken in very large numbers by the seine, not unfrequently causing a glut in the market; at such times the writer has seen fine fresh fishes of from twenty to thirty inches long, and weighing from six to eight pounds each, sold at the rate of two shillings per dozen, while many are given away to the poorer classes, no other possible means of getting rid of them being available. They take a bait freely and are frequently caught off the ocean beaches among the breakers, and Sherrin states that in New Zealand they afford good sport to anglers, as they rise to an artificial fly and are readily taken at sea with spoon bait.

Halfgrown examples are called "Salmon Trout" and are by no means to be despised for the table, but the adult fish is dry and rather tasteless, nevertheless from their size and abundance they are of considerable commercial value; Sherrin considers it "a fairly good fish for preserving in tins." Care should be taken to choose only the freshest fishes, as decomposition sets in very rapidly, and many cases of fish poisoning, some of them even resulting in death, are said to have been traced to this source. McCoy, however, it must in justice be said, does not agree with the above theory, stating that he has known several instances in which the effects were strongly marked after eating perfectly fresh examples, caught only an hour or so before cooking." Fishes, small swimming crabs, and *Sphæromidæ* were found in those whose stomachs were examined.

The Salmon has a wide range throughout the southern portion of the Australian Region, occurring along the entire southern seaboard of Australia, and along the New South Wales coast as far north at least as the Clarence River District, beyond which I have failed to trace it, nor is it even mentioned by Saville Kent in his Preliminary Report on the Food Fishes of Queensland. On all the shores of Tasmania it is "abundant all the year round" (Johnston), as also it is at Lord Howe, Norfolk, and Raoul Islands. It is abundant around New Zealand, "avoiding only that portion of the coast which is washed by the cold south-east current" (Sherrin). The Maori name for it is "Kahawai."

Family IV.—PRISTIPOMATIDAE.

Branchiostegals five, six, or seven (four only in *Chætopterus*): pseudobranchiæ present or rudimentary. Body oblong or ovate, more rarely elevated or cylindrical. Eyes lateral, of moderate size. Opercle with or without spines: preopercle serrated or entire. Mouth in front of the snout, with variously directed lateral cleft. Teeth in the jaws in villiform bands, with or without canines, rarely edentulous, with no molar or trenchant teeth: teeth on the vomer and palatines present or absent, in some genera deciduous: no lingual teeth. Dorsal fin continuous: ventrals thoracic: lower rays of pectorals branched. Scales moderate or small, feebly ctenoid or cycloid. Lateral line continuous, not extending on to the caudal fin. Airbladder present, with or without a median contraction. Pyloric appendages in small or moderate numbers (numerous in *Hyperoglyphe*).

Geographical distribution.—Marine and freshwater fishes of tropical and temperate regions.

Genus I.—CTENOLATES.

Ctenolates, Gnth. Proc. Zool. Soc. 1871, p. 320.

Branchiostegals seven: pseudobranchiæ present. Body oblong-ovate and somewhat compressed. Opercle with two spines, the lower of which is frequently subdivided into two or more points: preopercle serrated on the vertical limb; angle and lower limb with patches of coarser denticles. Teeth villiform on the jaws, vomer, and palatines: tongue smooth. One dorsal fin, moderately notched, with ten spines: the anal with three. Scales small, ctenoid, present on the occiput: vertical fins with a basal scaly sheath. Pyloric appendages in moderate numbers.

Geographical distribution.—Murray River and its tributaries; Mary River, Queensland.

CTENOLATES AMBIGUUS.

Datnia ambigua, Richards. Voy. Erebus & Terror, Fish. p. 25, pl. xix, 1846.
Dules ambiguus, Gnth. Catal. Fish. i. p. 270; Klunz. SB. Ak. Wien, lxxx. Abth. i. p. 337, pl. i. f. 1.
Ctenolates macquariensis, Guth. Proc. Zool. Soc. 1871, p. 390, pl. xxxiii.
Dules auratus, Casteln. Proc. Zool. Soc. Vict. i. p. 55.
Ctenolates ambiguus, Macleay, Catal. Austr. Fish. i. p. 54; Woods, Fisher. N. S. Wales, p. 103.

Golden Perch.
Plate V.

B. vii. D. 10/10–11. A. 3/8. V. 1/5. P. 16–17. C. 17. L. lat. 53–58. L. tr. 13–14/28–30. Cœc. pyl. ca. 11.

Length of head 3·40–3·60, of caudal fin 5·33–6·20, height of body 3·20–3·66 in the total length. Diameter of eye 4·75–6·00 in the length of the head, 1·10–1·50 in that of the snout, and 0·90–1·25 in the interorbital space, which is convex. Nostrils moderately close together, the anterior circular and closed by a valve, the posterior subpyriform and patent. Upper profile of head deeply concave. Lower jaw the longer. Cleft of mouth moderate and oblique; the maxilla reaches to beneath the middle of the orbit. Preorbital sinuous and serrated on its lower margin: vertical limb of preoperele serrated, the angle rounded with stronger denticulations, the horizontal limb with coarse teeth in patches: opercle with two strong spines, the lower of which is much the longer, and is frequently subdivided: its margin below very finely serrated: posttemporal and clavicle with some strong teeth. Teeth villiform in the jaws; in an obtusely angular band on the vomer; palatines with a long narrow band. The dorsal fin commences above the base of the pectoral, and ends opposite the termination of the anal; the spines are strong, the fifth the longest, subequal in height to the rays, from 1·80–2·50 in the length of the head; the last spine is about five sevenths of the longest spine, and three fourths of the first ray; base of rayed dorsal 1·33–1·50 in that of the spinous: the anal commences beneath the second or third dorsal ray; the second spine is the longest and strongest, not so long as the rays, and from 2·25–3·00 in the length of the head: ventral well developed, the filament of the outer ray reaching to or beyond the vent, its length from 1·33–1·50 in that of the head; the spine is strong, equal in length to the third dorsal spine: pectoral moderate, rounded posteriorly, 1·60–1·75 in the same: caudal rounded, the least height of the pedicle one third of the height of the body. Snout, preorbital, upper surface of head to midway along the occiput, outer edges of the preopercle, and temporal fossa scaleless; dorsal and anal fins scaly at their bases: there are from eighty two to eighty five series of scales above the lateral line, which is parallel to the curvature of the back.

Colors.—Upper surfaces olive green, the sides and lower surfaces golden.

Owing to the difficulty experienced in obtaining perfect* specimens of our freshwater fishes in a recent state, and the paucity of reliable data on the subject, original information as to the season of the year in which the ova are deposited, the localities selected for such deposition, and the means employed to ensure so far as possible the safety of the ova, whether by forming a nest in the river bed or by attaching the spawn to aquatic plants, is not forthcoming.†

The Golden Perch, which is also known to the colonists as the "Yellow-Belly," and, according to Macleay is the *Kaakaalain* of the Aboriginals of the Murrumbidgee, is abundant in all the rivers and lagunes connected with the Murray River and its tributaries, while the naturalists attached to the Challenger Expedition discovered that it was also a resident of the Mary River, Queensland. As food it is delicious, and it is, therefore, eagerly sought for both by hook and net.

Large specimens attain a length of at least twenty three inches, and a weight of nine pounds.

---

* All the specimens sent to the Sydney markets or consigned direct to dealers in the city are scaled and cleaned previous to their transmission here.
† These important considerations in the economy of our freshwater fishes will never be properly understood until a competent officer shall be appointed by the Government to report fully on these and all other matters connected with the fishes and fisheries of our transmontane river systems.

Genus II.—MACQUARIA.

Macquaria, Cuv. & Val. Hist. Nat. Poiss. v. p. 377, 1830.
Murrayia, Casteln. Proc. Zool. Soc. Vict. 1872, i. p. 61.
Riverina, Casteln. Proc. Zool. Soc. Vict. 1872, i. p. 64.

Branchiostegals six: pseudobranchiæ present. Body oblong-ovate and somewhat compressed. Head with distinct muciferous channels. Opercle with two spines, either or both of which may be subdivided into two or more points: edges of sub- and interopercles finely serrated: preopercle serrated on the vertical limb, the angle and lower limb with patches of coarser denticles. Teeth villiform on the jaws and vomer: a few teeth present or absent on the palatines. One dorsal fin moderately notched, with eleven or twelve spines: the anal with three. Scales moderate, ctenoid, present on the occiput: bases of vertical fins scaly. Pyloric appendages in small numbers.

Geographical distribution.—Murray River system.

MACQUARIA AUSTRALASICA.

Macquaria australasica, Cuv. & Val. Hist. Nat. Poiss. v. p. 377, pl. cxxxi 1830; Less. Voy. Coquille, Zool. ii. p. 194, pl. xiv. f. 1; Gnth. Catal. Fish. i. p. 286; Macleay, Catal. Austr. Fish. i. p. 59.
Dules riverinus, Krefft, Proc. Zool. Soc. 1867, p. 943.
Murrayia guntheri, Casteln. Proc. Zool. Soc. Vict. 1872, i. p. 61; Macleay, Catal. Austr. Fish. i. p. 56.
Murrayia cyprinoides, Casteln. Proc. Zool. Soc. Vict. 1872, i. p. 62; Macleay, Catal. Austr. Fish. i. p. 57.
Murrayia bramoides, Casteln. Proc. Zool. Soc. Vict. 1872, i. p. 63; Macleay, Catal. Austr. Fish. i. p. 57.
Murrayia riverina, Macleay, Catal. Austr. Fish. i. p. 58.
Riverina fluviatilis, Casteln. Proc. Zool. Soc. Vict. 1872, i. p. 64; Macleay, Catal. Austr. Fish. i. p. 58.

Macquarie's Perch.
Plate IV.

B. vi. D. 12-11/11-12. A. 3/8-9. V. 1/5. P. 16. C. 17. L. lat. 47-52. L. tr. 8-9/17-19. Cæc. pyl. 4. Vert. 12/18.

Length of head 3·40-3·70, of caudal fin 5·25-5·70, height of body 3·20-3·66 in the total length. Diameter of eye 3·50-4·80 in the length of the head, 1·00-1·50 in that of the snout, which is broad and truncate, and 1·00-1·40 in the convex interorbital space. Nostrils distant, the anterior subcircular, tubular, and pierced on a higher level than the posterior, which is oval and horizontal. Tip of the snout rounded, thence to between the posterior margins of the eyes flat or very slightly concave; occiput and anterior dorsal profile gibbous. Upper jaw a little the longer. Cleft of mouth rather small, transverse, and oblique, the maxilla reaching to beneath the posterior nostril. Upper surface of head with regular series of large pores in pairs, two on the front of the snout, two above the nostrils, and two inside the supraciliary edge; the median cephalic groove with a single pore in front and behind; sides of the head with two series, the upper skirting the suborbital ring, the lower from the chin to the upper angle of the preopercle. Preorbital serrature almost obsolete in large examples: vertical limb of preopercle slightly concave, serrated; the angle rounded with rather larger teeth; horizontal limb with coarser denticles, which are generally arranged in groups: opercle with two strong, broad, flat spines, subdivided at the tip into from three to ten spinelets, inter- and subopercular margins finely serrated: posttemporal and clavicle with a variable number of short strong denticulations. Teeth villiform; the jaws with a narrow band, separated at the symphyses; vomer with a triangular patch; a minute patch present or absent on the anterior edge of the palatines; tongue smooth. The dorsal fin commences opposite to or a little behind the angle of the opercle, and ends slightly in advance of the termination of the anal; the spines are strong, with the outer portion free, especially in front; the first is small, about half the height of the second, which bears the same proportion to the third; the fifth the longest, but little longer than the fourth or sixth and from 1·75–2·00 in the length of the head; the last spine is equal in height to that which precedes it, and 1·70 in the longest; the outer margin of the rayed dorsal is strongly convex, the middle rays being the longest, and equal to the longest spine; the base of the soft dorsal is from 1·40–1·50 in that of the spinous: the anal commences beneath the third or fourth dorsal ray; the second spine is the longest and very strong, equal in length to the eighth dorsal spine, and from 2·33–2·50 in the length of the head and 1·33–1·50 in that of the anterior rays: ventral fins well developed, with the outer margin rounded; the first ray with a moderate filament reaching nearly to the vent, its length 1·25–1·40 in that of the head; the spine is strong, equal in length to the ninth dorsal spine: pectorals gently rounded posteriorly, reaching to beneath the seventeenth to eighteenth scale of the lateral line, its length 1·50–1·75 in that of the head: caudal slightly rounded, the least height of the pedicle 2·70 in the height of the body. Snout, interorbital space, orbital ring, hinder limb of the preopercle, and a muciferous fossa surrounding the scaly occiput, except across the dorsal profile, naked: bases of the vertical fins scaly: a series of smaller scales extending upwards between the rays. Lateral line gently curved from beneath the posttemporal bone to opposite the end of the dorsal fin. Airbladder large and simple.

Colors.—Reddish-brown above, shading into yellowish-brown beneath.

The fish which is here described as *Macquaria australasica*, is undoubtedly that figured by Lesson in the Voyage of the Coquille, and the great confusion that has arisen over the genus is due to the statement made in the Histoire Naturelle des Poissons that it is absolutely devoid of teeth (*par le manque absolu de dents*). That the fish here figured, the *Macquaria* of Cuvier and Valenciennes, and the *Murrayia* and *Riverina* of Castelnau are one and the same genus admits of no dispute.

Having arrived at this conclusion there only remains to be seen how many of the five species described by Krefft and Castelnau can be considered as worthy of recognition. Leaving aside entirely the question of the dentition—and it must be remembered that since Lesson's time no edentulous Percid has been discovered in Australian rivers—the only other important difference that we find is that Cuvier in his description enumerates the branchiostegal rays at five, whereas in fifteen specimens personally examined, varying in length from three and three fourths to twelve and a third inches, the number was invariably six as given above.

Comparing the above description, taken from so many specimens of various ages, it is impossible to avoid coming to the conclusion that Castelnau's three species of *Murrayia*—*M. guentheri*, *M. cyprinoides*, and *M. bramoides*—are merely the same species with slight individual variations unduly magnified, and that they are inseparable from *Macquaria australasica*. Castelnau's type, a half skin wretchedly preserved and measuring over thirteen inches is in the collection of the Australian Museum, and differs in no way from our specimens.

In the type specimen of Krefft's *Dules riverinus*, now lying before me, and which measures a trifle over five inches, the scales of the lateral line number on the one side forty nine on the other fifty one to the base of the caudal fin, the difference between these and Krefft's published numbers having been caused by that author's inclusion of the tubular scales on the caudal fin. This being so it is manifest that the sole objection to including this fish with those of Castelnau is removed.

The accidental occurrence of an extra dorsal spine, which is always accompanied by the loss of a ray, the first ray having in point of fact become spinate, and the want of palatine teeth, which have been previously shown to be in all cases either almost or wholly obsolete, being the only differences which separate Castelnau's *Riverina fluviatilis* from the same author's *Murrayia bramoides*, it follows that this too must share the fate of the others, and sink into a synonym of *Macquaria australasica*.

Nothing is known as to the breeding habits of this species, but doubtless they do not materially differ from those of the other Murray Perches; as to the season we have only the negative evidence that no signs of spawn were present in any of a fine series of specimens, netted during October, and specially forwarded from Yulpa Creek, near Deniliquin, from which place also Castelnau received some of his specimens.

They are excellent fish for the table, and according to Castelnau are sent regularly to the Melbourne market, but they are never sent to those of Sydney. In the specimens examined remains of shells, water beetles, worms, and entomostraca were detected.

The range of Macquarie's Perch is limited to the waters of the Murray River system. They attain a length of at least fourteen inches.

Genus III.—THERAPON.

Therapon, Cuvier, Règne Anim.; Cuv. & Val. Hist. Nat. Poiss. iii. p. 125, 1829.
Datnia, Cuv. & Val. Hist. Nat. Poiss. iii. p. 138.
Pelates, Cuvier, Règne Anim.; Cuv. & Val. Hist. Nat. Poiss. iii. p. 145.

Branchiostegals six: pseudobranchiæ present. Body oblong or oblong-ovate, compressed. Eyes of moderate size. Opercle spiniferous: preopercle and sometimes preorbital serrated. Teeth villiform in both jaws: deciduous on the vomer and palatine bones. One dorsal fin, more or less deeply notched, with from ten to thirteen spines: the anal with three. Scales of moderate or small size. Airbladder divided transversely into two parts, separated by a constriction. Pyloric appendages in small or moderate numbers.

Geographical distribution.—Coasts and fresh waters of Australia; from the Malay Archipelago northwards through the Chinese seas to Japan, and westwards along the coasts of Asia to the Red Sea; east coast of Africa to the Cape.

THERAPON QUADRILINEATUS.

Holocentrus quadrilineatus, Bl. pl. ccxxxviii. fig. 2, 1797.
Pristipoma sexlineatum, Quoy & Gaim. Voy. Uranie, Poiss. p. 320.
Therapon quadrilineatus, Cuv. & Val. Hist. Nat. Poiss. iii. p. 134; Richards Ichthyol. China, p. 239; Bleek. Perc. p. 51; Guth. Catal. Fish. i. p. 282; Kner. Voy. Novara, Fisch. p. 46; Peters, Mon. Ak. Berl. 1868, p. 256; Day, Fish. Ind. p. 70, pl. xviii. fig. 5.
Therapon xanthurus, Cuv. & Val. Hist. Nat. Poiss. iii. p. 135.

Pelates quadrilineatus, quinquelineatus, and *sexlineatus,* Cuv. & Val. Hist. Nat. Poiss. p. iii. 146; Less. Voy. Coquille, ii. p. 223; Cuv. Règne Anim. Illus. Poiss. pl. xii. fig. 1; Griff. An. King. Fish. pl. xii. fig. 1.
Helotes polytænia, Bleek. Halmaheira, p. 53, *and* Atl. Ichthyol. Perc. pl. xiv. fig. 2: ? Gnth. Catal. Fish. i. p. 285.
Therapon cuvieri, Bleek. Timor, p. 211, *and* Atl. Ichthyol. Perc. pl. xxxvii. fig. 2: Gnth. Catal. Fish. i. p. 282: Macleay, Catal. Austr. Fish. i. p. 62.
Therapon sexlineatus, Steindachn. SB. Ak. Wien, liii. p. 429.

Trumpeter Perch.

B. vi. D. 12/10. A. 3/10. V. 1/5. P. 14-(15). C. 17. L. lat. 58-65. L. tr. 13-15/26. Cœc. pyl. 7. Vert. 10/15.

Length of head 4·00-4·25, of caudal fin 5·00-5·25, height of body 3·33-3·66 in the total length. Diameter of eye 3·40-3·75 in the length of the head, 1·25-1·10 in that of the snout, and about equal to the width of the interorbital space, which is convex. Upper profile of head slightly convex. Upper jaw the longer. Cleft of mouth small and oblique, the maxilla extending to beneath the posterior nostril. Preorbital serrated on its inferior margin: vertical limb and posterior third of horizontal limb of preopercle serrated, the denticles being coarsest at the rounded angle: opercle with two rather weak subequal spines: posttemporal and clavicle coarsely denticulated. Three or four series of small teeth in the upper jaw, two or three series in the lower, the outer maxillary row enlarged. The dorsal fin commences above the base of the pectoral and ends on the same plane as the termination of the anal; the spines are moderately strong, the fifth (fourth to sixth) the longest, 2·00-2·50 in the length of the head, and 1·10-1·25 in that of the longest ray; the base of the rayed portion is from 1·66-1·75 in that of the spinous: the anal commences beneath the eleventh or twelfth dorsal spine; the spines are rather weak, the third the longest, from 2·80-3·10 in the length of the head, and 1·50-1·75 in that of the longest ray: ventrals not nearly reaching to the vent, their length 1·50-1·75 in that of the head: pectorals short and rounded posteriorly, 1·40-1·66 in the same: caudal emarginate, the length of the pedicle from 1·25-1·33 in its height. Upper surface of head, preorbital, and outer margin of preopercle scaleless.

Colors.—Olive green above, darkest on the head; sides greyish-green; belly silvery; from four to six brown or brownish-orange longitudinal bands; a dusky blotch on the shoulder present or absent: fins hyaline, the dorsal with a narrow blackish margin.

The Trumpeter Perch, or as it is frequently but erroneously termed the "Mado,"—a name which properly applies to *Chætodon strigatus* and *Atypichthys strigatus,* which fishes are not recognised as distinct by the ordinary fisherman—is common in the neighborhood of Sydney, and is sent to market sometimes in considerable quantities in company with Yellowtails (*Caranx trachurus*); it is also taken with the hook off wharves and jetties, and is said to be particularly partial to the mouths of drains.

Specimens from Botany Bay examined during February were found to have the roe fully developed, while in others from the same locality, captured during the last week of September, it was about half developed; others again from Port Jackson showed no signs of breeding at Christmas.

T. quadrilineatus has a wide range, being found in all the seas of continental Australia except the extreme southern seaboard, ranging on the east coast at least as far south as Botany, where it is common; it is also present in all the seas of New Guinea and the Malay Archipelago, as well as of India and China.

The ordinary size of market specimens is from six to nine inches, but larger examples occasionally occur.

THERAPON ELLIPTICUS.

Datnia elliptica, Richards. Voy. Erebus & Terror, Fish. p. 118, pl. lii. ff. 4-8, 1846.

Therapon ellipticus, Gnth. Catal. Fish. i. p. 276;. Macleay, Catal. Austr. Fish. i. p. 63.

Therapon richardsonii, Casteln. Proc. Zool. Soc. Vict. 1872, i. p. 60; Macleay, Catal. Austr. Fish. i. p. 64; Woods, Fisher. N. S. Wales, p. 104.

Therapon niger, Casteln. Proc. Zool. Soc. Vict. i. p. 59; Macleay, Catal. Austr. Fish. i. p. 65.

Therapon macleayanus, Ramsay, Proc. Linn. Soc. N. S. Wales, vi. p. 831.

Silver Perch.

Plate VI.

B. vi. D. 12/11-12. A. 3/7-8. V. 1/5. P. 17. C. 17. L. lat. 55-60. L. tr. 17/31-34.

Length of head 4·00-4·33, of caudal fin 5·15-5·50, height of body 3·66-4·25 in the total length. Diameter of eye 3·50-4·50 in the length of the head, 1·00-1·40 in that of the snout, which is moderately pointed, and subequal to the width of the slightly convex interorbital space. Nostrils moderately close together, the anterior rounded, tubular, and directed forwards; the posterior oval and vertical. Occiput slightly concave. Upper jaw the longer. Cleft of mouth small, transverse, and horizontal; the maxilla reaches to the posterior nostril. Preorbital finely serrated: preopercle serrated, the denticulations on the angle and vertical limb coarser than those on the horizontal limb; the vertical limb slightly concave: opercle with two spines, the lower the larger and frequently split up into two or more points: posttemporal and clavicle coarsely denticulated. Teeth in the jaws villiform, with an enlarged outer row. The dorsal fin commences above the base of the pectoral, and ends a little behind the anal; the spines are strong, the fifth or sixth the highest, a little higher than the rays, from 1·70-2·00 in the length of the head; the last spine is about two thirds of the longest spine and three fourths of the first ray; the base of the rayed dorsal is from 1·40-1·60 in that of the spinous: the anal commences beneath the second dorsal ray, the second spine is very strong, equal to or rather higher than the rays, and from 1·50-1·75 in the length of the head: ventrals well developed, not quite reaching to the vent, the second ray the longest and with a slight filamentary appendage, its length from 1·25-1·40 in that of the head; the spine is strong equal in length to the last dorsal spine: pectoral rather short, rounded posteriorly, from 1·50-1·75 in the length of the head: caudal emarginate, the least height of the pedicle one third of the height of the body. Scales ctenoid: snout, preorbital, interorbital space, and the outer edges of the preopercle naked: dorsal and anal fins with a basal scaly sheath. The lateral line follows the dorsal curvature; it has fifty five to sixty tubular scales, and there are from eighty five to ninety series of scales above it between its inception and the base of the caudal.

Colors.—Silvery, the upper surfaces washed with brown, and sometimes with scattered black spots, which may be present or absent on the vertical fins.

The "Silver Perch" or "Silver Bream" of the colonists is the "Kooberry" of the Murrumbidgee Aboriginals.

Although Castelnau's name *richardsonii* seems to have been generally accepted by Australian authors for the eastern form, we fail to see what characters of sufficient importance are present to authorise its separation from Richardson's well known *ellipticus*, under which name it has, therefore, been placed here.

Never having seen this fish in a fresh state, I extract the following paragraph from the Report of the Royal Commission on Fisheries, 1880 : "The 'Silver Perch' or 'Bream' (*Therapon richardsonii*) is the perfection of fishes, extremely rich and delicate in flavor. It frequents running streams more than the last mentioned fish, *i.e.*, *Ctenolates ambiguus*, which is often found in lagunes and billabongs, and it affords good sport to the angler. A full grown fish attains a size of five or six pounds. It is not caught often with the hook, the very small size of its mouth preventing its taking the hooks in common use."

This fish inhabits the Murray River and its tributary streams, and if I am correct in joining it with Richardson's species it also occurs in the rivers of Western Australia, the original type, seventeen inches in length, having come from thence, while it is noteworthy that a second specimen in the British Museum was obtained in the Namoi River, a southern tributary of the Darling.

Genus IV.—HISTIOPTERUS.

Histiopterus Schlegel, Faun. Japon. Poiss. p. 86 (1844–46).
Richardsonia, Casteln. Proc. Zool. Soc. Vict. 1872, i. p. 112 (*not Steindachner*).

Branchiostegals six : pseudobranchiæ present. Body more or less elevated and strongly compressed. Snout much produced : the anterior profile of the head deeply concave. Mouth small, situated at the end of the snout. Preopercle, posttemporal, and clavicle obsoletely serrated. Small teeth in the jaws : vomer, palatines, and tongue toothless. One dorsal fin with from seven to nine spines : anal with two or three : some of the spines and rays more or less produced. Scales small and cycloid.

HISTIOPTERUS LABIOSUS.

Histiopterus labiosus, Gnth. Proc. Zool. Soc. 1871, p. 658, pl. lix ; Macleay, Catal. Austr. Fish. i. p. 74.
Richardsonia insignis, Casteln. Proc. Zool. Soc. Vict. 1872, i. p. 112.

Boar Fish.
Plate VII.

B. vi. D. 7/17. A. 2/9–11. V. 1/5. P. 17. C. 17. L. lat. 94–110.

Length of head 3·40–3·60, of caudal fin 5·33–5·40, height of body 3·50–3·60 in the total length. Diameter of eye 5·60–6·40 in the length of the head, and 3·00–3·33 in that of the snout: interorbital space convex and narrow, 2·25 in the diameter of the eye. Nostrils approximate, elongate-oval, and oblique, the posterior the larger. Upper profile of the head to above the hinder margin of the orbit concave, of the occiput nearly straight. Lower jaw the longer; the lips, which are thick and fleshy, and the chin densely covered with short papillæ. Cleft of mouth moderate and oblique, the maxilla extending to beneath the anterior nostril. Opercles sculptured: preopercle with both margins indistinctly serrated in adult examples, and with the vertical margin concave and the angle produced: posttemporal and clavicular bones with obsolete denticulations. Both jaws with bands of small teeth, those in front being cardiform and slightly curved backwards, those on the sides granular. The dorsal fin commences above the hinder margin of the opercular flap; the three anterior spines are short, and connected by a low membrane; the fourth is elongate and strongly compressed, its length 2·55–2·75 in that of the head, and about twice as long as the anterior rays; the four last spines are provided with more or less elongate filamentary appendages; the length of the spinous dorsal is from 1·75–1·90 in that of the rayed portion: the anal commences beneath the seventh dorsal ray; its first spine is very short, the second very powerful and strongly compressed, almost or quite equal in height to the anterior ray, and 2·33–2·55 in the length of the head: the ventral fin does not quite reach the vent; the spine is strong, compressed, and falcate, almost equalling the adjoining ray, and 1·80–2·10 in the length of the head; dorsal, anal, and ventral spines deeply striated: pectorals pointed, reaching as far back as the ventrals, their length 1·50–1·75 in that of the head: caudal emarginate with the lobes slightly produced; the least height of the pedicle one fourth of the height of the body. Body scales small and deeply imbedded; opercular bones, except the extreme upper edge of the opercle, scaleless; cheeks scaly, the scales almost concealed by the skin. Anterior portion of lateral line abruptly ascending to beneath the middle of the spinous dorsal, thence mostly following the curvature of the back, though in a more or less wavy line to between the terminations of the dorsal and anal, where it descends as abruptly on to the caudal pedicle. Airbladder large. Gill-rakers very short and stout.

Colors.—Back and sides dull greenish-gray, below lighter, sometimes with indistinct, darker, longitudinal bands: upper surface of head darker with a slight metallic gloss: fins violet, the spines dull yellow; the caudal edged with grayish-green.

Nothing is known of the breeding habits of this fine fish, but as in specimens examined during the month of June the ova was found to be but little developed it may be inferred that the spring or early summer months are those selected for shedding the spawn; that this is not deposited in our shallow bays and estuaries is manifest from the fact that no instances of the capture of the young, even in the over netted bays in the neighborhood of Sydney, have been recorded, adults only, of from twenty inches upwards, appearing in the market, these being taken by handlines in deep water, and that at but rare intervals, owing to the size of the hook used in fishing for Snapper and other line fish being as a rule too large for the comparatively small mouth of the Boarfish. The baits employed are also probably unsuitable, as the stomachs of those examined by us contained in no case anything but worms, small crustaceans and shells, and remains of brittle-stars, all mixed up with large quantities of sand which had evidently been taken into the œsophagus while the fish was engaged in rooting out the creatures concealed beneath it. The Boarfish is an excellent fish for the table, and it is much to be regreted that the supply is so inadequate, but for the reasons given above, and because of the probability that it normally frequents localities having a sandy bottom at a moderate depth, and, therefore, but rarely comes into contact with the Snapper fisher, no remedy is likely to be found until our magnificent stretches of outside sandy grounds are properly surveyed, and scientifically fished by powerful steam trawlers.

This species is a native of the southern coast of Australia, the first example described having been obtained on the coast of South Australia, and extends its range northwards along our own seaboard at least as far as Cape Hawke, beyond which I have been unable to trace it. Macleay records it from Tasmania, but Johnston in his more recently published Catalogue of the fishes of that colony makes no mention of it; it is, however, certain to occur in Tasmanian seas. A closely allied but very distinct species—*H. recurvirostris*, Richardson—characterised by an increased number of dorsal spines, and a broad curved black band extending from the origin of the dorsal to the end of the anal, occurs there and on the Victorian coast, but has not as yet been recorded from New South Wales waters, whence, however, a third easily distinguished species, recently described as *H. elevatus*, Rms. & Ogl., but which is probably the Japanese *H. typus*, Schleg., has been taken on two occasions by the trawl in from thirty five to seventy fathoms between Botany and Port Hacking Heads; this species may be easily recognised by the greatly increased number of dorsal and anal rays, and especially by the great comparative height of the body, which is contained only two and a third times in the total length.

Family V.—PRIACANTHIDÆ.

Branchiostegals six: pseudobranchiæ present. Body oblong. Eyes large and lateral. Opercles finely serrated, the angle spiniferous. Lower jaw with prominent chin: cleft of the mouth approaching the vertical. Villiform teeth in the jaws, vomer, and palatines: no canines: tongue smooth. Dorsal fin continuous: ventrals thoracic. Scales small, strongly ctenid, rough. Airbladder present, simple. Pyloric appendages in small numbers.

Geographical distribution.—All tropical seas; on the east coast of Australia extending its range at least as far southward as Port Jackson.

Genus.—PRIACANTHUS.

Priacanthus, Cuv. & Val. Hist. Nat. Poiss. iii. p. 96, 1829.

Branchiostegals six: pseudobranchiæ present. Body oblong and somewhat compressed. Eye large. Lower jaw prominent. Opercle with an indistinct point: preopercle serrated on both limbs and with a more or less prominent and flattened, serrated spine at the angle. Villiform teeth on the jaws, vomer, and palatines: tongue smooth. One dorsal fin with nine or ten spines: anal with three. Scales small and ctenid, extending on to the snout. Pyloric appendages in small numbers.

Geographical distribution.—As in the family. One genus only.

PRIACANTHUS BENMEBARI.

Priacanthus benmebari, Schleg. Faun. Japon. Poiss. p. 19, pl. vii. fig. 1;
   Krusenstern, p. 53, fig. 2; Richards. Ichthyol. China & Japan. p. 237;
   Gnth. Catal. Fish. i. p. 218, *and* Ann. Nat. Hist. (3) 1867, xx. p. 57;
   Macleay, Catal. Austr. Fish. i. p. 37; Woods, Fisher. N.S. Wales,
   p. 35, pl. iv. (*as Wirrah*).

Bullseye.

B. vi. D. 10/13. A. 3/14. V. 1/5. P. 18-19. C. 16. L. lat. 74-82. L. tr. 12/10-42. Cœc. pyl. 11. Vert. 9/13.

Length of head 4·00-4·33, of caudal fin 4·75-5·20, height of body 3·50-4·00 in the total length. Eye very large, its diameter 2·25-2·50 in the length of the head: snout short and very obtuse, 1·25-1·75 in the diameter of the eye: interorbital space very slightly convex, 1·85-2·20 in the same. Nostrils approximate, the anterior small, oval, and vertical; the posterior large, elongate-oval, and oblique. Upper profile of head flat, or with a very slight concavity. Chin prominent. Cleft of mouth very oblique, the maxilla reaching to beneath the anterior third of the eye, and greatly dilated posteriorly: the postorbital portion of the head is only two thirds of the diameter of the orbit. Preorbital roughened below and above: preopercle finely denticulated on both limbs; its angle obtuse, and bearing a strong serrated spine, whose length is from 2·80-3·25 in the diameter of the eye: subopercle with fine denticulations posteriorly: opercle with two weak spines, the lower being the longer, and with its hinder margin serrated in patches: clavicle coarsely serrated. Both jaws with a narrow band of villiform teeth, having the outer series much enlarged; vomerine teeth in an acutely angular band; on the palatines in a narrow elongate band. The dorsal commences above the opercle; the spines are slender, the anterior ones serrated in front above the membrane; the last is the longest from 2·00-2·25 in the length of the head, and equal in height to the rays, and the base of the rayed portion is five eighths of that of the spinous; dorsal and anal rays rough: the anal commences beneath the eighth dorsal spine and ends a little behind that fin; its spines are similar to those of the dorsal, the third the longest, from 2·00-2·50 in the length of the head, and not nearly so long as the rays: ventral pointed, extending to the origin of the anal, and 1·00-1·20 in the length of the head; the spine is serrated and well developed, much longer than the last dorsal spine: pectoral short and rounded, not reaching to above the vent, its length 1·66-1·75 in that of the head: caudal slightly emarginate, the least height of the pedicle 4·33 in the height of the body. Lateral line pointing obliquely upwards for a short distance anteriorly, thence almost straight to the free tail.

Colors.—Brick red: dorsal, anal, and ventral fins hyaline, profusely ornamented with round yellow spots.

Nothing is known of the breeding habits of this species on our coasts, but from the fact of small specimens having been trawled as far up the Parramatta River as Ryde we may infer that these fishes push their way to a considerable distance up our estuaries before depositing their spawn. They commence to arrive in Port Jackson as stragglers about the latter end of November, but are not taken in any numbers until the autumn months when they appear in moderate shoals in some years, but are totally absent in others, as for instance in the preceding year; as these schull fishes show little or no signs of breeding it is probable that they make only a short stay in the waters of the harbor and push on with all possible despatch to the closed waters of the upper reaches, where their presence would remain undetected, and they would be left to their parental duties unmolested by man. The flesh of the "Bullseye" is of good quality.

This species was originally described from Japan and it has, therefore, an extensive range to the south.

Large examples measure as much as twelve inches in length.

Family VI.—MULLIDÆ.

Branchiostegals four: pseudobranchiæ present. Body rather elongate, slightly compressed. Profile of head more or less parabolic. Eyes lateral, of moderate size. Mouth rather small, with lateral cleft. Two erectile barbels below the chin, belonging to the hyal apparatus, and received between the rami of the mandible and the opercles. Teeth feeble, variously placed. Two short dorsal fins, remote from one another, the first with feeble spines: anal similar to the second dorsal. Scales large, feebly ctenid, rather deciduous. Airbladder, when present, simple. Stomach siphonal. Pyloric appendages few or in moderate numbers.

Geographical distribution.—Seas between the tropics principally; some species, however, extending northwards to the Scandinavian and Japanese coasts, and southwards to those of Tasmania. Much more numerous in the eastern than in the western hemisphere. Many of the species enter rivers.

Genus.—MULLUS.

Mullus, Linn. Syst. Nat. i. p. 495, 1766; Cuv. & Val. Hist. Nat. Poiss. iii. p. 419, 1829.

One genus only; characters and distribution as in the family.

Synopsis of Australian Subgenera.

Teeth in both jaws, on the vomer, and on the palatines (*Hypeneoides*).
Teeth in both jaws, and on the vomer; none on the palate (*Hypeneichthys*).
Teeth in both jaws in several series; none on the vomer or palate (*Mulloides*).
Teeth in both jaws in a single series; none on the vomer or palate (*Hypeneus*).

Only one other Subgenus, the true *Mullus*, has been differentiated, the members of which are found in the Mediterranean and Eastern Atlantic only. Eleven species belonging to the family are known to occur in Australian waters, but it may confidently be predicted that this number will still further be extended when the riches of our intertropical fauna have been more thoroughly investigated.

MULLUS POROSUS.

Upeneus porosus, Cuv. & Val. Hist. Nat. Poiss. iii. p. 455, 1829; Less. Voy. Coquille, Zool. p. 216; Gnth. Ann. Nat. Hist. (3) 1867, xx. p. 59; Macleay, Catal. Austr. Fish. i. p. 105.
Upeneichthys porosus, Gnth. Catal. Fish. i. p. 400; ? Casteln. Proc. Zool. Soc. Vict. i. 1872, p. 65, *and* Proc. Linn. Soc. N.S. Wales. iii. p. 371.
Upeneichthys vlamingii, Hector, Trans. N.Z. Inst. ix. p. 465, pl. ix. fig. 5, *and* Ann. Nat. Hist. (4) xix. p. 340.
Hypeneus vlamingii, Ogilby, Catal. N.S. Wales Fish. p. 17.
Hypeneus porosus, Ogilby, Catal. N.S. Wales Fish. p. 17.
Upeneoides vlamingii, Sherrin, Handb. N.Z. Fish. p. 81.

Blue-striped Red Mullet.

B. iv. D. 8. 1/S. A. 2/6. V. 1/5. P. 15–16. C. 15. L. lat. 28–30. L. tr. 2/6. Cœc. pyl. 17. Vert. 10/14.

Length of head 3·40–4·25, of caudal fin 4·25–5·00, height of body 3·50–4·33 in the total length. Diameter of eye from 3·50 in immature to 5·00 in adult examples in the length of the head, and similarly from 1·40–2·33 in that of the snout: interorbital space convex, 1·00-1·50 in the diameter of the eye. Upper jaw the longer: breadth of preorbital three fifths of its height. Barbels well developed, extending to the opercular flap, or even beyond it in immature examples. Maxilla almost hidden by the preorbital when the mouth is closed, not dilated posteriorly, reaching to the anterior margin of the orbit or not quite so far. Upper profile of head rounded, with a slight concavity on the snout. Preopercle entire: opercle with two weak spines. Two rows of conical teeth anteriorly in both jaws, one row laterally; vomerine teeth in two series, each numbering from four to six; palate edentulous. Second or third spine of the first dorsal the longest, 1·25-1·60 in the length of the head; rayed dorsal one half the height of the spinous, but with a slightly longer base: the anal commences beneath the second or third dorsal ray, its second spine being nearly as long as the first ray: the ventrals do not quite reach to the vent, and are four fifths of the length of the head: pectorals short, about equal in length to the ventrals, extending backwards to the ninth or tenth scale of the lateral line: caudal forked, the least height of its pedicle somewhat less than the intradorsal space. Scales in four series between the dorsal fins, in three between the eye and the angle of the preopercle, and in two on the opercle. Tubes of the lateral line profusely branched, especially anteriorly.

Colors.—General color carmine, the upper surfaces, especially the head, with a purple gloss; abdominal region silvery; cheeks ornamented with narrow light blue bands: fins immaculate, or with faint silvery spots and lines.

None of the Red Mullets examined in the preparation of this work showed any signs of breeding, that is from December to March inclusive, and as nothing is mentioned on the subject in the report of the Royal Commission, it may be inferred that nothing is known regarding this important function so far as our two species are concerned. Writing of the British species (*Mullus barbatus*) Dunn (*vide* Day, Brit. Fish. i. p. 24) states:—"They shed only a little at a time, continuing their spawning probably over a month, and differing from all other fish I know. They get very fat at this time." It would be interesting to ascertain whether our species have the same curious habit.

Their food consists of small crustaceans, isopods, worms, molluscs, &c. As a table fish the European Red Mullet has been noted as a luxury since the time of the Roman Empire, but though we have frequently eaten both the species included in this work, having had them cooked in various ways, we are constrained to class them as, at the best, but second rate fishes; when obtained in a perfectly fresh state they are tolerably well flavored, but soft, and so quickly deteriorate. The Red Mullets rarely take a bait, the principal means of capturing them being by the trawl and trammel nets, and until these are in more common use in our seas our markets are not likely to receive more than an intermittent supply of these fishes, and that only during the summer months when they come shorewards into the warm waters of our bays and estuaries.

They are probably common around the greater part of the Australian coast, but they have not as yet been recorded from the northern or western shores. They occur along the entire seaboard of New South Wales, and penetrate rivers as far as the influence of the tide is felt. In Victoria, where according to Castelnau it is called "Red Gurnet," it is "greatly esteemed, and realises a high price in the Melbourne fish market" (Saville Kent), while Lucas adds that it is "not very common," this being probably due to inadequate methods of fishing, a remark which also applies to Johnston's note regarding Tasmania:—"Rare. I have not seen any specimens." Its range extends eastwards to the shores of New Zealand, where it is known to the Maoris as "Pakurakura."

The largest specimen observed on our coast measured twelve inches, but a pair seen in Adelaide approximated to fourteen.

MULLUS SIGNATUS.

Upeneus signatus, Gnth. Ann. Nat. Hist. (3) 1867, xx. p. 59; Macleay, Catal. Austr. Fish. i. p. 106.

Hypeneus signatus, Ogilby, Catal. N.S. Wales Fish. p. 17.

Spotted Red Mullet.
Plate XI.

B. iv. D. 8. 1/8. A. 2/6. V. 1/5. P. 16. C. 15. L. lat. 27–30. L. tr. 2/6. Vert. 10/14.

Length of head 3·66–4·20, of caudal fin 4·40–5·00, height of body 3·60–4·40 in the total length. Diameter of eye from 3·40 in immature to 4·33 in adult examples in the length of the head, and similarly from 1·50–2·15 in that of the snout: interorbital space convex, from 1·00–1·33 in the diameter of the eye. Upper jaw the longer; height of preorbital half of its breadth. Barbels moderately developed, extending a short distance behind the angle of the preopercle. Maxilla not hidden by the preorbital, dilated and fan-shaped posteriorly, not quite or only just reaching to the anterior margin of the eye. Upper profile of head rounded, with a slight concavity on the snout. Preopercle entire: opercle with two weak spines, the lower the stronger. A single row of small conical teeth in each jaw; vomer and palate edentulous. Third spine of the first dorsal the longest, 1·45–1·75 in the length of the head; rayed dorsal three fourths of the height of the spinous, its base about one fourth less than the base of that fin: the anal commences beneath the second or third dorsal ray, and its posterior spine is two thirds of the first ray: the ventral fins do not quite reach to the vent, and are 1·15–1·40 in the length of the head: pectorals equal in length to the ventrals, extending backwards to the twelfth or thirteenth scale of the lateral line: caudal forked, the least height of the pedicle equal to or rather more than the distance between the base of the last spine of the first dorsal and the origin of the second. Two or three series of scales between the dorsal fins, nine between the rayed dorsal and the caudal, three between the eye and the angle of the preopercle, and two on the opercle. Tubes of the lateral line profusely branched, more numerously and conspicuously so anteriorly.

Colors.—Red, the upper surfaces clouded with olive brown; a broad, rather obscure, dusky band from the opercles to beneath the rayed dorsal; caudal pedicle with a large black spot extending over its upper surface, and frequently preceded by a pinkish blotch.

The Spotted Red Mullet is rather more plentiful than *M. porosus* in Port Jackson, and numbers of the young, along with those of other more or less valuable fishes, are frequently left to decay on our sandy beaches by the seine fishers. The adults are not so often seen; the remarks made on the preceding species apply equally to this fish.

Little is known of the range of this species; the only localities from which it has been recorded being Port Jackson and Botany Bay; recently, however, it has been found to occur at Lord Howe Island, whence it was brought by the Australian Museum Expedition of 1888. These specimens were the largest seen as yet, one of them measuring up to ten inches.

Of the two other species—*Hypeneoides tragula* and *H. vlamingi*—mentioned by Macleay as inhabitants of Port Jackson, the former is very rare, only one immature specimen, taken with prawns in the Parramatta River, having come under our notice. As to *Mullus vlamingi*, the authority for the occurrence of which in Port Jackson we are unable to trace, we are inclined to think that some confusion has arisen between it and *M. porosus*, as originally happened to the writer.

Family VII.—CHÆTODONTIDÆ.

Branchiostegals six or seven (four in *Zanclus*): pseudobranchiæ well developed. Body elevated and compressed. Eyes lateral and of moderate size. Mouth situated in front of the snout, generally small, and with a lateral cleft. Teeth in villiform or setiform bands, without canines or incisors: palate edentulous in most genera. Soft portion of the dorsal fin generally of greater extent than the spinous, sometimes considerably more so: anal with three or four spines, the soft portion similar to that of the dorsal: the lower pectoral rays branched: ventrals thoracic with one spine and five rays. Scales cyclid or very finely ciliated, extending to a greater or less extent over the vertical fins, but occasionally absent from the spinous portions. Airbladder present and generally simple. Intestines usually with many convolutions: stomach cœcal. Pyloric appendages in moderate numbers.

Geographical distribution.—Marine carnivorous fishes, mostly of small size and brilliant coloration, inhabiting tropical and subtropical regions, chiefly haunting coral reefs, from which habit they have received the name of "Coral Fishes." A few species have been recorded from rivers and estuaries, but they rarely penetrate beyond reach of the tide.

Genus I.—SCATOPHAGUS.

Scatophagus, Cuv. & Val. Hist. Nat. Poiss. vii. p. 136, 1831.
Cacodoxus, Cantor, Catal. Malay. Fish. p. 163, 1850.

Branchiostegals six: pseudobranchiæ present. Body elevated and much compressed. Snout of moderate length. Preopercle without spine. Palate edentulous. Two dorsals, united at their bases, the first with ten or eleven spines, and with a recumbent spine directed forwards anteriorly: anal with four spines: pectorals short. Scales very small, absent on the spinous portions of the vertical fins. Airbladder simple. Pyloric appendages numerous.

Geographical distribution.—From the east coast of Africa through the seas of India, China, and the Malay Archipelago to Australia.

SCATOPHAGUS MULTIFASCIATUS.

Scatophagus multifasciatus, Richards. Voy. Erebus & Terror, Fish. p. 57, pl. xxxv. ff. 4-6; Gnth. Catal. Fish. ii. p. 60; All. & Macl. Proc. Linn. Soc, N.S. Wales, i. p. 277; Casteln. Proc. Linn. Soc. N.S. Wales, ii. p. 235. *and* iii. p. 376; Macleay, Catal. Austr. Fish. i. p. 96.

Butter Fish.

B. vi. D. 11. 1/16.   A. 4/15-16.   V. 1, 5.   P. 17. C. 16. Vert. 11/12 or 10/13.

Length of head 4·00-4·33, of caudal fin 4·00-4·50, height of body 2·10-2·25 in the total length. Diameter of eye 3·80-4·20 in the length of the head, 1·25-1·40 in that of the snout, and 1·33-1·75 in the interorbital space, which is slightly convex. Nostrils approximate, the anterior round and surrounded by a low raised edge, the posterior oval and a little larger. Snout in front of the anterior margins of the orbits greatly swollen, the occiput rising abruptly from the middle of the interorbital space. Upper jaw a little the longer. Cleft of mouth small and transverse, the maxilla extending to beneath the anterior nostril, or a little further. Postero-inferior angle of preorbital minutely serrated: preopercle rough. Villiform teeth in the jaws, with an outer enlarged row of tricuspid teeth, the central cusp being the longest. The dorsal commences above the posterior angle of the base of the pectoral; the fourth spine is the longest, from 1·20-1·60 in the length of the head, and subequal to the anterior rays; the first spine is about a third of the length of the second, which is two fifths of that of the third: the anal commences beneath the last dorsal spine; its spines are strong but short, the first and second the longest, scarcely as long as the second dorsal spine, and not half the length of the anterior rays; outer margin of rayed dorsal and anal truncated: the ventral does not reach to the origin of the anal; its length is 1·33-1·66 in that of the head; the spine is nearly as long as the outer ray and about equals the seventh dorsal spine in length: pectorals small and rounded, from 1·66-1·85 in the length of the head: caudal emarginate, the least height of the pedicle equal in length to the snout. Lateral line strongly curved to the caudal pedicle.

Colors.—General color silvery; upper surface and sides with six broad vertical dark green bands, composed of large elongated spots, the interspaces with bands of smaller, less conspicuous spots; sides of abdomen with two or three inconspicuous longitudinal bands; lips, occiput, and two intermediate bands, the anterior between the nostrils and joined mesially to the lips, the posterior crossing the interorbital space, a narrow band traversing the lower margin of the cheek, the upper part of the opercle, and the dorsal ridge dark green; rest of upper surface of the head yellow: dorsal and anal fin rays yellow, the membranes dark green; caudal yellowish anteriorly, dusky posteriorly.

During the autumn and summer months this fish appears, often in considerable numbers, from the northern fishing stations which supply the Sydney market. As a food fish it cannot be recommended, nevertheless it commands a ready sale in the market, and is doubtless sold to the uninitiated, after having been skinned and cooked, as " fried bream." It is reported to be a very foul feeder, and this habit has gained for it the generic name employed by the authors of the Histoire Naturelle des Poissons, which literally means "excrement eating." In this connection, not having any data concerning our own species in which to trust, it may be as well to record in what estimation its congener *S. argus*,—a species which is found throughout the seas of India, China, and the Malay Archipelago, and is common on the northern coasts of Australia, rare specimens having been recorded even as far south as Sydney—is held by other observers as regards its edible qualities.

Alluding to this latter species Day writes:—" It enters back waters and rivers, but is a foul feeder, and so far as I have observed is not in request as food"; quoting Hamilton Buchanan, he says:—" when newly caught it is a fish of great beauty, easy digestion, and excellent flavor, but after death it soon becomes soft and strong tasted"; Cantor states that at Penang " it is eaten by the natives, though many reject it on account of its reputed disgusting habits"; while Bennett remarks that in Ceylon " it is generally esteemed, its flesh partaking of the flavor of trout."

With such conflicting testimony as to the edible value of these fishes it is difficult to arrive at a just conclusion, but the probability is that examples captured in the open sea are wholesome and of good flavor when consumed fresh.

The Butterfish is plentiful on all the shores of Australia from King George's Sound, round West and North Australia, and extending its range southwards along the eastern coast at least as far as the latitude of Sydney; they have not been recorded from Victorian or Tasmanian waters.

Specimens measuring as much as sixteen inches are occasionally seen in the Sydney market, but the average length is about eight inches. The greater number of these fishes consigned to the market come from Lake Macquarie.

Genus II.—SCORPIS.

Scorpis, Cuv. & Val. Hist. Nat. Poiss. viii. p. 245, 1831.

Branchiostegals seven: pseudobranchiæ present. Body oblong-ovate and compressed. Snout of moderate length. Preopercle more or less finely serrated. Jaws with an outer series of enlarged teeth: teeth present on the vomer and palatines. One dorsal, with nine or ten spines: the anal with three. Scales small: soft portions of the vertical fins scaly, the spinous portions with a basal scaly sheath. Airbladder present. Pyloric appendages in very large numbers.

Geographical distribution.—Coasts of Australia, New Zealand, and Chili; Juan Fernandez.

SCORPIS ÆQUIPINNIS.

Scorpis æquipinnis, Richards. Voy. Erebus & Terror, Fish. p. 121, 1846; Gnth. Catal. Fish. ii. p. 64; Casteln. Proc. Linn. Soc. N. S. Wales, iii. p. 376; Macleay, Catal. Austr. Fish. i. p. 97; Woods, Fisher. N. S. Wales, p. 37, pl. vi.
Scorpis boops, Peters, SB. Ak. Berl. 1866, p. 519.
Scorpis lineolata, Kner, Voy. Novara, Fisch. p. 108, pl. v. fig. 3.

Sweep.

Plate X.

B. vii. D. 10/27-28. A. 3/25-27. V. 1/5. P. 19. C. 17. L. lat. 72-76. L. tr. 13-15/31-33. Cœc. pyl. num. Vert. 10/15.

Length of head 4·90-5·10, of caudal fin 3·66-3·90, height of body 2·75-3·00 in the total length. Eye moderate, its diameter 3·00-3·40 in the length of the head, and 1·00-1·25 in the convex interorbital space: snout short, obtusely rounded, 1·15-1·33 in the diameter of the eye. Nostrils oval, approximate, the anterior the larger, and on a slightly lower plane than the posterior. Jaws equal. Cleft of mouth small and oblique; maxilla triangular, convex behind, extending to a little behind the vertical from the anterior margin of the orbit. Lower limb and angle of the preopercle finely serrated, vertical limb rough, but without distinct serrations. Teeth villiform; jaws with minute teeth forming a broad but short patch in the upper, and a narrower but much longer band in the lower jaw; the outer row much enlarged and curved, with their tips yellow. Spinous portion of dorsal low, the spines, which are moderately strong and acute, increasing gradually in height to the last, which is three and a quarter to three and a half times the length of the first, and 2·50–2·75 in that of the head; the rays grow gradually shorter from the anterior ones, which are from one third to one fourth longer than the longest spine; length of base of spinous dorsal 1·75–1·85 in that of the rayed: anal similar in form to the dorsal, commencing beneath the last dorsal spine; its third spine longer than but not so strong as the second, equal in length to the longest dorsal spine or slightly shorter: the ventral reaches to the vent, its spine is half the length of the first ray, which is from 1·85–2·00 in that of the head: pectoral well developed, rounded, reaching to the vertical from the origin of the anal, and but little shorter than the head: caudal forked; the least height of its pedicle 1·50–1·66 in the height of the body. Scales finely ciliated; the entire head, except the lips, circumnasal membrane, and maxilla scaly; soft portions of the vertical fins clothed with minute scales, spinous portions with a basal scaly sheath. Lateral line in a long gentle curve, parallel to the dorsal profile.

Colors.—Silvery blue, darkest above, with a distinct dark blue axillary spot when alive; dull brown after death.

The Sweep occurs in the Sydney markets in moderate quantities throughout the year, but is in best condition during the summer and autumn months. The spawn is deposited in sheltered bays and harbors during the early winter months, and the young, to the length of three or four inches, are frequently taken by the trawl and seine in spring and summer. In the Report of the Royal Commission on Fisheries the following sentence occurs:—" It is seldom caught except in the seine, and is probably entirely a vegetable feeder." That the conclusion arrived at on this subject by the Commissioners is erroneous can be substantiated both from the personal examination of many specimens and from the testimony of Mr. Alexander Oliver, who states that " he has caught thousands with a live or meat bait." Remains of small crustaceans and worms were found in all the specimens examined by us, and in one example a small cuttle, *Octopus granulatus*, Lamarck, was present; in no case was vegetable matter detected in the intestines. As food it is only moderate, nevertheless it commands a ready sale in the market at fair prices.

The exact distribution of *S. æquipinnis* is difficult to determine, but specimens are in the British Museum from Swan River, West Australia, and King George's Sound, while, as has been shown, it is abundant on the New South Wales coast; Lucas, however, omits it from his Census of Victorian Fishes, as also does Johnston in his Catalogue of Tasmanian Fishes, the latter, however, including the western *S. georgianus*, with the remarks, " Rare. Not seen." How far it ranges to the north is also a matter of conjecture, Alleyne and Macleay having described as new a form, *S. vinosa*, from Darnley Island, north-eastern Queensland, which it is to be inferred from his Preliminary Report on the Food Fishes of that colony Saville Kent considers worthy of recognition. Its eastwardly distribution extends as far as Lord Howe Island.

Twelve inches is the maximum size to which the Sweep attains; and it may be here remarked that a very distinct fish, *Girella simplex*, goes by the name of "Sweep" in Tasmania.

Family VIII.—SPARIDÆ.

Branchiostegals five to seven: pseudobranchiæ present. Body oblong or oblong-ovate, compressed. Eyes of moderate size, lateral. Mouth in front of the snout, with lateral cleft. Bones of the head with a rudimentary muciferous system. More or less broad and trenchant or conical teeth in front of the jaws, with or without lateral series of molar teeth: palatines generally smooth. One dorsal fin formed by a subequally developed spinous and soft portion: anal with three spines: lower pectoral rays branched: ventrals thoracic, with one spine and five rays. Lateral line continuous, not extending along the caudal fin. Scales cycloid or feebly ctenoid.

Geographical distribution.—Seas of temperate and tropical regions; some species entering fresh water.

Genus I.—PIMELEPTERUS.

Pimelepterus, (Lacép.) Cuvier, Règne Anim.; Cuv. & Val. Hist. Nat. Poiss. vii. p. 254, 1831.

Branchiostegals seven: pseudobranchiæ present. Body ovate and but little compressed. Preopercle with or without serrature. Villiform teeth in the jaws, with an outer row of strong incisors: vomer, palatines, and tongue with small teeth. One dorsal fin with eleven spines: anal with three. Scales of moderate size, the soft portion of the vertical fins scaly. Airbladder divided posteriorly into two horns, and sometimes notched anteriorly. Pyloric appendages few or very numerous.

Geographical distribution.—Tropical and subtropical seas, more especially of the eastern hemisphere.

PIMELEPTERUS SYDNEYANUS.

Pachymetopon grande, Macleay, Catal. Austr. Fish. i. p. 106, 1881 (*nec Gnth.*).
Pimelepterus sydneyanus, Gnth. Ann. Nat. Hist. (5) 1886, xviii. p. 368.
Pimelepterus meridionalis, Ogilby, Proc. Zool. Soc. 1886, p. 539.

Drummer.
Plate XVI.

B. vii. D. (10)—11/12 A. 3/10. V. 1/5. P. 17. C 17. L. lat. 57–59. L. tr. 10/19 Cœc. pyl. very num. Vert. 11/15.

Length of head 4·85–5·15, of caudal fin 4·25–5·00, height of body 3·00–3·20 in the total length. Eyes moderate, 3·75–4·00 in length of the head, 1·33–1·75 in that of the obtusely rounded snout, and 1·80–2·30 in the convex interorbital space. Upper profile of head rather flat, with a transverse rounded protuberance in front of the eyes. Upper jaw rather the longer. Cleft of mouth small and transverse, the maxilla extending to beneath the anterior margin of the orbit. Opercular bones entire. A single row of strong curved teeth in the jaws, the posterior horizontal portion equal in length to the vertical; behind these a narrow band of similar but smaller and non-functional teeth, intended to replace losses in the outer cutting series; vomer, palatines, and tongue densely crowded with minute teeth. Dorsal spines of moderate strength, increasing in height to the sixth and seventh, which are 1·75–2·10 in the length of the head, and much higher than the rays: third anal spine the longest and strongest; anterior anal rays equal in length to the highest dorsal spine: pectorals short and rounded, as long as or a little longer than the ventrals, 1·33-1·50 in the length of the head: caudal emarginate, the least height of the pedicle two thirds of the distance between the last dorsal ray and the origin of the caudal. Scales feebly ctenid, extending on to the frontal protuberance, much larger on the body than on the head, those below the lateral line larger than those above it; eighteen scales between the origin of the ventral and the lateral line, and eight between the latter and the base of the sixth dorsal spine.

Colors.—Dark gray, washed with silver on the lower part of the sides; upper surface of head darkest: all the fins dark colored: irides golden and silvery about equally mixed.

The "Drummer" of the Sydney fishermen,—not of Macleay's Catalogue, p. 108, which is a perfectly distinct fish, not distinguished by them from the ordinary Blackfishes—is not uncommon in Port Jackson and Broken Bay, and though occasionally a dozen or more may be seen at one time in the market, this is certainly the exception, not because of the rarity of the fish, but owing to its habit of frequenting closely the neighborhood of rocky shores and inlets where the nets in vogue here cannot be used. As stated by the author in 1886 (*loc. cit.*), "it is a true rockfish, dwelling in the crevices and indentations of our rocky shores, where it finds abundant food and shelter; it is not given to roaming, and is only taken by the trammel, one end of which is attached to the shore, against which the mesh must actually lie or else the fish would assuredly pass inside, whence it happens that this fish is almost always caught within a few feet of the shore." So far as I can ascertain it is never known to take a bait.

The breeding season is about midsummer, and the ova is probably deposited in sheltered spots among weed covered rocks.

As food the Drummer is held in little estimation, and does not readily command a sale in the market, nevertheless halfgrown examples are quite equal in flavor to the other herbivorous Sparids.

Either the range of this fish is extraordinarily limited, or the local naturalists to the northward have failed to recognise this very distinct species; to the south no considerable extension of range is to be expected in a fish of this genus. From three localities only, namely, Port Jackson, Broken Bay, and Port Stephens have we been enabled to obtain any reliable record of its occurrence.

The Drummer grows to the length of thirty inches.

Genus II.—GIRELLA.

Girella, Gray, Illustr. Ind. Zool. 1830-35.
Melanichthys, Schleg. Faun. Japon. Poiss. p. 75, 1850.
Crenidens, sp. Richards.

Branchiostegals six: pseudobranchiæ present. Body oblong-ovate and compressed. Opercle with a small spine; preopercular armature rudimentary or absent. Jaws with one or more series of functional, usually, tricuspidate incisors, behind which is a pluriserial band of similar but less developed teeth, destined to replace losses in the former: vomer and palatines with or without a small patch of similar teeth. One dorsal fin, with from thirteen to fifteen spines, which are receivable into an incomplete groove: anal with three spines. Scales of moderate size, finely ctenid: cheeks, occiput, and upper portion of the opercle scaly: rows of small scales on the membranes of the vertical fins. Airbladder bilobed posteriorly. Pyloric appendages in large numbers.

Geographical distribution.—Australian, Chinese, and Japanese seas.

As nothing appears to be accurately known as to the place selected for the deposition of their ova by our herbivorous Sparid fishes, the following remarks, published by Mr. W. Saville Kent, in *Nature* (May 8, 1873), on the breeding habits of the allied genus *Cantharus* may prove of interest, and may induce some of our seashore residents to observe more carefully the time and place of spawning of these and other valuable food fishes of the Colony. Writing of *C. lineatus*, which curiously enough goes by the name of "Black Bream" on the south coast of England, he remarks concerning examples under his personal observation in the Brighton Aquarium, that the males, "retiring from the remainder of the shoal, select certain separate and prescribed areas at the bottom of the tank, where they commence excavating considerable hollows in the sand or shingle by the rapid and powerful action of the tail and lower portion of the body. A depression of suitable size having been produced, each male now mounts vigilant guard over his respective hollow, and vigorously attacks and drives away any other fish of the same sex that ventures to trespass within the magic circle he has appropriated to himself. Towards his companion of the opposite sex his conduct is far different. Many of the latter are now distended with spawn, and these he endeavors by all the means in his power to lure singly to his prepared hollow, now discovered to be a true nest or spawning bed, and there to deposit the myriad ova with which they are laden, which he then protects and guards with the greatest care."

GIRELLA TRICUSPIDATA.

Box tricuspidatus, Quoy & Gaim. Voy. Freyc. Zool. p. 296., 1824.
Oblata tricuspidata, Cuv. & Val. Hist. Nat. Poiss. vi. p. 372.
Crenidens triglyphus, Richards. Voy. Erebus & Terror, Fish. p. 36, pl. xxv. fig. 2.
Girella tricuspidata, Gnth. Catal. Fish. i. p. 428; Macleay, Catal. Austr. Fish. i. p. 107; Woods, Fisher. N. S. Wales, p. 39, pl. vii; Johnston Proc. Roy. Soc. Tas. 1882, pp. 69, 111.
Melanichthys tricuspidata, Casteln. Proc. Zool. Soc. Vict. 1872, i. p. 57.
Girella blackii, Casteln. Proc. Zool. Soc. Vict. ii. p. 41.

Blackfish.

Plate XII.

B. vi. D. 15/11-12. A. 3/11-12. V. 1/5. P. 16. C. 17. L. lat. 48-51. L. tr. 10/23-25. Cœc. pyl. num. Vert. 11/16.

Length of head 4·50-5·00, of caudal fin 4·75-5·00, height of body 3·00-3·75 in the total length. Diameter of eye 4·00-4·50 in the length of the head, 1·50-1·66 in that of the obtusely rounded snout, and 1·33-1·66 in that of the interorbital space, which is convex. Upper profile of the head slightly convex, much swollen in front of the eyes so as to form a marked concavity immediately behind the jaws. Upper jaw the longer. Cleft of mouth small and transverse, the maxilla reaching to or a little beyond the posterior nostril: the height of the preorbital is four fifths of its breadth. A small flat spine on the opercle: vertical limb of the preopercle slightly inclined backwards, and finely denticulated; lower limb smooth. A pluriserial band of tricuspid teeth in the jaws, the two outer rows functional, and separated from the others by an interspace ; a small patch of teeth, similar to the partially developed postlabial teeth, on the anterior part of the palatines. Dorsal spines increasing in length to the seventh or eighth, whence there is little or no difference to the last, which is 2·15–2·55 in the length of the head ; the rays are subequal to the spines in height ; the base of the rayed portion is five eighths of that of the spinous: the anal commences beneath the first dorsal ray and ends opposite the termination of the dorsal, the rays of which are not nearly so long as those of the anal ; the third spine is the longest, much stronger, and but little shorter than the longest dorsal spine, but not nearly so strong as the second anal spine: ventrals not extending to the vent, 1·33–1·60 in the length of the head: pectorals small, 1·25–1·33 in the same: caudal slightly emarginate, the least height of the pedicle equal to the distance between the last dorsal ray and the origin of the caudal. Scales moderate, feebly ctenid, adherent ; cheeks and upper third of opercle scaly, remainder of head naked : dorsal and anal fins with a basal scaly sheath : a row of small scales between the rays. Lateral line following the curvature of the back.

Colors.—Blackish or dark brown above, lighter below ; or silvery gray with a variable number of dark brown transverse bands.

This is by far the most common species of *Girella* sent to the Sydney market. It is not easy to arrive at any certainty, from published documents, as to locality made use of for depositing the spawn, but in Mr. Glover's report to the Royal Commission he states, writing from Twofold Bay, that "Bream, black, silver, and red, and the Black-fish . . . . spawn among weeds, and in deep holes with a muddy bottom"; so far as estuaries and creeks are concerned this is doubtless correct, but that they also spawn on the outer beaches is equally certain as the young, measuring from one to three inches, are to be found in rock pools during the autumn and winter months, As to the season of shedding the spawn that appears to be indisputably fixed for the first three months of the year from our own observations in the neighborhood of Sydney, those of Mr. Glover at Twofold Bay, and those of Mr. Hood Pegus at the Clarence Heads.

Like most, if not all, herbivorous fishes the Blackfish rapidly deteriorates in flavor after death, nevertheless when freshly caught it is by no means to be despised, especially if the contents of the stomach are immediately removed.

These fishes go in shoals and are chiefly taken for the market by means of the seine, and Tenison Woods writes "in certain seasons they may be caught in abundance in shallow water with the line, the only bait being a green confervid weed obtained on wood under sea water."

The Blackfish is very abundant along the entire coastline of the Colony, frequenting estuaries, creeks, and tidal rivers, as well as the open sea ; it is also common on the coast of Victoria, where it goes by the names of "Black Perch" and "Rock Perch" and, according to Castelnau, is "esteemed as an article of food." Speaking of it in Tasmania, Johnston mentions that it is common, but does not ascend estuaries as far as *Chrysophrys australis ;* it is called "Black Bream" in that colony. Of the extent of its range to the westward we have no certain record, while it is not mentioned by Saville Kent from the Queensland coast, though there can be little doubt of its occurrence in the southern waters of that colony at least.

The average length of examples forwarded to the Sydney markets is about twelve inches, but examples of the length of twenty one are occasionally obtainable.

GIRELLA SIMPLEX.

Crenidens simplex, Richards. Voy. Erebus & Terror, Fish. p. 120., 1846.
Girella simplex, Gnth. Catal. Fish. i. p. 429; Macleay, Catal. Austr. Fish.
    i. p. 107; McCoy, Prodr. Zool. Vic. dec. viii. pl. 73; Johnston, Proc.
    Roy. Soc. Tas. 1882, pp. 69, 111; Sherrin, Handb. N.Z. Fish. p. 71.
Melanichthys simplex, Casteln. Proc. Zool. Soc. Vict. 1872, i. p. 68.
Girella percoides, Hector, Trans. N. Z. Inst. vii. p. 243, pl. x. f. 6D, *and* ix. p.
    468, pl. viii. f. 6c.

Ludrick.

B. vi. D. 15-14/12-13. A. 3/12. V. 1/5. P. 17. C. 17. L. lat. 50-53. L. tr. 11/20-24. Cœc. pyl. num. Vert. 11/16.

Length of head 4·50-5·00, of caudal fin 4·75, height of body 2·75-3·00 in the total length. Diameter of eye 3·80-4·00 in the length of the head, 1·40-1·60 in that of the snout, and 1·50 in the convex interorbital space. Snout convex; occiput almost flat. Upper jaw the longer. Cleft of mouth small and transverse, the maxilla not quite extending to the posterior nostril. Opercle with a flat spine, which is sometimes bifid: vertical limb of preopercle straight, but inclining slightly backwards, the rounded angle distinctly serrated. Jaws with two or three irregular series of compressed incisors, having the cutting edge entire and moderately broad; behind them a broad band of small tricuspid ones; a curved band of minute teeth on the vomer present or absent; a small pyriform patch on the palatines. Dorsal spines rather strong, increasing in length to the eighth, which is about 2·66 in the length of the head; rayed dorsal subequal in height to the spinous, its basal length about half of the base of the same: the anal commences beneath the last or penultimate dorsal spine; its rays are much longer than those of the dorsal, and their outer margin is truncate; the third spine is a little longer than the second, and 3·20-3·33 in the length of the head: ventrals not extending to the vent, their length 1·50-1·66 in that of the head: pectoral moderate, 1·20-1·50 in the same: caudal emarginate, with moderately pointed lobes. Scales moderate, feebly ctenid, firmly adherent; those on the throat smallest and elongate; cheek scales small and deeply imbedded: streaks of small scales between the dorsal and anal rays, and the dorsal spines except the first three. Lateral line gently curved to the end of the dorsal; its tubes simple.

Colors.—Above brown, with a purple tinge, becoming lighter on the sides; abdominal region whitish or yellowish: sides of the head and the pectoral fins yellowish.

This species is not nearly so plentiful as is the preceding, from the dark variety of which it may usually be distinguished by its generally lighter colors and from the lighter variety by the absence of bands, which, if present at any stage of growth, do not appear to be ever persistent, as in its congener, which it resembles in all respects in habits, &c., and with which it is confounded by the fishermen.

It inhabits the entire seaboard of New South Wales and ranges northwards along the Queensland coast at least as far as Murray Island. In Victoria Lucas gives it as an inhabitant of the "Gippsland Lakes," and as "not very uncommon in Port Phillip." McCoy remarks:—"This is one of the best fishes for the table found in Victoria, but is not well known to the public or to the dealers, although abundant in the Gippsland Lakes." Further westward we have no record; in Tasmania it is common, and goes by the name of "Sweep." It is also a native of New Zealand waters, where it is known as the Perch.

The largest example obtained in our market measured twenty three inches.

In order to distinguish it from *G. tricuspidata* I have adopted the trivial name "Ludrick," which is given to it by the Gippsland Aborigines.

GIRELLA CYANEA.

Girella cyanea, Macleay, Catal. Aust. Fish. i. p. 108, 1881; Ogilby, Proc. Zool. Soc. 1887, p. 893.

Bluefish.

B. vi. D. 15–14/12–13. A. 3/11. V. 1/5. P. 19–20. C. 17. L. lat. 54–57. L. tr. 11/25–28. Cœc. pyl. num. Vert. 11/16.

Length of head 4·66–5·33, of caudal fin 4·00–4·80, height of body 2·75–3·60 in the total length. Diameter of eye 3·75–4·40 in the length of the head, 1·33–1·75 in that of the snout, and 1·25–1·75 in the convex interorbital space. Upper profile of head slightly convex. Upper jaw the longer. Cleft of mouth small and transverse, the maxilla reaching to beneath the posterior nostril: height of preorbital 1·00–1·25 in its length. Opercle with a flat spinous point, which is sometimes divided: vertical limb of the preopercle inclining slightly backwards, feebly denticulated, except in very old examples where it is entire; lower limb smooth. A pluriserial band of tricuspid teeth in the jaws, the outer row strong, compressed, and functional, separated from the others by an interspace; small patches of deeply imbedded teeth, similar to the non-functional incisors teeth, generally present on the vomer and on the anterior portion of the palatines. Dorsal spines of moderate strength, increasing in length to about the eighth, whence there is little or no difference to the last, which is 2·25–2·80 in the length of the head; the rays are subequal in height to the spines; base of rayed portion one half to four sevenths of that of the spinous: the anal commences beneath the origin of the soft dorsal, and its rays are much longer than those of that fin; the third spine is much stronger and but little shorter than the longest dorsal spines; the outer margin of the anal rays is obliquely truncated: ventrals not extending to the vent, 1·20–1·40 in the length of the head: pectorals moderate, 1·00–1·25 in the same: caudal deeply emarginate, with acute lobes; the least height of the pedicle equal to the distance between the base of the last dorsal ray and the origin of the caudal. Scales moderate, feebly ctenid, firmly adherent; those on the throat much smaller and more oblong in shape; head scales deeply imbedded: dorsal and anal fins with a basal scaly sheath, and rows of minute scales between the rays and spines, with the exception of the three anterior dorsal spines. Lateral line with a long slight curve to the end of the dorsal; its tubes simple.

Colors.—Upper parts bright blue, the body with numerous golden spots, which decrease in number with age; below pale blue.

The Bluefish is much less common in the Sydney market than either of the two species of *Girella* previously mentioned; and it is also noticeable that all the examples so obtained are very large; they are in all probability much more abundant than is generally supposed, but being purely ocean fishes, which do not enter rivers and estuaries for the purpose of spawning, they do not come within the scope of the ordinary net fishermen, and such as find their way to the market are taken by the professional line fishermen. A large female example caught off Botany Heads during the month of

December had the ova ready for extrusion, while another taken off Broken Bay within a few days was in poor condition and showed unmistakable signs of having shed its spawn but a short time previously; numerous examples examined between March and June showed no vestiges of spawn; we may, therefore, infer that the breeding season on this part of the coast is rather earlier than is the case with *G. tricuspidata* and *G. simplex*, and that the ova is deposited at a considerable depth, and, judging from the habits of the fish, probably in the vicinity of weed-covered rocks.

As referred to above, the Bluefish varies entirely from the Blackfish and Ludrick in its preference for the open sea; it delights in bold rocky coasts, and being a strong hardy fish is apparently indifferent to the wildest storms, a fact to which the configuration of the powerful caudal fin, which differs greatly from that of its congeners, probably bears some relationship; this divergence in habits is best illustrated by studying examples of the three species confined in the same tank in an aquarium, for while this species will be found to swim restlessly round and round the tank, the others are content to move sluggishly about or remain in the same spot with gently moving fins.

As food this species is much superior to its congeners, and this is easy to account for, not only because of its residence in the open sea, but also that it is not purely herbivorous, but apparently prefers a more or less flesh diet; for while the Blackfishes are almost invariably found to contain masses of green seaweeds, the intestines of the present species rarely contain any except the calcareous sorts, and these are always mixed with other substances, such as hydrid zoophytes, boltinias, prawns, squid, and the remains of fishes, among which were distinguished Yellowtail (*Caranx trachurus*), Hardyhead (*Atherina pinguis*), Whiting (*Sillago maculata*), and a Flatfish (*Lophonectes gallus*).

On the New South Wales coast they have not been recorded elsewhere than from the limited area comprised between Port Hacking Heads and those of Broken Bay, but I have little doubt that sooner or later they will be found in numbers further north. So far as our present knowledge goes the metropolis of the species is Lord Howe Island, where it is abundant at all seasons, and forms one of the staple articles of food among the inhabitants, being used either fresh, salted, or smoked. It is taken principally, if not altogether, by means of handlines, and grows to about thirty inches in length. The largest specimen measured by us was over twenty five inches and was caught off Broken Bay.

Genus III.—PAGRUS.

Pagrus. Cuv. Règne Anim.; Cuv. & Val. Hist. Nat. Poiss. vi. p. 141, 1830.
Chrysophrys, Cuv. Règne Anim.; Cuv. & Val. Hist. Nat. Poiss. vi. p. 81.

Branchiostegals six: pseudobranchiæ present. Body oblong-ovate and somewhat compressed. Jaws with an anterior row of conical or compressed canines, and from two to four lateral rows of rounded molars. A single dorsal fin, with from eleven to thirteen, rarely elongated, spines, which are receivable into a groove at their base: the anal with three. Scales of moderate size, cycloid or finely ctenid: cheeks scaly. Airbladder usually simple, but sometimes notched or with very short appendages. Pyloric appendages, when present, in small numbers.

PAGRUS UNICOLOR.

Chrysophrys unicolor, Quoy & Gaim. Voy. Uranie, p. 209.
Pagrus unicolor, Cuv. & Val. Hist. Nat. Poiss. vi. p. 160; Richards. Ichthyol. China, p. 242; Gnth. Catal. Fish. i. p. 468; Castelu. Proc. Zool. Soc. Vict. 1872, i. p. 70; Kner, Voy. Novara, Fisch. p. 85; Macleay, Catal. Austr. Fish. i. p. 116; Woods, Fisher. N. S. Wales, p. 39, pl. viii. *and Frontispiece*; Johnston, Proc. Zool. Soc. Tas. 1882, pp. 69, 111; Sherrin, Handb. N. Z. Fish. p. 85.
Pagrus guttulatus, Cuv. & Val. Hist. Nat. Poiss. vi. p. 160; Less. Voy. Coquille, Zool. ii. p. 188.

Snapper.

Plate XIII.

B. vi. D. 12/10. A. 3/8. V. 1/5. P. 15. C. 17. L. lat. 54-55. L. tr. 9-10/16-17. Cæc. pyl. 4. Vert. 10/14.

Length of head 4·25-4·50, of caudal fin 3·66-4·00, height of body 3·00-3·33 in the total length. Diameter of eye 3·50-4·00 in the length of the head, 1·40-1·80 in that of the snout, and 1·00-1·33 in the convex interorbital space. Nostrils at some distance apart, the anterior small and subcircular, the posterior much larger, elongate-ovoid, not entering the orbital ring. Upper jaw a little the longer. Cleft of mouth moderate and slightly oblique, the maxilla extending to beneath the anterior margin of the orbit or a little beyond it. Upper profile of head rounded in the young; mature examples with a conspicuous bony knob on the occiput, which in very old males attains to an enormous development, and is accompanied by a corresponding excrescence of smaller size on the snout. A short, compressed, blunt point on the opercle. Both jaws with four small canines in front, and with a lateral row of teeth, the anterior of which are conical, the others molariform; inside these are from one to three irregular series of small molars, with two or three enlarged ones about midway. Dorsal spines rather weak, flexible, the third, sometimes the fourth, the longest, 1·80-2·10 in the length of the head; the last spine about three fifths of the first ray, which is much lower than the longest spines: the anal commences beneath the anterior dorsal ray or last dorsal spine, and ends opposite or a little before the last ray; the third spine is the longest, not much longer but slightly weaker than the second, and from 2·75-3·15 in the length of the head; the rays are very little longer than the spines: the ventrals do not reach the vent; the outer ray is the longest, from 1·30-1·40 in the length of the head; the spine is long and slender, longer than the highest dorsal spine: pectorals elongate and falcate, reaching to above the first to fourth anal rays, and from one tenth to one fifth longer than the head: caudal forked, the least height of its pedicle about one fourth of the height of the body. Scales finely ctenid, in six series between the eye and the angle of the preopercle, and in eight across the opercle; rest of the head naked. Lateral line curved to about the anterior third of the spinous dorsal, from thence parallel to the dorsal profile.

Colors.—Varying with age from silvery red in the young to bright red in the adult, the upper parts of which, especially the head, are tinted with brown; the abdominal region is pinkish or silvery; the body is ornamented with pale blue spots, which are numerous in the young and entirely disappear in very old examples.

Owing to no systematic attempt having been made to obtain reliable evidence on the breeding of even our principal food fishes,—a subject which, affecting as it assuredly does the food supply and through it the material welfare of the masses, should long ago have received enlightened attention from the Government of the Colony—we are still in the same humiliating position that the Royal Commission of twelve years ago were placed when they authorised the printing of the following paragraph:—" The actual mode of the deposition or attachment of the spawn has never been observed, and the same may be said of the date of the first appearance of the young fry, but there can be little doubt that the deposition takes place in moderately deep water near the land, and that the young are probably hatched before the winter season."

Of the various special reports furnished to the Royal Commission three only make any attempt to solve the difficulty, and in these the evidence, if it merits such a title, is contradictory and extremely unsatisfactory; from Twofold Bay Mr. Glover reports:—" Their time of spawning is in November. They spawn out on the sandbank. I think they spawn loose on the top of the sand." Mr. George Mulhall, senr., writing from Broken Bay remarks:—" Snapper are very prolific with roe in this month (March), but when they spawn I am unable to say." And Mr. Wilson, refering to the Newcastle District, says:—" This—*i.e.*, the number of very small Snapper present inshore, where the school fish never appear—leads me to think that Snapper spawn on the roughest rocks close inshore, and I doubt not that they are better protected there from their chief enemies, the sharks." In this unsatisfactory state this most important subject must of necessity be left at present.

The Snapper is the premier sporting fish of New South Wales, for though occasionally captured by deeply sunken nets in Lake Macquarie and elsewhere, it is essentially a line fish, and pleasure parties and fishing clubs frequently set out from Port Jackson to the various sunken reefs, known as Snapper-grounds, within easy reach of that port, or even charter a steamer for a week, and make more extended excursions north or south; these fishes play most determinedly, and being possessed of great strength no little skill is requisite to safely land a large fish. The following observations from the pen of the late Mr. Edward Hill aptly describe the capture of an old male:—" The tugging, jerking motion of the Snapper is unmistakable, and when he gets his shoulder to the line he goes off with a rapidity that makes the cord whistle again, either through your fingers or over the boat's gunwale; a steady and continuous strain, no stray line, together with some skill, enables you to safely land him, at which time you can realize that your patience, toil, and anxiety are rewarded with a fish from twenty to twenty five pounds weight, fit to embellish a noble banquet." The same gentleman tells us that the bait for these fishes are starfish, squid, mackerel, yellowtail, mullet, tailors, and a variety of other fishes; the whole of these at particular time will be readily taken, but when the Snapper appears dainty, mackerel and squid may tempt him when all others fail.

It was long contended, and the opinion is still held by a few, that there were three kinds of Snapper, known popularly as "Red Bream," "Squire," and "Snapper"; these, however, have long been proved to be merely stages in the growth of the same species, the Red Bream being the young fish of under a year's growth, which are extremely numerous in all sheltered localities along the coast during the summer months, and form the chief sport of the juvenile population; the Squire is the half-grown fish up to two or three years of age, beyond which they have attained to the full dignity of Snapper.

In the condensed report of the Royal Commission the following passages occur:—"The Snapper is the most valuable of Australian fishes, not for its superior excellence, for we have many more delicious, but for the abundant and regular supply which it affords of a very nutritious and wholesome description of food. It is found on all parts of the Australian coast, but most abundantly on that of New South Wales. It is a deepwater fish, found generally on or near rocky points, or reefs running out for miles from the coast. Its food is chiefly the mollusca living on the rocks, though the readiness with which it will snap up bait of the most varied descriptions indicates tastes of a rather omnivorous character. Like all or most fishes, it has its periods of migration and accumulation in shoals. The time of the appearance of the 'School Snapper' is the early part of summer; it is then believed to be at least three years old, the previous stages of its existence being well known under the names 'Red Bream' at the age of one year and of 'Squire' at two. At a still greater age the Snapper seems to cease to school, and becomes what is known as the 'Native' and 'Rock Native' a solitary and sometimes enormously large fish." According to Tenison Woods the aboriginal name of these large examples is "Wollomai."

Referring to the Melbourne market Castelnau states:—"The Snapper is one of the largest and handsomest fishes (brought thither). It is found all the year round, but the specimens caught in the cold months of the year are generally small; in November and December it becomes much more abundant, and very large specimens are common."

On our own coast *P. unicolor* is very abundant in all suitable localities, but its exact range to the northwards has not been determined, and Saville Kent merely states, alluding apparently to the *Sparidæ* of the Brisbane fishmarket:—"It includes the celebrated Snapper." Lucas, in his Victorian "Census" gives the locality as "Port Phillip and off the south coast." Johnston, writing on its scarcity in Tasmania, remarks that it "is seldom seen in the southern waters of Tasmania, even where the reefs, depths of water, and other conditions seem to be favorable. The north coast of Tasmania lacks the deep fringing reefs which seem to be the favored resort of the Snapper." It occurs in all suitable localities along the southern and south-western coast line of Australia, but how far to the northward it extends in West Australian waters is rendered uncertain by the possibility of the species which occurs at Houtman's Abrolhos being distinct. The statement made by so many writers that the Snapper occurs in the seas all round Australia is certainly erroneous; those round the southern half of the continent would be more correct. It occurs both at Lord Howe and Norfolk Islands, but is said to be uncommon at the former place. Its habits in New Zealand, where its Maori name is "Tamure," differ much from those which prevail in this Colony as will be seen by the following quotations from Hector, extracted from Sherrin's Handbook:—"There are few fishes better known in the northern parts of the Colony than the Snapper." "The Snapper is not frequently reported to occur south of the Kaikoura Peninsula." "The Snapper frequents shallow water, and is generally caught with the net in Wellington Harbor, but the natives may often be seen catching them with a hook and line in the surf on exposed sandy beaches when the wind is off the shore. In clear shallow bays troops of this fish may be observed rooting up the shellfish that are buried in the sandy bottom, and crushing them with their powerfully armed jaws." Speaking mainly on the question of fish curing, Mr. M'Leod stated:—"I took nineteen hundred Snapper in one haul in a seine net, and in curing this large quantity there was not a single loss, although the month of January is the least adapted of all seasons for fish curing," while Capt. Robinson remarked :—" I considered Snapper (cured) equal to Cod, and far superior to Ling"; that is as ships' provisions.

The Snapper grows to at least twenty five pounds weight with a length of thirty inches. Castelnau's twice repeated statement that it "sometimes weighs up to fifty pounds" is altogether wrong.

PAGRUS SARBA.

Sparus sarba, Forsk. Descr. Anim. p. 31, 1775; Gmel. Syst. Nat. p. 1275.
Chrysophrys sarba, Cuv. & Val. Hist. Nat. Poiss. vi. p. 102; Rüpp. N. W. Fisch. p. 110, pl. xxviii. fig. 1; Gnth. Catal. Fish. i. p. 488; Kner. Voy. Novara, Fisch. p. 88; Day, Fish. Ind. p. 142, pl. xxxiv. fig. 6; Macleay, Catal. Austr. Fish. i. p. 118.

Tarwhine.

Plate XIV.

B. vi. D. 11/12–13. A. 3/11. V. 1/5. P. 15 (14). C. 17. L. lat. 58–61. L. tr. 7/14. Cœc. pyl. 3. Vert. 10/14.

Length of head 1·00–1·25, of caudal fin 3·85–4·20, height of body 2·66–2·80 in the total length. Eye rather large, its diameter 3·70–4·00 in the length of the head, 1·75–2·00 in that of the rounded snout, and 1·10–1·25 in that of the very convex interorbital space. Nostrils approximate, the anterior small, oval, and oblique, the posterior elongate and oblique, entering the orbital ring. Upper jaw the longer. Cleft of mouth moderate, horizontal; the maxilla extending to beneath the middle of the orbit or not quite so far. Upper profile of head parabolic, the preocular swelling but little apparent. Opercle with a single blunt point. Three pairs of broad cutting teeth in front of each jaw, behind which are several lateral series—four or five in the upper, and three or four in the lower jaw—of rounded molars, which gradually increase in size towards the base of the jaw; posteriorly there is a single enormously enlarged ovate tooth, situated in the middle line of the series. Dorsal spines rather weak and flexible, the fourth the longest, 2·15–2·50 in the length of the head, the last spine two thirds of the longest, and equal to the first ray: the anal commences beneath the third dorsal ray, and terminates a short distance behind that fin; the third spine is longer than but not so strong as the second, and is only two thirds of the length of the longest dorsal spine: the ventral fins do not nearly reach to the vent; the outer ray is without rudiment of filament, 1·50–1·66 in the length of the head: pectorals falciform, extending beyond the origin of the anal fin, one fourth to one half longer than the head: caudal emarginate, the height of the pedicle one fourth of that of the body. Scales feebly ctenoid, adherent: snout, preorbital, maxilla, and interorbital space scaleless: dorsal spines set in a deep groove, the rayed portion and the anal with a broad scaly sheath: a long narrow scale above the base of the ventral fin, as long as or longer than the spine. Lateral line forming a long gentle curve to the base of the pedicle, thence straight.

Colors.—Upper surface of head lead color; preorbital and preopercle silvery; cheeks and opercles with a golden tinge; body silvery, each scale with a broad, median, dull gold bar, forming together longitudinal bands, which become gradually fainter on the lower part of the sides; generally a bright golden band above the base of the ventral; dorsal fin dusky, with a basal hyaline spot between the rays; caudal dull yellow, with a broad dusky terminal band; ventrals golden; anal with the basal half silvery, the marginal half golden.

The generally accepted breeding season of the Tarwhine are the summer months, but that some at least deposit their ova at a different time is evident from the fact that specimens forwarded to the Sydney market from Gosford were found on examination to have the roe more than half developed during the first week in July.

They are sent in numbers to the market, chiefly from the northern fishing stations and command a ready sale. Though not by any means so good a fish as *P. australis*, it is nevertheless, when perfectly fresh and in good condition, a fairly well flavored fish.

The range of *P. sarba* is very extensive, embracing the greater part of the Australian coast, thence through the Malayan and Indian Seas westward to the Red Sea and the Ile de France. It is tolerably common in the neighborhood of Port Jackson, but it is impossible to state definitely how much further to the southward its range extends. Northwards it rapidly increases in numbers, and at Brisbane, according to Saville Kent it contributes extensively to the fish supply; it is abundant along the entire coastline of Queensland, Southern New Guinea, and Northern Australia, but there is no record as to its southerly range on the shores of West Australia.

PAGRUS AUSTRALIS.

Chrysophrys australis, Gnth. Catal. Fish. i. p. 494, 1859; Casteln. Proc. Zool. Soc. Vict. 1872, i. p. 71; McCoy, Prodr. Zool. Vict. dec. i. pl. 4; Macleay, Catal. Austr. Fish. i. p. 119; Johnston, Proc. Roy. Soc. Tas. 1882, pp. 69, 111.

Chrysophrys sarba, Casteln. Proc. Linn. Soc. N.S. Wales, iii. p. 373.

Black Bream.

Plate XV.

B. vii. D. 11–12/11–10. A. 3/7–9. V. 1/5. P. 15. C. 17. L. lat. 44–47. L. tr. 5/13–15. Cœc. pyl. 3–4. Vert. 10/14.

Length of head 3·60–4·33, of caudal fin 4·25–4·75, height of body 2·66–3·00 in the total length. Eye moderate, its diameter 4·00–4·66 in the length of the head, 1·50–2·00 in that of the rather pointed snout, and 1·15–1·50 in that of the convex interorbital space. Nostrils separated, the anterior small, round, and slightly tubular, the posterior a narrow oblique slit entering the orbital ring. Upper jaw slightly the longer. Cleft of mouth moderate, horizontal, the maxilla extending to beneath the anterior third of the orbit. Upper profile of head almost straight, much swollen above the posterior nostrils. A single blunt spine on the opercle. Three pairs of curved canines in front of either jaw, behind which are several series—four to six in the upper and three or four in the lower jaw—of rounded molars, the posterior teeth being the largest; the outer series in the upper jaw subconical. Dorsal spines strong, the fourth (or fifth) the longest, 2·00–2·33 in the length of the head, the last spine two thirds of the longest, and equal to the first ray: the anal commences beneath the third dorsal ray and terminates at a considerable distance behind the dorsal; the second spine is very strong and curved, subequal in length to the longest dorsal spine: the ventrals do not quite reach to the vent; the outer ray is filamentous, 1·25–1·50 in the length of the head: pectorals sickle-shaped, extending beyond the origin of the anal fin, and one sixth to two fifths longer than the head: caudal emarginate; the height of the pedicle 3·33–3·66 in that of the body. Scales feebly ctenid, adherent: snout, preorbital, maxilla, and interorbital space scaleless: dorsal spines set in a deep groove, the rayed portion and the anal with a basal scaly sheath: a long narrow scale above the base of the ventral fin. Lateral line sinuous anteriorly, subsequently following the curvature of the back, frequently with a slight sinuosity beneath the posterior dorsal rays. Airbladder large.

Colors.—Upper surface of head dark bluish-gray, lighter between the eyes, cheeks and opercles gray and gold with a tinge of pink; mandibular region silvery white; a dark gray arcuate band from the occiput to the origin of the lateral line; back, olive green; sides, silvery, each scale margined with dull yellow; lower surfaces white, tinged with yellow below the base of the pectorals: dorsal opaque, with a narrow black margin; anal yellow, basally tinged with pink, and with a broad dark gray median band; ventrals yellow; a black axillary spot; caudal yellowish-brown, with a moderately broad black marginal band: irides brown and gold.

The evidence elicited before the Royal Commission in connection with the spawning of the Black Bream is again very conflicting, so much so that the only conclusion arrived at is stated thus:—"The schooling season seems to be summer, but when or where they spawn has not been ascertained." From Twofold Bay Mr. Glover distinctly asserts that "February is the month for spawning, and the fish spawn among weeds, and in deep holes with a muddy bottom." This agrees fairly well as to the date with the observations of the late Mr. Edward Hill, who, referring probably to the Sydney District, says:—"These Bream visit our harbors from seaward periodically during the summer months of February, March, and April, and are adult fishes, being full roed at the time of their visit; probably they are migratory for the purpose of spawning." Writing from the Clarence Heads Mr. Hood Pegus states that "Black Bream spawn in July, and are found in the river all the year round." From my own notes I find that of two specimens examined during the month of August, both having been taken in the same haul of a seine, one was found to contain ova in a very early stage of development, while in the other the ova was fully developed, but exceptionally few in number; during the following month a specimen from the same locality showed not the faintest trace of spawning, nor did a specimen from Lake Macquarie captured in October, though in another example from the same Lake the roe was about half developed; a specimen, however, from Wollongong, taken during the same month, had the spawn ready for extrusion; lastly a specimen from Shellharbor, taken in December, scarcely showed any signs of breeding, while the roe was fully developed in Port Jackson examples purchased at the same time; it would appear, therefore, that even in fishes from the same locality much diversity occurs as to the spawning season.

Though occasionally taken on the outside Snapper-grounds, the favorite haunts of the Black Bream are the sheltered bays, lakes, and estuaries which are so frequent on the coast of the Colony; here they are taken by the seine in enormous numbers, the finest offered for sale in the Sydney market coming from Lake Macquarie. They are also great favorites with the amateur line fisher, as when plentiful and in a taking humor they afford fine sport, the best bait according to Mr. Hill being fresh or a day old mackerel, or better still the small prawns, popularly known as "nippers" (*Alpheus edwardsii*), which are procurable at low tide among seaweeds. Of their manner of taking a bait that gentleman remarks :—"They pick it up and rush off at full tilt (no nibbling with them), and pull hard and sheer about, with a full determination if possible to get away." Tenison Woods also bears witness to their value to the angler in the following words :—" It affords excellent sport to anglers in Victoria. The author remembers in January, 1860, catching an immense quantity with a line in the Glenelg River, Victoria, where the river was little more than brackish, though not far from the mouth. The bait used was a small crab, and no sooner was the line down than the hook was swallowed." McCoy remarks :—" The Bream is the chief sport of amateur fishermen, who catch great quantities by rod and line in the brackish water of the mouths of the rivers and creeks and sea entrances of the Gippsland Lakes, which they enter during the summer months, spawning there about November and December. They go down to the sea again about the end of June, when the cold weather comes on, and may be caught in the sea, commonly about the ends of piers, with rod and line during the winter months. The bait is usually small fish, or small shrimps, or worms. The fish is moderately good for the table, except at spring time, when the flesh becomes flabby and the colors dull."

The Black Bream is quite as valuable a species as its congener *P. unicolor*, for where that species, from the high prices which it commands in the market, owing to the limited supply, is of great value to the moneyed classes, the present comes in such numbers that the low prices (as prices run in Sydney) at which it is sold place it within reach of every householder.

It is a wholesome, nutritious, and well flavored fish, and is a general favorite with all. The stomachs of a number lately examined contained small fishes, among which could be detected a *Cristiceps* and a *Sillago*, crustaceans, molluscs such as Limpets, brittle-stars, worms, and Sertulariæ.

The Black Bream inhabits the coasts of Australia, Tasmania, and southern New Guinea. On our coast it is very abundant, and ascends rivers as far as the influence of the tide extends, and sometimes, if not habitually, above that point. It is also abundant in Victorian waters; referring to that colony Castelnau says :—" This fish is one of the most common in the Melbourne market throughout all seasons of the year. It is esteemed as food, but never attains to a large size, the longest specimens being about twelve inches. The Australian Bream is a sea fish, but often enters the rivers, and is common in the Lower Yarra and also in the Gippsland Lakes." Johnston remarks :—"The Silver Bream enters the brackish waters of creeks and rivers during the summer months in considerable numbers. They subsist chiefly upon crabs and other hard shelled animals, which abound in such places. They are supposed to shed their spawn in the brackish shallows during the months of November and December, returning to the sea before the close of June." Specimens are in the South Kensington Museum, taken in fresh water, from the Harvey River, West Australia, and a skin is also deposited there from Port Essington.

The average size of this fish may be placed at twelve inches, but much larger examples are common. The largest personally examined was caught in Port Jackson, and measured nineteen inches.

Family IX.—CIRRHITIDÆ.

Branchiostegals normally six, in one genus (*Nemadactylus*) three: pseudobranchiæ present. Body oblong or oblong-ovate, compressed. Eyes of moderate size, lateral. Mouth in front of the snout, with lateral cleft. Cheeks not cuirassed. Dentition variable, generally consisting of small teeth in both jaws, with or without canines: vomerine and palatine teeth present or absent. One dorsal fin composed of a spinous and a rayed portion of nearly equal extent: anal with three spines: ventrals thoracic, remote from the insertion of the pectorals, with one spine and five rays: lower pectoral rays simple and generally thickened. Scales cycloid: lateral line continuous. Airbladder absent or, when present, with many appendages. Pyloric appendages few.

Geographical distribution.—Tropical and temperate regions of the Indian and Pacific Oceans.

Genus I.—CHIRONEMUS.

Chironemus, Cuv. & Val. Hist. Nat. Poiss. iii. p. 78, 1829.

Branchiostegals six: pseudobranchiæ present. Body oblong and slightly compressed. Opercle spiniferous: preopercle entire. Small teeth in both jaws: teeth on the vomer: palate edentulous. One dorsal fin with fourteen or fifteen spines: the anal with three: the six or seven lower pectoral rays simple. Scales of moderate size, cycloid. Airbladder wanting. Pyloric appendages in small numbers.

Geographical distribution.—Coasts of Australia, Tasmania, and New Zealand.

CHIRONEMUS MARMORATUS.

Chironemus marmoratus, Gnth. Catal. Fish. ii. p. 76; Macleay, Catal. Austr. Fish. i. p. 121.

Kelpfish.

Plate XVII.

B. vi. D. 15/18. (14/19). A. 3/6. V. 1/5. P. 15. C. 15. L. lat. 55—58. L. tr. 11/20. Cœc. pyl. 2.

Length of head 3·50—3·75, of caudal fin 5·33—5·66, height of body 3·90—4·10 in the total length. Eye large and prominent, its diameter 4·50—4·80 in the length of the head, 1·50—1·66 in that of the snout, which is moderately pointed, and from 0·90—1·10 in the rather deeply concave interorbital space. Nostrils equal and horizontally oval, the anterior with a broad multiradiate flap both before and behind. Upper profile of head rounded. Jaws equal. Cleft of mouth moderate and horizontal, the maxilla reaching to the anterior margin of the orbit or not quite so far. Supraorbital margin well developed, terminating in a blunt point: preopercular margin evenly rounded: opercle with two prominent spinous points. A broad band of cardiform teeth in the jaws; villiform teeth in a narrower obtusely angular band on the vomer. The dorsal commences above the opercular spines; its spines are moderately strong, the sixth, rarely the fifth, the longest, from 2·25—2·50 in the length of the head; the height of the first spine is two sevenths of the longest, and a little shorter than the penultimate, which is five eighths of the last spine; the outer margin of the soft dorsal is obliquely truncated, the anterior rays being equal in height to the highest spine; the base of the soft dorsal is five sixths of that of the spinous: the anal commences beneath the fifth, and ends beneath the eleventh dorsal ray; the second spine is equal in length to, but stronger than, the third, which is from 2·75—3·00 in the length of the head, and 1·75 in the two anterior rays, which far exceed those of the dorsal in height; the outer margin of the fin is sinuous: the ventral commences beneath the eighth dorsal spine, and reaches to the origin of the anal; its spine is subequal in length to the longest dorsal spine, and 1·50 in the outer ray, which is from 1·50—1·60 in the head: the six lower pectoral rays are simple, the upper simple ray is the longest in the fin, and about one tenth shorter than the head; the posterior margin of the fin is rounded: the caudal is truncated, the least height of its pedicle one third of the height of the body.

Colors.—Olive green or yellowish-brown, blotched and marbled with rich dark reddish-brown; young and halfgrown examples with bright red spots of moderate size: spinous dorsal dark brown, immaculate; other fins spotted and speckled with reddish-brown.

The Kelpfish or Marbled Morwong is a true rock fish, and is only caught by hook and line or by meshing nets set close in along the rocks. They are said to breed in holes among seaweeds, to which they attach their spawn. Owing to the difficulties attending their capture they are not sought by the professional fishermen, and appear, therefore, but rarely in the market; they are, nevertheless, excellent table fish. Their food consists of small fishes, crustaceans, molluscs, and all such lower forms of life as live among seaweed.

South of Port Jackson the Kelpfish is common along the New South Wales coast, but to the northward we are unable to trace its presence beyond Port Stephens, whence we have seen one example. Of its occurrence in the Victorian waters, there cannot be the slightest doubt, though Lucas only gives it on the authority of Castelnau, whose description evidently refers to a species of *Haplodactylus*, as the tricuspid teeth, differently shaped dorsal fin, consumption of seaweeds, &c., abundantly prove. It occurs in Tasmania; "caught ocasionally at the mouth of the Derwent" (Johnston). *C. marmoratus* was originally described by Günther from western and north-eastern Australia, the types having been obtained from Swan River and Darnley Island. A single example from Lord Howe Island is in the Australian Museum.

The Kelpfish attains a length of fourteen inches.

Genus II.—CHILODACTYLUS.

Chilodactylus, Cuvier, Règne Anim.; Cuv. & Val. Hist. Nat. Poiss. v. p. 356, 1830.

Branchiostegals six (or five?): pseudobranchiæ present. Body oblong or oblong-ovate, more or less compressed. Opercular bones entire. Teeth in the jaws in villiform bands, with or without an outer enlarged series: vomer and palate edentulous. One dorsal fin with numerous spines: anal of moderate length or rather short: one simple pectoral ray more or less produced beyond the rest of the fin. Scales of moderate size, cycloid; cheeks scaly. Airbladder large, and frequently multilobate. Pyloric appendages few.

Geographical distribution.—Tropical and subtropical parts of the Indian and Pacific Oceans.

CHILODACTYLUS CARPONEMUS.

Sparus carponemus, Parkinson.
Chilodactylus carponemus, Cuv. & Val. v. p. 362, pl. cxxviii.; Richards. Proc. Zool. Soc. 1850, p. 61, *and* Ann. Nat. Hist. (2) 1851, vii. p. 277; Guth. Catal. Fish. ii. p. 78; Macleay, Catal. Austr. Fish. i. p. 122; McCoy, Prodr. Zool. Vict. dec. xviii. pls. 173, 174.
Chilodactylus morwong, Rms. and Ogl. Proc. Linn. Soc. N. S. Wales (2) i. p. 879.

Morwong.

Plate XVIII.

B. vi. D. 17-19/26-30. A. 3/15-17. V. 1/5. P. 15. C. 17. L. lat. 55-59. L. tr. 7/18. Cœc pyl. 2. Vert. 15/20.

Length of head 3·85-4·20, of caudal fin 4·33-4·70, height of body 3·20-3·40 in the total length. Eye large and prominent, its diameter 4·00-5·00 in the length of the head, 2·00-2·66 in that of the snout, and from 0·90-1·25 in the convex interorbital space. Nostrils equal, subcircular, the anterior with a broad, simple, lanceolate flap on its hinder margin. Upper profile of head sinuous, the forehead swollen. Lips thick and fleshy. Upper jaw the longer. Cleft of mouth small and transverse, the maxilla not reaching to the anterior nostril. Jaws with a band of villiform teeth, and an outer series of enlarged conical ones. The dorsal fin commences above the upper angle of the opercle; the spines are moderately strong, the sixth or seventh the longest, 2·90-3·20 in the length of the head; the first spine is the shortest, about two fifths of the sixth, and the last is shorter than the one preceding it, about equal to the second, and a little shorter than the first ray; all the rays short; the basal length of the rayed portion is about six sevenths of that of the spinous: the anal fin commences beneath the third to fifth dorsal ray, and ends beneath the twentieth; the spines are short but very strong, the second the longest, 5·40-5·75 in the length of the head, and one fifth of the first ray; anterior rays much longer than the median ones, but considerably shorter than the last three, which are abruptly elongated : the ventral commences beneath the eighth dorsal spine, and reaches to or within a fractional distance of the vent; its spine is moderately strong and considerably longer than the highest dorsal spine; the outer ray is the longer, its length 1·66-1·75•in that of the dorsal : the two upper and seven lower pectoral rays simple ; the second lower simple ray the longest, reaching to between the sixth and twelfth anal rays ; its length is from 2·66-2·90 in the total length, and about one half longer than the head : caudal deeply forked, the least height of the pedicle 5·33 in the height of the body. Preorbital naked ; the scales on the upper profile of the head encroaching on the snout to beyond the nostrils: vertical fins with a narrow basal sheath covered with several series of small scales. Lateral line gently curved, entering the caudal pedicle very near to its upper margin.

Colors.—Above purplish-gray, darkest on the head; each of the scales with a greenish-golden dark edged spot, forming inconspicuous bands; lower part of the sides and the abdominal region silvery ; a golden band, margined above and below by iridescent purple from below the middle of the eye along the snout.

Of this, one of the best food fishes of the Colony, nothing whatever is known of the breeding habits, nor has a single example come under our notice in which the slightest rudiments of spawn could be detected ; neither are the young ever found among the *débris* of the seine nets in the harbor nor washed ashore with other fishes on the outer beaches after stormy weather. They are only caught by parties fishing for Snapper in deep water on the ocean reefs, and do not, therefore, so often appear in the market as might be expected ; nevertheless, as many as half a dozen may occasionally be seen there together. These examples are almost invariably of large size, specimens of fifteen inches and under being very rare. Their food consists of small crustaceans, molluscs, polyzoa, &c.

Either this species is everywhere uncommon or else we have hitherto failed to ascertain the centre of its distribution. On our own coast it has been shown to be nowhere common, nor can it be traced further northwards than the Port Jackson District; McCoy and Lucas mention it as rare on the Victorian coast, while Johnston omits it entirely from his Tasmanian list. It has also been recorded from South Australia and New Zealand, so that it is known to have a fairly wide distribution, and as, from the facts stated above, it is evidently not a shore frequenting fish, it is just possible that extensive fishing grounds, of which we at present know nothing, may lie between this and the last named Colony, which may prove to be the metropolis of this valuable fish.

The largest Morwong examined in the Sydney market measured a trifle over twenty eight inches.

CHILODACTYLUS MACROPTERUS.

Sciæna macroptera, Forster.
Cichla macroptera, Bl. Schn. p. 342.
Cheilodactylus macropterus, Richards. Proc. Zool. Soc. 1850, p. 62, and Ann. Nat. Hist. (2) 1851, vii. p. 278.
Chilodactylus macropterus, Gnth. Catal. Fish. p. 78. and Study of Fish. p. 411, f. 177; Casteln. Proc. Zool. Soc. Vict. 1872, i. p. 74; Macleay, Catal. Austr. Fish. i. p. 122; Johnston, Proc. Roy. Soc. Tas. 1882, pp. 76, 112; Sherrin, Handb. N. Z. Fish. p. 98.

Jackassfish.

B. vi. D. 17–18/25–27. A. 3/12–15. V 1/5. P. 15. C. 15. L. lat. 53–55. L. tr. 6/14–17. Cœc. pyl. 3.

Length of head 4·00–4·25, of caudal fin 4·20–4·50, height of body 3·50 3·70 in the total length. Diameter of eye 3·33–3·50 in the length of the head, and 1·30–1·40 in that of the snout: interorbital space slightly convex, from 1·10–1·20 in the diameter of the eye. Upper profile of the head sinuous. Lips fleshy. Upper jaw the longer. Cleft of mouth almost horizontal, the maxilla reaching to the anterior margin of the eye. Jaws with a broad band of villiform teeth, and an outer series of enlarged conical ones. The dorsal fin commences above the opercular flap; the spines are moderately strong, the seventh, rarely the sixth, the longest, 1·90–2·05 in the length of the head, and much longer than the rays: the anal fin commences beneath the third or fourth dorsal ray, and terminates beneath the seventeenth to nineteenth; the spines are moderate, the second very strong and slightly longer than the third, from 3·60–3·85 in the length of the head, and three fourths of the first rays, which are much longer than the median ones; posterior rays but little elongated: the ventral commences beneath the eighth dorsal spine, and reaches to within a short distance of, or slightly beyond, the vent; its spine is strong, and equal in length to the longest dorsal spine; the outer ray is the longest, 1·50–1·60 in the length of the head: the two upper and six lower pectoral rays are simple; the first lower simple ray is the longest, reaching to the third or fourth anal ray, its length 3·33 in the total length, and from one fourth to two fifths longer than the head: caudal deeply forked, the least height of the pedicle 4·75–5·00 in the height of the body. Cheeks, opercles, and the upper surface of the head to in front of the anterior nostrils scaly. Lateral line with a very slight curvature, entering the caudal pedicle near to its upper margin.

Colors.—Silvery, the back washed with purple; a broad purple transverse band, which becomes inconspicuous with age, from the origin of the dorsal, across the shoulder and posterior lobe of the opercle, but not reaching the pectoral fin.

Both the Report of the Royal Commission on Fisheries and Tenison Woods' "Fisheries of New South Wales" are responsible for the confusion which exists concerning the three very distinct species included in this work; these three species are fully recognised as distinct by the professional fishermen, not as a rule very discriminating authorities, under the names of "Morwong," "Jackassfish," and "Carp," and it is hoped that all such confusion as to the identity of the fishes so named will now be set at rest.

This species is equally as scarce as the preceding in our markets, and like it is only an accidental capture in an adult state on the Snapper-grounds; one reason for this immunity from capture is that, not being by habits a rock loving fish, it does not habitually frequent the ocean reefs, as do the Snapper and kindred fishes, but prefers a sandy bottom at a moderate depth, while another reason which might be deduced from the contents of the stomachs of many specimens of all three species examined, taken in conjunction with the weak dentition, and especially with the absence of teeth on the roof of the mouth, leads inevitably to the conclusion that the baits in use are quite unsuitable to the fishes of this genus.

In a fresh specimen, sent for identification to the Australian Museum during the month of August, the ova appeared to be about one third developed, but since other specimens caught during the same and the two following months showed no symptoms of spawning, we must again acknowledge our inability to fix the date of the performance of this important function. Though abundant on the shores of Tasmania and New Zealand neither Messrs. Johnston or Sherrin refer to this subject; the former, however, remarks:—"It is most probable that the mature fish spawn in five to six fathoms of water; that, like the Trumpeters (*Latris*), the young immediately after seek the upper shallow banks of estuaries, remaining there until they are halfgrown, when they again gradually return to the parent ground, toward the mouth of the estuaries."

As food in a fresh state they are excellent, and according to the Report of the Royal Commission they "are equal to Cod or Ling for salting"; this statement is possibly correct, but needs verifying, since they are too scarce in this Colony to admit of any practical experiment being attempted, while in the two above mentioned, where they are abundant, no special industry of the sort is noted by their historians. As with *C. carponemus* its food consists of small molluscs and crustaceans, mixed with polyzoa and similiar minute organisms.

These fishes are usually taken by hook and line, and where plentiful afford good sport. "In the various bays in the immediate vicinity of Hobart" Johnston writes, "the young Silver Perch, seven to eight inches long, afford ample sport to amateur fishermen. The fish take bait readily—the mussel, boiled, being a favorite; and during the months of March, April, and May, it is not uncommon for a party of two or three persons to catch from ten to twenty dozen in a couple of hours"; and again:—"Although some are caught in nets with the Bastard Trumpeter they are usually caught by hook and line." On the same subject Hector writes:—"Throughout the whole year the Tarakihi may be caught with the hook in ten to twenty five fathoms water with a sandy bottom."

The range of this species is considerable; in the British Museum Catalogue it is given as "Australian Seas," but we have no evidence whatever of its occurrence on the northern, western, or south-western shores of the continent, while the occurrence of a single specimen at Port Essington, as recorded by Günther, cannot be regarded, supposing the locality to be correct, but as accidental for a fish which is so markedly a denizen of cold water strata. Of its scarcity on the New South Wales coast it is unnecessary to say more than that the high price which both this and the preceding species command in the Sydney market is ample evidence of the estimation in which both species are held. Of its abundance or otherwise on the Victorian coast it is difficult to judge, as Lucas, who does not appear to know the fish, merely mentions it tersely as found "off South Coast, Castelnau," while from the latter author's words we might infer that it is a common market fish in Melbourne. In Tasmania the "Silver Perch," (*C. macropterus*) as it is there called is, Johnston writes, "next in importance to the Trumpeter group as regards quality and supply. . . . The young are to be caught on the numerous rocky banks, in three to four fathoms water, in the upper bays of the estuaries, especially in those of the Derwent. They are in this state found in more or less abundance all the year round, and are highly esteemed for the breakfast table." Referring to New Zealand Hector writes of the Tarahiki, the Maori name for our Jackassfish:—"This is a very common fish in the market, and comes into season in September. Two sizes are generally sold during the spring months—the smaller ones, three or four to the pound, being the best; the flesh of the larger fish, which are three to six pounds weight, being considered rather tasteless.

Johnston considers that the Silver Perch (*C. macropterus*) and the Black Perch (*C. aspersus*) are merely local varieties of a most variable species, and from the evidence adduced I see no reason to doubt the correctness of his surmise. To quote his own words:—"The Black Perch (*C. aspersus*) is most probably a mere variety of *C. macropterus*. The former is found invariably upon a rocky bottom, and the latter upon a sandy bottom, and the color is, undoubtedly, the result of the difference in local environment." "The Black Perch is only distinguished from the Silver by its condition and quality"; and, "Generally the Black Perch is found in deeper water, and attains a greater size."

The Jackassfish grows on our coast to a length of at least eighteen inches.

CHILODACTYLUS FUSCUS.

Chilodactylus fuscus, Casteln. Proc. Linn. Soc. N. S. Wales, 1879, iii. p. 376; Woods, Fisher. N. S. Wales, p. 46, pls. x. xi.
Chilodactylus annularis, Casteln. Proc. Linn. Soc. N.S. Wales, iii. p. 377.

Carp.

Plate XIX.

B. vi. D. 17/31–33. A. 3/9–10. V. 1/5. P. 14. C. 15. L. lat. 58–62 L. tr. 8–9/18–19. Cœc. pyl. 4. Vert. 14/21.

Length of head 3·75–4·25, of caudal fin 4·50–5·00, height of body 3·00–3·40 in the total length. Eye large and prominent, 4·00–4·60 in the length of the head, 1·25–2·00 in that of the snout, and about equal to the interorbital space, which is almost flat. Upper profile of head concave from above the posterior half of the eyes. Lips fleshy. Upper jaw the longer; the maxilla extends to beneath the posterior nostril, or between that and the eye; a blunt process in front of the antero-superior margin of the eyes; and in old examples a similar process anteriorly on the snout. Snout with a median and a pair of lateral longitudinal grooves, in the latter of which the nostrils are pierced; nostrils with a raised skinny margin, the anterior elongate-oval, oblique, provided posteriorly with a flap, which entirely conceals its hinder moiety; posterior oval and much smaller; both nostrils directed backwards. Jaws with a band of villiform teeth, which are scarcely visible above the gums. The dorsal fin commences above the angle of the preopercle; the spines are rather weak, longer than the rays, the fourth or fourth and fifth the longest, 2·50-2·70 in the length of the head; base of the spinous portion three fourths of that of the soft: the anal commences beneath the eleventh or twelfth dorsal ray, and terminates beneath the seventeenth to twentieth; the second spine is not so long as but is stronger than the third, which is from 3·25-3·75 in the length of the head, and not half the length of the anterior ray; outer edge of anal rays truncate with a posterior rounded margin, the anterior more than twice as long as the middle dorsal rays: the ventrals commence opposite to the tenth dorsal spine, and reach to or not quite to the vent, their length being from 1·50-1·75 in that of the head: pectoral fins with normally six, sometimes seven, simple rays, the second the longest, reaching to or but little beyond the vent, and equal to, or as much as one fourth longer, than the head: caudal forked, the least height of its pedicle 4·66 in the height of the body. Snout and preorbitals naked; remainder of the head covered with small scales: vertical fins with a narrow basal scaly sheath. Lateral line gently curved through out its entire length, entering the caudal pedicle near its dorsal margin.

Colors.—General color of the body bluish-silvery, each scale with a reddish-brown margin which is much broader above than below; two or three oblique silvery bands on the posterior portion of the tail, which are very conspicuous in immature examples but almost obsolete in adults; head reddish-brown; an orange band, broadest in front, round the eye, except on the supraorbital region; chin and branchiostegals silvery, with a chestnut patch between them; anterior margin of pectoral region orange: dorsal reddish-brown, the rays narrowly edged with orange; anal and ventrals black, with or without a bluish submarginal band; pectorals pale brown, with a small axillary spot and the elongate portions of the simple rays red; caudal reddish-brown basally, deepening almost to black behind, and with a broad orange posterior margin.

The Australian Carp differs so much from all the other *Chilodactyli* that it is difficult to understand how Tenison Woods has so confounded it with its congeners, as to figure the same species twice under different names.

Notwithstanding that the Carp is found in moderate numbers along our coast at all seasons of the year, and freely enters our harbors and estuaries, where it doubtless breeds, since the young are taken there by seine, trawl, and hook, nothing definite can be learned as to its manner of breeding. As stated by the Royal Commission, it " is more of a rockfish (than the two preceding species), being frequently taken in the harbor in nets," but with the next sentence " it seems to be only an occasional visitor" we can by no means agree; the adults are in fact fairly common on the outside reefs and rocky shores throughout the year, though apparently in greater numbers during the warmer months; in such places they are chiefly caught by hook and line; they are among the most common as well as the most handsome fishes to be found in our aquaria. Tenison Woods states that the aboriginal name is " Bingátti."

As food this is one of the best fishes of the Colony, and is obtainable at a moderate price, but, as is unfortunately the case with so many of our fishes, there is no special fishery for them, and, except in the case of the immature examples which frequent the shoal waters of our inlets, they, therefore, escape capture. The food of those examined consisted of small worms, finely triturated masses of foraminifera, and small shells, with a single perfect example of *Gena striatula*.

This again is one of those species whose range is either very limited, or the centre of whose distribution has not yet been discovered, the coastline lying between Lake Macquarie and Shoalhaven being so far the only locality from which it has been recorded.

This species should, however, be critically compared with *Chilodactylus spectabilis*, Hutton (=*C. allporti*, Gnth. and *C. rubrofasciatus*, Casteln.), for it seems quite probable that they are but color varieties of the same species, in which case Hutton's name takes precedence. Should this surmise prove correct its range must be extended to Victorian, Tasmanian, and New Zealand waters.

Family X.—SCORPÆNIDÆ.

Branchiostegals five to seven: pseudobranchiæ present. Body oblong-ovate, subcylindrical, or compressed. Eye lateral. Cleft of mouth lateral. Some of the bones of the head armed: suborbital ring articulated with the preopercle. Teeth in villiform bands. A single dorsal fin in two distinct portions: anal usually similar to the soft dorsal: ventrals thoracic. Body with or without scales. Airbladder generally present. Pyloric appendages, when present, few or in moderate numbers.

Geographical distribution.—Almost all seas; some of the species living in fresh water.

Genus I.—SEBASTES.

Sebastes, Cuv. & Val. Hist. Nat. Poiss. iv. p. 326, 1829.
Pseudosebastes, Sauvage, Nouv. Arch. Mus. (2) 1878, i. p. 113.

Branchiostegals seven: pseudobranchiæ present. Body oblong-ovate and somewhat compressed. No occipital groove, but usually a few small spines. Opercle spiniferous: preopercle armed. Villiform teeth on the jaws, vomer, and generally on the palatine bones. Fins not elongated: one dorsal having the spinous and soft portions separated by a more or less deep notch, and with from twelve to fourteen spines: anal with three: lower pectoral rays simple: no pectoral appendages. Scales of moderate or small size, extending forwards to the orbit or even beyond it: no skinny appendages. Airbladder usually present. Pyloric appendages few or in moderate numbers.

Geographical distribution.—Inhabitants of almost all seas; not as yet recorded from the Atlantic shores of tropical America, nor from the east coast of Africa.

SEBASTES PERCOIDES.

Scorpæna percoides, Solander.
Sebastes maculatus, Richards. Trans. Zool. Soc. iii. p. 93 (*not Cuvier, nor Smith*).
Sebastes percoides, Richards. Ann. Nat. Hist. 1842, ix. p. 384, *and* Voy. Erebus & Terror, Fish. p. 23, pl. xv. ff. 1, 2; Gnth. Catal. Fish. ii. p. 101, *and* Study of Fish. p. 412. f. 178; Casteln. Proc. Linn. Soc. N.S.W. iii, p. 379; McCoy, Prodr. Zool. Vict. dec. iv. pl. 33; Hutton, Trans. N.Z. Inst. v. pl. viii. f. 14; Macleay Catal. Austr. Fish. i. p. 129; Woods, Fisher, N. S. Wales, pl. xiv.; Sherrin, Handb. N.Z. Fish. p. 88.
Sebastes allporti, Casteln. Proc. Zool. Soc. Vict. i. p. 40.

Red Gurnard Perch.

B. vii. D. 12/12. A. 3/5. V. 1/5. P. 18. C. 13. L. lat 56-65. L. tr. ca. 10/23.

Length of head 2·75–3·10, of caudal fin 4·90–5·40, height of body 3·10–3·60 in the total length. Width of head at the base of the longest preopercular spine 1·80–2·00 in its length. Eye large, situated high up on the head, its diameter 3·15–3·50 in the length of the head: snout short, 1·25–1·50 in the diameter of the eye: interorbital space concave, narrow, 2·20–2·75 in the same. Nostrils but little separated, the anterior pierced in a low tube and with a short tentacle behind, the posterior simple, oval, and vertical. Jaws equal. Cleft of mouth large and oblique, the maxilla reaching to beneath the posterior fourth of the orbit. Preorbital with two strong, compressed, blunt points inferiorly: turbinal bone armed with a strong spine: a rather larger one on the antero-superior angle of the orbit, and two at the postero-superior angle: interorbital space with two curved ridges, terminating in spines: occiput with two divergent ridges terminating in two spines each: three temporal spines, the anterior pair placed one above the other, the third at the origin of the lateral line: a low ridge from beneath the eye to the upper preopercular spine bearing a single spine mesially: preopercle with five strong spines, the second counting from above the largest: two acute spines on the opercle. Teeth villiform in the jaws; in a rectangular band on the vomer, and in narrow anteriorly curved bands on the palatines. The dorsal commences above the inner angle of the opercle, its spines are strong and sharp, the third the longest, 2·00–2·60 in the length of the head, and considerably longer than the longest rays; the height of the eleventh spine is from 1·25–1·33 in that of the last, which is 1·25–1·40 in that of the second; the base of the rayed dorsal is from 1·85–2·00 in that of the spinous, and the last ray is attached to the tail by a short membrane: the anal commences beneath the second and ends beneath the tenth dorsal ray; the second anal spine is much the longest and strongest, equal in length to the sixth dorsal spine, 2·70–3·00 in the length of the head, and much shorter than the rays, the last of which is not attached by membrane to the tail: ventral pointed, the second ray the longest, reaching to the vent, and 1·75–1·90 in the length of the head; its spine equal to the seventh or eighth dorsal spine: seven, sometimes eight, simple pectoral rays, the branched portion truncate, the simple portion rounded posteriorly; upper simple rays the longest, 1·50–1·75 in the length of the head: caudal rounded, the least height of its pedicle about 3·33–3·66 in the height of the body. Scales rather small, finely ctenid, adherent, extending on the head to about midway along the interorbital space, and on to the bases of the soft dorsal and anal fins. Eight series of scales between the last dorsal spine and the lateral line. Lateral line with a gentle downward curve along its entire length.

Colors.—Above reddish-orange, gradually shading into the white of the lower surfaces; upper part of head dusky owing to numbers of small semi-coalescent dark specks; a bluish spot on the inner margin of the opercle; sides with four irregular broad dark transverse bands, the two anterior not reaching to the abdominal profile, and the last of which crosses the base of the caudal: fins red, the lateral bands generally extending a short way on to the dorsal and anal; a dusky spot on the pectorals rather below the centre usually present.

In the Sydney District this species has no vernacular name among the fishermen and salesmen, by whom, owing to a general resemblance in coloration, it is confounded with *Plectropoma nigrorubrum*; I have, therefore, adopted the name by which it is known in Victoria. With us it is only found in moderately deep water, in the neighborhood of sunken ocean reefs, and, consequently, is only occasionally captured, and that by hook and line alone. Examples brought to the Sydney market during the early months of summer are well advanced in roe.

Alluding to Victoria McCoy remarks that it is "rather rare"; Johnston, however, speaking of it in Tasmania, where it is called the "Rock Gurnard," says that it is "found more abundantly on the northern coasts, is held in great esteem for the table, and is obtained in the vicinity of George Town in considerable numbers."

In New Zealand it is known to the settlers as "Sea Perch," its Maori name being "Pohuiakaroa." Hector says:—"It is one of the most frequent and troublesome fishes, caught in a moderate depth of water round the coast, and especially in rocky waters, being almost worthless as food."

It does not exceed twelve inches in length on our coast.

Genus II.—SCORPÆNA.

Scorpæna, Artedi, Genera. Pisc. p. 47, 1738; Cuv. & Val. Hist. Nat. Poiss. iv. p. 286, 1829.

Branchiostegals seven: pseudobranchiæ present. Body ovate and slightly compressed. Head large, with a naked groove on the occiput, armed with spines, and bearing skinny flaps. Villiform teeth on the jaws, vomer, and palatines. One dorsal fin, more or less deeply notched, with twelve spines: anal with three spines: pectorals large and rounded, with some of the lower rays unbranched; no free pectoral appendages. Scales moderate or rather small, mixed with more or less numerous skinny appendages. Airbladder absent. Pyloric appendages in small numbers.

Geographical distribution.—Tropical seas, extending northwards to the Mediterranean, New York, and Japan, southwards to Tasmania and New Zealand.

SCORPÆNA CRUENTA.

Scorpæna cruenta (Solander) Richards. Ann. Nat. Hist. 1842, ix. p. 217; Guth. Catal. Fish. ii. p. 112; Castelu. Proc. Linn. Soc. N. S. Wales, iii. p. 378; Hutton. Trans. N. Z. Inst. v. pl. viii. f. 15; Macleay, Catal. Austr. Fish. i. p. 130.
Scorpæna ergastulorum, Richards. Ann. Nat. Hist. 1842, ix. p. 217.
Scorpæna militaris, Richards. Voy. Ereb. & Terror, Fish. p. 22, pl. xiv. ff. 1, 2.

Black-spotted Red Rock-Cod.

Plate XX.

B. vii. D. 12/10. A. 3/5. V. 1/5. P. 17. C. 14. L. lat. 20–21. L. tr. 8/15–17.

Length of head 2·80, of caudal fin 4·50, height of body 3·90 in the total length. Width of head at the base of the upper preopercular spines 1·85 in its length. Diameter of eye 3·85 in the length of the head, and equal to that of the short, broad, rounded snout: interorbital space deeply concave, its width at the median orbital spine 1·85 in the diameter of the eye. Nostrils separated; the anterior of moderate size, with a low fleshy rim surrounding it except for a short space in front, and with a well developed fimbriated tentacle behind; the posterior small and oval, pierced at the base of the orbital ring. Jaws equal, the lower with a short bony tubercle below the symphysis. Cleft of mouth wide and a little oblique, the maxilla reaching to beneath the posterior third of the orbit. Preorbital with from one to three small spines at the middle of its upper margin, from which radiate ridges terminating in short stout spines along its inferior margin, some of which are ornamented with tentacles, that of the last being always present, long, and fringed, and with a pair of small bilobate tentacles posteriorly: a turbinal spine: one anterior and two posterior supraorbital spines: a short compressed ridge commences behind the intermaxillary processes, and ends between the front margins of the eyes: interorbital space with a low ridge on each side, which is absorbed into a much more prominent ridge rising at the base of the second supraorbital spine, and meeting at the anterior margin of the vertical groove, which after their junction they partially divide by a much lower ridge: a strong spine on each side in the groove, followed by a pair on the occiput in contact with one another: a temporal ridge consisting of three strong spines, the last of which marks the origin of the lateral line, and preceded by a pair of small spines, below which, at some distance, are a similar pair: a deep naked groove below the eye, bordered inferiorly by a strongly spinate ridge, which terminates in the upper and longest preopercular spine: preopercle with five spines, which grow gradually shorter inferiorly: opercle with two divergent ridges traversing its entire length and ending in strong spines, the upper of which is the longer. A broad band of cardiform teeth in the jaws, those in the lower being somewhat the stronger; vomerine teeth in an obtusely angular band; one or two series of incurved teeth on the palate. The dorsal commences above the middle of the opercle; its spines are strong and acute, the third the longest, 2·25 in the length of the head; height of the eleventh spine 1·90 in that of the last, which is a little shorter than the second, and 1·50 in the height of the third; anterior dorsal rays not quite so long as the longest spine; the base of the rayed portion is 2·00 in that of the spinous, and the posterior ray is attached by membrane to the tail: the anal commences beneath the second dorsal ray, the second spine is the longest and strongest, equal in length to the fifth dorsal spine, and 2·66 in that of the head; the rays are longer than those of the dorsal, and the posterior one is not attached by membrane to the tail: the ventral reaches to the vent, its length being 1·80 in that of the head; the spine is moderately strong, about equal in length to the seventh dorsal spine: the ten lower pectoral rays are simple, the upper one the longest, but little longer than the last divided ray, and 1·60 in the length of the head: caudal gently rounded, the least height of the pedicle 4·33 in the height of the body. Head scaleless. Lateral line with twenty one tubular scales behind the opercular flap, and with forty four series above it; eight series between the last dorsal spine and the lateral line.

Colors.—General color carmine, brightest above; abdominal region pearly white; a broad transverse pink spot, narrowest mesially, on the occiput immediately behind the vertical groove; lower surface of the head pale red marbled with yellow, with which color the lips are banded; from one to three pink tentaculated spots on the lateral line; lower part of the sides with scattered dark brown spots margined with carmine, most conspicuous underneath the pectorals: spinous dorsal bright red with silvery blotches and stripes, and a black spot on the outer half between the sixth and tenth spines present or absent; rayed portion with the outer half profusely marbled with silvery, and generally with a small black spot at the base of the two last rays, behind which is a pink spot; caudal marbled red and yellow, with a, frequently V-shaped, row of black spots basally; pectorals mottled red, yellow, and silvery, with blackish spots on the upper half; ventrals and anal yellow, with spots and blotches of carmine.

All our Rock Cods belonging to this family are ground fishes, haunting the vicinity of weed-covered rocks in more or less shallow water. In such places they prowl about in search of food, or lie motionless and concealed among the seaweeds, and here doubtless they deposit their ova.

They are voracious fishes, and readily take a fish or shrimp bait, their natural food being small fishes, crustaceans, soft molluscs, and worms. As food they vary greatly, sometimes barely meriting the definition "a fair food fish," applied to them by the writer in his Catalogue of the Fishes of New South Wales, 1886; the flesh of others, however, which we have since tasted was found to be firm, white, flaky, and well flavored.

This species is common along the entire seaboard of New South Wales, and, according to Saville Kent, extends northwards into Queensland waters, but as to its extension of range in that direction he gives no clue. It occurs on the coast of Victoria according to Macleay, but the naturalists of that colony give no data as to its abundance or scarcity; in Tasmanian waters, however, Johnston states that it is "common on a shallow rocky bottom all round the coasts and estuaries."

S. cruenta grows to the length of eighteen inches, but the usual length of market specimens is under twelve.

SCORPÆNA BYNOENSIS.

Scorpæna bynoensis, Richards. Voy. Erebus and Terror, Fish. p. 22, pl. xiv. ff. 4-5, 1846; Gnth. Catal. Fish. ii. p. 113, *and* Study of Fish. p. 414, f. 180; All. and Macl. Proc. Linn. Soc. N. S. Wales, i. p. 278; Macleay Proc. Linn. Soc. N. S. Wales ii. p. 353, *and* Catal. Austr. Fish. i. p. 131.
Scorpæna jacksoniensis, Steindachn. SB. Ak. Wien, liii. 1866, p. 438, pl. iii. f. 2.

Bynoe's Rock-cod.

B. vii. D. 12/9. A. 3/5. V. 1/5. P. 17. C. 13. L. lat. 22-24. L. tr. 8/15.

Length of head 2·90, of caudal fin 4·40, height of body 3·40 in the total length. Width of the head at the base of the upper preopercular spines 1·66 in its length. Diameter of eye 4·00 in the length of the head, and 1·10 in that of the broad, rounded snout: interorbital space very deeply concave, its width at the median supraorbital spine 1·40 in the diameter of the eye. Nostrils separate; the anterior circular, surrounded by a low fleshy rim, which is developed behind into a broad simple tentacle; the posterior smaller and oval, with a low fringed rim. Jaws equal, the symphyseal tubercle of the lower scarcely developed. Cleft of mouth wide and a little oblique; the maxilla reaching to beneath the posterior fourth of the orbit. Preorbital ridged, with three spines on the lower and one on the posterior margin, that at the angle with a moderate, pointed, simple tentacle having a basal lobe: an upright acute turbinal spine: one anterior and two posterior supraorbital spines, the latter having a narrow, elongate, bifid tentacle between them: upper part of postorbital ring with a series of small spines: interorbital space with two inconspicuous ridges, forming posteriorly a rounded junction, which is surmounted by an elevated skinny flap: vertical groove but moderately developed, a little broader than long, with a conical spine on each margin: two compressed spines in contact on the occiput: temporal ridge as in *S. cruenta*, but without small spines below the anterior pair: no

E

groove below the eye: cheek traversed by a spinate ridge terminating at the upper and longer preopercular spine: preopercle with five spines: opercle with two equal spines, the lower of which is preceded by an acute elevated ridge. Jaws with a band of villiform teeth, the inner series being rather the largest; vomerine and palatine teeth in a single series, the former obtusely angular, the latter short. The dorsal commences above the middle of the opercle; the spines are strong, the anterior ones deeply grooved on their outer half, the third and fourth the longest, 2·35 in the length of the head; height of eleventh spine 1·75 in that of the last, which is equal to the eighth, much longer than the second, and 1·33 in the longest spines, which are equal to the anterior rays; the base of the rayed portion is 2·00 in that of the spinous, and the last ray is joined for about two thirds of its length by membrane to the tail: the anal commences beneath the last dorsal spine; the spines are grooved throughout their entire length, the second is the longest and strongest, curved, longer than the longest dorsal spines, 2·20 in the length of the head, but not so long as the rays; the posterior ray is not attached to the tail: the ventral reaches to or slightly beyond the vent, its length being 1·75 in that of the head; the spine is moderately strong and grooved, equal in length to the sixth dorsal spine: pectoral rounded, the eleven lower rays simple, the upper of these the longest, 1·50 in the length of the head: caudal rounded, the least height of the pedicle 3·40 in the height of the body. Head scaleless; three series of small scales in front of the dorsal; body with fine filaments, which are most numerous near the base of the dorsal fin and on the lateral line. Lateral line with twenty two to twenty four tubular scales, and forty four to forty six series above it.

Colors.—Upper surface reddish-brown, the brown decreasing on the sides, the lower surface pale yellow; lower jaw with brown and pearly spots; cheeks with a large dusky patch; a narrow black band across the anterior margin of the snout; lower part of sides with scattered, round, blackish spots: dorsal fin pale violet with black streaks and a conspicuous pearly basal spot between the third and fourth spines; anal silvery with an oblique black cross band, outside of which it is spotted and tipped with pink; ventrals pinkish with brown spots; pectorals and caudal, variegated with black.

Bynoe's Rock Cod and the allied Cardinal Rock Cod (*Scorpæna cardinalis*) are much less commonly sent to the Sydney market than the preceding species. They do not attain to the size of *S. cruenta*, but as they frequent similar localities, and are taken by similar means, it may be inferred that their habits are also similar.

This species is widely distributed, ranging from north-western Australia, whence the species was first described, through Torres' Straits, and down the east coast, at least as far as Port Jackson. It is also found on the shores of New Zealand.

Genus III.—CENTROPOGON.

Centropogon, Günther, Catal. Fish. ii. p. 128, 1860.

Branchiostegals six or seven: pseudobranchiæ present. Head and body rather strongly compressed. No groove on the occiput. Preorbital and preopercle with strong spines: opercle armed. Villiform teeth in the jaws, vomer, and palatine bones. One dorsal fin with more spines than rays: anal with three spines: pectoral without simple rays: all the articulated fin rays branched. Scales present. A narrow cleft behind the fourth gill. Pyloric appendages in small numbers.

Geographical distribution.—Seas of Australia, Malaysia, and India, entering rivers, and at least one species—*C. robustus*—having become permanently established in fresh water.

CENTROPOGON ROBUSTUS.

Centropogon robustus, Gnth. Catal. Fish. ii. p. 128, 1860, *and* Ann. Nat. Hist. (3) 1867, xx. p. 60; Krefft, Proc. Zool. Soc. 1861, p. 182; Macleay. Catal. Austr. Fish. i. p. 136, *and* Proc. Linn. Soc. N. S. Wales, viii. p. 203; Woods, Fisher. N. S. Wales, p. 48.
Centropogon troschelii, Steindachn, SB. Ak. Wien, 1866, liii. p. 440.

Bullrout.

B. vi. D. 15/9–10. A. 3/5. V. 1/5. P. 12. C. 14. L. lat. 83–88. L. tr. 21/50–58. Cœc. pyl. 4. Vert. 8/14.

Length of head 3·00–3·25, of caudal fin 4·50–5·00, height of body 3·33–3·66 in the total length. Width of head at the base of the upper preopercular spines 2·20 in its length. Diameter of eye 4·10–4·25 in the length of the head, and a little shorter than that of the snout: interorbital space concave, its width at the anterior supraorbital spine 1·60–1·75 in the diameter of the eye. Nostrils separate, the anterior small and oval, pierced in the summit of a lower rounded prominence; the posterior circular and much larger, surrounded by a low rim. Upper surface of the head flat. Lower jaw very slightly the longer. Cleft of mouth wide and oblique, the maxilla reaching to beneath the middle of the eye or a little further. Preorbital with two strong spines, the anterior short and triangular, the posterior long, thorn-shaped, and very acute, directed backwards and downwards, erectile at will, and from 1·50–2·00 in the diameter of the eye: a small sharp turbinal spine: one anterior and two posterior supraorbital spines, more acute and prominent in small examples: interorbital space with a ridge on each side and a lower median ridge, the latter bifurcating posteriorly, and forming with the lateral ridges parallel arcuate ridges on the vertex: a pair of spines on each occipital ridge: a temporal ridge bearing three strong spines, the last of which marks the origin of the lateral line: suborbital ridges with a single spine inferiorly above the preorbital spine, and broken up posteriorly into numerous low ramose ridges: preopercle with five strong spines, the upper the longest: interopercle with a low ridge terminating in a hidden spinate point at its upper margin: opercle with two prominent spines, the margin between them moderately indented, and the space between and above them carinated: a strong spine on the posttemporal and another, pointing upwards and backwards, on the clavicular bone, which is closely striated. Villiform teeth on the jaws, vomer, and palatines; on the latter in a narrow band; vomerine band subcrescentic. The dorsal commences above the middle of the opercle, its origin being midway between the tip of the snout and the tenth spine; the spines are acute and moderately strong. the fourth normally the longest, but scarcely differing in height from the third and fifth, 2·25–2·33 in the length of the head; beyond these the spines grow gradually shorter, the last not being perceptibly longer than its predecessor, and but very little less than the second; the first spine is the shortest, 2·40 in the height of the fourth; the rays are equal in height to the spines, and their outside contour forms a high and regular arch; the last ray is the shortest, and is attached by membrane to the caudal pedicle by two-thirds of its length; the basal length of the rayed portion is from 3·20–3·33 in that of the spinous: the anal commences beneath the thirteenth or fourteenth dorsal spine, and ends in front of the termination of the dorsal; the third spine is a little longer than the second, equal to the eighth dorsal spine, and 2·50–2·75 in the length of the head; the rays are much longer than those of the dorsal, and their outer margin is truncate; the last ray is attached to the pedicle by a short membrane: ventral slightly cuneate, reaching to or beyond the vent; the spine strong, equal in length to the last anal spine; the second ray the longest, 1·40–1·50 in the length of the head; the inner ray firmly attached along half its length to the abdomen: pectoral rounded, the middle rays the longest, a little longer than the ventral: caudal rounded, the least height of its pedicle 3·20 in the height of the body. Head scaleless. Lateral line with from twenty six to thirty raised tubes.

Colors.—Brown, irregularly marbled with black, which sometimes takes the form of broad vertical bands, and frequently with yellow spots and blotches; a chestnut spot frequently present on the vertex: all the fins mottled with grey and black; a large black spot always present in front of the middle of the spinous dorsal.

The Bullrout deserves a place in this work, firstly because it is as a fact an edible fish, its flesh being firm and of an excellent flavor, and secondly because though originally a marine form it has taken to a brackish and purely fresh water existence, having ascended and colonised many of our rivers far beyond the influence of the tide; for instance, they are found in the Nepean above the falls at Norton's Basin, which though but a few feet in height, would prove an insurmountable barrier to such a fish as this; they also occur above the weir on the Parramatta River.

So far as our personal knowledge at present goes the range of this species is limited to the rivers draining the eastern watershed of the colony with their estuaries, between the Parramatta and the Upper Macleay, from both which rivers we have handled specimens; the collectors employed by the scientists of the Challenger Expedition have, however, obtained specimens from the Mary River, Q., and we may, therefore, conclude that it is distributed through all the rivers discharging into the seas of eastern Australia.

It is by no means the "very ugly" fish Tenison Woods calls it; on the contrary, the different shades of yellow and brown and black are generally so beautifully blended in fresh examples as to make it a strikingly handsome fish; the fry of an inch long and under are very pretty little fishes, their colors being bright yellow blotched with dark brown. "There are two remarkable peculiarities about this fish," continues Tenison Woods, "one is that it emits a loud and harsh grunting noise when it is caught, so that if by chance it takes a bait, the fisherman knows what he has got by the noise before he brings his fish to the surface of the water. When out of the water the noise of the Bullrout is loudest." If this be correct it affords a more simple and probable explanation of the vernacular name, than the suggestion of its being "a corruption of some native name" advanced by that author. The second peculiarity, he says, is "that the spines about the head are venomous, and inflict most painful stings." No doubt any such wound would cause pain, but the state of the sufferer's health, his nervousness, and his belief in the superstition of its poisonous qualities are all factors, which must be taken into consideration. Personally the writer has been "stung" on many occasions, both by the allied Fortescue —which is *Centropogon australis*, not *Pentaroge marmorata*, this latter fish being so rare in Port Jackson that we have never seen a recent specimen— and by the British Weever (*Trachinus vipera*) and never felt any more inconvenience than would result from a similar stab of a knife. The fact is the wound is merely a deeply punctured and viciously inflicted one, without any venomous properties whatever.

They attain to a length of nine inches.

Family XI.—BERYCIDÆ.

Branchiostegals normally eight, in one genus (*Polymixia*) four. Body oblong or rather elevated, compressed. Eyes large, except in *Melamphaës*, lateral. Cleft of mouth lateral, oblique. Opercular bones more or less armed. Villiform teeth in both jaws: present or absent on the vomer and palatine bones. Ventral fins thoracic, with more that five rays, except in *Monocentris*. Scales normally ctenid; bony in *Monocentris*, absent in *Anoplogaster*, and cyclid in *Melamphaës*.

Geographical distribution.—Tropical and temperate seas.

Genus.—BERYX.

Beryx, Cuv. Règne Anim.; Cuv. & Val. Hist. Nat Poiss. iii. p. 226, 1829.

Branchiostegals normally eight, exceptionally seven or nine: pseudobranchiæ present. Eyes large. Snout short, with oblique cleft of mouth and prominent chin. Body short and rather elevated, compressed. Opercular bones serrated: preopercle without elongated spine at the angle. Villiform teeth in both jaws, on the vomer, and on the palatine bones. One dorsal fin with several spines: ventrals with seven or more rays. Scales moderate or rather small, ctenid. Airbladder simple. Pyloric appendages in moderate numbers.

Geographical distribution.—Australian Seas; Indian Ocean; Madeira; Japan.

The genus *Beryx* is of exceptional interest, since to fossil forms of this and closely allied genera belong the oldest known Teleostean Fishes; "the majority of the Acanthopterygians found in the chalk being representatives of this family" (*Günther*).

BERYX AFFINIS.

Beryx affinis, Gnth. Catal. Fish. i. p. 13, 1859; Casteln. Proc. Linn. Soc. N. S. Wales, ii. p. 225, *and* iii. p. 365; Hector, Ann. Nat. Hist. 1877 (4) xix. p. 341; Macleay, Catal. Austr. Fish. i. p. 147; Woods, Fisher. N. S. Wales, p. 51, pl. xv.; Sherrin, Handb. N. Z. Fish. p. 68.

Nannygai.

Plate XXI.

B. viii. D. 7/12. A. 4/12-13. V. 1/7. P. 13. C. 19. L. lat. 41-44. L. tr. 6/13.

Length of head 3·50-3·75, of caudal fin 3·45-3·55, height of body 3·25-3·33 in the total length. Eye very large, its diameter one third of the length of the head: snout short and rounded, deeply indented mesially, 1·50-1·66 in the diameter of the eye: interorbital space convex, 1·25-1·40 in the same. Nostrils approximate, subequal in size, the anterior subcircular, the posterior ovate and pierced on a higher plane. Upper profile of the head rounded. Jaws equal, the lower with a prominent bony chin. Cleft of mouth large and very oblique, the maxilla greatly dilated posteriorly, its hinder margin sinuous; it is, with the exception of the postero-inferior angle, entirely overlaid by the supernumerary bone, the surface of which is rugose, and which is posteriorly denticulated, extending to beneath the posterior margin of the orbit. A lanceolate pentagonal groove between the anterior half of the eyes, from the outer angles of which a pair of rough diverging ridges are continued backwards along the temporal region, on which they terminate in serrated spinous processes. Preorbital very finely serrated anteriorly: turbinals with a deep, naked indentation on the lower margin, and with the anterior and inferior edges strongly denticulated; their entire surface coarsely granulated: orbital ring rough, more coarsely so inferiorly, and with several strongly denticulated spines behind the eye: preopercle with two margins; the anterior finely serrated on both limbs, and with two strong spines at the angle; the posterior with fewer but coarser serrations on the vertical limb, with strong denticulations below, and crossed by three or four serrated ridges, which terminate in coarse spines on the rounded and produced angle: posterior margin of subopercle concave, the angle produced and spiniferous: interopercle finely serrated and bearing a deep naked notch posteriorly: opercle serrated, and furnished with two strong spines, the upper of which is the longer; there is a shallow marginal notch above the spines and a second below them: posttemporal with a single strong spine posteriorly and small serrations above. Both jaws with a few small conical teeth in front, and a single series of very fine teeth laterally; vomerine patch small and triangular; a cuneiform band, broadest anteriorly, on the palatines. The dorsal commences above the sixth scale of the lateral line and ends above the twenty seventh to twenty ninth scale; the distance between its first spine and the tip of the snout is about seven eighths of that between the same point and the origin of the caudal; the spines are moderately strong and acute, some of them being laterally grooved; they increase gradually in height to the last, which is from four and a half to five times longer than the first, and 2·00-2·33 in the length of the head; the rays gradually decrease in height from the first, which is a little longer than the last spine and twice as long as the last ray; the length of the base of the dorsal fin is equal to or rather more than that of the head: the anal commences beneath the second dorsal ray, and ends some distance behind that fin, which it resembles in shape; its fourth spine is the highest, equal in height to the fifth dorsal spine, and from 2·50-2·66 in the length of the head, while its base is about two thirds of the same length, and its outer margin is slightly convex: the ventral reaches to the vent: the spine is strong, smooth, and laterally grooved, three fourths of the length of the rays, and 1·66-1·75 in that of the head: pectorals pointed, reaching to the nineteenth or twentieth scale of the lateral line, and from 1·25-1·33 in the length of the head: caudal deeply forked, the base above and below with four recumbent graduated spines; the upper lobe is slightly longer than the lower, and the least height of its pedicle is two sevenths of the height of the body. Anterior margin of the opercle, and the cheek, scaly; the scales on the occiput extend forwards as far as the middle of the orbit: vertical fins with a low scaly sheath; a small elongated scale at the base of the ventral outside. Lateral line nearly straight.

Colors.—Red, with violet reflections, each longitudinal series of scales with a large median spot, which is golden on the back and grows gradually paler on the sides, becoming silvery below, and forming well defined bands; abdominal region dirty white: fins red.

Though a fairly common and first rate edible fish nothing is known of the economy of the Nannygai, except that it appears on our coast in considerable numbers during the warmer months of the year, frequents the neighborhood of sunken reefs, is taken, when present, plentifully with hook and line, and commands a high price in the market. It is said to be a great delicacy when slightly corned and smoked.

Like all its congeners *B. affinis* is an inhabitant of moderate depths, only approaching the shore at intervals, and the reason for this periodical migration is not quite apparent, for, since those which are sent to the market do not show any signs of breeding, it does not appear that the exercise of this important function is in any way connected with this seasonal indrawing to our coasts and estuaries.

In the Report of the Royal Commission the following paragraph occurs:— "It is seldom seen full roed, and we have not found that the very young fish are even seen in our harbors or on our coasts, so that it may be fairly infered that the Nannygai does not as a rule spawn in this vicinity;" with the first sentence our experience entirely coincides; but with the second we are unable to agree so cordially, having obtained specimens on several occasions both from Port Jackson and Botany Bay, which did not exceed two inches in length, while we have seen one measuring five inches, which was taken by hook and line in Port Jackson, the season being about midwinter. In the same Report the statement is made that " to the north its range seems to be unlimited," but we can find no authority for this, nor do we think it is at all likely to be correct; Saville Kent makes no mention of it among the edible fishes of Queensland. As a matter of fact we do not know its exact northern limit in the seas of our own Colony, while we do know that it makes periodical visits to the whole extent of our southerly seaboard, and even extends its range in that direction to the Tasmanian coast, where, however, Johnston considers it rare. As it also inhabits New Zealand waters, the occurrence of this deep sea form on both shores strengthens the suggestion made on p. 57 that between that colony and Australia extensive deep sea banks and reefs are present, which have only to be discovered and worked to make them a source of incalculable profit to the Colonies at large. Of course the methods of fishing now prevalent in these Colonies must be revolutionized before such a consummation can be hoped for.

The Nannygai attains a length of at least twenty inches.

Family XII.—SCIÆNIDÆ.

Branchiostegals seven: pseudobranchiæ present, concealed, or absent. Body compressed and rather elongate. Mouth in front of or below the snout. Eye lateral, of moderate size. Cheeks without armature. Preopercle without bony stay: opercle not or feebly armed. Barbels sometimes present. Muciferous system of the head well developed. Teeth in villiform bands, with or without canines: cutting or molariform teeth never present in the jaws: palate edentulous. Two dorsal fins, the spines of the first usually feeble; the second much more developed than the first: anal with one or two spines: pectoral rays branched and without free filaments: ventrals thoracic, with one spine and five rays. Scales ctenid or cyclid, covering the head and snout. Lateral line complete, often continued on to the caudal fin. Stomach cœcal. Airbladder, when present, with branching or elongate appendages. Pyloric appendages in small or moderate numbers.

Geographical distribution.—Tropical and subtropical seas, less common in the South Pacific. Günther remarks that they "are chiefly coast fishes of the tropical and subtropical Atlantic and Indian Oceans, prefering the neighborhood of the mouths of large rivers, into which they freely enter, some of the species having become so completely naturalised that they are never found nowadays in the sea. Some of the larger species wander far from their orginal home, and are not rarely found at distant localities as occasional visitors. In the Pacific and on the coast of Australia, where but few large rivers enter the ocean, they are extremely rare, and in the Red Sea they are absent. Many attain a large size, and almost all are eaten." This statement, published in 1880, regarding their extreme rarity on the Australian coast is, of course, founded on error, one or more species, forming a considerable portion of the food supply, being common on all the explored parts of our shores.

Genus I.—SCIÆNA.

Sciæna, sp (Artedi) Cuvier, Règne Anim.; Cuv. & Val. Hist. Nat. Poiss. v. p. 28, 1830.
Corvina, Cuvier, Règne Anim.; Cuv. & Val. Hist. Nat. Poiss. v. p. 81.

Branchiostegals seven: pseudobranchiæ present. Body oblong and rather elongate, compressed. Eyes of moderate size. Interorbital space broad and convex. Snout rounded, sometimes overhanging the upper jaw. Jaws equal, or the lower the longer. Cleft of mouth nearly or quite horizontal. Teeth villiform, with an outer enlarged row: no distinct canines. Two dorsal fins, the first with eight to thirteen spines, and connected at its base to the second, which is of moderate length: anal with one or two spines. Scales ctenid or cyclid, extending over the head and snout. Airbladder present or absent. Pyloric appendages in small numbers.

Geographical distribution.—Tropical and temperate seas, much more numerous in the former; absent from the South Pacific, except on the shores of Australia and South America. Fresh waters of the United States

SCIÆNA AQUILA.

Labrus hololepidotus, Lacép. iii. p. 517, pl. xxi. f. 2, 1802.
Sciæna umbra, Lacép. iv. p. 314; Cuv. Mém. Mus. i. p. 1, *and* Règne Anim.; Bonap. Faun. Ital. Pesc. pl. —. f. 1.
Cheilodipterus aquila, Lacép. v. p. 685.
Perca vanloo, Risso, Ichthyol. Nice, p. 298, pl ix. f. 30.
Sciæna aquila, Risso, Eur. Mérid. iii. p. 411; Cuv. & Val. Hist. Nat. Poiss. v. p. 28, pl. c.; Gnth. Catal. Fish. ii. p. 291, *and* Fisch. Sudsee, p. 105; Day, Brit. Fish. i. p. 150, pl. 1.
Sciæna hololepidota, Cuv. & Val. Hist. Nat. Poiss. v. p. 53; Quoy & Gaim. Voy. Astrolabe, Poiss. p. 697, pl. xii f. 1.
Sciæna capensis, Smith, Illustr. S. Afric. Zool. Fish. pl. xv.
Sciæna antarctica, Casteln. Proc. Zool. Soc. Vict. 1872, i. p. 100, *and* Proc. Linn. Soc. N. S. Wales, ii. p. 232, *and* iii. p. 381; Macleay, Catal. Austr. Fish. i. p. 154; Woods, Fisher. N.S. Wales, p. 53, pl. xvi.
? *Sciæna (Corvina) novæ-hollandiæ*, Steindachn. SB. Ak. Wien, 1866, liii. p. 445, pl. v. f. 2.
Sciæna neglecta, Rms. and Ogl. Proc. Linn. Soc. N.S. Wales (2) i. p. 941.

Jewfish.
Plate XXII.

B. vii. D. 10. 1/27–28. A. 2/7. V. 1/5. P. 17. C. 17. L. lat. 51–54. L. tr. 9–10/19–21. Cœc. pyl. 8.

Length of head, 4·10–4·50, of caudal fin, 5·50–6·25, height of body 4·33–5·33 in the total length. Diameter of eye 5·00–5·50 in the length of the head, 1·25–1·60 in that of the snout, and from 0·80–1·30 in the slightly convex interorbital space. Nostrils moderately approximate, the anterior circular, the posterior much larger, suboval, and vertical. Upper profile of head slightly concave. Cleft of mouth slightly oblique, the maxilla not quite reaching to beneath the posterior margin of the orbit. Vertical limb and angle of the preopercle serrated, the serrations becoming obsolete in large examples: opercles with two flattened spines. A row of strong, pointed, slightly curved teeth in the jaws, rather stronger in the upper than in the lower, and with a narrow band of finer teeth inside them. Dorsal spines weak; the third or fourth the longest, from 2·15–2·40 in the length of the head; the rayed portion lower than the spinous: the anal commences beneath the ninth or tenth dorsal ray; its first spine is short, the second about equal to the seventh dorsal spine and half the length of the contiguous ray; the anterior rays much longer than those of the dorsal: ventrals pointed from 1·45–1·70 in the length of the head: pectorals from 1·40–1·50 in the same length: caudal truncate or rounded, the least height of its pedicle from 3·00–3·25 in the height of the body. Lateral line gently curving to above the anal fin, beyond which it is straight, and is continued to the extremity of the caudal fin; the tubes branched posteriorly. Airbladder large, with numerous branching lateral processes.

Colors.—Deep steel blue above, gradually changing through the silvery of the sides into the white of the lower surfaces; head not so brilliantly tinted above as the back, its sides suffused with gold; a black axillary blotch: all the fins, except the ventrals which are white, pale brown: irides golden and brown: inside of jaws and lower margin of the opercular region orange.

In the seas of Europe, as in our own seas, little is known of the breeding habits of this fish. In neither is the locality selected known, and the only evidence elicited by the Royal Commission as to the spawning season in this Colony is that of Mr. Hood Pegus, who, referring to the Clarence River writes:—" Jewfish are plentiful all the year round, but especially in March, April, and May. They spawn in May, and are caught with hook and line as well as with the net and trap." Of five specimens examined three, sent to market from Broken Bay and Port Jackson during the months of August and September, contained barely visible ova, while two others from Broken Bay and Botany obtained in November and December were without any trace of it. It is probable, therefore, that even in the same localities there is considerable individual variation in the date for depositing the spawn, or it may be that, as with the Mullet, there are two different spawning seasons selected by the different schools of the same species.

The Jewfishes are bold, cunning, and voracious, ascending rivers to, or even beyond, the extreme limit of the tide; this, however, is only for predatory purposes, as it certain that they do not breed in such places; they are regular attendants on the breeding grounds of the Mullets, and commit great ravages both among the young fish and the ova. Their food consists chiefly of fishes, cephalopods, and crustaceans, and in fact of all suitable creatures which they can overtake and overpower, and their great swiftness and strength enables them with ease to satisfy even their voracity. As food those measuring less than two feet are the best for the table, and whether fried or boiled are excellent; it is at this stage that they are known as "Silver Jew"; they are then coming in shoals along the coast, seeking the harbors, estuaries, and salt water lakes, with which our coast abounds, and in which instinct teaches them that they will find a more plentiful and more easily obtainable supply of food, and, man excepted, fewer enemies than they are likely to meet outside.

It has long been known to European and American fishermen and sailors that this and the allied species, especially *Pogonias chromis* from the Atlantic shores of the United States, emit noises when under water, which, it is stated, may be heard at a depth of twenty fathoms; the means used to produce these drumming sounds is not, however, distinctly known, all the theories which have been put forward being mere conjecture. We do not know whether this peculiarity has been noticed in the Colony, where every facility for detecting the occurrence of the phenomena is present in abundance.

The airbladder of these fishes is exceptionally large and thick, and a fair quality of isinglass is obtainable from it; on this subject the Report of the Royal Commission says:—"The airbladder of some of the same genus of fishes is of great value for isinglass, and forms a valuable article of export on the Indian and Malacca coasts, the merely dried bladder being worth equal to three shillings per pound." Needless to say this valuable product is wasted here, thousands of bladders being annually thrown away as refuse.

The Jewfish is abundant along the entire coast line of New South Wales; it is gregarious, ascends rivers beyond the influence of the tide, and is most destructive to spawning fish. The limit of its northern range has not been accurately ascertained, but it does not probably extend much beyond the Queensland frontier. In Victoria Castelnau considered it as a rare fish in Bass' Straits, but as it is found as far westward as the mouth of the Murray, its apparent scarcity is probably due to the want of large rivers flowing into the sea on the Victorian coast. Johnston, under the name of *S. antarctica*, catalogues it as, "rare in Tasmanian waters," and makes some remarks as to its specific difference from *S. aquila*, which, however, will not bear the test of investigation; he writes:—"As Dr. Günther recognises an important difference in the number of scales on the lateral line as of specific value, there is no doubt but that Castelnau's *S. antarctica* is distinct from the *Maigre* of Europe"; this is apparently conclusive, but the solution is that Castelnau, without giving any notice of having done so, has counted the lateral line scales to the end of the caudal fin, instead of those to the end of the hippural bone. All things considered the middle zone of the New South Wales coast may be taken as the centre of distribution of this species in the South Pacific.

The Jewfish grows to a length of at least five feet, but the more common market size is from two to three feet.

Genus II.—OTOLITHUS.

Otolithus, Cuvier, Règne Anim.; Cuv. & Val. Hist. Nat. Poiss. v. p. 59, 1830.

Branchiostegals seven: pseudobranchiæ present. Body oblong. Eyes of moderate size. Snout obtuse or a little pointed, with the lower jaw the longer. Preopercle crenulated, serrated, or denticulated. Villiform teeth in both jaws, with the outer row in the premaxillaries enlarged: more or less well developed conical canines, either in both jaws, or in the upper only, usually received, when the mouth is closed, into fossæ in the opposite jaw: a single row of widely separated conical teeth in the lower jaw, with occasionally a single outer row of villiform ones. Two dorsal fins, united at their bases, the first with nine or ten weak spines: anal with one or two small spines and but few rays. Scales ctenid or cyclid, of moderate or small size. Airbladder present, in some with a horn-like, forwardly directed process on each side, in others with numerous lateral appendages. Pyloric appendages in small numbers.

Geographical distribution.—Nearly all tropical and subtropical seas; south-eastern coast of Australia; some species permanently resident in fresh water.

OTOLITHUS ATELODUS.

Otolithus atelodus, Gnth. Ann. Nat. Hist. (3) 1867, xx. p. 60; Macleay, Catal. Austr. Fish. i p. 156; Woods, Fisher. N. S. Wales, p. 54, pl. xvii.
Otolithus teraglin, Macleay, Proc. Linn. Soc. N. S. Wales. v. p. 48.

Teraglin.
Plate XXIII.

B. vii. D. 10. 1/29-30. A. 2/9. V. 1/5. P. 19. C. 17. L. lat. 74-77. L tr. 16/33. Cœc. pyl. 5. Vert. 13/12.

Length of head 4·15—4·33, of caudal fin 5·50-5·90, height of body 4·90-5·10 in the total length. Eyes prominent, the diameter 5·80-6·25 in the length of the head, 1·50-1·66 in that of the snout, and 1·33-1·50 in that of the convex interorbital space. Nostrils moderately approximate, pierced in a naked groove, the anterior circular, the posterior elongate-oval and vertical. Upper profile of head flat, or very slightly concave. Lower jaw the longer. Cleft of mouth wide and but little oblique, the maxilla reaching to or slightly beyond the hinder margin of the orbit. Opercle with two weak spines, having a deep indentation between them. Teeth in the upper jaw in a villiform band, broadest in front, with a symphysial patch of recurved conical teeth, and with one or two series of strong lateral teeth; the lower jaw with a large anterior patch of recurved teeth, and two lateral series, the inner of which contains the strongest teeth in either jaw. The dorsal commences slightly behind the opercular flap; the spines are feeble, the fourth the longest, from 2·50-2·75 in. the length of the head, and much longer than any of the rays; the first spine is minute, and the basal length of the spinous dorsal is two thirds of that of the rayed fin: the anal commences beneath the nineteenth to twenty first dorsal ray; its spines are small, and the anterior rays are subequal to the highest dorsal spine: ventrals pointed, their length about one third of the distance between their origin and the vent, and from 1·85-2·00 in the length of the head: pectorals small, 1·60-1·90 in the same length: caudal emarginate, the least height of its pedicle one third of the height of the body, and rather less than the distance between the last dorsal ray and the base of the caudal. Maxilla scaleless; soft dorsal with a low adipose sheath. Lateral line gently curved throughout its entire length.

Colors.—Upper surface and sides silvery, below white: dorsals yellowish-gray with darker spots at the base; caudal yellowish-gray with the outer margins dark; pectorals with a black spot at the base inside; ventrals pink; anal silvery with the elongate rays dusky: inside of mouth and inner margin of opercle orange.

The difficulty of formulating any general rule as to the breeding season of our marine fishes, and especially of those which, like the present species and the Jewfish, are confirmed wanderers, is well exemplified by the examination of several specimens recently obtained in the market, which led to the following results:—During the earlier part of September examples, forwarded for sale to the Sydney market from Lake Macquarie, were found to be in a forward state of spawning, the ova being almost fully developed, whilst in others, taken in Port Jackson during the following November, the contents of the ovaries were not more than half developed. As with the preceding, the spawning grounds are quite unknown, nor is it known whether the ova, when shed, is buried beneath sand or gravel, attached to the fronds of seaweeds, or floats; the whereabouts and manner of life of the young fishes are equally unknown, all we know being that they appear from seaward in large shoals during the late winter and the spring months, varying at this time from one to three feet in length, the smaller fishes usually preceding their more mature brethren by a few days.

Referring to the Teraglin, the Royal Commission's Report has the following sentence:—"In our species the airbladder is of great size and excellent quality, and treated in the same way, that is without any preparation or outlay except that of drying in the sun, would probably add from threepence to sixpence to the value of each fish caught."

The Teraglin is of equally rapacious habits as the Jewfish, but does not ascend rivers to a similar extent, and is not, therefore, so great a pest to the estuarine breeding grounds. As a table fish it is infinitely superior to the Jewfish, even in the young, or Silver Jew, stage of that species, and always commands a high price in the market.

So far as we know at present the Teraglin is only found on the New South Wales coast, where it is abundant, and grows to a maximum length of about three feet.

Family XIII.—CARANGIDÆ.

Branchiostegals normally seven (six to ten): pseudobranchiæ present, except in *Lichia* and *Trachynotus*. Body generally compressed, oblong, elevated, or subcylindrical. Eyes lateral. Gill-openings wide. No bony articulation between the preopercle and infraorbital. Dentition variable: teeth, when present, conical. Spinous dorsal less developed than the rayed portion or than the anal, either continuous with or separated from the rayed portion, and sometimes formed of isolated spines: the anal spines, when present, may or may not be continuous with the fin: the posterior rays of the dorsal and anal fins sometimes detached: ventrals thoracic, sometimes rudimentary or absent. Scales generally small or absent. The lateral line may be partially or entirely armed with shield-like plates. Airbladder present. Pyloric appendages usually numerous.

Geographical distribution.—Tropical and temperate seas of both hemispheres.

Günther lays great stress on the uniformity of the number of vertebræ in this family, fixing this number at ten abdominal and fourteen caudal, with, however, a limitation in favor of *Temnodon* and *Chorinemus*, which have, the former twelve abdominal, the latter fifteen or sixteen caudal vertebræ; to these must be added *Naucrates*, in which there are also sixteen, while, even in the typical genus *Caranx*, our White Trevally (*C. georgianus*) has constantly fifteen caudal vertebræ, and *Seriola lalandii* sometimes has eleven abdominal. Until, therefore, the vertebral column of the numerous little known species of *Caranx*, much less of *Carangidæ*, has been thoroughly investigated, it would be well not to place too much reliance on this as a diagnostic character of the family.

In many of the Carangid genera the head in the young is armed with spines, as in *Naucrates*, but these are absorbed before they attain to maturity.

Of the true *Carangidæ* many recent genera, such as *Caranx*, *Argyriosus*, *Lichia*, and *Trachynotus*, are present in various Tertiary formations, while of the more aberrant forms *Platax* occurs as far back as the Cretaceous, and reappears in the Tertiary in company with *Zanclus* and *Equula*.

Genus I.—CARANX.

Caranx (Commerson), Lacép. Hist. Nat. Poiss. iii. p. 60, 1802.
Trachurus, Cuv. & Val. Hist. Nat. Poiss. ix. p. 6, 1833.
Carangichthys, Bleek. Celebes, iii. p. 760

Branchiostegals seven: pseudobranchiæ present. Body oblong. or elevated, or subcylindrical, more or less compressed. Cleft of mouth moderate. Eyes lateral, with or without adipose lids. Dentition feeble, more or less complete. Two dorsal fins, the first continuous, with about eight feeble spines which are sometimes rudimentary, and having in front of its origin a recumbent spine directed forwards: the second dorsal more developed than the first, and similar to the anal; the posterior rays of both these fins sometimes wholly or partially detached: two preanal spines, which are sometimes rudimentary, separated by an interspace from the anal fin. Scales minute. Lateral line with an anterior curved and a posterior straight portion, the latter covered with large plate-like scales, which are usually keeled, and sometimes spinate; these are rarely continued on to the anterior curved portion. Airbladder bifurcated posteriorly. Pyloric appendages in large numbers.

Geographical distribution.—Almost all temperate and tropical seas, more especially abundant in the latter.

This is a very large and complex genus, embracing species with little or no external resemblance to one another, and might conveniently be subdivided into two or more genera.

CARANX TRACHURUS.

Scomber trachurus, Linn. Syst. Nat. i. p. 494, 1766; Bloch, pl. lvi.
Caranx trachurus, Lacép. Hist. Nat. Poiss. iii. p. 60; Risso, Ichthyol. Nice, p. 173, *and* Eur. Mérid. iii. p. 421; Cuv. & Val. Hist. Nat. Poiss. ix. p. 11, pl. cexlvi.; Gay, Hist. Chile, Zool. ii. p 233; Richards. Ichthyol. China, p. 273, *and* Ann. Nat. Hist. 1843, xi. p. 25; Day, Brit. Fish. i. p. 124, pl. xliv.
Trachurus vulgaris, Flem. Brit. Anim. p. 218.
Caranx trachurus, var. *japonicus*, Schleg. Faun. Japon. Poiss. p. 109, pl. lix. f. 1.
Selar japonicus, Bleek. Japan, pl. viii. f. 1.
Caranx symmetricus, Ayres, Proc. Calif. Acad. Nat. Sc. i. 1855, p. 62.
Caranx cuvieri, Lowe, Trans. Zool. Soc. ii. p. 183.
Caranx declivis, Jenyns, Zool. Beagle, Fish. p. 68, pl. xiv.
Trachurus trachurus, Casteln. Anim. nouv. ou rares, Poiss. p. 23; Gnth. Catal. Fish. ii. p. 419; Kner, Voy. Novara, Fisch. p. 150; Kner & Steindachn. SB. Ak. Wien, liv. p. 364; Steindachn. SB. Ak. Wien, lvii. p. 382; Macleay, Catal. Austr. Fish. i. p. 166; McCoy, Prodr. Zool. Vict. dec. ii. pl. 18; Johnston, Proc. Roy. Soc. Tas. 1882, pp. 85, 119; Sherrin, Handb. N.Z. Fish. p. 46.
Trachurus declivis, Casteln. Proc Linn. Soc. N. S. Wales, iii. p. 383; Woods, Fisher. N. S. Wales, p. 58, pls. xviii, xxii.

Yellowtail; Scad.

B. vii. D. 8. 1/32. A. 2. 1/29. V. 1/5. P. 21. C. 17. L. lat. 71–73. Cœc. pyl. 12–20. Vert. 10/14.

Length of head 4·75–5·00, of caudal fin 5·00–5·33, height of body 4·75–5·00 in the total length. Eye with an adipose lid, the posterior part extending forwards to or nearly to the margin of the pupil, the anterior portion narrow; its diameter 3·40–3·60 in the length of the head, and 1·00–1·25 in that of the snout: interorbital space convex with a central ridge, 1·20–1·33 in the diameter of the eye. Nostrils approximate, oval, oblique, the anterior slightly the larger. Upper profile of head slightly convex. Cleft of mouth oblique; lower jaw the longer, the maxilla extending to beneath the anterior third of the orbit. A narrow band of minute teeth in the jaws, on the vomer, and palatine bones, and along the middle of the tongue. Dorsal spines weak, increasing in length to the fourth, which is from 1·60–1·90 in the length of the head; a short interspace between the fins; second dorsal much lower than the spinous and similar to the anal: detached anal spines strong: ventral fin not extending to the vent, its length being from 1·10–1·33 in the distance between its origin and the vent, and 1·60–1·75 in that of the head: pectoral falcate, extending backwards to above the preanal spines, 1·15–1·25 in the same length: caudal forked, the height of its pedicle less than its width. Head naked in front of the eyes. Lateral line abruptly curved downwards below the anterior third of the rayed dorsal, behind this straight; anteriorly it is crossed by large scale-like plates much deeper than long, and without keel, while the plates on the straight portion, thirty six to thirty nine in number, are keeled, most strongly so posteriorly.

Colors.—Adult dark blue, young bright green, above the lateral line, below which it is silvery tinted with metallic pink and gold; opercle with a black spot: irides bronze above, with orange reflections; silvery below.

It is difficult to ascertain the exact season or seasons of breeding of the Yellowtail, since the adult fishes rarely enter our bays and harbors, and are, therefore, very seldom seen in our fishmarkets; the fact that the immature fishes, however, from three to six or eight inches in length, are always to be found there in numbers, proves that their breeding stations are not far distant from the coast. That the Report of the Royal Commission is erroneous in its suggestion that " It is most probable that this fish spawns in the inlets and harbors of the coast, from the fact that the young fish of five or six inches in length are always to be found in such localities " is easily demonstrable seeing that, if this were the case, the adult fishes, when breeding, would be taken by the seine fishermen in countless numbers, and forwarded in due course to the market, and this, as we have before shown, is an almost unknown occurrence. It is much more probable that the shoals passing along the coast shed their spawn in the open sea, that the spawn floats, and is carried by the combined action of wind and tide into our bays and inlets, in the warm, quiet waters of which they quickly come to maturity; and that a continuous supply of these small fishes is kept up throughout the year leads us to the inference that either the Yellowtail breeds twice in the year, or, more probably, that the different shoals do not all breed at the same time. The adult fishes are said to pass along the coast in enormous shoals about midsummer, but they are on the coast at other seasons, the two largest we have examined having been taken in Lake Macquarie during the month of August; in neither of these examples, however, could distinct evidences of breeding be detected.

In the same Report it is stated that " The very young fry have a most extraordinary and ingenious way of providing for their safety and nutrition at the same time; they take up their quarters inside the umbrella of the large *Medusæ*, where they are safe from their enemies, and are, without any exertion on their part, supplied with the minute organisms which constitute their food, by the constant current kept up by the action of the curtain-like cilia of the animal." We are unaware upon whose authority this statement is made, and, though it is very possibly correct, we think that confirmatory evidence, drawn from thoroughly reliable sources, that is from the personal observation of individuals competent to recognise the very young stages of *C. trachurus*—must be forthcoming before this can be accepted as a constant habit of the species. It has never, so far as we are aware, been observed on the British coast, where the ordinary life history of the fish has been fully worked out, though it is well known that several members of the True Cod family (*Gadidæ*) make use of this means of concealment and protection, and are thus carried in safety to the shallow waters near the shore where the earlier stages of their existence are necessarily passed.

Their food consists of the fry of other fishes, small crabs and molluscs, &c. As food the adults, when perfectly fresh, are firm and well flavored, but they soon deteriorate, and become tasteless and insipid. The principle use, however, to which the Yellowtail is put is as bait for the line fishermen; it forms a good bait for Snapper, but is not so good as Mackerel. They readily take a bait, either artificial or natural, more especially if it is kept moving through the water so as to represent a small fish. They may also be taken by "whiffing," that is by trailing a line, or better still several lines, after a boat in moderately rapid motion, or anchored in a strong tideway so as to cause the lines to stream out behind.

These fishes almost without exception suffer from being the host of an isopodous crustacean of the genus *Anilocra*, which lives in the throat, and thus obtains both sustenance and protection for itself; though it is common to take this commensal from the Scad with its developed ova attached we have never found more than one in a single fish.

Though immense shoals of large Scad are known to frequent the open sea along our coast, they do not make themselves so conspicuous as those which at irregular intervals visit the British coasts, probably because, in the warmer waters washing the shores of the Colony, the supply of suitable food is more constant.

The range of this species is very wide, embracing all the temperate coasts of Europe, Madeira, along the west coast of Africa to the Cape of Good Hope, the Chinese seas, Chili, the temperate parts of Australia, and New Zealand.

As has been stated it is very abundant on the coast of New South Wales, but the large shoals which are off the coast during the warmer months probably seek the open sea at a greater depth after spawning, as they have not been noticed on the Queensland coast, and the species is only incidentally mentioned by Saville Kent as being the "Yellowtail" of the Sydney market. McCoy considers it to be "a very rare visitor" to Hobson's Bay, but in Tasmanian waters Johnston says:—"The Horse Mackerel occurs in these waters in vast numbers. The young are seen all round the bays of the upper waters of the Derwent during the autumn. The mature fish are in fair esteem in the market;" and again:—"They appear in immense shoals at times between January and June, and might with proper appliances become the source of a valuable industry."

In New Zealand, according to Sherrin, "this fish appears in Wellington Harbor about the end of November, and is one of the commonest offered for sale throughout the summer." The Maori name of our Yellowtail is "Haunture," and its habits on the New Zealand coast are, we gather from the same authority, similar to those which prevail in British waters; he says:—"Immense shoals of Scad are occasionally driven on the beaches round the harbor by their impetuosity when following their prey into shallow water." So far Mr. Sherrin is undoubtedly correct, but that the succeeding sentence, " or from their sufferings caused by an irritating isopod crustacean that infects their gills at this season," is erroneous, is clearly demonstrable by the facts that the equally infected New South Wales fishes do not seek relief from their sufferings, if such there be, by any such suicidal policy, while those which frequent the British coasts, where the commensal is unknown, are notable in following it. In the southern provinces of New Zealand the species is rare.

The Yellowtail grows to a length of twenty inches, but the more usual size of the adult fish is about twelve ; the largest we have seen from the Colony did not quite measure sixteen inches.

CARANX GEORGIANUS.

Caranx georgianus, Cuv. & Val. Hist. Nat. Poiss. ix. p. 85, 1,833; Jenyns, Voy. Beagle, Fish. p. 71; Richards. Ann Nat. Hist. 1843, xi. p. 27, *and* Voy. Ereb. & Terror, Fish. p. 135, pl. lviii. ff. 1-3 ; Gnth. Catal. Fish. ii. p. 440 ; Casteln. Proc. Zool. Soc. Vict. i. 1872, p. 117 ; All. & Macl. Proc. Linn. Soc. N.S. Wales, i. p. 327 ; Macleay, Catal. Austr. Fish. i. p. 168, *and* Proc. Linn. Soc. N.S. Wales, viii. p. 204; Johnston, Proc. Roy. Soc. Tas. 1882, pp. 85, 119 ; Sherrin, Handb. N.Z. Fish. p. 99.

Caranx chilensis, Gay, Hist. Chile, Zool. ii. p. 235, Ictiol. Atl. pl. vi. f. 2 ; Steindachn. SB. Ak. Wien, 1875, lxxi. p. 459.

White Trevally.

Plate XXIV.

B vii. D. 8. 1 25–27. A. 2. 1/22–24. V. 1/5. P. 20–21. C. 19. L. lat. 79–81/19–22. Cœc. pyl. 15. Vert. 10/15.

Length of head 4·00–4·40, of caudal fin 4·20–4·75, height of body 3·00–3·50 in the total length. Eye rather small, with rudimentary adipose lid, its diameter 4·00–4·75 in the length of the head, 1·33–1·75 in that of the pointed snout, and 1·20–1·50 in the convex interorbital space. Nostrils approximate, oval, subequal. Upper jaw slightly the longer ; cleft of mouth moderate and a little oblique ; the maxilla dilated posteriorly, reaching to beneath the front margin of the orbit, or not quite so far. Upper surface of head very slightly convex ; a low longitudinal ridge extending from the interorbital space to the horizontal anterior spine. A single row of short stout conical teeth in each jaw, usually supplemented by a few extra ones at the symphyses : narrow bands of villiform teeth on the vomer, palatines, and tongue. Dorsal spines weak, much higher than the rays, the third the longest, 2·00–2·40 in the length of the head ; the distance between the base of the first ray and the origin of the caudal is equal to that between the same spot and the posterior margin of the orbit : the anterior anal spine rises beneath the third or fourth dorsal ray : ventral fins reaching to the vent, 1·90–2·25 in the length of the head : pectorals long and falcate, reaching to the vertical from the sixth to eighth anal ray, its length from one seventh to one fourth longer than that of the head : caudal deeply forked, the height of its pedicle much less than its width, which is equal to the distance between its origin and the base of the last dorsal ray. Scales minute and adherent, the breast scaly ; bases of the vertical fins with an adipose sheath. Lateral line arched to beneath the middle of the rayed dorsal. Airbladder moderate.

Colors.—Steel blue above, silvery on the sides and below; a black spot on the operele, behind which along the median line of the body a broad golden band is present or absent: tip of spinous dorsal blackish.

The White Trevallies are full of spawn in October, and the principal breeding season occurs during this and the succeeding month, large specimens obtained in the Sydney market during December being as a rule without trace of spawn. From Twofold Bay Mr. Glover also fixes the same two months as the spawning season, and these may, therefore, be taken as the normal period for the southern half of the Colony at least. As their habits during this important season are similar to those of *C. trachurus*, so likewise we find the immature fishes, up to about ten inches in length, abundant in our sheltered harbors and estuaries for the greater part of the year, whence they are sent in numbers to the market, where they meet with a ready sale at fair prices; the adults too are much more commonly sent to market than those of the Yellowtail, as they do not confine themselves so exclusively to the open sea as does that species, but by freely entering the indentations of the coast place themselves within reach of the seine fishermen.

We are at a loss to know why it is stated in the Report of the Royal Commission that the Trevally "is not much esteemed as food." In our opinion it, especially when large, is a firm, well flavored fish, rightly deserving to hold a high rank among the edible fishes of the Colony. Its food consists of small fishes, squid, swimming crabs, and such like.

Though not so generally affected by the presence of *Anilocra* as its congener, it is by no means uncommon to find its throat similarly tenanted by this curious Isopod.

The White Trevally is abundant along the entire coast line of New South Wales, and is also found along the Queensland coast northwards to Torres Straits, where, referring to it, Saville Kent says:—"The White or Silver Trevally of the Southern Colonies grows to a weight of ten to twelve pounds and undoubtedly represents one of the most delicate and finest flavored fishes in Australian waters." It is very common on the Victorian coast, where it is called "Silver Trevally" and, according to Castelnau, is "particularly so in the cold months of the year." As it is also common in all the seas of southern and western Australia it may be fairly considered as constituting one of the most important sources of food supply for the entire Australian seaboard. Johnston remarks of their occurrence in Tasmanian waters, that they "are very much prized for food, and are caught in considerable quantities in the Tamar and at South Arm during the autumn. Although it is said that they grow to a considerable size, the smaller ones are alone seen in local markets. They are caught by graball and seine, as a rule, but they take bait readily, and may be caught with hook and line." In New Zealand, where its native name is "Arara," it is, Hector remarks, " a highly esteemed fish, that is very common in every part of the Colony during the summer months, but is in best condition at the commencement and close of the season. . . . The flesh is very delicate, but less so in the larger sized fish, about twelve inches in length being the best size for the table. The Trevalli frequents shallow water and feeds among the rocks, so that it may sometimes be caught by the hand at low water." According to Mr. Wilson (*vide* Sherrin) they "smoke splendidly, though they are not adapted for canning." They are also found at Lord Howe, Norfolk, and Raoul Islands, and at the former are very common and grow to a large size, specimens measuring 30 inches having been recorded. It is considered one of the best food fishes, and is used fresh, salted, or smoked. It has been recorded by Gay from Juan Fernandez.

F

Genus II.—SERIOLA.

Seriola, part, Cuvier, Règne Anim.; Cuv. & Val. Hist. Nat. Poiss. ix. p. 200, 1833.

Branchiostegals seven: pseudobranchiæ present. Body oblong and moderately compressed, with the abdomen rounded. Cleft of mouth moderate. Preopercle entire or very feebly serrated. Bands of villiform teeth on the jaws, vomer, and palatine bones. First dorsal fin with rather feeble spines, which are connected by membrane: second dorsal and anal much more developed, without detached finlets; the latter generally with a pair of preanal spines separated from the rest of the fin. Scales small or rudimentary. Lateral line unarmed. Airbladder large and simple. Pyloric appendages in large numbers.

Geographical distribution.—Nearly all the seas of the tropical and temperate zones.

SERIOLA LALANDII.

Seriola lalandii, Cuv. & Val. Hist. Nat. Poiss. ix. p. 208, 1830; Gnth. Catal. Fish. ii. p. 463; Macleay, Catal. Austr. Fish. 1872, i. p. 174; Woods, Fisher. N. S. Wales, p. 59, pl. xix; McCoy, Prodr. Zool. Vict. dec. xviii. pl. 172; Sherrin Handb. N. Z. Fish, p. 39.
Seriola aureo-vittata, Temm. & Schleg. Faun. Japon. Poiss. p. 115, pl. LXII. fig. 1.
Seriola dubia, Lowe, Proc. Zool. Soc. 1839, vii. p. 81, *and* Trans. Zool. Soc. iii. p. 5.
Seriola grandis, Casteln. Proc. Zool. Soc. Vict. 1872, i., p. 115; Macleay, Catal. Austr. Fish i., p. 175: Johnston, Proc. Roy. Soc. Tas. 1882. p. 119.
Seriola simplex, Rams. & Ogl. Proc. Linn. Soc. N. S. Wales, x., p. 757.

Kingfish.

B. vii. D. 6-7. 1/32-34. A. 0-2. 1/20-21. V. 1/5. P. 21. C. 19. L. lat. 156-160. Cœc. pyl. num. (113). Vert. 10-11/14.

Length of head 4·40-4·60, of caudal fin 5·25-5·80, height of body 4·66-5·25 in the total length. Eye rather small, with the adipose lid but little developed, its diameter 4·75-5·75 in the length of the head, and 1·50-2·00 in that of the snout, which is elongate, conical, and equal in length to the convex interorbital space. Nostrils approximate, of equal size, oval and vertical. Upper profile of head slightly convex. Jaws equal, or the lower a little the longer. Cleft of mouth slightly oblique, the maxilla extending to beneath the anterior third of the orbit, or not quite so far. Jaws with broad bands of villiform teeth; vomerine teeth in a sagittate patch, palatine in bands; pterygoid bones with small scattered patches; tongue with an oblong median patch, and with numerous small lateral patches. Dorsal spines low and feeble, the fourth the longest, one-sixth of the length of the head; the anterior rays the longest, from 2·10-2·33 in the same; the base of the first dorsal ray is equidistant from the tip of the snout and the origin of the caudal fin: the anal commences beneath the fifteenth or sixteenth dorsal ray; the anterior rays are similar to those of the second dorsal, their length being 2·75 in that of the head; the detached spines in front of the anal are sometimes absent: the ventral fins reach to midway between their origin and the vent, and their length is from 1·66-1·90 in that of the head; in specimens under a foot in length they are, however, much longer proportionately; the outer ray is partially attached to the body by membrane: pectorals rather small, from 1·85-2·00 in the length of the head: caudal deeply forked, the least height of the pedicle, which is feebly keeled, equal to its width, and three fifths of the distance between the last dorsal ray and the origin of the caudal fin: a distinct pit in front of the caudal fin above and below. Entire head, with the exception of the cheeks, the upper margin of the opercles, and some isolated patches on the temporal region, naked. Lateral line curved and wavy to beneath the anterior third of the rayed dorsal, thence straight.

Colors.—Brilliant purplish blue above, the head darker and with a distinctly greenish tinge; sides silvery; abdominal region pearly white; a broad golden band commencing behind the eye, and traversing the median line of the body may or may not be present: soft dorsal and anal olive green, the elongate anterior rays tipped with yellow, the latter fin with a narrow white margin, and with a pearly spot between the bases of each pair of rays; caudal olive green with the lobes yellow; ventrals white outside, yellowish-green inside: pectorals and spinous dorsal gray: irides silvery, clouded in parts with golden brown.

From the examination of specimens, obtained in the Sydney market, it is apparent that the main body of Kingfishes shed their spawn in October, though individuals having the spawn ready for extrusion are not infrequently met with both in September and November. That the ova is shed as a rule out to sea, and possibly at some considerable distance from the land, is probable, while it may be taken for granted that it floats, nevertheless, unlike the two preceding species, the fry are never found in our harbors nor even on our outer shores; where, therefore, they remain, during the period elapsing between their emergence from the egg and their appearance in shoals along the coast during the latter end of summer, when they measure from twelve to eighteen inches, is merely matter for conjecture. In the Twofold Bay District they are reported to spawn in deep water outside about the month of September, after which "they make for a large sandbank which exists about twelve miles out from the Heads, where they are found in great numbers." Mr. Glover, from whom the above extract is taken, also claims to have "seen the young fry out at the Heads in December, at which time they also come into the shoal waters of the bay." He also credits them with being "one of the greatest enemies to the spawn (*sic*) of the smaller fish we have."

The Kingfish visits our shores in large shoals at irregular intervals throughout the year, the large fishes not, however, consorting with those of smaller size. At all ages their voracity is very great, and they do much damage to such fishes as the Mullet, both by harassing the parents when on the breeding grounds, and subsequently by the enormous consumption of fry.

Their food consists almost exclusively of small fishes, and Hardyheads (*Atherina pinguis*), Yellowtails (*Caranx trachurus*), Whitings (*Sillago, sp.*), and Mullet (*Mugil dobula*), have been taken by us from the intestines of a single large individual. As a table fish it varies much with the season, and its size, examples measuring two feet and under being firm and palatable while the larger fishes grow increasingly coarse, tough, and flavorless. In this connection Mr. Edward Hill remarks:—"When the Kingfishes are in good condition and perfectly fresh, the belly part, cured and smoked, is far superior to any of the imported fish cured in that way; and that portion cured alone and used immediately, before it gets too salt, boiled, and served up with egg sauce, is a choice morceau." As a game fish for sporting purposes it ranks high in the estimation of the same author, who is also of opinion that half a dozen large Kingfishes from fifty to sixty pounds weight caught by one angler form a fair day's work.

It must not be lost sight of when referring to this fish under its trivial name, that the Kingfish of Victoria is *Sciæna aquila*, while that of Tasmania is *Thyrsites solandri*.

The entire coast of New South Wales is subject at all seasons to the incursion of shoals of this species, of which the most marked is a run of large breeding fish commencing during August and lasting till about the middle of November; from this time during the summer and autumn months large shoals of immature and halfgrown fishes make their appearance, these in their turn retiring, with the approach of cold weather, to more open, deeper, and consequently warmer waters. Even, however, during the depth of winter some few examples, chiefly of large size, may constantly be met with in our market.

How far northwards it ranges we are unable to say, there being no available catalogue of Queensland Fishes, but we gather from Saville Kent's Preliminary Report that it is a "large and valuable foodfish of the Queensland market," and is "not unfrequently taken in Moreton Bay. It is a school fish readily taken with hook and line, or, as in some localities, with the harpoon. It is much esteemed for the table."

Writing of its occurrence on the Victorian coast under the heading, *S. grandis*, Castelnau remarks that the Yellowtail—by which name it is there known—"plays a conspicuous figure in the Melbourne market, particularly during the hottest months of the year." Referring to Tasmania, Johnston says:—"Appears in schools; abundant off the George Town Heads regularly during a brief season (autumn) every year. Takes bait greedily." For a similar reason to that given when discussing its distribution in Queensland waters, we are also unable to determine how far its range extends to the westward, no South Australian naturalist having as yet published a Catalogue of the Fishes of their Colony or even of the Gulf of St. Vincent; we think it probable, however, that it occurs along the entire seaboard of southern Australia.

At Lord Howe Island it is common, and much esteemed either fresh, salted, or smoked. It is found in the seas of New Zealand, but its distribution there does not appear to be at present accurately determined; the Maori name is "Haku." Sherrin remarks:—"In the months of January and February in each year large shoals of this fish visit Cook Strait, and occasionally enter Wellington Harbor. They are generally of two dsitinct sizes, the smaller about six pounds weight and twenty inches long, and the larger about four feet in length and weighing about forty pounds. The flesh is very rich and well flavored, but, like all fishes of this class, must be eaten quite fresh. These fishes are often caught in Moki* nets, to which they do great damage. They also drive on to exposed beaches, several of them being generally cast up together. Natives value them very highly, and eagerly search the coast for them at the proper season, and have been known to carry choice specimens far into the interior as gifts to their friends. * * * In New Zealand it is not mentioned as having been seen further south than Cook Strait, but in all probability it must occur along the whole of the west side of the island. In its habits it is migratory and gregarious, like the Tunny." He goes on to say that in the Auckland District it is not so plentiful as

---

The "Moki" is the Bastard Trumpeter, *Latris ciliaris*, Forster.

Kahawai (*Arripis salar*) or Snapper, but that they are to be obtained in the open sea if sought for, while in the Dunedin market they were observed but once in three years.

The Kingfish has an extensive range outside of the Australian Colonies; it was originally described from the coast of Brazil, from whence it crosses the Atlantic to the Cape of Good Hope, and it also occurs, but rarely, at St. Helena, and, if we are correct in assigning Lowe's *S. dubia* to this species, at Maderia also; while, under the name of *S. aureovittata*, Schlegel has recorded it from the seas of Japan.

The Kingfish grows to a length of at least fifty two inches, and a weight of sixty pounds.

SERIOLA HIPPOS.

Seriola hippos, Gnth. Ann. Nat. Hist. (4) 1876, xvii. p. 392; Macleay, Catal. Austr. Fish. i. p. 176; Woods, Fisher. N. S. Wales, p. 60.

Seriola nigrofasciata, Castelu. Proc. Linn. Soc. N. S. Wales, iii. p. 352; (*not Rüppell*) Macleay, Catal. Austr. Fish. i. p. 174.

Samsonfish.

B. vii. D. S. 1/23–25. A. 2. 1/16. V. 1/5. P. 20–22. C. 19. Cœc. pyl. num. Vert. 10/14.

Length of head 3·75–4·20, of caudal fin 4·40–4·80, height of body 3·00–3·80 in the total length. Eye moderate, the adipose lid scarcely overlapping the iris, its diameter 3·70–4·00 in the length of the head, 1·20–1·40 in that of the snout, and 1·25 in the convex interorbital space. Nostrils approximate, the anterior oval and protected by a flap, the posterior much larger, subcircular, exposed. Jaws equal. Cleft of mouth moderate, and very slightly oblique; the maxilla greatly dilated posteriorly, extending to beneath the middle of the orbit. Upper profile of head with a slight concavity on the snout, and rounded on the occiput; a low longitudinal ridge on the interorbital space and the occiput, beyond which it extends but a short distance. Teeth in the jaws in villiform bands, with several of the outer rows enlarged; the bands separated at the symphyses, broad in front and gradually narrowing posteriorly; a patch of villiform teeth on the vomer; palatines and pterygoids toothed; tongue with an oval median band, and numerous detached lateral patches. Dorsal spines low, the fifth the longest, one fourth to one fifth of the length of the head; the anterior rays elongate, five eighths of the same; the origin of the rayed dorsal is nearer to that of the caudal than to the end of the snout: the anal commences beneath the eleventh dorsal ray; the anterior rays are elongate, and rather more than half of the length of the head: ventral fins reaching two thirds of the distance between their origin and the vent, which distance is subequal to the length of the head; the anterior ray attached to the body by a skinny flap: pectorals short, about five ninths of the length of the head: caudal forked, the least height of the pedicle equal to its width, and three fourths of the distance between the base of the last dorsal ray and the origin of the caudal; a well marked pit in front of the origin of the caudal above and below. Entire head, with the exception of the cheeks scaleless: bases of the vertical fins naked. Lateral line irregularly waved, following the curvature of the back.

Colors.—Bluish above, the head darkest; sides golden; lower surfaces silvery: spinous dorsal dusky, hyaline basally; rayed dorsal pale yellowish-brown, darkest marginally; ventrals, pectorals, and anal dusky, with a silvery base, and a narrow whitish outer margin.

The Samsonfish occurs not unfrequently in the Sydney market, but always singly and taken by hook and line. None of the specimens personally examined contained ova in any stage of growth, nor is there any published account of the season or manner in which the spawning is accomplished, but it is not probable that these differ materially from what obtains among their congeners. That, however, the fry are very rarely found upon our shores, along with the solitary habits of the individuals brought to our market, and the limited distribution which we can at present ascribe with certainty to the species, leads to the inference that the localities where the main shoals of these fishes habitually shed their spawn is in the open sea, or if near land have not as yet been discovered.

Mr. Hill, referring to Port Jackson, writes:—"The Samsonfish is occasionally caught either in the harbor or off the headlands outside; its habits are similar to those of the Kingfishes, except that it moves about in deep water, and is more fond of the northern latitude." What this last sentence is intended to convey would be difficult to determine, for, unless its author had distinct evidence of its greater abundance to the northward, which we have now no means of judging, it must be taken for what it is worth as a mere expression of opinion. It was possibly a perusal of this sentence which induced Saville Kent to say that its "range probably extends to Queensland waters." Mr. Hill also notices as remarkable the great strength of these fishes, and assumes, with all probability, that it is from this characteristic that they have acquired their trivial name.

So far as can be ascertained from public records and from our own experience, the purely Port Jackson District, stretching from Broken Bay in the north to Port Hacking in the south, can alone be given as the acknowledged habitat of this species on our coast.

The Samsonfish attains a length of at least twenty inches.

Genus III.—TEMNODON.

Temnodon, Cuv. & Val. Hist. Nat. Poiss. ix. p. 225, 1833.

Branchiostegals seven: pseudobranchiæ present. Body oblong, compressed. Preopercle with some slight denticulations. Jaws armed with strong teeth: villiform teeth on the vomer and palatines. Two dorsal fins, the first with seven feeble spines: the second and the anal more developed: one or two small detached spines in front of the anal. Scales moderate, cycloid. Pyloric appendages very numerous. Airbladder simple.

Geographical distribution.—Temperate and tropical seas of both hemispheres.

TEMNODON SALTATOR.

Gasterosteus saltatrix, Linn. Syst. Nat. i. p. 491, 1766; Shaw, Zool. iv. p. 609.
Scomber saltator, Bl. Schn. p. 35.
Chilodipterus heptacanthus, Lacép. Hist. Nat. Poiss. iii. p. 542, pl. xxi. fig. 3 (bad).
Pomatomus skib, Lacép. Hist. Nat. Poiss. iv. p. 436, pl. viii. fig. 3.
Scomber plumbeus, Mitch. Trans. Lit. & Phil. Soc. New York, i. p. 424, pl. iv. fig. 1.
Temnodon heptacanthus, Quoy & Gaim. Voy. Freycinet, Zool. p. 400, pl. lxi. fig. 2.

Temnodon saltator, Cuv. & Val. Hist. Nat. Poiss. ix. p. 225, pl. cclx; Cuv. Règne Anim. Ill. Poiss. pl. lvi. fig. 3 ; Storer, Report, p. 57; De Kay, New York Fauna, Fish. p. 130, pl. xxvi. fig. 81 ; Baird, Ninth Smithson. Report, p. 337; Holbr. Ichthyol. S. Carol. p. 62, pl. ix. fig. 2 ; Gay, Hist. Chil. Zool. ii. p. 244; Lowe, Trans. Zool. Soc. ii. p. 183 ; Nordm. *in* Demidoff, Voy. Russ. Merid. iii. p. 394 ; Guichen. Explor. Algér. Poiss. p. 63; Webb & Berthel. Hist. Nat. Iles Canar. Poiss. p. 58, pl. xiii. fig. 2 ; Gnth. Catal. Fish. ii. p. 479 ; Casteln. Proc. Zool. Soc. Vict. 1872, i. p. 118 ; Macleay Catal. Austr. Fish. i. p. 179; Woods, Fisher. New South Wales, p. 60, pl. xx.

Tailor.

Plate XXV.

B. vii. D. 7–8. 1/24–26. A. 1–2. 1/26–28. V. 1 5. P. 17. C. 17. L. lat. 90–100. L. tr. 8–9/19–21. Cæc. pyl. num. Vert. 12/14.

Length of head 4·20–4·33, of caudal fin 4·50–5·15, height of body 4·50–4·75 in the total length. Eye with the adipose lid but little developed, its diameter 4·50–6·25 in the total length, 1·10–1·60 in the length of the snout, and 1·10–1·70 in the interorbital space, which is strongly convex. Nostrils approximate, separated by a narrow bridge of skin only ; the anterior oval and vertical ; the posterior a long, narrow, vertical slit. Upper profile of head gently rounded. Lower jaw the longer. Cleft of mouth wide and oblique, the maxilla extending to beneath the posterior margin of the eye, or not quite so far. Preopercle finely denticulated on the lower limb, and with a notch on the vertical limb immediately above the angle ; opercle with a weak bony point. Jaws with a single series of strong subulate teeth ; the upper with a series of smaller teeth anteriorly, separated by a considerable interval from the outer series : villiform teeth on the vomer in a triangular patch ; on the palatines in a band, which is broadest about the middle. Dorsal spines very feeble, the fourth the longest, 4·50–5·00 in the length of the head, and 2·00–2·33 in that of the anterior rays, which are much longer than the posterior ones : the anal commences beneath the fourth dorsal ray ; it is of similar shape to the rayed dorsal, and extends slightly beyond that fin : ventrals rather small, their length from 2·00 in half-grown to 2·75 in adult examples in the distance between their origin and the vent, and from 2·20–2·50 in the length of the head ; its spine long and slender, 2·66–3·33 in the same length : pectorals small and pointed, 1·50–1·75 in the same : caudal forked, the least height of its pedicle 3·00–3·50 in the height of the body. Cheeks and opercles scaly ; a few scales on the temporal region and on the hinder part of the occiput : soft dorsal and anal scaly. Curve of the lateral line very slight. Airbladder large.

Colors.—Pale green above, silvery below : soft dorsal, anal, and posterior half of caudal tinged with yellow.

During the spring months the Tailor arrives off our coasts in countless numbers for the purpose of shedding their spawn ; this function takes place in the open sea, but well within the influence of the tides, and the impregnated ova float on the surface in large masses, where they become the prey of numerous predaceous fishes and birds; owing to the combined warmth of the sun and water, and influenced doubtless by the action of the tides, the ova mature quickly, and the young fish on their emergence soon find their way into sheltered harbors and inlets, though, should stormy weather intervene during their passage, thousands of fry under two inches in length are frequently washed ashore on the outer beaches, those, however, which survive the perils of the journey, and reach the comparatively safe shelter of our harbors and salt water lakes rapidly increase in size, and are taken by the seine at all seasons of the year, measuring from four to ten inches in length, and are sent to market along with Yellowtail, to be sold as bait, for which purpose they are excellent.

Writing from Twofold Bay Mr. Glover remarks:—"They are seen between the Heads in September and October in large shoals. I think they spawn in November in deep water outside; I have often seen the spawn floating on the surface, and surrounded by gulls, shags, &c. The young fry are caught in the bay in March, varying from two inches upwards, accompanied by full grown ones eighteen inches in length. In June they leave the Bay till the following September." From the Clarence River Heads Mr. Hood Pegus reported that they come in October and spawn during the same month.

As a table fish the Tailor is in great request, and is bought up with avidity in the market; indeed we have few more delicate or well flavored fishes on the coast; the flesh, however, deteriorates very rapidly, and care should, therefore, be taken when choosing one for consumption to select an example which has but recently been captured.

The Tailor appears to subsist almost exclusively upon smaller fishes, and as its voracity is boundless, the destruction caused by shoals of adults to their own fry and those of the other species must be enormous. On two occasions only have we found food other than fishes; these were, on one occasion a squid, on another several small swimming crabs.

Consequent on their rapacity they take a bait of almost any kind freely, and afford good sport to the angler. The great majority of those brought to market are, however, taken by the seine net, but, though commanding a remunerative price, the enclosure of a shoal of large Tailors is frequently no great cause for congratulation on the part of their captors, as their strong subulate teeth, aided by their strength and determination, enable them in an incredibly short time to cut through the meshes, and not only escape themselves, but by rendering the net useless cause the loss of that night's fishing, not to speak of the trouble and expense incurred in mending the nets. In connection with this Oliver (*vide* Tenison Woods) states:—"This fish is very destructive to the fishermen's nets. A school of Tailors enclosed in a seine generally involves wholesale destruction to the net. After such a haul a considerable expenditure of time and twine is necessary to repair the rents made by the sharp teeth of these very active and determined fishes. Instances have been known where the entire bunt of a net has been torn to shreds by a few dozen Tailors."

Speaking generally of its distribution Günther states that it "is spread over nearly all the tropical and subtropical seas; it frequents principally the coasts, but is also met with in the open sea. On the Atlantic coasts of the United States it is well known by the name of ' Bluefish,' being highly esteemed as food, and furnishing excellent sport. It is one of the most rapacious fishes, destroying an immense number of other shore fishes, and killing many more than it can devour."

The Tailor is very abundant along the whole of our coastline from north to south, and though as before stated the catch is greatest during the spring and early summer months, there are nevertheless not many days throughout the year on which they are absent from the market. On the Queensland coast we are again left in uncertainty as to the extension of its northerly range, but Saville Kent mentions it as "requiring classification among the representative fishes of Moreton Bay"; he also remarks that it is locally known as the "Diarbi" or "Pombah," is closely allied to *Seriola*, associates in a similar way in shoals, grows to a weight of about seventeen pounds, affords excellent sport, is very voracious and extremely destructive to fishing nets, is an excellent table fish, and is in best season during the winter months. In hot weather the flesh decomposes very rapidly.

According to Castelnau the Skipjack, as this species is called in Melbourne, "is one of the most common fishes in the market. It is generally found at Melbourne of a small size, but I have seen one in September which was two and a half feet in length." In view of this account of its abundance in Victorian waters, and of the silence one way or other of McCoy on this point, it is surprising to find the species dismissed by Lucas with the brief intimation, "Loc.—Queenscliff." In all probability the Tailor is common along our entire southern coastline, and we know that it is found on the West Australian coast at least as far north as the Swan River. Johnston, refering to the Tasmanian coast, merely remarks:—"An odd individual caught occasionally in the Derwent."

So far the Tailor has not been recorded from the shores of New Zealand; neither does it occur among any of the numerous collections from the Pacific Islands, nor can we find it noticed from the western shores of North America. It is not mentioned by Indian zoologists, yet there is an example in the British Museum from the Molucca Sea. It is abundant along the shores of the Eastern States of North America, and crosses the Atlantic to the Canary Islands at least. It is very common at the Cape, and according to Castelnau is known there as "Elftvish."

It is credited by Günther with attaining to a length of five feet, but the ordinary size of adults in our market does not exceed twenty four inches, while the largest seen measured but thirty three.

Genus IV.—TRACHYNOTUS.

Trachinotus (Lacép.) Cuv. & Val. Hist. Nat. Poiss. viii. p. 398, 1831.

Branchiostegals seven: pseudobranchiæ absent. Body more or less elevated, compressed. Cleft of mouth small: snout obtuse and swollen. Eyes lateral. Teeth on the jaws, vomer, and palatine bones, generally lost with age. Two dorsal fins: the first composed of a few small spines, connected by a low membrane, and with an anterior horizontal spine directed forwards: second dorsal and anal similar, and more developed than the first dorsal: two preanal spines, separated from the fin by an interspace: no finlets. Scales very small. Lateral line without armature. Airbladder bifurcate posteriorly. Pyloric appendages in large or moderate numbers.

Geographical distribution.—Atlantic coasts of tropical and temperate America; East and West coasts of Africa; from the Red Sea, through the Indian Seas to those of China and Japan, the Malay Archipelago, and Australia.

TRACHYNOTUS RUSSELLI.

Scomber botla parah, Russell, Fish. Vizag. ii. p. 32, pl. cxxxvi.
Scomber botla, Shaw, Zool. iv. p. 591.
Trachinotus russelii, Cuv. & Val. Hist. Nat. Poiss. viii. p. 436; Jerdon. Madras Journ. L. & Sc. 1851, p. 136.
Trachinotus oblonqus, Cuv. & Val. Hist. Nat. Poiss. viii., p. 437.
Trachynotus oblonqus, Gnth. Catal. Fish. ii. p. 484.
Trachynotus russellii, Day, Fish. Ind. p. 233, pl. li. B. fig. 3.

Dart.

B. vii. D. 6. 1/23-25. A. 2. 1/22-24*. V. 1/5. P. 18. C. 17. L. lat. 85-95. Cæc. pyl. 10. Vert. 10/14.

Length of head 5·10-5·50, of caudal fin 3·33-3·75, height of body 3·00-3·25 in the total length. Eye moderate 3·33-3·75 in the length of the head, and 1·10-1·25 in the interorbital space, which is convex: snout short and obtusely rounded, rising abruptly from the jaws, 1·10-1·20 in the diameter of the eye. Nostrils separated by a narrow band of skin, vertical, the posterior the larger. Jaws equal. Cleft of mouth moderate and slightly oblique, the maxilla extending to beneath the middle of the orbit, or not so far. Upper profile of head very slightly convex, the interorbital space and the occiput with a low longitudinal ridge which extends backwards to the recumbent dorsal spine. A narrow band of villiform teeth in each jaw, the outer row enlarged : a triangular patch on the vomer, and a short elongate band on the palatines. The anterior dorsal rays reach, when laid back, almost to the end of the fin, and are from one seventh to one third longer than the head : the anal is similar to the dorsal ; its anterior rays are even longer, reaching when intact to or even slightly beyond the end of the fin, and from one third to three fifths longer than the head : ventrals small, reaching to the vent, 2·25-2·75 in the length of the head : pectorals small, 1·40-1·66 in the same length : caudal deeply forked, the least height of the pedicle four fifths of the distance between the last dorsal ray and the base of the caudal. Entire head, except the cheeks and a narrow band along the upper margin of the opercle, scaleless : vertical fins with a low scaly sheath. Lateral line nearly straight, the anterior half wavy.

Colors.—Bluish-gray above, silvery on the sides and below; a series of six or seven indistinct dusky spots immediately above the lateral line : elongated rays of the dorsal and anal, and caudal lobes blackish.

As a food fish the Dart belongs more especially to the northern districts of the Colony, but we occasionally find it forwarded to the Sydney market in considerable numbers from such fishing grounds as Port Stephens and Lake Macquarie; these visits occur during the latter months of spring and the summer, but in no case could we detect any symptoms of spawn in the ovaries of a considerable number examined.

This handsome fish has received its popular name from the alleged rapidity of its motions. Judging by the contents of the stomachs of those dissected the major portion of its food would appear to be the young of other fishes, though small squid are not unfrequently present, and on one occasion the author detected the remains of a swimming crab As a table fish they cannot be highly recommended, nevertheless they are by no means unpalatable when eaten perfectly fresh.

On the New South Wales coast the Dart occasionally finds its way as far south as Port Jackson according to Macleay, but to the northward it quickly increases in numbers and importance, though even in Port Stephens and Lake Macquarie, where it is sometimes met with in considerable shoals, its appearance must be considered irregular, none of the fishes sent to market being full grown, nor likely to spawn in the district; it occurs also at Lord Howe Island. Curiously enough the genus *Trachynotus* is not even mentioned by Saville Kent in his Preliminary Report on the Food Fishes of Queensland, though, from their numbers and the size to which they attain,

---

* In one example there were nineteen rays only, though the base of the fin was of equal length to similarly sized specimens having twenty four rays.

they might have been expected to form no unimportant item among the food-producing resources of the northern parts of the Colony at least; they are abundant in Torres' Straits, and along all our northern and north-western seaboard, while in West Australian seas they may safely be predicted to extend at least as far to the southward as we know them to do on the east coast. This species ranges westward through the seas of the Malay Archipelago to those of India.

The Dart grows to the length of twenty two inches in tropical seas, but on our coast rarely attains to more than half that length.

Day states that *Trachynotus russelli* may be easily distinguished from the closely allied *T. bailloni* by the position of the lateral series of spots, which on the former are above, on the latter across, the lateral line, and by the development of the ventral fins, which are much longer in *T. russelli* than n its congener.

Genus V.—PSETTUS.

Psettus (Commerson) Cuv. & Val. Hist. Nat. Poiss. vii. p. 240, 1831.

Branchiostegals six: pseudobranchiæ present. Body much compressed and elevated. Cleft of mouth small: snout short. Eyes lateral. Villiform teeth on the jaws, vomer, palatine bones, and tongue. One dorsal fin with seven or eight spines: anal continuous, with three spines: ventrals rudimentary. Scales small, covering the vertical fins. Lateral line unarmed. Airbladder bifurcate posteriorly. Pyloric appendages numerous.

Geographical distribution.—From the Red Sea, east coast of Africa, and the Mascarene Archipelago through the seas of India to those of China, Malaysia, and Australia, and eastwards to Samoa and Fiji: west coast of Africa.

PSETTUS ARGENTEUS.

Chætodon argenteus, Linn. Ann. Acad. iv. p. 249; Bl. Schn. p. 230.
Psettus rhombeus, Cuv. & Val. Hist. Nat. Poiss. vii. p. 245.
Psettus argenteus, Richards. Voy. Erebus. & Terror, Fish. p. 57, pl. xxxv. ff. 1-3; Gnth. Catal. Fish. ii. p. 487, Fisch. de Sudsee, p. 140, *and* Study of Fish. ff. 198, 199; Kner, Voy. Novara, Fisch. p. 161; Day, Fish. Ind. p. 235, pl. li. B. fig. 5; Castelu. Proc. Linn. Soc. N. S. Wales, ii. p. 235; Macleay, Catal. Austr. Fish. i. p. 181, Proc. Linn. Soc. N. S. Wales, iv. p. 63, *and* viii. p. 266; Woods, Fisher. N. S. Wales, pl. xlv.

Batfish.

B. vi. D. 8/28-29. A. 3/28-30. V. 1/ 2-3. P. 16-17. C. 17. L. lat. 68-75. L. tr. 18/50 ca. Cæc. pyl. 120 ca. Vert. 9/14.

Length of head 3·80–4·10, of caudal fin 4·00, height of body 1·60–1·85 in the total length. Eye large, 2·50–2·75 in the length of the head: snout short and obtusely rounded, 1·50–1·75 in the diameter of the eye: interorbital space convex, 1·10–1·25 in the same. Nostrils approximate, oval, the anterior not much smaller than the posterior. Jaws equal. Cleft of mouth small and oblique, the maxilla extending to beneath the anterior margin of the orbit or a little further, and expanded behind. Upper profile of head very slightly convex; occipital ridge obtuse, inconspicuous. Angle and lower portion of the posterior limb of the preopercle feebly serrated, the denticulations lost with age. Villiform teeth in a narrow band in both jaws, in a subcircular patch on the vomer, and a short band on the palatines;

pterygoids densely clothed with minute teeth; a central suboval patch on the tongue. Last dorsal spine the longest, about three sevenths of the anterior rays, which are produced and from 1·00-1·33 in the length of the head : the anal is similar to the soft dorsal, its anterior rays are equal in length to those of that fin, and the third spine is longer and stronger than the last dorsal spine: ventral fins rudimentary, the short stout spine reaching midway to the vent, which is situated nearer to their origin than to that of the anal: pectorals small, about three fourths of the length of the head: caudal emarginate, the least height of its pedicle five eighths of the same length. Scales small and cycloid, the greater part of the vertical fins scaly, the snout and maxilla naked. Lateral line with a long gradual curve to below the middle of the rayed dorsal.

Colors.—Pale yellowish-brown with violet reflections on the upper surfaces and the caudal region; abdominal region silvery; a black band from the nape to the eye, and a second from the origin of the dorsal fin to the opercle, present in immature, but indistinct in adult examples: dorsal and caudal fins dusky; anal tinged with yellow.

The Batfish appears on the coast of New South Wales, north of Port Jackson, in considerable shoals, during the spring and earlier summer months. They are heavy with spawn about midsummer, but we are unacquainted with the manner in which the spawn is deposited, nor have we as yet seen the fry brought ashore in our harbors or estuaries, those sent to market being all adult and of about equal size.

Their food consists of minute marine animals, crustaceans, molluscs, worms, &c., the smallness of the mouth precluding the possibility of their swallowing other food, while their comparatively limited powers of locomotion prevent them from capturing swifter prey. As food they are of good quality.

On the Australian coast it is found at least as far to the south-eastward as Port Jackson, sometimes in considerable shoals. It has not been recorded from Victoria, Tasmania, or New Zealand, but is abundant on the Queensland coast, and, according to Saville Kent, is "commonly taken in Moreton Bay, and is classified among the food fishes of that Colony." It occurs in numbers along the northern seaboard of Australia, but the limit of its southerly range on the western coast has not been recorded.

Beyond these Colonies its range is very extensive, stretching from the Red Sea, the east coast of Africa, Madagascar, and Rodriguez, through the seas of India and Malaysia, eastward to Samoa and Fiji.

The Batfish attains to a length of nine inches, but rarely exceeds six in our seas.

Family XIV.—SCOMBRIDÆ.

Branchiostegals seven or eight: pseudobranchiæ present. Body oblong or fusiform, more or less compressed. Eyes lateral. Gill-openings wide. No bony articulation between the preopercle and infraorbital bones. Teeth always present in the jaws: vomer and palatine bones with or without teeth. Two dorsal fins: the spinous less developed than the rayed portion or than the anal, either continuous with or separated from the rayed dorsal, sometimes (as in *Echeneis*) modified into a sucking disc: finlets present or absent: ventrals thoracic. Tail with or without a lateral keel. Scales small or absent. Airbladder present or absent. Pyloric appendages in large numbers.

Geographical distribution.—Carnivorous pelagic fishes of the tropical and temperate seas of both hemisphere.

According to Günther all true Scombrid fishes have more than ten abdominal, and more than fourteen caudal vertebræ. Along with the *Gadidæ*, *Clupeidæ*, and *Salmonidæ*, the members of this family are most useful to mankind. He goes on to say:—" They are fishes of prey, and unceasingly active, their power of endurance in swimming being equal to the rapidity of their motions. Their muscles receive a greater supply of blood vessels and nerves than in other fishes, and are of a red color, and more like those of birds or mammals. This energy of muscular action causes the temperature of their blood to be several degrees higher than in other fishes. They wander about in shoals, spawn in the open sea, but periodically approach the shore, probably in pursuit of other fishes on which they feed." And again:— " Mackerel, like other marine fishes, birds, and mammals of prey, follow the shoals of young and adult Clupeids in their periodical migrations ; on the British coasts it is principally the fry of the Pilchard and Sprat which wanders from the open sea towards the coast, and guides the movements of the Mackerel."

Day remarks:—" Fishes of the Mackerel family are pelagic forms, readily distinguishable by their elegant shapes and brilliant colors, while they are mostly highly prized for the table. Carnivorous and exceedingly active, their shapes are well adapted to enable them to glide rapidly through the water ; while to obviate the least impediment, we even find, in some, depressions for the reception of the pectoral fins."

Fossil Scombridæ are not uncommon in tertiary formations, the existing genera *Scomber*, *Thynnus*, and *Cybium* being represented in the Eocene and Miocene.

Genus I.—SCOMBER.

Scomber, sp. Artedi, Genera Pisc. p. 30, 1738.
Scomber, Cuvier, Règne Anim. ; Cuv. & Val. Hist. Nat. Poiss. viii. p. 6, 1831.
Cordylus, Gray, in Gronow's Syst. Ichthyol. 1854.

Branchiostegals seven : pseudobranchiæ present. Body fusiform, compressed. Cleft of mouth deep. Eyes lateral, with adipose lids. Teeth in the jaws small and deciduous : similar teeth present or absent on the vomer and palatine bones. Two dorsal fins, the first continuous, with feeble spines, and separated by an interspace from the second ; the spines fewer in number than the rays of the second dorsal or the anal : five or six finlets behind the rayed dorsal and anal : a preanal spine generally present. Two slight ridges on each side of the root of the caudal fin. Scales very small, equally covering the whole body as a rule. Airbladder present or absent, simple. Pyloric appendages in large numbers.

Geographical distribution.—Almost all the tropical and temperate seas of both hemispheres ; not, as yet, recorded from the Atlantic shores of temperate South America.

SCOMBER PNEUMATOPHORUS.

Scomber pneumatophorus, De la Roche, Ann. Mus. Hist. Nat. 1809, xiii. pp. 315, 334 ; Cuv. & Val. Hist. Nat. Poiss. viii. p. 36 ; Guichen. Explor. Algér. Poiss. p. 56 ; Gnth. Catal. Fish. ii. p. 359 ; McCoy, Prodr. Zool. Vict. dec. iii. pl. 28.
Scomber grex, Mitch. Trans. Lit. & Phil. Soc. N. York, p. 422 ; Cuv. & Val. Hist. Nat. Poiss. viii. p. 45 ; Dekay, N. York Faun. Fish. p. 103, pl. xi. f. 32.

Scomber australasicus, Cuv. & Val. Hist. Nat. Poiss. viii. p. 49; Gnth. Catal. Fish. ii. p. 359; Macleay, Catal. Austr. Fish. i. p. 190; Johnston, Proc. Roy. Soc. Tas.1882, pp. 84,118; Sherrin, Handb. N.Z. Fish. p. 61.
? *Scomber capensis*, Cuv. & Val. Hist. Nat. Poiss. viii. p. 56.
Scomber pneumatophorus major, Schleg. Faun. Japon. Poiss. p. 94, pl. xlvii, f. 1.
Scomber pneumatophorus minor, Schleg. Faun. Japon. Poiss. p. 94, pl. xlvii, f. 2.
? *Scomber saba*, Bleek. Japan, p. 405, *and* Verh. Batav. Gen. xxvi. p. 95.
Scomber janesaba, Bleek. Japan, p. 406, *and* Verh. Batav. Gen. xxvi. p. 96; Gnth. Catal. Fish. ii. p. 359; Macleay, Catal. Austr. Fish. Suppl. p. 27.
Scomber tapeinocephalus, Bleek. Japan, p. 407, *and* Verh. Batav. Gen. xxvi. p. 97, pl. vii. f. 2; Gnth. Catal. Fish ii. p. 361; Macleay, Catal. Austr. Fish. Suppl. p. 27.
Scomber antarcticus, Casteln. Proc. Zool. Soc. Vict. 1872, i. p. 106.

Mackerel.

B. vii. D. 10–12. 1/11 + v–vi. A. 1. 1/11 + v–vi. V. 1/5. P. 21. C. 19. Cœc. pyl. num. Vert. 14/17.

Length of head 4·00–4·25, of caudal fin 6·00–7·00, height of body 5·50–6·00 in the total length. Thickness of body from 1·25–1·40 in its height. Diameter of eye 3·00–3·40 in the length of the head, equal in length to the snout, and 1·40–1·60 in the interorbital space, which is flat; the anterior adipose lid reaches slightly beyond the front margin of the pupil, and inferiorly crosses over the posterior lid, which latter extends forward over one fourth of the pupil. Upper surface of head flat, with a broad median longitudinal groove; occiput with a short ridge. Jaws equal. Cleft of mouth large and slightly oblique; maxilla entirely covered by the preorbital, extending to beneath the anterior third of the orbit. Posterior limb of preopercle oblique and convex. A single row of small curved teeth on the jaws and palatines: two small patches on the vomer: tongue toothless. The spinous dorsal commences above the posterior angle of the base of the ventral; the distance between its origin and the tip of the snout is 3 10–3·25 in the total length; the spines are of moderate length, but weak; the second the longest, from 2·00–2·50 in the length of the head; second dorsal low: the anal commences beneath the third or fourth dorsal ray, and is preceded by a single short strong detached spine: ventral small, its length from 3·00–3·50 in the distance between its origin and the vent, and 2·40–2·60 in the length of the head: pectoral short and pointed, its length from 2·00–2·20 in the same: caudal deeply forked, each lobe with a basal keel. Scales minute, in fifteen to seventeen series between the lateral line and the base of the first dorsal: largest on the pectoral region, where they form an indistinct corselet: a row across the cheek. Lateral line gently curved. Airbladder present, of moderate size

Colors.—Upper surfaces bright green, frequently becoming dark blue after death, with numerous, irregular, wavy, transverse bars; sides paler green, with darker spots and short streaks; lower surfaces pearly white, washed with orange and pink, and ornamented with many more or less indistinct dark gray blotches and spots: interorbital space pale: cheeks with a golden tinge.

Large shoals of Mackerel appear upon our coast at irregular intervals during the year, but these visits, which may number as many as three or even four in the twelve months, or may be entirely wanting during a similar period, are much too uncertain in their recurrence to allow of any such profitable fishery—as that pertaining to the industry, as carried on in European and American waters—being held here, even were any adequate means for their capture employed by our fishermen. These shoals, which periodically appear in the bays and inlets of our deeply indented coast, consist entirely of immature fishes, never or very rarely exceeding twelve inches in length, and showing no trace of their having spawned in the past, nor of any likelihood of their so doing in the near future; we are, therefore, indebted for these visits solely to the abundance or scarcity of suitable food, which consists chiefly of the fry of other fishes, and, according to Mr. Edward Hill, of shrimps and young prawns. Taking into consideration the thousands of individuals which go to comprise a single shoal, and their extreme voracity, necessitated by an exceptionally active mode of life, it is not to be wondered at that these sources of food supply are quickly exhausted, and this having been effected the shoals disappear as suddenly as they had previously made their appearance. There seems, however, to be a general consensus of opinion that enormous shoals of Mackerel annually pass along our coast about midsummer, heading in a northerly direction, but whether these shoals consist of adult and breeding fishes, or what their ultimate destination is, can only be conjectured. It is, however, more than probable that the "shoals of enormous magnitude" mentioned in the Report of the Royal Commission, as causing the sea, "sometimes for miles, to have the appearance of being almost a solid mass of them," are, when so observed, engaged in the very act of shedding their spawn. Of the habits of the common Atlantic Mackerel (*Scomber scomber*), when engaged in perpetuating its species, it has been remarked by Sars (*v.* Day, Brit. Fish. i. p. 89) that the ova are "deposited some leagues from the shore, and at the very surface of the waves, where a great quantity of these fishes may often be met with, engaged in spawning." There is no reason to doubt that the breeding operations of our species are carried out in a similar manner. Though normally a fish of very rapid growth, such may be retarded by the absence of suitable food, or by a long continuance of cold and stormy weather.

Mackerel give excellent sport to the line fisher, either from a boat under easy sail or anchored in a strong tideway, so as to permit of the lines, of which it is always best to use several in each boat, streaming away behind, the sinkers used being of course graduated to the swiftness with which the boat is moving or the strength of the tide; nor must it be lost sight of that the present species is much more liable to be taken near the bottom than is *S. scomber*. Mackerel are not by any means choice in their selection of a bait, almost any glittering substance being sufficient to attract them, but we have never found any lure so deadly as a strip cut off the side of the tail of another mackerel, and termed a lask or lashing, and which, when in motion through the water, has a wonderful resemblance to the sinuous movements of a small fish, and being exceedingly tough a single bait may with care be used for the capture of a number of individuals.

In pursuit of their prey Mackerel do not follow it up, as most fishes do, but strike across the line of its flight, as has been observed by us on several occasions, when large shoals entered the harbor of Portrush on the north coast of Ireland, and were taken by hundreds off the quays by means of a rod and line with three or more large white flies attached; all the fish observed, and these were often within a few feet, struck at the flies at an angle to their course.

The confusion, which has caused several writers on our food fishes, such as Tenison Woods and even Saville Kent, to confound our common Mackerel with Castelnau's *S. antarcticus*, is directly attributable to the Royal Commission Report above quoted. There it is stated :—"The genus *Scomber* is represented in Australia by two species, *S. australascius*, Cuv. & Val., and *S. antarcticus*, Castelu. The last named is the one best known in these seas as the 'Mackerel'." How so grave an error could have been made it is difficult to imagine, since Castelnau distinctly states that his species has no airbladder, while the most cursory examination is sufficient to reveal the presence of a well developed one in our species. Though he has not been followed by other colonial authors this question was practically decided by McCoy many years ago. The only question, therefore, which need concern us now is whether Castelnau is to be relied upon in his statement as to the absence of an airbladder in the unique example of *S. antarcticus* which he examined, and judging from the carelessness which characterises many other descriptions of Australian fishes by the same author, and the fact that no other colonial scientist has since met with his fish, we must conclude that the Count's conclusion is open to grave doubt; nevertheless there is no reason whatever why a Mackerel without an airbladder should not be coexistent in our seas with one possessed of that organ, as is the case in European waters; should this be so *S. antarcticus* will probably prove to be a more southerly form. We are, however, of opinion that Castelnau was mistaken as to the absence of an airbladder in his supposed species, which will in that event merge in the present form.

The food of the Mackerel consists of the fry and ova of other fishes, small crustaceans, &c., while as a table fish it is universally esteemed, care being, however, taken that they are eaten quite fresh, as they decompose very rapidly, soon become soft and tasteless, and develop deleterious qualities; they are also excellent when pickled fresh. They are of great value too in providing the best bait for all other predaceous fishes.

This Mackerel is common along our coast from south to north, and is "occasionally taken in Queensland waters" according to Saville Kent. McCoy states that it appears "rarely in Hobson's Bay, but in considerable numbers when it does appear"; to the westward it can be traced through King George's Sound whence it was described by Cuvier and Valenciennes to Swan River and northwards, from both which places specimens have been received by the British Museum. Of its occurrence in Tasmanian waters Johnston writes :—" I have not seen specimens, but the fishermen assure me that a fish, called by them the English Mackerel, is seen in immense shoals, after long irregular intervals of time, on the east coast"; and again :—The English Mackerel is seen on the east coast, occasionally in large numbers, each year, moving in a northerly direction. They have been known to enter the estuary of the Derwent in large numbers as far as Bridgewater, but owing to the absence of proper means for capturing them, they rarely find their way to the market." In New Zealand, where its native name is "Tawatawa," its occurrence on the coast seems to be much more regular than on our shores; Sherrin remarks :—" The appearance of Mackerel shoals is of more frequent and regular occurrence than is generally regarded, or was at least in past years, as it was the usual Maori habit in summer to station men on cliffs to watch the shoals coming to land."

Many good observers consider that Gmelin's *Scomber colias* is identical with this fish, but as this is by no means proved to be correct, and as that species has constantly but seven dorsal spines only, we have considered it advisable to keep them separate. The synonymy given is compiled from descriptions only.

Genus II.—PELAMYS.

Pelamys. Cuv. & Val. Hist. Nat. Poiss. viii, p. 149, 1831.

Branchiostigals seven: pseudobranchiæ present. Body elongate-oblong. Cleft of mouth deep. Teeth in the jaws of moderate strength: small teeth present or absent on the vomer, present on the palatine bones. Two dorsal fins, the first formed of rather feeble spines, and reaching almost to the base of the second dorsal, behind which and the anal are from six to nine finlets. Scales minute: enlarged and forming a corselet on the anterior part of the body. A longitudinal keel on each side of the tail. Airbladder absent. Pyloric appendage dendritical.

Geographical distribution.—Temperate and tropical seas.

PELAMYS CHILENSIS.

Pelamys chilensis, Cuv. & Val. Hist. Nat. Poiss. viii. p. 163; Gay, Hist. Chile, Zool. ii. p. 224; Gnth. Catal. Fish ii. p. 368; Steindachn. SB. Ak. Wien, lvii. p. 353; Day, Fish. Ind. p. 253, pl. lvi. f. 1.
Pelamys orientalis, Schleg. Faun. Japon. Poiss. p. 69, pl. lii.; Gnth. Catal. Fish. ii. p. 368.
Pelamys australis, Macleay Catal. Austr. Fish. i. p. 192.
Pelamys schlegeli, McCoy, Prodr. Zool. Vict. dec. xvi. pl. 155.

Horse-Mackerel.

Plate XXVI.

B. vii. D. 18–19. 2–3/12–13.+vii–viii. A. 3–4/12–13.+vi. V. 1/5. P. 25–27. C. 24. Vert. 23/22.

Length of head 4·00–4·20, of caudal fin 5·75–6·00, height of body 4·50–4·80 in the total length. Eye with a very narrow adipose lid, its diameter 5·20–5·40 in the length of the head, 1·75 in. the length of the snout, which is conical and slightly depressed, and 1·40 in the convex interorbital space. Upper jaw very slightly the longer. Cleft of mouth deep and almost horizontal; maxilla slightly expanded behind, reaching to beneath the posterior margin of the orbit. A single row of distant, incurved teeth in the jaws increasing in size posteriorly, fifteen to twenty in number in the upper jaw, ten to thirteen in the lower; lower jaw with one, sometimes two, pair of canines behind the symphysis, and inside of the outer row, directed inwards and backwards; a small circular patch of stout teeth, curving in all directions on the head of the vomer; these teeth are deciduous, but two or three are always present. A short row of recurved teeth on the palatines. Dorsal spines weak, the second the longest, three sevenths of the length of the head, gradually decreasing in length from thence the posterior ones being very short, and the last very close to the origin of the rayed dorsal; the latter fin high in front, its height about two thirds of the length of its base: the anal commences beneath the last dorsal ray or first finlet, and is similar to the rayed dorsal, its height, however, is equal to the length of its base: ventrals short, their length from 4·50–4·75 in the distance between their origin and the vent, and 3·10–3·30 in the length of the head; pectorals short and falcate, extending backwards to beneath the ninth dorsal spine, from 9·00–9·60 in the total length, and 2·15–2·33 in the length of the head: caudal with pointed lobes; posterior portion of caudal pedicle strongly depressed, and bearing a lateral longitudinal keel, without supplementary keels above and below. Scales small, covering the entire body, anteriorly forming a distinct corselet, which sends backwards three prolongations, the upper passing along the base of the spinous dorsal, the central one along the middle of the side to immediately behind the pectoral, the upper edge of which is sunk in a groove, and the lower, which is also grooved, passing along the median line of the abdomen to a short distance behind the termination of the ventrals. Airbladder absent.

Colors.—Back green with violet reflections, below silvery; a broad dusky band covering the upper surface of the head and extending along the dorsal profile to the base of the rayed dorsal, growing gradually narrower posteriorly; five to eleven dark longitudinal wavy bands on the sides, the lower ones faint or wanting: dorsal fins dusky, the upper third of the anterior spines, darkest, of the rays yellowish, as also are the tips of the finlets; anal and ventral fins whitish; pectorals and caudal blackish: irides silvery.

The Horse Mackerel, as this fish is invariably called here both by fishermen and dealers, appears on our shores in considerable shoals at irregular intervals, and even ascends our shallow bays and estuaries to some distance in pursuit of fry. Specimens obtained from Port Jackson and Botany during the month of March, contained ova in an early stage of development.

Like all its allies these fishes are exceedingly active and voracious, nothing which it can swallow coming amiss to its appetite, while as food it is moderate when quite fresh.

So far the Port Jackson District is the only recorded Australian habitat of this species, with the exception of a single specimen, in which the lower body bands are very strongly marked, obtained by McCoy in Port Phillip. It is, therefore, to be hoped that the figure given by him (Prodr. Zool. Vict. dec. xvi. pl. 155) and the accompanying description, along with those presented here, will draw attention to our larger striped Scombrids, and enable us shortly to gain a clearer insight into their distribution in Australian seas. It is also found in Indian and Japanese waters, and was originally described from the coast of Chili.

With us eighteen inches is the maximum size to which it attains, but the type specimen is twenty six inches in length.

Pelamys chilensis is included in Sherrin's "List of Fishes in New Zealand" (p. 301), but is not mentioned in the index or the letterpress; we are, therefore, unable to say whether it is common or otherwise.

Family XV.—TRACHINIDÆ.

Branchiostegals five to seven: pseudobranchiæ present. Body more or less elongate, compressed posteriorly. Cleft of mouth varying from small to very deep, and from almost horizontal to nearly vertical. Eyes more or less lateral. Some of the bones of the head usually armed: preopercle without bony stay. Teeth in the jaws small and pointed, with or without canines: vomerine teeth present: palate edentulous or dentigerous. One or two dorsal fins, the rays generally greatly outnumbering the spines: the anal similar to the rayed dorsal: ventrals thoracic, with one spine and five rays: lower pectoral rays simple or branched. Scales present or absent. Airbladder generally absent. Pyloric appendages in small numbers.

Geographical distribution.—Cosmopolitan. All the *Trachinidæ* are of small size, and, with the exception of *Bathydraco*, are littoral forms, some of which enter rivers. Almost all are slow and inactive in their movements, and keep entirely to the bottom. This, however, is not invariably the case; as instances to the contrary our whitings (*Sillago*) may be taken, while the European *Trachinus vipera* will rise to a white fly after sunset (see Proc. Roy. Dublin Soc. 1885, p. 512.)

Several fossil forms have been described from tertiary deposits.

Genus I.—SILLAGO.

Sillago, Cuvier, Règne Anim.; Cuv & Val. Hist. Nat. Poiss. iii. p. 398, 1829
Sillaginodes, Gill, Proc. Ac. Nat. Sc. Philad. 1861, p. 504.
Sillaginopsis, Gill, Proc. Ac. Nat. Sc. Philad. 1861, p. 505.

Branchiostegals six; pseudobranchiæ present. Body elongate and somewhat cylindrical. Head conical, with the muciferous system well developed. Cleft of mouth small: the upper jaw rather the longer. Eyes lateral directed slightly upwards. Gill-openings wide. Preopercle serrated or crenulated: opercle terminating in a spinous point. Villiform teeth in the jaws, with an outer subconical series, and on the vomer: palatine bones edentulous. Two dorsal fins, the first with nine to twelve spines: the second more developed, similar to the anal: ventrals thoracic: the lower pectoral rays branched. Scales moderate or small, ctenoid. Lateral line not continued on to the caudal fin. Airbladder simple. Pyloric appendages in small number.

Geographical distribution.—From the Red Sea, the east coast of Africa, and the Seychelles, through all the seas of India and Malaysia, to those of Australia and Tasmania.

The great confusion, which exists in the works of Australian authors, as to the correct names to which the two species mentioned below are referable, has made it a task of exceptional difficulty to select from the writings of these authors the true species to which they allude, and thus present an amended, and we trust more accurate, synonymy to our readers. That many of these errors have been caused by the confused account given in the Report of the Royal Commission, pp. 16, 17, is undoubted, but in justice to the gentlemen who drew up that Report it is but fair to say that they were probably misled by the statement made by Günther (Catal. Fish. ii. p. 245, *foot-note*) that the Astrolabe figure shows twenty one rays, whereas it really shows two spines and nineteen rays, and as one of the spines is as often absent as present, it necessarily follows that, so far as this character is concerned, the fish in question is intermediate between *S. maculata* and *S. ciliata*. Johnston also throws some additional light on the subject by the statement that in the Tasmanian form the "sides are faintly marked with yellowish bars, which become obsolete towards the belly," and, it might be added, probably disappear in specimens preserved in alcohol. Until, therefore, a careful comparison of the Tasmanian fish with undoubted specimens of our two species has been made, it seems to us unadvisable to consider *S. bassensis* as a proved synonym of *S. maculata*. The Melbourne Whiting, *S. punctata*, occasionally occurs as far north as Port Jackson.

SILLAGO MACULATA.

Sillago maculata, Quoy & Gaim. Voy. Freycinet, Zool. p. 261, pl. liii. f. 2;
Cuv. & Val. iii. p. 411; Bleek. Perc. p. 62, *and* Revis. Sill. 1874, p. 71;
Gnth. Catal. Fish. ii. p. 245; Kner, Voy. Novara, Fisch. p. 127: Day,
Fish. Ind. p. 265, pl. lviii. f. 4; Bleek. Atl. Ichthyol. pl. ccclxxxix. f.
5; All. & Macl. Proc. Linn. Soc. N. S. Wales, i. p. 279; Castel. Proc.
Zool. Soc. Vict. 1872, i. p. 94, *and* Proc. Linn. Soc. N. S. Wales, iii. p.
380; Macleay, Catal. Austr. Fish. i p. 201; Woods, Fisher, N. S. Wales,
pl. xxiii.
? *Sillago bassensis*, Cuv. & Val. Hist. Nat. Poiss. iii. p. 412; Quoy & Gaim.
Voy. Astrolabe, Poiss. p. 672, pl. i. f. 2.
? *Sillago ciliata*, Johnston, Proc. Roy. Soc. Tas. 1882, pp. 80, 116.

Trumpeter Whiting.

B. vi. D. 11. 1/19–20. A. 1–2/20–21. V. 1 5. P. 15. C. 17. L. lat. 70–72. L. tr.
6 14. Cœc. pyl. 4. Vert. 14/21.

Length of head 3·75–4·25, of caudal fin 5·50–6·00, height of body
5·00–5·66 in the total length. Diameter of eye 3·50–4·25 in the length of
the head, and 1·33–1·80 in that of the snout: interorbital space flat,
1·25–1·50 in the diameter of the eye. Nostrils approximate, subcircular, the
anterior protected by a flap, the posterior patent. Upper profile of head
slightly rounded. Upper jaw a little the longer. Cleft of mouth small and
transverse, the maxilla extending less than half way along the snout.
Preopercle finely denticulated: opercle with a single blunt point. Teeth in
the jaws in villiform bands, with the outer row a little enlarged; an arcuate
band on the vomer. Dorsal spines weak, the second the longest, 1·75–2·25
in the length of the head: second dorsal not so high as the first, its base
about one eighth longer than that of the anal: the anal commences opposite
the third dorsal ray, and ends beneath the penultimate ray: ventral fin
with the outer ray filamentous, its length from 1·25–1·50 in the distance
between its origin and the vent, and 1·50–2·00 in that of the head: pectorals
1·66–2·00 in the same: caudal emarginate, the least height of the pedicle
from 2·33–2·75 in the height of the body. Preorbital, maxilla, and snout in
front of the nostrils naked; a row of minute scales behind each dorsal and
anal ray. Lateral line gently curved to beneath the anterior dorsal rays,
thence straight.

Colors.—Sandy brown above, silvery below; the sides with a conspicuous,
median, longitudinal silvery band, and with seven or eight irregular dusky
blotches directed obliquely forwards, which are sometimes very faint or
even absent: cheeks golden, a dark green blotch on the opercles: spinous
dorsal blotched, rayed dorsal spotted, with olive green; anal and ventrals
golden; pectorals and caudal cloudy gray, the former with a deep black spot
in front of the base.

So great is the confusion existing with regard to this and the succeeding
species of Whiting, that it is very difficult to ascertain to which of them the
various authors refer; it is, however, generally conceded that the two species
shed their ova at different seasons, and this accords with our own observations.
Examples of this species obtained during January and February have the roe
about half developed, and the months, March and April, given as the breeding
season in the Royal Commission Report, are therefore correct. The ova is
deposited on sandy beaches in sheltered bays and lakes, and in estuaries, water

of no great depth being selected. In the Report above referred to it is stated:—
"There is a similar want of reliable evidence as to the time of the appearance of the young fry, but we believe that there are sufficient grounds for concluding that the spawn deposited at the end of summer does not germinate until the warmth of spring." This remark is worthy of all consideration, the only alternative suggestion being that during the winter months the coldness of the shallow water in which the ova are deposited, retards their growth on their emergence from the egg. Be this as it may, the young fish, measuring from one to two inches, may be found abundantly on shallow, sheltered, sandy flats and lagunes—such as Manly Lagune, where great facilities for their observation are available—during the early summer months; each of these young fish is in possession of a hole in the sand, but whether self-excavated, or having been deserted by, or taken from, its rightful owner, we are not in a position to state; at the mouth of the hole, which is only just large enough to admit of the passage of its body, the little creature lies, and on the approach of danger, or even the passage of a dark cloud over the sun, immediately disappears, the anterior half of the head, however, as quickly reappearing, thus showing that close beneath the surface a chamber must exist, sufficiently large to permit of their turning round with ease; should any movement occur in their neighborhood to cause them further alarm when in this position they are able to back down again into their hiding place with great celerity, but if perfect quiet is maintained, they soon emerge and take up their original position near the opening. These were undoubtedly *S. maculata*, as several specimens were caught.

Though not numerically so abundant nor attaining to such a size as the succeeding species, the flesh of this Whiting is of equally excellent quality, and few, if any, of our food fishes are so universally appreciated, while none command so certain a sale, and none with the exception of its congener, for their size so high a price in the local market. Their food consists of worms, small crustaceans, isopods, and foraminifera.

The Trumpeter Whiting is found along the entire seaboard of New South Wales, but becomes more numerous to the northward. It is mentioned by Saville Kent as frequenting Moreton Bay, but no more inappropriate name than that of "Sydney Whiting" could have been devised for it, *Sillago maculata* being the only species of our Whitings which can boast of an extended range; *S. punctata* being confined, so far as our present records go, to Victoria and South Australia; *S. bassensis*, if a good species, inhabiting Tasmanian waters only; while *S. ciliata* is found along our entire eastern and perhaps nothern coast-lines; what species is found in West Australia we are unable to state at present.* In virtue of its wide northerly and westerly range, the Trumpeter Whiting should be abundant along the shores of Queensland and North Australia. From Victoria it has been recorded as "once seen" by Castelnau, and it does not appear from Lucas' Census that it has been observed since; while Johnston records it doubtfully from Tasmania. Of the common Whiting of the island colony, it is, however, necessary to speak at greater length; Johnston, who refers it to *S. ciliata*, writes:—"The Tasmanian Whiting is a most valuable market fish; it fetches a higher price in the market, for its size, than any other fish. These fishes are usually taken in seine nets, during the months of November, December, and January, in the Derwent, and along the east coast. They also may be taken with hook and line, and

---

* A report on the Food Fishes of West Australia from the pen of a competent ichthyologist is greatly needed. No more fertile and almost unworked field for the study of this branch of zoological science exists on the face of the globe, than the varied and extensive seaboard of that magnificent Colony.

a dozen or so are frequently captured in this way at odd times in the upper waters about Sandy Bay as late as July. They go in schools, but they are stated to have greatly fallen off in numbers during the last year or two; the reason for this decrease has not yet been satisfactorily determined. They are delicious little fishes, averaging a quarter of a pound in weight, silvery, with elongate snout and body. The sides are faintly marked with yellowish bars, which become obsolete towards the belly." Further on the same author remarks :—" When (freshly) caught, however, there are six to seven faint irregularly oblique bars running across the side in a forward direction from the dorsal to the lateral line. Faint oblique streaks of olive ornament the interspaces between the dorsal rays. There are invariably seventy rows of scales along the lateral line. Average length ten inches." Mr. Johnston, presumably from personal examination, gives the formula of the anal fin in the Tasmanian species as 2/18-19; in all the specimens of *S. ciliata* which have passed through our hands, that formula was 2/16, while in *S. maculata* it was 1-2/20-21, the Tasmanian fish being, therefore, intermediate in this character. We may at once withdraw *S. ciliata* from the discussion, as from Johnston's remarks we have ample evidence that his fish does not belong to that species, the number of scales on the lateral line, the coloration, and the average size and weight, all combining to preclude such a belief. The whole question, therefore, rests on the identity or otherwise of *S. bassensis* with *S. maculata*, and this can only be settled finally by a direct comparison of the Tasmanian form with the undoubted *S. maculata* of our own coast. We may, however, remark that the anal formula as given by Johnston, agrees with the figures of *S. bassensis* in the voyage of the Astrolabe, but by a clerical error the authors of the Histoire Naturelle des Poissons, are represented as giving that formula as 1/12, though in the next line they assert that it has two anal spines (*Il y a deux épines à son anale*).

It is a resident of the seas of the Malay Archipelago, and ranges westward as far as the Andaman Islands, but has not as yet been recorded from the mainland of India.

This species attains to a length of twelve inches, but the more usual market size is under ten inches.

SILLAGO CILIATA.

Sillago ciliata, Cuv. & Val. Hist. Nat. Poiss. iii. p. 415 ; Cuv. Règne Anim. Ill. Poiss. pl. xiii. f. 2; Gnth. Catal. Fish. ii. p. 245; Castelu. Proc. Zool. Soc. Vict. ii. p. 113 ; Kner, Voy. Novara, Fisch. p. 127 ; All. & Macl. Proc. Linn. Soc. N. S. Wales, i. p. 279; Macleay, Catal. Austr. Fish. i. p. 202 ; Woods, Fisher. N. S. Wales, pl. xxiv.

Sillago terræ-reginæ, Casteln. Proc. Linn. Soc. N. S. Wales, ii. p. 232.

Sillago bassensis, Casteln. Proc. Linn. Soc. N. S. Wales, iii. p. 380; Macleay, Catal. Austr. Fish. i. p. 202.

Sand Whiting.

Plate XXVII.

B. vi. D. 11. 1/17-18. A. 2/16. V. 1/5. P. 16. C. 17. L. lat. 61-65. L. tr. 6/12-13. Cœc. pyl. 3. Vert. 14/19.

Length of head 4·00-4·20, of caudal fin 5·20-5·75, height of body 5·66-5·85 in the total length. Diameter of eye, 4·00-5·25 in the length of the head, and 1·75-2·50 in that of the snout: interorbital space flat, 1·00-1·40 in the diameter of the eye. Nostrils approximate, the anterior crescentic and protected by a flap, the posterior circular and patent. Upper profile of head slightly rounded. Upper jaw a little the longer. Cleft of mouth small and transverse, the maxilla not extending to more than half way along the snout. Preopercle finely denticulated on the vertical limb: opercle with a blunt point. Teeth in the jaws villiform with an outer enlarged row; on the vomer in an angular band. Dorsal spines weak, the second the longest, 1·50–1·75 in the length of the head; second dorsal not nearly so high as the first, its base one fifth longer than that of the anal: the anal commences opposite the second or third dorsal ray, and ends opposite the fifteenth: ventral fin extending from five sevenths to one half of the distance between its origin and the vent, its length, 1·50–2·00 in that of the head; the outer ray slightly filamentous: pectorals from 1·50–1·75 in the same: caudal emarginate, the least height of the pedicle 2·15–2·33 in the height of the body. Scales adherent; none on the preorbital or anterior half of the snout; rows of minute scales behind the dorsal and anterior anal rays.

Colors.—Sandy brown above with purple and green reflections; upper surface of head and the snout olive green; a broad but rather indistinct yellowish band along the middle of the sides: spinous dorsal with faint dusky blotches, the rayed with rows of blackish spots: anal and ventral golden; pectorals pale brown with a darker base; caudal yellowish with blackish margins.

The principal breeding season of this *Sillago* extends from the middle of October nearly to Christmas, according to the bulk of the specimens examined by us, and this is fairly in harmony with the evidence of Mr. Glover, who states that in Twofold Bay:—" They spawn in December, up the river, and also on sand-banks in the bay. I have caught them very small in April"; and of Mr. Hood Pegus, who, speaking of the Clarence Heads, remarks:—" Whiting are most plentiful in January, and spawn in November, December, and January." Relying on the evidence of Mr. C. Smith, the Royal Commissioners say:—" We are inclined to think that this Whiting"— undoubtedly *S. ciliata*, not *S. maculata* as supposed by the Commission— " has two spawning seasons in the year, but if so, and there is little reason to doubt it, the spring" (winter?) " spawning is much the least important." That there are two distinct seasons during which this species, and in all probability *S. maculata* also. sheds its spawn, admits of no doubt, but, as mentioned before, the main body of adult fish deposit their ova during the early months of summer, while those which utilise June and July for this purpose are. as a rule, smaller, not fully adult, fish, which are possibly obeying the instincts of nature for the first time; there is, therefore, we consider, but one breeding season in the year for each individual fish. We are not in a position to state whether the fry of this fish protects itself by seeking refuge in holes in the sand, as mentioned in the account of the preceding species.

In its habits this species does not materially differ from *S. maculata*, but, being a larger and more handsome fish, it commands an even higher price in the market, and is, of all our food fishes, the one which is most in request for the breakfast table of those who can afford its price. The bulk of the Whitings sent to the Sydney Market are captured by means of the seine net. but they are also taken by hook and line.

Mr. Hill, referring to this species under the name of *S. maculata*, says:— " The Whiting may be caught with hook and line off sandy beaches or sand-spits, and in open sandy bays on the coast, in smooth water. The best bait is a live earthworm, although they will also take a fish bait, but not so readily; rarely, however, is the adult Whiting caught by hook and line; the medium size is the rule, except on the open sea beaches, where some of the very large ones may be taken by these means." So far as this goes it is doubtless correct, but the remainder of the paragraph* is hardly what one would expect to find countenanced by a Royal Commission specially appointed for the purpose of protecting our food fishes during the earlier stages of their existence, and developing our fishing industries; neither of these important ends are likely to be attained by advocating this unprincipled destruction of the fry of our finest food fish.

The Sand Whiting is far more abundant on the shores of the Colony than the preceding species, and is found along the coast from north to south; but like *S. maculata* appears to increase in numbers towards our northern boundary, while the finest consignments of these fishes forwarded to the Sydney market come from Lake Macquarie. Macleay has still further accentuated the confusion existing between the Australian Whitings by enumerating our common form as *S. bassensis*, and giving northern Australia as the restricted habitat of *S. ciliata*; this further confusion, it is but just to say, is probably traceable to Castelnau's papers on the subject.

S. ciliata is common on the coast of Queensland, and extends its range northward to York Peninsula and probably to the shores of southern New Guinea; but the extent of its range to the westward cannot be determined until a series of examples from our northern and north-western waters have been placed in the hands of a competent authority. This species has not been recorded as yet from Victoria; but it is palpable that a fish which is abundant at Twofold Bay is sure to occur in at least the eastern waters of that Colony. Although Johnston is in error as to the fish which he catalogues as *S. ciliata* (see p. 101), the true *S. ciliata* does, as might be expected, occur on the Tasmanian coast, a specimen from that Colony being in the collection of the British Museum.

This fine species grows to the length of twenty inches, and it is no uncommon sight to see in the Sydney market several dozens of these fishes, each individual of which would exceed fifteen; twelve inches is, however, about the average size.

Family XVI.—COTTIDÆ.

Branchiostegals five to seven: pseudobranchiæ present. Body oblong or subcylindrical. Cleft of mouth lateral. Eyes lateral or directed upwards. Some of the bones of the head armed. Preopercle connected to the suborbital ring by a bony stay. Dentition generally feeble, and consisting of villiform bands: vomer and palate with or without teeth. One or two dorsal fins, the spinous portion less developed than the soft portion or the anal: ventrals thoracic, with five or less rays: pectorals with or without free rays. Body naked, scaly, or with series of bony plates. Airbladder present or absent. Pyloric appendages, when present, few or in moderate numbers.

Geographical distribution.—Cosmopolitan.

This family contains a number of carnivorous fishes, none of which attain to a large size, belonging chiefly to the littoral zone; some, however, are inhabitants of fresh water only, and one Japanese species (*Cottus bathybius*) is found at a depth of at least five hundred fathoms.

Fossil representatives, among which the recent genus *Trigla* occurs, have been described from various tertiary formations.

---

* The very young Whiting, from three to four inches long, in the beginning of the year, and at early morning flood tide, will readily take a worm bait. These, nicely cleaned, and fried crisp and brown, are not easily to be beaten, and would fairly vie with the famous Whitebait of England.

Genus I.—PLATYCEPHALUS.

Platycephalus, Bl. Schn. p. 58, 1801; Cuv. & Val. Hist. Nat. Poiss. iv. p. 226.
Neoplatycephalus, Casteln. Proc. Zool. Soc. Vict. 1872, i. p. 87.

Branchiostegals seven: pseudobranchiæ present. Head broad, much depressed, more or less armed. Body depressed anteriorly, subcylindrical posteriorly. Cleft of mouth wide: lower jaw the longer. Eyes lateral or directed upwards. Jaws, vomer, and palatine bones with bands of villiform teeth, the former sometimes intermixed with larger ones. Two dorsal fins, the first with the anterior spine small and isolated: a similar spine sometimes present between the fins: anal similar to the rayed dorsal: ventrals thoracic, remote from the root of the pectorals: no pectoral appendages. Scales small or of moderate size, ctenid. Lateral line complete: in some species armed with spines. Airbladder absent. Pyloric appendages in moderate numbers.

Geographical distribution.—From the seas of Australia and Polynesia, through those of Malaysia, northwards to Japan, and westwards through those of India to the east coast of Africa.

Day remarks:—"These fishes are termed 'Crocodile-fishes' in Malabar, and wounds from their spines are dreaded, because of the violent irritation they occasion." He also notices the peculiarity of the eyes, "in that the iris possesses two semicircular flaps, one above and the other below, the upper being usually the larger; they can be brought close, one to the other, probably due to the stimulus of light." Günther, referring to the genus, says:—"This genus represents in the tropical Indian Ocean the *Cotti* of the Arctic and the *Nototheniæ* of the Antarctic zone. Like these, they live on the bottom in shallow water, hidden in the sand, the colors of which are assimilated to those of their body. Therefore, they are very scarce near coral islands which are surrounded by great depths; whilst the numbers of species is considerable on many points of the shelving Australian coasts. Their long and strong ventral fins are of great use to them in locomotion."

PLATYCEPHALUS FUSCUS.

Platycephalus fuscus, Cuv. & Val. Hist. Nat. Poiss. iv. p. 241; Quoy & Gaim. Voy. Astrolabe, Poiss. pl. x. f. 1; Casteln. Proc. Zool. Soc. Vict., 1872, i. p. 86, *and* Proc. Linn. Soc. N. S. Wales, iii. p. 379; Sauv. N. Arch. Mus. (2) i. p. 150; Macleay, Catal. Austr. Fish. i. p. 217: Woods, Fisher. N. S. Wales, p. 67, pl. xxv.
? *Platycephalus cinereus*, Gnth. Proc. Zool. Soc. 1871, p. 661; Macleay, Catal. Austr. Fish. i. p. 219.

Common Flathead.

Plate XXVIII.

B. vii. D. 2·7. 1/13. A. 13. V. 1/5. P. 19–20. C. 14. L. lat. ca. 100. Cæc. pyl. 11. Vert. 11/16.

Length of head 3·50–3·75, of caudal fin 6·66–7·00, height of body 8·50–9·00 in the total length: breadth of head at the base of the preopercular spines 1·80–2·00 in its length. Diameter of eye 6·66–7·33 in the length of the head, and 1·80–2·00 in that of the snout, which is broad and depressed, rounded in front, its length one fourth of that of the head: interorbital space slightly concave, from 1·10–1·33 in the diameter of the eye. Nostrils small, rounded, separated by a moderate interspace, the anterior pierced in the summit of a low tube. Upper surface of head flat. Lower jaw the longer. The maxilla extends to below the middle of the orbit. Preorbital with two short, stout, blunt spines, directed forwards, at its antero-inferior angle, from the bases of which rise two prominent parallel ridges, which terminate at the preopercular spines, and the upper of which bears a very minute spinous point at the anterior angle of the preopercle: no turbinal spines: a broad low ridge, ceasing between the eyes, behind the turbinal bones: a minute spine at the antero-superior margin of the orbit: a pair of convergent ridges from above the eyes terminate on the anterior part of the occiput in a minute point: five other short occipital ridges, the anterior pair profusely branched, the posterior pair ending in a minute spine: a temporal ridge from the postero-superior margin of the orbit to the origin of the lateral line, bearing several minute points, and a short strong terminal spine: opercle with a single weak spine: preopercular spines slightly divergent, the lower a little longer than the upper, and two thirds of the diameter of the eye: a skinny flap, not quite equal in length to the interorbital space and ending in an acute point, on the subopercle. Maxilla with a broad band of villiform teeth and a short strong canine at the inner angle of the symphysis on either ramus, and several pairs of similar but much smaller teeth in front of and outside it; mandible with a narrow band of villiform teeth in front, and an inner row of short sharp teeth continued back as far as the maxillary bands; two small patches of villiform teeth on the vomer, connected mesially by a single series, and terminating on either side in three strong conical teeth, the median one being much the longest; a single series of small, stout, conical, acute teeth on the palatines, extending backwards to behind the angle of the mouth. Two partially isolated spines in front of the spinous dorsal, the first very minute and about as long as the last spine; the second strong, 5·50 in the length of the succeeding spine, which is the longest, from 2·00–2·15 in the length of the head, and rather more than the distance between the tip of the lower jaw and the posterior margin of the eye; the remaining dorsal spines flexible; a short, stout, isolated spine in front of the second dorsal; anterior dorsal ray the longest and unbranched, not quite so long as the longest spine; the distance between its base and the origin of the caudal 1·25 in that between the same point and the tip of the snout: the anal commences opposite to the origin of the soft dorsal, and reaches some distance further back than that fin; the posterior rays, except the last, are the longest, but not nearly so long as the anterior rays of the dorsal: the fourth ventral ray is the longest, reaching to the second or third anal ray, its length from 1·33–1·50 in that of the head: pectoral rather short and rounded, reaching to the vertical from the fourth flexible dorsal spine, its length from 2·00–2·30 in that of the head; the lower five, six, or seven rays equal: caudal gently rounded, the height of the pedicle at the base of the last anal ray two thirds of its width at the same spot. Lateral line smooth: fourteen series of scales between it and the first dorsal ray, and one hundred and thirty series above it.

Colors.—Rich brown above and on the upper half of the sides, the head lighter with numerous reddish-brown spots; sides of head and subopercular flap spotted with pale olive green; lower half of sides pale greenish-yellow with indistinct blotches of olive green; white below: first dorsal with a series of small chestnut spots in front of each spine; second with the spots crossing the rays, forming interrupted bands; upper third of caudal similar to the dorsals, but with much larger spots; the remainder dark bluish-gray, unspotted, and narrowly edged below with white; pectorals grayish, thickly freckled with reddish-brown; ventrals similar, but with much larger spots, and with the spine and a narrow margin white; anal white.

Of the several species of Flathead inhabiting the seas of New South Wales not one can claim any title to commercial rank except the one which is here described and figured.

So far as our own observation goes, the main body of the Flatheads, consigned to the Sydney market from the coast line between Shoalhaven to the south and Lake Macquarie to the north, shed their ova during the two first months of the year, and this is generally in accordance with the evidence given before the Royal Commission. Writing from Twofold Bay, under date February, 1880, Mr. Glover states :—" Flathead are plentiful here all the year round in the shallower parts of the bay. They are caught with hook and line, and they spawn, I think, about March, as they are very full of ova now, and I have caught very small ones soon after March. The fish spawn in the usual fishing places and the spawn lies loose." This notice must, however, be considered as possibly applying to *Platycephalus bassensis* and *P. lævigatus* as well as to the present species. In the Clarence River the date of spawning is said to be January, February, and March. The ova are deposited on sand or mud banks in water of a moderate depth.

The flesh of the Flathead is of excellent quality, firm, flaky, and well flavored; in fact all the species must be ranked among our best food fishes; its appearance is unfortunately somewhat against it, but once the prejudice excited by this is overcome, it will not intentionally be cast aside in future. Being essentially a ground fish its food principally consists of squid, prawns, and other crustaceans, worms, and smaller fishes; among the latter we have recognised *Callionymi*, a *Petroscirtes*, young *Pseudorhombi*, *Stigmatophora*, and in a large specimen an eight inches example of its own species.

Though properly a marine fish inhabiting sand and mud banks at a moderate depth in our bays and estuaries, the Flathead is also found on the shelving and sandy tracts of our ocean shores to the depth of at least 80 fathoms, but it is needless to say that, until the trawl net comes into general use, these valuable fishing grounds must remain idle; this fish does not, however, confine itself solely to salt water, as it is well known to ascend many of our rivers far above the influence of the tide, and Tenison Woods remarks that " *P. fuscus* comes up the Hunter River as far as West Maitland, where it is caught abundantly by the anglers in summer."

They are considerable contributors to the sport of the amateur line fisher, the most sportsmanlike method of capturing them being to allow the boat to drift with the tide broad side on across a bank, when, if the fish be plentiful on the ground, good sport, with the not unpleasant resultant of a large number of excellent table fish, may frequently be obtained; unfortunately, where fish are plentiful sharks are rarely distant, and many a good hour's fishing is spoiled by these pests; the writer formed one of a boat's crew which decided to drift over a well known bank in the hope of making a material and welcome accession to their Christmas dinner; all went favorably for the first five minutes when half a dozen fine Flathead had been brought to bag; then the School Sharks (*Galeus*) made their appearance, and not another fish was caught. Mr. Hill, writing of Flathead fishing, remarks :—"They are ground fishes, and bite freely in the summer season, but retire into deeper water during the colder months of the year, where they might also be caught with the line. Of a calm day it is usual to let the boat drift over the ground which is generally sandy, when occasionally they bite freely. I have often known fifteen or twenty dozens hauled up as fast as the lines could be put over. They are sluggish fishes and do not give much sport; the very large ones, of three to four (?) feet in length, which are at times caught with the line, have pretty good strength but are soon exhausted. The flesh is good, white, firm, and flaky, and is preferable when boiled." The same author also warns anglers against the "great pain and inflammation consequent on a wound inflicted by the preopercular spines, with which they strike viciously, and which they can erect to a certain degree at will, when stirred by anger or fear."

How far to the northward the species is found it is difficult to say, but we have seen specimens from Maryborough, while Saville Kent, alluding presumably to the Brisbane Market, writes that Flatheads "yield a substantial contribution to the general fish supply. The most abundant and familiar type is the Common Flathead, *Platycephalus fuscus*." From Port Phillip Lucas records this species as the "Grass Flathead," while Castelnau, states that it is found on a weedy bottom; a conclusion which does not tally with our experience in this Colony, but which would seemingly be more applicable to the Rock Flathead, *P. lævigatus*.

If we are correct in our suggestion that Günther's *P. cinereus* is the same fish as this of which we are now treating, and the differences between his description and ours are trifling, the range of this species would be extended in a westerly direction at least to South Australia, while the anomaly of its absence from Tasmanian waters, where Johnston gives it as "not uncommon, but rarely brought to market," would disappear.

This species attains a length of forty inches, but the majority of examples sent to market are little more than half that size.

Genus II.—TRIGLA.

Trigla, Artedi, Gen. Pisc. p. 42, 1738; Cuvier, Règne Anim.; Cuv. & Val. Hist. Nat. Poiss. iv. p. 9.
Lepidotrigla, Günther, Catal. Fish ii. p. 196, 1860.

Branchiostegals seven: pseudobranchiæ present. Head parallelopiped, with its upper surface and sides bony, the large infraorbital covering the cheek. Villiform teeth in the jaws and normally on the vomer: palate edentulous. Two dorsal fins, the first being of less extent than the second: three free pectoral filaments. Airbladder well developed, usually provided with lateral muscles, and sometimes partially divided internally. Pyloric appendages in small numbers.

Geographical distribution.—Coasts of Australia, Tasmania, and New Zealand. Beyond these limits Day gives its distribution as follows:—"Coasts of Europe, being especially abundant in the Mediterranean. One species extending across the North Atlantic is found on the eastern shores of North America. To the south it passes round the west coast of Africa, and from the Atlantic to the Indian Ocean, apparently avoiding the east coast of Africa, the shores of India, and the contiguous islands."

One of the most noticeable characteristics of *Trigla* is the presence of three free pectoral filaments, which are employed as organs of touch and locomotion, and it is most interesting to watch these fishes balancing themselves by means of their expanded pectoral fins, slowly draw themselves forward by these filaments, and at the same time carefully testing every particle of the ground over which they are passing in order to detect their concealed prey. For the adequate execution of such complex functions it is manifest that these filaments must be supplied with specially strengthened nerves, and accordingly we find Günther (Study of Fishes, p. 108) observing: "The additional function which the (five) anterior spinal nerves of *Trigla* have to perform, in supplying the sensitive pectoral appendages and their muscles, has caused the development of a paired series of globular swellings of the corresponding portion of the spinal chord. A similar structure is found in *Polynemus*."

TRIGLA KUMU.

Trigla kumu, Less. & Garn. Voy. Coquille. Poiss. pl. xix., 1826; Cuv. & Val. Hist. Nat. Poiss. iv. p. 50; Jenyns, Voy. Beagle, Fish. p. 27; Schleg. Faun. Japon. Poiss. p. 37, pl. xiv. A. f. 3; Owen, Osteol. Catal. i. p. 55; Bleek. Verhand. Batav. Genootsch. xxvi. Japan, p. 74; Gnth. Catal. Fish. ii. p. 204; Kner, Voy. Novara, Fisch. p. 124, pl. vi. f. 2 (*air bladder*), *and* SB. Ak. Wien, lviii. p. 318; McCoy, Prodr. Zool. Vict. dec. i. pl. 5; Casteln. Proc. Linn. Soc. N. S. Wales, iii. p. 380; Macleay, Catal. Austr. Fish. i. p. 225; Woods, Fisher. N. S. Wales, p. 68, pl. xxvii.; Sherrin, Handb. Fish. N.Z. p. 36.
Trigla spinosa, McClell. Calc. Journ. Nat. Hist. iv. p. 396, pl. xxii. f. 2.
Trigla kumu, var. *dorsomaculata*, Steindachn. SB. Ak. Wien, lxxiv. p. 216.

Red Gurnard.
Plate XXIX.

B. vii. D. 9-10/15. A. 14-15. V. 1/5. P. 10-11+3. C. 12. L. lat. 75-82. Cœc. pyl. 6. Vert. 12/22.

Length of head 4·00-4·25, of caudal fin 5·15-5·66, height of body 5·66-6·50 in the total length: breadth of head immediately behind the preopercle 1·40-1·66 in its length. Eye large, situated so high up as to rise above the dorsal profile, its diameter 3·85-4·00 in the length of the head, and 1·80-2·00 in that of the snout, which is rather elongate, and flat or slightly concave above: interorbital space concave, 1·50-1·75 in the diameter of the eye. Nostrils remote, the anterior small and subcircular, protected by a low skinny flap; the posterior open, forming a moderately long subhorizontal slit, and pierced slightly nearer to the orbit than to the tip of the preorbital. Occiput slightly convex. Upper jaw the longer. Cleft of mouth moderate and horizontal, the maxilla reaching to beneath the anterior margin of the orbit, or not quite so far. Preorbital granulose and bearing anteriorly several small blunt spinous points: armature of snout ornamented with numerous series of small granules radiating from a common centre: supraorbital ridge anteriorly with two or three strong spines, the upper of which is rather the larger; posteriorly roughened or obscurely spinose: a naked patch anteriorly on the snout, from whence a narrow naked band runs backwards through the nostrils to beneath and behind the orbit, and thence below the occipital bone to the opercular flap: cheeks with horizontal, preopercle with vertical series of granules: preopercle with two spines at the angle, the upper the longer; no distinct ridge between the preorbital and the angle of the preopercle: an interopercular spine: opercle with a broad, naked margin, the bony portion with radiating striæ composed of small granules, and armed with two spines, the lower of which is much the stronger and longer: occipital bone lunate behind, each horn terminating posteriorly in a strong spine: clavicle with a single strong spine. Both jaws with a band of villiform teeth, interrupted at the symphyses: vomerine teeth in two small circular patches. The dorsal fin commences above the free portion of the clavicular spine, and ends above the fourteenth anal ray; the first spine is roughened anteriorly; it is not so long as the second, which is normally the longest, 1·50–1·66 in the length of the head; the tenth spine, when present, is minute and may easily be overlooked; the first ray of the soft dorsal is unbranched, and its base is from one fifth to one seventh nearer to the origin of the caudal than to the tip of the snout; the third or fourth ray is the highest, about three fifths of the highest spine; the last ray is undivided: the anal commences beneath the second dorsal ray; all the rays, except the last three, are simple, the last being divided to its base: in small examples the ventral fin reaches to the vent, but in the adult fish it falls a little short of it; the spine is stronger than those of the first dorsal, the fifth of which is about equal in length to it; the third and fourth rays are equal and longest, from 1·10–1·33 in the length of the head: the pectoral is rounded posteriorly, and the middle rays, which are longest, are from one fourth to two fifths longer than the head, and reach back as far as the fourth to the seventh anal ray: caudal emarginate in small, truncated with the outer rays slightly produced in large, examples; the least height of the caudal pedicle equal to its width at the same spot, and about three sevenths of the distance between the dorsal fin and the base of the caudal. Scales minute. Lateral line almost straight, the scales smooth: the series of keeled scales along each side of the bases of the dorsal fins well developed, and numbering about twenty three pairs.

Colors.—Upper surfaces and sides of the head red, with or without an admixture of brown; lower surfaces white washed with pink: dorsal and caudal fins reddish with a strong tinge of yellow, the latter color frequently predominating on the posterior half of the caudal; anal and ventral fins white or pinkish; pectorals externally pale red, the membrane frequently tinged with violet, and with a broad pale blue marginal band posteriorly; the inner or posterior side olive green or purple, with more or less numerous light blue spots on its outer half, and with a large black blotch on the lower third of the fin, the spots on which are milk white.

There is not, so far as we are aware, any recorded notice of the spawning season of this fish on the Australian coast, and the only light which we can throw on the subject is, therefore, from our own necessarily limited observations; these fix the season at or about the two last months of the year, specimens examined during the last week in October being full of ripe ova, while others were found to have spawned towards the latter end of December; others again dissected during May and June contained no ova. The fry are never seen in our harbors, nor have I ever found it occurring among the *débris* of the seine net. Little is known as to the place and method of shedding the spawn, but since Sars' discovery that the ova floats, it is probable that these do not differ materially from other fishes dwelling at moderate depths, such as the Cod (*Gadus morrhua*), the flotation of whose ova is unquestionable. We have ourselves noticed that about July and August the Gray Gurnards (*Trigla gurnardus*) off the north coast of Ireland were full of roe, and schooled on the surface of the water.

As a food fish our Red Gurnard is excellent, the best way of preparing it being undoubtedly by stuffing and baking. Their food consists of worms, small molluscs, crustaceans, and fishes.

Notwithstanding the large size of the pectoral fins these fishes have not the power of sustaining themselves in the air, and can only leap out of the water and immediately fall back again like other fishes, and this power even they do not often exert, or only at least when striving to escape from an enemy, and perhaps at the schooling season.

Though but seldom appearing in our market the Red Gurnard is probably not uncommon on the coast of the Colony, but being an inhabitant of water of considerable depth, and with a sandy or shingly bottom, we have at present no appliances for capturing it, and it is only when a stray individual is taken by men engaged in fishing for Snapper that we ever see a specimen. It is found along the coast of Queensland from north to south, and is the fish mentioned by Saville Kent as *Trigla polyommata*, but not the species figured by him under that name, which is possibly *Trigla buergeri*. Tenison Woods has also confounded these two unmistakable fishes, so that the names on Plates xxvi and xxvii must be reversed. It occurs on the shores of Victoria and Tasmania, but is not common. Although we have no record of its occurrence in the seas of South and West Australia, its extensive range, through Malaysia to the Chinese and Japanese seas, leads us to infer its existence in those waters, and its gradual increase in numbers in a northerly direction Kner has recorded it from the Cape of Good Hope.

Our Red Gurnard is found also in New Zealand waters, where it is known to the Maoris by the name of Kumukumu, and is much more abundant than is the case in the other Colonies. Sherrin remarks:—"The Red Gurnard or Kumukumu is very abundant during the summer months in the harbors of the North, and full nets are sometimes drawn in Wellington with no other fish in them. The full grown fish weighs about four pounds, and all sizes are used as food, the smaller ones, however, being preferred. The flesh is firm and white but rather dry. The grunting noise which this beautifully colored fish makes when caught, is a great source of amusement to amateur fishermen. It is rarely seen in the Dunedin market. Though found all around the North Island, they are not so plentiful in many places as at Wellington. They can be caught with hook and line if fished for, and are found in some fifteen fathoms of water." Further, he says that "in flavor it is similar to Snapper when fresh in tins, and will put up well in small casks." The grunting noise above refered to is caused, says Günther, " by the escape of gas from the airbladder through the open pneumatic duct."

This species grows to a length of twenty inches.

TRIGLA POLYOMMATA.

Trigla polyommata, Richards. Proc. Zool. Soc. 1839, p. 96, *and* Trans. Zool. Soc. iii. p. 87, pl. v. f. 2; Gnth. Catal. Fish. ii. p. 204; Casteln. Proc. Zool. Soc. Vict. 1872. i. p. 88; Macleay, Catal. Austr. Fish. i. p. 226 (*fin formula incorrect*); Woods, Fisher. N. S. Wales, pl. xxvi.; Johnston, Proc. Roy. Soc. Tas. 1882, pp. 80, 115.
Hoplonotus polyommatus, Guichen. Ann. Soc. Linn. Maine-et-Loire, ix. Ichthyol.
? *Trigla amœna*, Proc. Zool. Soc. Vict. ii. p. 131; Macleay, Catal. Aust. Fish. ii. p. 226.

Sharp-beaked Gurnard.

B. vii. D. 8/12. A. 12. V. 1/5 P. 12 + 3. C. 13. Cœc. pyl. 8. Vert. 13/14.

Length of head* 3·33–3·60, of caudal fin 5·20–5·33, height of body 4·50–4·75 in the total length : breadth of head 1·90–2·33 in its length. Eye very large, rising far above the dorsal profile, its diameter 3·00–3·66 in the length of the head, and 1·33–1·50 in that of the snout, which is short, abruptly descending, and concave ; interorbital space deeply concave, 1·00–1·20 in the

---

* Measured from the tip of the preorbital to that of the occipital spine.

diameter of the eye. Nostrils separated by a short interspace, the anterior minute and rounded, the posterior of moderate size, elongate-oval, and oblique, very much nearer to the orbit than to the extremity of the preorbital spine. Occiput flat. Upper jaw the longer. Cleft of mouth moderate, and slightly oblique, the maxilla reaching to the anterior margin or as far as the first third of the eye. Preorbital granulose, its anterior extremity produced into a strong, longitudinally striated, spine; armature of snout densely granulose, without radiating striæ: supraorbital ridge simple: the naked patch on the snout subovate in shape, and extending backwards to between the anterior nostrils; the sulcus between the preorbital and turbinal bones, very narrow, much broader beneath the occipital bones: armature of the cheeks granulate, and ornamented with striæ which radiate from the hinder apex of the preorbital: preopercular striæ radiating from the base of the spine: preopercle with from one to three spines at the angle, the upper being always present: no distinct ridge between the preorbital and the angle of the preopercle: posterior margin of interopercle rounded: opercle with a broad, naked margin, the bony part coarsely granulated anteriorly, finely so posteriorly; bearing two spines, the lower of which is much the stronger: occipital bone lunate behind, enclosing a membranous space, and terminating at each edge in a very strong acute spine: clavicle with a very strong ridged spine, about equal in total length to the diameter of the eye. Jaws with a band of villiform teeth, interrupted at the symphyses; vomerine teeth in a single patch much broader than long. The dorsal fin commences above the expanded portion of the clavicle, and ends slightly in front of the anal; the spines are strong, the three first minutely granulated on their lower portion anteriorly, the third the longest, but little longer than the second and fourth, and from 1·90-2·10 in the length of the head; the eighth spine is minute; the two first rays of the soft dorsal are unbranched, the anterior being one half the length of the second, and the distance between its base and the origin of the caudal is 1·75 in that between the same spot and the tip of the snout: the fourth ray is the highest, and five sevenths of the third spine; the last ray is undivided: the anal commences beneath the origin of the soft dorsal; the first seven rays are simple, the last divided almost to its base, and the middle rays are the longest: the ventral fin barely reaches to the vent; its spine is equal in length to, but more flexible than, the first dorsal spine, and the middle ray is the longest, from 1·40-1·80 in the length of the head: the pectoral is rounded posteriorly, and its middle rays are from one sixth to one tenth longer than the head, and extend to between the fifth and seventh anal rays: caudal deeply emarginate; the least height of the pedicle greater than its breadth at the same spot, and rather less than one half of the distance between the dorsal fin and the origin of the caudal. Scales exceedingly small, absent on the throat and chest. Lateral line smooth and slightly sinuous. A series of seven stout, flat, roughened plates supporting the base of the spinous dorsal, the anterior of which is crescentic, the convex portion being in front; rayed dorsal without supporting plates.

Colors.—Upper parts red or reddish-brown, the sides sometimes tinged with yellow; below silvery: dorsal and caudal fins uniform red; ventral pale pink or yellow; pectorals outwardly dull purple with occasionally a few scattered white spots, and with the inner surface olive green ornamented with purple bands, which run parallel to the hinder margin of the fin, and are much narrower than the interspaces; two large, oblong, white edged black spots, the lower of which is about twice as long as the upper, near its base inferiorly; anal white.

The breeding season of this species differs from that of *Trigla kumu*, examples obtained in the Sydney market having the ova fully developed during the months of July and August; in no other respects does it differ in its habits from that species.

Speaking generally, this is a southern, while the Red Gurnard is a northern, form. The Sharp-beaked Gurnard is not so common on our coast as its congener, and only large specimens occur, while Port Stephens appears to be approximately its northward range. Both on our own coast and that of the sister Colonies, this species is commonly, but erroneously, known as the Flying Gurnard, this name being shared by, and with more propriety applied to, *Dactylopterus orientalis*. On the Victorian coast, Castelnau says:—"Without being common in the Melbourne market, this fish appears at all seasons; but often for months there are none to be seen, and then several will be caught together." On the Tasmanian coast they are "not uncommon, during May and June, in the estuaries of the Derwent and Tamar." Johnston, who has had special facilities for observing this species, gives the following interesting account, interesting because the Gurnards, not being strictly littoral fishes, do not come under supervision in their natural state as do shore fishes; he says:—"At times during the winter season these beautifully colored fishes, with their gaudily-painted pectoral wings, may be seen around our wharves in small schools, dashing, or rather flying, through the water, with sudden bounds, after their prey. . . . . . They are rarely captured, however, on our coasts; and are, therefore, unimportant here, from a commercial point of view." Macleay records it from West Australia, but we are unaware upon what evidence. Castelnau's *Trigla amœna* is very closely allied to, if not identical with, our fish, the black spot on the spinous dorsal being the most prominent distinctive character mentioned in the description.

This species attains to a length of twenty inches.

Family XVII.—SPHYRÆNIDÆ.

Branchiostegals seven: pseudobranchiæ present. Body elongate, sub-cylindrical or compressed. Eyes of moderate size, lateral. Cleft of mouth wide. Jaws armed with strong, trenchant teeth, with or without a villiform band: teeth present on the palate, absent or present on the vomer. Two dorsal fins remote from each other: anal similar to the second dorsal. Ventrals abdominal, composed of one spine and five rays. Scales small or of moderate size, cycloid. Lateral line continuous. Airbladder present, bifurcate anteriorly. Pyloric appendages in moderate or large numbers.

Geographical distribution.—Seas of the tropical and temperate regions; carnivorous.

Genus I.—SPHYRÆNA.

Sphyræna, Artedi, Synon. Pisc, p. 112, 1738; Cuvier, Règne Anim.; Cuv. & Val. Hist. Nat. Poiss. iii, p. 325.

Branchiostegals seven: pseudobranchiæ present Body elongate, sub-cylindrical. Cleft of mouth wide. Eyes lateral. Large trenchant teeth in both jaws and on the palatine bones: vomer edentulous. Two short dorsal fins, separated by a long interspace: anal with a single spine, similar to the second dorsal: ventrals opposite, or nearly opposite, to the anterior dorsal. Scales small, cycloid, adherent. Airbladder large, bifurcate anteriorly. Pyloric appendages in moderate or large numbers.

Geographical distribution.—Almost all temperate and tropical seas.

These fishes are very voracious, and some of them grow to a large size and are greatly dreaded by the inhabitants of those shores which they frequent. Cuvier and Valenciennes, quoting some of the older writers, relate of the West Indian Barracuda (*Sphyræna picuda*), that " it must be included in the number of marine monsters which are greedy for human flesh " ; that " it attains to the length of seven or eight feet, and rushes with fury upon the men whom it perceives in the water. Its teeth often inflict mortal injuries " ; that " it is more dangerous than the shark, inasmuch as noise and movement, far from intimidating it, serve to incite it the more to rush upon its victims."

SPHYRÆNA NOVÆHOLLANDIÆ.

Sphyræna novæhollandiæ, Gnth. Catal. Fish. ii. p. 335 ; Macleay, Catal. Austr. Fish. ii. p. 32 ; Casteln. Proc. Zool. Soc. Vict. i. p. 96.

Short-finned Pike.
Plate XXX.

B. vii. D. 5. 1/9. A. 2/9. V. 1/5. P. 13. C. 17. L. lat. 127–136. L. tr. 11/16–17. Cœc. pyl. 47. Vert. 12/12.

Length of head 4·25–4·50, of caudal fin 7·33–7·80, height of body 9·50–9·75 in the total length. Eye large, its diameter 5·66–6·50 in the length of the head, and 2·10–2·80 in that of the snout : interorbital space flat, with two pairs of lateral longitudinal grooves, its width from 1·20–1·33 in the diameter of the eye. Nostrils small ; the anterior pierced in a low tube, which is directed forwards ; the posterior about twice as large and with an anterior skinny flap, which, when decumbent, completely conceals the orifice. Upper profile of head flat. Lower jaw much the longer. Cleft of mouth very slightly oblique ; the posterior portion of the maxilla sharply separated from the attenuated anterior portion, quadrilateral, the posterior margin slightly concave, the inferior margin convex, reaching to the posterior nostril in young specimens, and one fourth of its own length in front of the eye in large examples. Two to four pairs of strong recurved conical teeth in the upper jaw anteriorly, behind which are a single closely set row of minute teeth ; a pair of strong recurved fangs in the middle of the lower jaw in front, followed by a row of conical teeth, numbering about sixteen in each ramus and strongest posteriorly ; palatine teeth in a single series, five strong ones on each side, preceded by one or two, and succeeded by numerous, small ones. Dorsal spines weak and flexible, the first and second the longest, 3·15–3·50 in the length of the head ; the distance between the origin of the fin and the tip of the snout is 1·15 in that between the same point and the base of the caudal, while that between the origins of the two dorsal fins is 1·10 in the length of the head ; the second dorsal ray is the longest, 1·30 in the postorbital portion of the head, and 1·20 in the longest spines: the anal commences beneath the third dorsal ray, and extends back slightly beyond that fin, the basal length of the latter being about one fifth more than that of the former ; the anal rays are equal in height to those of the dorsal, and the posterior ray in both fins is slightly elongated : ventrals small, inserted beneath the anterior half of the first dorsal, the outer ray the longest, their length 2·50 in the distance between their origin and the vent, and 3·20–3·66 in the length of the head : pectorals small, equal in length to the postorbital portion of the head, or 2·40–2·75 in the length of the head : caudal deeply forked, the least height of the pedicle 2·30 in the height of the body. Lateral line almost straight.

Colors.—Green above, silvery below : soft dorsal and caudal yellow, the latter with a black marginal band posteriorly.

These fishes occur in the Sydney market during all seasons of the year, generally in small numbers and rather irregularly; occasionally, however, they appear in fair quantity, this being almost invariably in August or September when they are in fine condition and full of ripe ova; by the end of October these small schools have disappeared. We are unable to say how or where the spawn is shed. They are very voracious, swim rapidly and high in the water, and feed principally on small fishes, of which they destroy large numbers; it is probable that nothing in motion through the water, which they can swallow, comes amiss to them; we have taken the following fishes from their intestines; Yellowtail (*Caranx trachurus*), Tailor (*Temnodon saltator*), Hardyhead (*Atherina pinguis*), Mullet (*Mugil peroni*), and Garfish (*Hemirhamphus regularis*), besides numbers of fry too small or too much decomposed to be readily recognisable; no other substances have as yet been found by us. As table fish they are excellent. Like the Barracoutas of Tasmania, these fishes, where plentiful, afford excellent sport to the line fisher by trailing baited hooks or artificial lures after a boat kept sailing at a moderate rate of speed.

Exactly how far to the northward this Pike is found is not known, but it is not included in Saville Kent's list of Queensland Food Fishes; to the southward, however, it increases rapidly in numbers, and is common on the coast of Victoria, where Castelnau says that it "is considered by many as the most delicate of the Victorian fishes"; and again, writing in 1872, he remarks:—"The fishmongers say that, some years ago, this fish used to be generally larger than now, and that it was quite common to get them over a yard long. It is only rarely that such specimens appear on the market now." Mr. North, however, informs me that he has frequently caught them in Western Port measuring considerably more than three feet, in fact, approaching to, if not exceeding, four feet. To the westward it occurs at least as far as Adelaide. It is not included in Johnston's Catalogue of Tasmanian Fishes.

The largest specimen seen in market measured thirty five inches.

Genus II.—DINOLESTES.

Dinolestes, Klunzinger, Arch. f. Nat. 1872, p. 29, pl. iii.
Neosphyræna, Casteluau, Proc. Zool. Soc. Vic., i. p. 96 1872.
Lanioperca, Günther, Ann. Nat. Hist. (4) 1872, x. p. 183.

Branchiostegals seven: pseudobranchiæ present. Body moderately elongate, compressed. Cleft of mouth wide. Eye lateral. Jaws, vomer, and palatine bones with narrow bands of villiform teeth, the former with an outer enlarged series: one or two pairs of very strong canines anteriorly in the upper jaw. Two dorsal fins, the anterior small: the posterior and the anal well developed, the latter with two spines: ventrals situated considerably in front of the first dorsal. Scales moderate, cycloid, deciduous.

Geographical distribution.—Australian seas.

DINOLESTES MUELLERI.

Dinolestes muelleri, Klunz. Arch. f. Nat. 1872, p. 29, pl. iii.
Neosphyræna multiradiata, Castelu. Proc. Zool. Soc. Vict. i. p. 96.
Lanioperca mordax, Gnth. Ann. Nat. Hist. (4) 1872, x. p. 183; Macleay, Catal. Austr. Fish. ii. p. 36; Woods, Fisher. N. S. Wales, pls. xxviii. xxix. McCoy, Prodr. Zool. Vict. dec. xii. pl. 115.
Esox? lewini, Griff. An. Kingd. Ed. p. 465, pl. lx. 1834; Gill, Ann. Nat. Hist. (4) 1874, xiv. p. 159.

Long-finned Pike.

B. vii. D. 5. 1/18-19. A. 2/25-26. V. 1/5. P. 16. C. 17. L. lat. 61-67. L. tr. 6/11.

Length of head 3·40, of caudal fin 6·00, height of body 6·00 in the total length. Eye large, its diameter 5·00 in the length of the head, and 2·00 in that of the obtusely rounded snout: interorbital space flat, 1·33 in the diameter of the eye. Nostrils small, oval, approximate, the anterior tubular, the posterior simple. Upper profile of head flat. Lower jaw much the longer. Cleft of mouth slightly oblique, the maxilla reaching to beneath the anterior margin of the orbit; in shape it is elongate-pyriform, with the lower edge emarginate, and the posterior rounded. Upper jaw with two pairs of strong canines in front, the anterior pair erect with recurved tips, the posterior similar but much larger and inclined backwards; both jaws with a broad band of villiform teeth, having an outer enlarged series, which in the upper are subequal and throughout much smaller and more numerous than those of the lower, in which the four or more rarely five posterior teeth are remote and caninid; teeth on the vomer in a horseshoe-shaped band, with the arc in front, and two or three posterior ones on either side greatly enlarged; a narrow elongate band of small teeth on the palatines. The dorsal spines are small and weak, the second and longest not being equal to the diameter of the eye, and the distance between the origin of the fin and the tip of the snout is 1·33 in that between the same spot and the base of the caudal; the second dorsal ray is the longest, and equals the postorbital portion of the head: the anal commences beneath the origin of the second dorsal and extends back far beyond it, the basal length of the latter being 1·30 in that of the former, and equal to the distance between the origins of the two dorsals; the anal rays are not quite so high as those of the dorsal: ventrals small, the outer ray the longest, reaching midway to the vent, its length 3·20 in that of the head; pectorals reaching as far back as the ventrals, and equal in length to the maxilla: caudal emarginate, the least height of its pedicle 2·25 in the height of the body. Lateral line slightly curved downwards above the pectorals, thence straight.

Colors.—Above brown with a tinge of gold, the head darkest; silvery below the lateral line; the caudal peduncle deeply tinted with yellow: vertical fins yellow; inside of jaws anteriorly, and upper surface of tongue purple: teeth dull red.

Full-roed examples of this fish are often obtainable in our market during the winter months, and except that with us it frequents deeper water and keeps closer to the bottom, it does not differ materially in its habits from the *Sphyrænæ*. Its much shorter and deeper body makes it recognisable when lying on the floor of the market, even when the fins cannot be seen.

Though from the small number of specimens of this fish and *Sphyræna novæhollandiæ*, which we have so far had an opportunity of examining intestinally, it would be presumptuous to draw a hard and fast line as to the food, it is a fact that, in the majority of specimens of this species, remains of crustaceans and molluscs were plentifully present, while in no case were they discernible in the Short-finned Pike. As a food fish it is equally as good as, if not better than, that species.

The outward resemblance which this fish bears to the other members of the family, all the species of which, *Dinolestes* included, are grouped together by fishermen, dealers, and market officials as "Pike," makes it difficult to gauge, even approximately, the northern limit to which this species attains. We have known it to occur in small numbers both in Botany and

Broken Bays, but beyond the latter no record exists, and it does not appear to have been observed on the Queensland coast. In the Melbourne market, where it goes by the name of " Skipjack Pike " this species, writes Castelnau is " common in the months of May, June, and July. .... It is considered equal to *Sphyræna norœhollandiæ* for the use of the table." Johnston dismisses it from the shores whence it was originally described with a curt " not uncommon in the Derwent."

The Long-finned Pike is said to grow to twenty four inches; the largest we have examined was seventeen inches, and was considered exceptionally large.

Family XVIII.—MUGILIDÆ.

Branchiostegals four to six: pseudobranchiæ present. Gill-openings wide; gills four. Body oblong and compressed, the head sometimes depressed. Mouth in front of the snout, narrow or of moderate width. Eyes lateral, with or without adipose lids. Opercles generally unarmed. Dentition feeble: sometimes absent. Two dorsal fins separated by an interspace, the anterior consisting of four stiff spines: anal a little longer than the rayed dorsal; ventral fins abdominal, suspended from an elongated coracoid bone. Scales cycloid, rarely ctenoid, extending on to the snout. No lateral line. Airbladder large, simple. Pyloric appendages in small numbers. Vertebræ twenty four to twenty six.

Geographical distribution.—Seas of the temperate and tropical regions entering fresh waters; some species apparently confined to the latter.

Day remarks:—"In India and Burma I have observed that in such forms as *Mugil corsula*, *M. cascasia*, and *M. hamiltonii*, which mostly or entirely reside in fresh water, the scales are strongly ctenoid, while the two last have merely two pyloric appendages."

Genus I.—MUGIL.

Mugil, Artedi, Gen. Pisc. p. 32, 1738.

Branchiostegals four to six: pseudobranchiæ present. Mouth more or less transverse, with a shallow lateral cleft, and the anterior margin of the mandible sharp and sometimes ciliated. Eyes with or without adipose lids. Teeth, when present, minute. Pyloric appendages in small numbers. Upper portion of stomach very muscular: intestinal tract long.

Geographical distribution.—All temperate and tropical regions.

The majority of the species pass a portion of the year in the sea, whence they migrate to the brackish water of estuaries for the purpose of depositing their spawn; some, however, are now confined to purely fresh water, but it is probable that, like the land-locked Salmon, some cause, other than their own volition, necessitated so important a departure from their natural mode of life.

For the benefit of Australian students Dr. Günther's clear enunciation of the means by which the Mullet obtains its microscopic food, and the special mechanism employed to insure the perfect attainment of that object, may be advantageously reproduced here; he says:—"They frequent brackish waters in which they find an abundance of food, which consists chiefly of the organic substances mixed with mud or sand; in order to prevent larger bodies from passing into the stomach, or substances from passing through the gill-openings, these fishes have the organs of the pharynx modified into a filtering apparatus. They take in a quantity of sand or mud, and, after having worked it for some time between the pharyngeal bones, they reject the roughest and indigestible portion of it."

Refering to *Mugil chelo* he continues:—"The upper pharyngeals have a rather irregular form; they are slightly arched, the convexity being directed towards the pharyngeal cavity, tapering anteriorly and broad posteriorly. They are coated with a thick, soft membrane, which reaches far beyond the margin of the bone, at least on its interior posterior portion; this membrane is studded all over with minute horny cilia. The pharyngeal bone rests upon a large fatty mass, giving it a considerable degree of elasticity. There is a very large venous sinus between the anterior portion of the pharyngeal and the basal portion of the branchial arches. Another mass of fat, of elliptical form, occupies the middle of the roof of the pharynx, between the two pharyngeal bones. Each branchial arch is provided on each side, in its whole length, with a series of closely set gillrakers, which are laterally bent downwards, each series closely fitting into the series of the adjoining arch; they constitute together a sieve, admirably adapted to permit a transit for the water, retaining at the same time every other substance in the cavity of the pharynx.

'The lower pharyngeal bones are elongate, crescent-shaped, and broader posteriorly than anteriorly. Their inner surface is concave, corresponding to the convexity of the upper pharyngeals, and provided with a single series of lamellæ, similar to those of the branchial arches, but reaching across the bone from one margin to the other.

'The intestinal tract shows no less peculiarities. The lower portion of the œsophagus is provided with numerous long thread-like papillæ, and continued into the oblong ovoid membranaceous cæcal portion of the stomach, the mucosa of which forms several longitudinal folds. The second portion of the stomach reminds one of the stomach of birds; it communicates laterally with the other portion, is globular, and surrounded by an exceedingly strong muscle. This muscle is not divided into two as in birds, but is of great thickness in the whole circumference of the stomach, all the muscular fasciculi being circularly arranged. The internal cavity of this stomach is rather small, and coated with a tough epithelium, longitudinal folds running from the entrance opening to the pyloric, which is situated opposite to the other. A low circular valve forms a pylorus. There are five rather short pyloric appendages. The intestines make a great number of circumvolutions, and are seven feet long in a specimen thirteen inches in length.'"

The lateral line being absent in the fishes of this family, while the number of scales is of great importance in differentiating the various species, of which very many have been described, it is necessary to define the method by which the number of lateral and transverse scales is arrived at; in the former the series of scales running from the upper angle of the operculum to the base of the caudal fin is counted, in the latter the oblique series which commences at the base of the first dorsal ray.

MUGIL DOBULA.

Mugil dobula, Gnth. Catal. Fish. iii. p. 420, 1861, *and* Fisch. de Sudsee, p. 214, pl. cxx. fig. A.; Casteln. Proc. Linn. Soc. N. S. Wales, iii. p. 387; Macleay, Proc. Linn. Soc. N. S. Wales, iv. p. 415.

Mugil waigiensis, Casteln. Proc. Zool. Soc. Vict. 1872, i. p. 140 (*not Quoy & Gaimard*).

Mugil grandis, Casteln. Proc. Linn. Soc. N. S. Wales, iii. p. 386, 1878; Macleay, Proc. Linn. Soc. N. S. Wales, iv. p. 412.

Mugil cephalotus, Johnston, Proc. Roy. Soc. Tas. 1882, p. 122 (*not Cuv. & Val*).

Sea Mullet: Hard-gut Mullet.

Plate XXXI.

B. vi. D. 4. 1/8. A. 3/8. V. 1/5. P. 16. C. 14. L. lat. 40-42. L. tr. 14-15. Cœc. pyl. 4. Vert. 11/13.

Length of head 4·80 to 5·40, of caudal fin 4·33 to 5·00, height of body 4·00-5·00 in the total length. Eye with the adipose lid extending to or beyond the front margin and well beyond the hinder margin of the pupil; its diameter 3·40-4·00 in the length of the head, and 1·66-2·15 in that of the interorbital space, which is almost flat: snout short and very broad, its length from 1·00-1·20 in the diameter of the eye. Lips thin: jaws fringed with minute cilia. Nostrils distant, the anterior minute and rounded, about equidistant from the eye and the tip of the snout; the posterior oval or pyriform, three times as large as the anterior, with which it is connected by a naked shallow groove. Free space below the chin broadly lanceolate, equal to or rather less than the distance between the end of the snout and the posterior margin of the orbit. The maxilla extends to beneath the anterior margin of the orbit. Preorbital minutely denticulate, the denticulations becoming almost obsolete in large examples, not expanded behind. The distance between the origin of the spinous dorsal and the base of the caudal is equal to that between the same point and the end of the snout; the first dorsal spine is the longest, 1·75-2·00 in the length of the head; the distance between the origins of the two dorsal fins is equal to or rather more than the length of the head: the anal commences beneath the origin of the soft dorsal, and its anterior rays are subequal to those of that fin; the posterior rays are produced beyond the median, thus forming a deep emargination on the outer edge of the fin: the length of the ventral is from 2·00-2·40 in the distance between its origin and the vent, and from 1-50-1·75 in the length of the head: the pectoral reaches to the ninth or tenth body scale, and is 1·40-1·60 in the length of the head: caudal forked, the least height of the pedicle less than the distance between the last dorsal ray and the base of the caudal, and 2·33-2·50 in the length of the head. Thirteen or fourteen scales between the occiput and the origin of the spinous dorsal, four or five on the interspace between the dorsals, and eight between the rayed dorsal and the caudal: first dorsal, pectoral, and ventral fins with enlarged pointed axillary scales.

Colors.—Steel blue, with a tinge of green or olive above; sides and lower surfaces silvery; a small black axillary spot, and a golden spot on the upper angle of the opercle: dorsal and pectoral fins dark bluish-gray, caudal and anal yellowish-green.

As with some of our other food fishes this Mullet has two distinct breeding seasons in each year, that of the autumn, which lasts from some time in March until about the middle of May, being, however, by far the most important. At this time they enter the estuaries, inlets, and saltwater lakes, which indent our coastline from south to north, in almost incredible numbers, and push on at once to the spawning grounds, which mainly consist of the mud flats, which margin our rivers. Here, according to Macleay, the ova remain undeveloped until the spring months, when they mature, and he instances an occasion on which large shoals of young Sea Mullet, measuring up to an inch and a half in length, were observed along the shores of Port Jackson about the middle of October, from which fact he draws the following deduction:—
"As the time of spawning is never later than May, and as these fish could not have been more than a day or two old, the inference is that the spawn had remained in the mud near that spot (Elizabeth Bay) during the winter, and

until the increasing heat of spring caused the ova to germinate." As, however, this author does not seem to have been aware of the second or spring breeding season of this species, the conclusion above mentioned must be taken with reservation: it seems more probable to us that these fry were the progeny of fishes which had shed their ova during August or the first half of September, while the large shoals of young mullet, which undoubtedly appear during the winter months are the result of the autumn spawning.

In his excellent report to the Royal Commission, Inspector Cain fixes the date of spawning at "between the latter end of February and the middle of April" for Brisbane Water, while at Shoalhaven March and April are given as the breeding season. Referring to the Clarence River district, Mr. Hood Pegus writes:—"Sea mullet commence to enter the river in March, and proceed up the river as far as the salt water goes. They come in in immense shoals, and continue entering in and out with the tides up to July. They are observed several miles off the coast before they make for the river to spawn." He further states that they spawn in April, May, and June in the river on sandy banks in shoal water, the ova being deposited in circular holes in the sand, and the young fry make their appearance in July or sometimes as late as August. Such of the breeding fish as survive the perils of the river make their way to the open sea about July; Mr. Thurgate also gives May as the breeding season in the Richmond River.

The young Mullet on their emergence from the ova remain quiescent until the absorption of the yelk-sac, after which they wander in small schools along the shore in shallow water, mostly working up stream frequently into purely fresh water; in such places they pass the two first years of their existence, during which they increase rapidly in size; they then drop quietly down the rivers and for the first time seek the open sea about the early autumn months, returning, however, much improved in flavor and condition during the months of January and February, at which time they are sent in large numbers to the Sydney market, where they are sold as "Hard-gut Mullet." It is scarcely necessary to say that this title is ridiculous, there being no difference in the hardness of the œsophagus of the immature and the adult fish; if, therefore, a distinctive appellation is necessary for the former, River, or better still, Estuary, Mullet would be far more appropriate.

The Sea Mullet are fortunately most prolific fishes, else they could not have withstood the drain on their numbers caused by the numerous enemies of the ova and young fry—which comprise, along with sea birds and other fishes, starfishes, echinoderms, Actineæ, &c.—as well as the persecution which they undergo from the fishermen in their endeavor to reach the breeding grounds. In both adult and immature fishes the ovaries are, however, very large, and as each individual ovum is exceedingly small, the quantity shed by each fish, which, in an adult female, is computed to number between two and three millions, is apparently large enough to bear the great and ever increasing strain on their resources: and in view of future developments, which must necessarily take place in the direction of utilising the surplus catch of this fine fish by canning, smoking, &c., it is to be hoped that the New South Wales Commissioners of Fisheries will not shrink from their plain duty of stringently conserving the breeding grounds, *and the approaches to the breeding grounds*, of a species which, with proper fostering care, is destined to play no unimportant part in both the intercolonial and the export trade of the Colony.

In connection with this no place can be more advantageously chosen than the present to point out, that few, if any, fishes can be more easily domesticated than those belonging to the Mugilidæ, and, glancing at the wealth of sheltered bays, creeks, and backwaters which fringe the margins of our estuaries and salt water lagunes, it is marvelous that so great and profitable a trade, one which in the nature of things must be ever increasing in its scope, and which year by year would necessarily absorb more and more labor, has not hitherto commended itself to either the public or the private financiers of the Colony.

Their hardiness, their adaptability to various conditions of life, their indifference to the density of the element which they inhabit, the fact which has been proved that they breed and thrive equally well in enclosed freshwater ponds as under normal conditions, the ease with which they may be brought to perfection at a minimum of cost, since no artificial method of supplying food would be required, all point to our Gray Mullet as the pioneer of a fishing industry, which is capable of becoming a not unworthy rival of the Salmon-canning industry of the Western States of America, did our Australian capitalists possess but a tithe of the indomitable energy and perseverance of our transpacific cousins.

A steady supply of fish, regulated to meet all local requirements, would then be daily available for delivery in the market in such a condition that the most hypercritical could find no ground for cavilling; and so far as this fish is concerned, would make us practically independent of the forces of nature—such, for instance, as the terrible floods which have recently devastated Eastern Australia—and the constitutional indolence of the colonial fishermen.

But little capital would be requisite to inaugurate a fish farm on the lines here advocated, the initial expense being merely the enclosure of a suitable sheet of water—preferably one having a stream of fresh water emptying into it—so thoroughly as to admit of no incursion of the larger predaceous fishes, such as the Kingfish and Tailor, while at the same time allowing free entry to the Mullet fry, and permitting no outlet to the marketable fish.

This primitive method having been proved to be a profitable speculation it would need but little commercial enterprise to advance and enlarge the industry by enclosing suitable localities by a boundary wall, leaving a few well protected gates to admit of the ingress and egress of the tides, and being as copiously as circumstances would allow supplied with fresh water. The enclosed space should of course be of considerable extent, and the bed should consist of sand and mud, in order to satisfy the requirements of the contained Mullet as to nutrition and reproduction. To farms, such as are briefly sketched out here, the fry, when roaming in schools along the foreshores, as is their habit, might with ease be transfered in almost illimitable numbers, and being there freed, so far as is possible, from their natural enemies, being supplied without cost with an abundance of their natural food, and being practically undisturbed by any disquieting influences, their growth would be materially accelerated, and their condition proportionately improved. With a few such establishments in working order in the Port Jackson District, and with the unlimited range of choice, which even the close neighborhood of Sydney affords, dozens of such establishments might with ease be formed, and a great and profitable canning industry might with but little effort be built up in our midst; nor should we ever again hear of the "boat loads of the finest fish thrown away, because they were not worth the trouble of conveying to market" as mentioned by Macleay; in addition to this would be the advantages that the local market or individual dealers could be supplied from the farms with so many fish as would be requisite for the day's consumption and no more, and that these would be delivered to the customer in a fresh and cleanly state; furthermore the enormous and inexcusable destruction of fry, which takes place daily without let or hindrance along our foreshores, would by the advent of some such system be reduced to a minimum.

The young fish having been introduced into the enclosed waters, and being undisturbed by the presence of such enemies as Sharks, Kingfishes, &c., and the depredations of rapacious birds, such as Cormorants, Herons, and Gulls, being easily kept in check, would gain so rapidly in size as to enable them quickly to defy the attacks of less conspicuous, but no less insidious enemies, such as starfishes, Sea-Anemonies, and the like, which also could be greatly reduced in numbers by the application of suitable remedies.

By means of proper appliances also many inland towns, where a meal of fresh fish is now a rarity or even unknown, could be supplied weekly; but apart from this it would be well worth trying as an experiment whether the Sea Mullet could be introduced into ponds, lagunes, and tanks in the transmontane districts of the Colony, and there acclimatised; and whether the ova would germinate there and the fry grow to maturity; under such conditions it is hardly to be expected that the fish would grow to so large a size as it does in its normal state, but if it is possible to breed them in such places, and of its practicability there can be but little doubt, we have here, neglected at our very doors, a fish far surpassing in excellence the European Perch, Carp, and Tench—all of which have been introduced at great expense, and with no practical results so far as a fish food supply to the Riverine Districts is concerned—and which with its other natural advantages, would not interfere in any way with our native fauna.

The question of the acclimatization of the Sea Mullet to purely fresh water is not one which should be productive of any great difficulty, for since, as has been shown above, the fry instinctively make their way upwards from the spawning beds to the utmost limit of the tide or even beyond it, it would be only necessary to establish a suitable number of farms above the furthest influence of the tides, and allowing the young fishes to grow to maturity and breed therein, to secure eventually from the progeny of such parents a hardy race suitable for introduction into our transmontane waters.

Another advantage to be gained by the establishment of such a system, combined with the passage of more stringent regulations, enforced by exemplary punishments, for the more thorough conservation of the breeding grounds and the approaches leading thereto, would be found in its tendency to check in a great degree the grave deterioration which is taking place in the size and quality of the spawning fishes; this deterioration is very noticeable and has been during the last ten years as rapid as it is lamentable; for instance, five or six years ago the average weight of school fish was quite four pounds and much larger ones were daily procurable during the season; the fishes at that time taken at any haul of the seine were of the same general size, and the intestines were imbedded in a dense layer of pure fat: now similar school fish do not average three pounds, and a five pounds example is quite exceptional; the small fishes, of a pound weight or even less, are indiscriminately mingled with the larger, and the necessary reserve of strength, requisite for undergoing the weakening process of spawning, as gauged by the presence of the internal fat, is almost absolutely wanting.

There can be no reasonable doubt as to the causes which tend to produce this unhappy state of affairs; overfishing night after night the same grounds in the vicinity of the spawning beds, and the disturbance of and want of adequate protection to the fishes when engaged in depositing their ova, are the plain causes of the ruinous decadence of this valuable fishery; if a peremptory stop is not put upon these short-sighted practices, the Mullet-harvest, so much vaunted, will, so far as the metropolitan district is concerned, be a thing of the past within the next decade.

Having once established these Mullet farms on a sound basis, similar farms for the reception of such other of our littoral fishes as are not of a roving disposition, as, for example the Whiting, Flathead, Flounder, Sole, and Eel would soon follow.

In the Report of the Royal Commission the following sentences which require some explanation, occur:—" When the period at length arrives for the mature fish to go to the sea preparatory to spawning, the instinct which actuates them appears to be irresistible. In one instance, some years ago, when Tuggerah Beach Lake was for a time shut up at its sea mouth, the Mullet pressed in such masses in the direction in which the outlet should have been that thousands of them were forced up on the land and perished. An occurrence of the same kind is mentioned as having happened at Lake Illawarra under similar circumstances. It is doubtful how long it is between the rush of the fish to the sea and their reentrance into the same or other rivers; the belief is that the time is very short, that the movement is only from one part of the coast to another, and always from south to north. There can be little doubt that the fishes, after spawning, find their way back to their old haunts, but they have very seldom been seen so returning."

The above would seem to denote that in the opinion of the Commission the adult as well as the immature fishes spend their whole lives, with the exception of the "very short time" elapsing between the "rush of the fish to the sea and their reentrance into the rivers," in our estuaries; this view we cannot hold, nor do facts warrant its adoption; it is well known that enormous shoals of these Mullet appear off the coast during the late summer and early autumn months; if the Commissioners' opinion were correct, the question which would naturally suggest itself to anyone would be,—where do these huge shoals come from? The answer is not difficult; as soon as each fish has shed its spawn it, having become greatly exhausted in the process, immediately seeks deeper and more quiet waters and with each ebbing tide drops unobserved down to the bays and thence finally to the open ocean; this migration, being composed of individual fish, is carried out so quietly and at such a depth as to have escaped observation, and probably lasts more or less continuously during the late autumn and the winter months; once having gained the outer beaches these individuals unite into small bands, which, retiring into water of a moderate depth and keeping strictly to the bottom, gradually drop down the coast, receiving from every estuary and inlet which they pass a fresh accession to their numbers; thus during the spring and summer these ever increasing bands are aimlessly drifting along, keeping, however, a general southerly direction, until about the New Year, when the migratory instinct, consequent upon the ripening of the ova, forces them more and more to the surface, and, a common impulse leading them all in the one direction, the various bands unite as they proceed, and form the enormous schools, whose presence on the surface has been described as a "truly marvellous sight." From these schools as they move slowly up the coast in a northerly direction more or less important bodies detach themselves and seek each its own well known spawning ground.

Between what parallels these great congregations of Mullet, as distinct from other surface-schooling families,—such as the Herring, the Mackerel, and the Scad,—exist, is a matter of great interest, whether viewed from a scientific or commercial standpoint, and an appeal to the officers of our coastal merchant service, to make notes of any such occurrence, specifying date, state of tide, trend of current, direction of wind, calmness or otherwise of the surface water, along with the direction in which the shoal is believed to be moving, would be certain to produce good results, and would fix incontrovertably the southern and northern range of this fine *Mugil*.

The Tuggerah Lake and Lake Illawarra cases cited do not in any way militate against the contention here advanced, since under the circumstances of the closure of the natural outlets the individual fishes on their way to the sea were blocked, and becoming massed together within a small area, those that were in the rear, in their uncontrolable anxiety to gain the safety and seclusion of the more open waters, pressing forwards in large masses with this object, absolutely forced the vanguard ashore.

We must again join issue with the Commissioners on their assertion that the Mullet, after spawning, simply move from one river or inlet to the other, remaining presumably in the latter until the breeding season again draws near, when they go out to sea, school, and then return to the rivers in which each was originally bred ; such an idea, we contend, is preposterous, is unsupported by facts, and is utterly opposed to the known habits of all anadromous or semianadromous fishes; from the account given by Macleay, it appears that this idea is borrowed from the professional fishermen, than whom, with rare exceptions, no more unreliable body of men, as to the facts connected with their own calling, can be found the world over.

Notwithstanding the enormous shoals which are known to occur as surface fishes off our shores during the earlier months of the year, no systematic attempt, so far as we are aware, has yet been made to capture them before their arrival on, or in the vicinity of, the spawning beds; then, however, the destructive seine net comes to the front, and good and bad, adult and young, salable and unsalable species are alike immolated on the altar of the Mullet. It is easy to see that an obstinate continuance in such a course, must end, and indeed is already far advanced theretowards, in the depletion, if not absolute denudation, of fish life in our metropolitan waters, and all others round which large centres of population have gathered, or may in the future so do. The fact is that the rising generation of fishermen have to be taught that the harvest of the sea must be gathered in the open, and that they must not be content, as their fathers are, to drag the same harbor beaches and estuarine mud flats, day after day, month after month, and year after year; failing their capacity to learn this it will eventually become necessary to import a sufficient number of our north country men with their families, or of the equally hardy and daring fishermen of Canada and the New England States, to work our ocean fisheries, who by the exercise of greater skill, and the employment of superior methods for placing the catch on the market would gradually supersede the haphazard system at present in vogue.

It is generally considered that the Sea Mullet will not take a bait, but this is denied by Tenison Woods, who, in his account of the species, states that it "affords good sport to anglers in the Hunter and other eastern rivers." "The bait," he continues, "is a small worm, but a far better kind is the fine silky green conferva which grows on the surface of stones or logs which have been long in the water. Mullet will take this with great avidity. The weed must be cut rather long and wound around the hook. It must not be confounded with the coarse green wooly conferva which covers the bottom like a blanket; Mullet will not touch this; the other they eat so greedily that not a particle can be found on the stones and logs of the rivers where these fishes are abundant." This statement, which is not only unsupported but directly contradicted by all other authorities, needs confirmation. According to Ramsay, however, it will take a dough bait.

As a food fish this Mullet, both in its adult and immature state, is deservedly popular, the flesh being always rich and nutritious, nor does that of even the largest examples ever become coarse, as is so often the case with other fishes. In a commercial sense this is undoubtedly the premier fish of New South Wales, and when smoking and canning operations are more extensively and scientifically cultivated, is capable of becoming no inconsiderable a source of national wealth, and of being an influential competitor with the smoked and canned fishes, which we are now compelled to import. The roe is of very large size, and are most delicious, whether they are consumed in a fresh or smoked state. Mr. Edward Hill mentions that "experiments have been tried by boiling them—the Mullet—down," which resulted in the discovery that "each fish yielded nearly a pint of fine clear oil"; we are not aware, however, that any practical attempt has ever been made to utilise the intestinal fat in this direction, though it is probable that such oil would possess valuable medicinal properties.

This fine species frequents in enormous numbers the entire length of the seaboard of the Colony. Of its occurrence on the Queensland coast Saville Kent remarks:—"Taken in the order of their economic importance, precedence is almost universally conceded to the Sea Mullet, a magnificent fish growing to a weight of ten or twelve pounds and upwards. This species arrives in Moreton Bay about the last week in April, continues plentiful till the middle of July, and by August has passed away to the north." In that Colony the immature fish is known as the "Mangrove Mullet" a title infinitely preferable to that of "Hard-gut Mullet" in use here. He also observes that the Mangrove or Sea Mullet is apparently the species most easily accessible and best adapted for the purposes of canning and exportation." Along the coastline of Victoria this species is said to be known as "Sand Mullet,"—a name which is with more propriety applied in the home Colony to *Myxus elongatus*,—and is everywhere common; Castelnau, speaking of it under the name of *Mugil waigiensis*, says that it is "much esteemed as food." The omission of South Australian scientists to give even so fragmentary a list of the fishes inhabiting the waters geographically pertaining to their Colony, as wash its southern shores, places us again in the unsatisfactory position of being obliged to infer, not record as a fact, its presence in those seas, but since the British Museum possesses specimens from Perth, West Australia, it cannot be doubted that it occurs in more or less abundance along the entire length of our southern and south-western seaboard. As to the latitude to which it attains in our north-western equatorial regions we are equally in the dark, for judging from its occurrence so far to the northerly and easterly as the New Hebrides and Sandwich Islands, we might well suppose that it would even more easily have penetrated to the more distinctly accessible shores of those groups of islands which belong to the Austro-Malayan section of the Archipelago. From Tasmania Johnston records this species, which he refers to *Mugil cephalotus*, as being "common along the north-eastern coast, George's Bay, Seamander River," and elsewhere states that it is very highly prized in the market, attains to a much greater size than *Agonostoma forsteri*, but owing to its distance from the chief centres of population is scarce in the markets, where, however, it always commands a good price.

Until a more exact system of trivial names shall have been established throughout the Australian Colonies for such fishes as, from commercial or other reasons, are considered worthy of a distinctive vernacular nomenclature, it is almost hopeless to expect to educate the general public, who go entirely by these trivial and frequently senseless names, into a due appreciation of the differences which constitute a species; in our opinion the various forms should be as carefully described in the vernacular as in the scientific designation. This species, for instance, which is appropriately the "Sea Mullet" of the mother Colony and Queensland is the miscalled "Sand Mullet" of Victoria and Tasmania, and while the "Sea Mullet" of the latter Colony is the comparatively worthless *Agonostoma forsteri*, the "Sand Mullet" of New South Wales is the *Myxus elongatus* of Günther, more commonly known as "Tallegalane," while to complicate matters, in all ways bad enough, nothing will persuade most persons that the immature stages of the present species do not specifically differ from the adult, and both in this Colony and in Queensland grant to them that rank by the respective titles of "Hardgut" and "Mangrove Mullet."

These fishes attain to a length of at least twenty four inches.

It is not an uncommon occurrence to find examples of the Sea Mullet, which through some accident in early youth have had the snout cut off in front of the eyes; a remarkable specimen was sent to the Australian Museum a short time ago, in which the entire front of the head was so far cut away as to have destroyed all vestiges of the mouth and nostrils proper, and to have left a mere small longitudinal slit on the right side of the ventral axis of the snout, which slit had developed around it a series of moderately strong acute teeth; this tends to the belief that originally the *Mugilidæ* possessed teeth, which, owing to their peculiar method of feeding, have fallen into desuetude, but are still lying dormant, ready to appear and become functional on such an emergency as at present cited In this case, as in all others observed, the sufferer was found to be in excellent condition.

The immature fish, before it has visited the open sea, is not unfrequently infested by a species of *Anilocra*, which usually attaches itself to the inner side of the axil of the pectoral fin.

MUGIL PERONI.

Mugil peroni, Cuv & Val. Hist. Nat. Poiss. xi. p. 138; Gnth. Catal. Fish. iii. p. 452; Castelu. Proc. Zool. Soc. Vict. ii. p. 151, *and* Proc. Linn. Soc. N. S. Wales, iii. p. 387; Macleay, Proc. Linn. Soc. N. S. Wales iv. p. 421.

Flat-tailed Mullet.

Plate XXXII.

B. vi. D. 4. 1/8 A. 3/10. V. 1/5. P. 16. C. 14. L. lat. 35–38. L. tr. 14. Cœc. pyl. 2. Vert. 11/13.

Length of head 4·33–4·85, of caudal fin 4·25–4·50, height of body 4·50–4·80 in the total length. Eye with the adipose lid but little developed, its diameter 4·25–4·75 in the length of the head, 1·20–1·45 in that of the snout, which is obtusely rounded, moderately broad, and very slightly convex, and 1·60–2·00 in the interorbital space, which is convex. Lips thin: jaws fringed with minute cilia. Nostrils approximate, upright, suboval, the anterior slightly nearer to the orbit than to the tip of the snout; the posterior about twice as large as the anterior. Free space below the chin lanceolate, equal to or rather longer than the distance between the end of the snout and the posterior margin of the orbit. The maxilla extends to between the hinder nostril and the orbit. Preorbital minutely denticulate along its inferior, more strongly so on its posterior edge, expanded behind. The distance between the origin of the spinous dorsal and the base of the caudal is 1·25-1·50 in that between the same point and the top of the snout; the first dorsal spine is the longest, 1·75-2·15 in the length of the head; the distance between the origins of the two dorsal fins is much less than the length of the head: the anal commences considerably in front of the soft dorsal, and its anterior rays are longer than those of that fin; the posterior rays are not produced beyond the median: the ventral extends midway between its origin and that of the anal, and is 1·60-1·80 in the length of the head: the pectoral reaches to the tenth or eleventh body scale, and is 1·40-1·60 in the length of the head: caudal deeply emarginate, the least height of the pedicle is more than the distance between the last dorsal ray and the base of the caudal, and one half or rather more than one half of the length of the head. Fifteen to seventeen scales between the occiput and the origin of the spinous dorsal, six on the interspace between the dorsals, and seven or eight between the rayed dorsal and the caudal; no enlarged axillary scale.

Colors.—Steel blue above, silvery on the sides, white below; scales of the back with a narrow median longitudinal streak forming bands, and often with golden reflections; a small black axillary spot preceded by a golden blotch: soft dorsal, anal, and caudal fins tinged with gold on the outer margin.

Though the Flat-tailed Mullet does not attain to a commercial importance similar to that of its larger relative, the Sea Mullet, nor possesses the exceptional richness of flesh peculiar to that species, it forms no inconsiderable part of our food resources, and is abundant, and in good condition throughout almost the whole year.

The spawning season appears to be spread over a number of months, specimens examined during December having been ripe for spawning, while others of the same catch had the ova in all different developments between that and the barely possible discernment of its formation in the ovaries; the main body, however, appears to shed their spawn about the latter end of spring or during the early winter months, but at any time between December and June, inclusive, spawning fishes may be observed. This prolongation of the breeding season doubtless accounts for the fact that they are rarely noticed to arrive in the enormous shoals, for which we are accustomed to look in the case of *Mugil dobula.* The Flat-tailed Mullet does not penetrate up the rivers to such an extent as does the preceding species, but prefers shallow sandy bays in the various inlets which indent our coasts.

In habits, feeding, &c., it differs in no wise from the other species of *Mugil.* As food it is excellent, and not being so oily as the Sea Mullet is more delicate in flavor, and more adapted for these reasons to the use of invalids.

This fish is found along our coast from south to north, but in the former direction quickly decreases in numbers, and though originally described from Western Port, Victoria,—erroneously stated by its describers as being situated on the north-western coast of New Holland (*pris sur la côte nord-ouest de la Nouvelle-Hollande dans le port Western**)—is so scarce in that Colony that it only seems to have been recorded in one instance, by Castelnau,

---

* This is evidently an error, since Dumont D'Urville's expedition only explored the southern coast of Australia and Tasmania.

since, and so far not at all in Tasmania. It is not mentioned, at least under its scientific name by Saville Kent from the coast of Queensland, but there can be little doubt as to its presence along the whole eastern seaboard of Australia.

The average size at which this species appears in the market is about twelve inches, but examples measuring as much as sixteen occasionally occur.

Genus II.—MYXUS.

Myxus, Günther, Catal. Fish. iii. p. 466, 1861.

Branchiostegals six : pseudobranchiæ present. Cleft of mouth extending on to the sides of the snout, but not reaching to the orbit: anterior margin of the mandible sharp. Eyes without adipose lids. A single series of small teeth in the upper jaw: similar teeth sometimes present in the lower jaw, on the vomer, and on the palatine bones. Pyloric appendages in small numbers.

Geographical distribution.—Coasts of Australia and western South America.

MYXUS ELONGATUS.

Myxus elongatus. Guth. Catal. Fish. iii. p. 466 ; Kner. Voy. Novara, Fisch. p. 230; Macleay, Proc. Linn. Soc. N.S. Wales, iv. p. 426.

Tallegalane : Sand Mullet.

Plate XXXIII.

B. vi. D. 4. 1/8 A. 3/9. V. 1/5. P. 16. C. 14. L. lat. 43–46. L. tr. 15. Cœc. pyl. 2. Vert. 11/13.

Length of head 4·40–4·75, of caudal fin 4·66–4·90, height of body 4·60–4·85 in the total length. Eye moderate, with the adipose lid but little developed, its diameter 4·20–4·60 in the length of the head, 1·20–1·40 in that of the obtusely rounded snout, and 1·10–1·60 in the interorbital space, which is very slightly convex. Lips thin. Nostrils approximate, the anterior circular and set in a low tube, a little nearer to the eye than to the tip of the snout ; the posterior upright and oval, about twice as large as the anterior. Free space behind the mandible lanceolate, its length equal to the distance between the eye and the tip of the snout. The maxilla extends to between the posterior nostril and the orbit. Preorbital denticulated along the posterior half of its lower margin and the hinder margin, the denticulations strongest at the angle, not much expanded behind. A single series of small, rarely tricuspid teeth in the upper jaw ; lower fringed with minute ciliæ ; a narrow transverse band of small teeth on the head of the vomer, and a similar, but smaller, patch on the palatines. The distance between the origin of the spinous dorsal and the base of the caudal is equal to that between the same point and the anterior margin of the eye ; spinous dorsal small, the first spine the longest, 2·00–2·33 in the length of the head ; the distance between the origins of the two dorsal fins is a little less than the length of the head ; the rayed dorsal commences opposite to the middle of the anal fin : the anterior anal rays are longer than those of the dorsal, and the posterior ray is produced beyond the median rays, forming a shallow emargination on the outer edge of the fin : the length of the ventral is from 2·00–2·33 in the distance between its origin and that of the anal, and from 1·75–1·90 in that of the head : the pectoral reaches to the tenth body scale, and is 1·50–1·66 in the same length :

caudal deeply emarginate, the least height of the pedicle much less than the distance between the base of the last dorsal ray and the origin of the caudal, and 2·40–2·60 in the length of the head. There are seventeen or eighteen scales between the occiput and the origin of the spinous dorsal, nine on the interspace between the dorsals, and ten between the rayed dorsal and the caudal; no enlarged axillary scale; elongate scale above the base of the ventral small.

Colors.—Light reddish-brown or dark green above; sides pink; lower surfaces silvery; a small black axillary spot.

The Sand Mullet, or, to use the more euphonious aboriginal name, Tallegalane, does not materially differ in its habits from its congeners.

Like the preceding species they deposit their spawn on sandy beaches during the autumn months, and these ova do not seem to germinate until the succeeding spring, when we have seen the fry swept ashore by thousands in the back wash of a seine net, along with those of *Stigmatophora*, *Sillago*, and others.

The Tallegalane is found along the entire coastline of New South Wales, but is more abundant towards the northern boundaries of the Colony; in Victoria, from whence Gunther received one of his types, it is so scarce that is has not since been recorded, nor have the Tasmanian authorities as yet obtained examples from their seas. Writing of Queensland, Saville Kent says:—"A member of the genus Myxus—*M. elongatus*, *Gnth.*—is also a native of Queensland; it, however, rarely measures a foot in length, and is but little esteemed as food." We are not, however, told how far its range extends in a northerly direction. At Lord Howe Island this species is abundant at all seasons, and forms a staple article of food among the islanders, either fresh, salted, or dried.

This is a common fish in the Sydney market, but does not average more than eight inches; it is not, therefore, of much value, and has consequently attained a bad reputation as a food fish; nevertheless we consider that large examples, from twelve to fourteen inches in length, are equally as good as the preceding species, and in fact that when cooked it would take an expert to detect a difference between the two fishes.

Family XIX.—LABRIDÆ.

Branchiostegals five or six: pseudobranchiæ present. Gills three and a half. Body oblong or elongate. Teeth in the jaws: palate edentulous: lower pharyngeal bones ankylosed into one along the median line, and without median suture. One dorsal fin with the spinous portion as well developed as the rayed, or more so: the anal rays generally similar to those of the dorsal: ventral fins thoracic, with one spine and five rays. Scales cycloid. Lateral line complete or interrupted. Airbladder present, without pneumatic duct. Stomach without cœcal sac. Pyloric appendages absent.

Geographical distribution.—Marine fishes inhabiting the shores of all tropical and temperate seas.

As the food of the *Labridæ* consists chiefly of molluscs and crustaceans, they are provided with exceedingly strong teeth, which are admirably adapted to crush the hard outer coverings of these animals, and even the corals on which some species feed; many Labrids are in addition possessed of a strong, pointed, generally curved tooth, directed forwards, and rising from the posterior end of the premaxillary, which is supposed to be employed for pressing shells and other hard substances against the front and lateral teeth, by which they are broken up; zoophytes enter largely into the food supply of some species, while others, such as the *Scarina*, feed principally on fuci and other seaweeds.

In many of the genera the lips are abnormally thickened, and even folded internally, a peculiarity which has suggested for them the family name of *Labridæ*, and, among the Germans, that of "Lip-fishes."

In the majority of species beautiful tints prevail, "the intensity of which," says Day, "are greatly augmented during the nuptial season." The same author continues:—"They are subject to great individual variations in the mode in which they are colored, while in some the livery of the two sexes is very dissimilar."

Genus I.—CHŒROPS.

Chœrops, Rüppell, Verz. Mus. Senckenb. Fisch. p. 20, 1852; Bleek. Proc. Zool. Soc. 1861, p. 416.
Hypsigenys, Günther, Ann. Nat. Hist. 1861, viii. p. 383.
Torresia, Casteln. Res. Fish. Austr. p. 36, 1875.

Branchiostegals five or six: pseudobranchiæ present. Body oblong-ovate, compressed. Snout more or less obtuse. Cheeks high. Preopercle serrated or entire. Four strong free canine teeth anteriorly in each jaw: lateral teeth confluent into a more or less obtuse osseous ridge: posterior canines present or absent: inferior pharyngeal teeth not confluent or pavement-like. Dorsal fin with thirteen spines and seven rays: anal with three spines and nine or ten rays. Scales large, cycloid: cheek scales generally non-imbricate: opercles scaly: base of the dorsal and anal fins with a low scaly sheath. Lateral line continuous. Airbladder large, simple.

Geographical distribution.—From tropical and subtropical Australia, through Malaysia to the seas of China and Japan; and through India to the Red Sea and the east coast of Africa.

CHŒROPS OMMOPTERUS.

? *Cossyphus schönleinii* (Agass.) Cuv. & Val. Hist. Nat. Poiss. xiii. p. 143, 1839.
Cossyphus ommopterus, Richards. Ichthyol. China, p. 257, 1846.
? *Crenilabrus leucozona*, Bleek. Biliton, iv. p. 238.
Cossyphus schönleinii, Bleek. Celebes, v. p. 252.
Chœrops ommopterus, Gnth. Catal. Fish. iv. p. 94, 1862; Macleay, Catal. Austr. Fish. ii. p. 72; Ogilby, Proc. Zool. Soc. 1889, p. 158.
Chœrops schoenleini, Bleek. Atl. Ichthyol. i. p. 163, pl. xlvi. f. 1.

Blue-spotted Groper.

B. vi. D. 13/7. A. 3/10. V. 1/5. P. 16. C. 14. L. lat. 29–30. L. tr. 4/9–10. Vert. 11/16.

Length of head 3·50–3·90, of caudal fin 4·60–4·85, height of body 3·20–3·40 in the total length: height of head equal to or rather more than its length. Diameter of eye 5·00–5·66 in the length of the head, 2·40–3·00 in that of the pointed snout, and 1·20–1·66 in that of the interorbital space, which is strongly arched. Nostrils distant, minute. Jaws equal. Cleft of mouth slightly oblique, the maxilla reaching to beneath the internasal space. Preorbital very high: vertical margin of preopercle finely but distinctly serrated. Anterior canine teeth very strong and curved; no posterior canine. The dorsal fin commences above the opercular flap, the spines are moderately strong and are noticeably compressed, subequal in length, the last 3·25–4·00 in the length of the head; the rays are longer than the spines, the fifth the longest, one half longer than the last spine: the anal commences beneath the eleventh dorsal spine, and extends further back along the caudal pedicle; the third spine is the longest, 3·80–4·50 in the length of the head, and five ninths of the eighth and longest ray; all the dorsal and anal spines with a short, free, terminal flap: ventral reaching to the vent, the two outer rays the longest, produced considerably beyond the others, 1·50–1·70 in the length of the head; the spine weak, longer than the longest dorsal spine, and but little more than half the length of the outer ray: pectoral well developed, pointed above, rounded below, the third ray the longest, 1·10–1·20 in the length of the head: caudal truncated, with the upper lobe produced; the least height of the pedicle about one third of the height of the body. Scales on the cheeks non-imbricate; in four series on the opercle. Lateral line tubes more or less ramose.

Colors.—Upper part of head green, becoming gradually more tinged with blue towards the snout; cheeks and opercles olive; mandibular region pale violet; chin sky blue; edge of the maxillary lip with a narrow outer golden and inner blue stripe; anterior margin of the preorbital very narrowly edged with blue; an oval sky blue spot in front of the orbit, and extending to about one third of its diameter: body olive brown above the lateral line, rose-colored below, most of the scales on the back and caudal pedicle with a medium-sized, round, blue spot; a broad dark band runs from the fifth scale of the lateral line forwards and downwards in an arcuate shape to the inferior margin of the opercle: dorsal fin golden, the spinous portion with a basal, median, and marginal band of blue, the two outer of which are exchanged on the rays for wavy, anastomosing lines of the same shade; anal fin gray, with broad basal and marginal blue bands, bordered on the inner edge by a narrower golden stripe; ventrals bluish, the membrane between the first and second rays golden; pectorals gray, with two transverse golden bands in front of the base, and the two outer rays and the basal third of the others blue; caudal brownish with the outer rays blue, and the bases of the remainder green: irides golden and crimson, with sky blue marginal spots: basal half of canines and lateral teeth light blue.

It is only during the winter months that this fish is obtainable in the Sydney market, as, except at that season, no consignments come to the metropolis from the northern rivers. Of those examined only one, caught in July, showed any signs of breeding, and in this the ova were about half developed, and were small and numerous. As food they are excellent, the flesh being white, firm, and flaky, and in no case was any substance, except the coarsely broken up remains of shells, found in the intestines.

So far we have not received this Groper from any locality south of the Clarence River, but as it appears to be common there, it doubtless occurs in the estuaries of some of our more southern rivers, such as the Bellinger and Macleay. That it does not, however, confine itself so the mouths of rivers, or even to the vicinity of land, we are aware, from the fact that the naturalists of the "Rattlesnake" captured a specimen off Cape York with hook and line at a depth of sixty three fathoms. It is strange that, notwithstanding the size to which they grow and their excellence as food, no mention is made of this or any other species of *Chærops* in Saville Kent's list of Queensland Food Fishes.

Beyond the Australian coasts it is found through the Molucca Sea to those of China.

The Blue-spotted Groper attains a length of at least twenty six inches.

Genus II.—PLATYCHŒROPS.

Platychœrops, Klunzing. SB. Ak. Wien, lxxx. Abth. i. p. 399, 1879.

Branchiostegals six : pseudobranchiæ present. Body rather short, oblong or ovate, not much compressed. Snout moderately rounded. Preopercle entire. Four transversely flattened canines anteriorly in each jaw : lateral teeth connected by an osseous ridge : posterior canine present or absent. One dorsal fin with eleven spines and ten or eleven rays : anal with three spines and eleven or twelve rays. Scales of moderate size, those of the cheeks non-imbricate : bases of the vertical fins partially scaly. Lateral line continuous.

Geographical distribution.—Coasts of temperate Australia and Tasmania.

PLATYCHŒROPS GOULDI

Labrus gouldii, Richards. Ann. Nat. Hist. 1843, xi. p. 353.
Cossyphus vel *Lachnolaimus gouldii*, Richards. Voy. Erebus & Terror, Fish. p. 132.
Cossyphus gouldii, Richards. Ann. Nat. Hist. (2) 1851, vii. p. 288, *and* Proc. Zool. Soc. 1850, p. 72, pl. iii. fig. 3 ; Gnth. Catal. Fish. iv. p. 111 ; Macleay, Catal. Austr. Fish. ii. p. 78 ; Woods, Fisher. N.S. Wales, p. 74, pl. xxxi.
Platychœrops mülleri, Klunzing. SB. Ak. Wien, lxxx Abth. i. 1879, p. 399, pl. viii. f. 2.

Blue Groper.
Plate XXXV.

B. vi. D. 11/11. A. 3/11. V. 1/5. P. 16. C. 14. L. lat. 39–41. L. tr. 10/17.

Length of head 4·00, of caudal fin 5·50, height of body 3·50 in the total length. Eye rather small, its diameter 4·60 in the length of the head, 2·00 in that of the moderately rounded snout, and 1·60 in the convex interorbital space. Nostrils slightly separated, the anterior minute, rounded, and with a low, fleshy valve, more developed behind ; the posterior much larger, oval, horizontal, and patent. Upper profile of head flat. Lips thick and fleshy, the lower with a well developed rounded lateral flap. Upper jaw slightly the longer. Cleft of mouth small and slightly oblique, the maxilla reaching to beneath the anterior nostril : intermaxillary processes reaching to between the anterior margins of the eyes, their length 2·33 in that of the head. Preorbital a little longer than deep. Preopercle entire. Two pairs of strong flattened canines anteriorly in each jaw : lateral teeth visible, but connected by a sharp osseous ridge, beyond which the tips slightly protrude : posterior canine present or absent. The dorsal fin commences above the base of the pectoral and terminates above the eighth anal ray ; the spines are somewhat curved backwards, and, with the exception of the two or three posterior ones, strongly compressed ; the last spine is slightly longer than those preceding it, 3·15 in the length of the head, and 1·60 in the longest rays, which are situated in the posterior half of the fin : the anal commences beneath the first dorsal ray ; its spines are stronger than those of the dorsal, the third the longest, 2·40 in the length of the head and 1·33 in that of the longest rays : ventral small, the second ray the longest, 2·00 in the distance between its origin and that of the anal, and bearing the same proportion to the length of the head ; the spine stout and strongly compressed, equal in length to the second anal spine. pectoral well developed rounded posteriorly, 1·40 in the length of the head : caudal truncate, the least height of its pedicle one half of the height of the body. Snout, preorbital, interorbital space, and preopercle naked: cheek scales small, oval, and non-imbricate; those of the opercle of moderate size, of the occiput, nape, and throat minute: vertical fins, partially enveloped in a deep, basal, scaly sheath, which in the dorsal includes the three last, in the anal the two last spines, and in both ceases about the eighth ray. Lateral line gently curved to the caudal pedicle, the tubes, especially the posterior ones, profusely branched.

Colors.—Above purplish-brown, sides and lower surface yellowish-brown, each scale with an orange spot or vertical bar; a narrow orange band encircles the eye; sides of snout with three similar bands, one of which crosses the cheek, separated by blue bands: fins purple, the membranes of the anterior rays of the dorsal and anal with orange spots; all these markings are most conspicuous in the young, but almost totally disappear in adult examples.

The Blue Groper is essentially a rock-loving fish, its favorite haunts being rocky points, rising from a moderate depth, and with the bottom shelving somewhat rapidly into deep water; in such spots they may always be found, coming in with the flood tide to search every crevice and channel worn by the waves for the molluscs, crustaceans, echinoderms, and starfishes, which form the bulk of their food, and retiring with the ebb to the deeper waters in the vicinity; they are unsociable fishes, not more than two being found about the same spot, and that possibly only during the spawning season, and each one appears to confine itself to its own particular stretch of shore.

Nothing positive is known of its breeding habits, but it may be taken for granted that the ova is deposited in crannies among weed-covered rocks, but whether or not a nest is formed for the reception of the eggs—as has been observed on the French coast by Moreau to be the case among members of the typical genus, *Labrus*—must be left for further investigation.

Though an excellent table fish the Blue Groper, notwithstanding that it is of common occurrence on our coast is but rarely to be seen in the market, even though, when obtainable, it commands a high price; for this apparent scarcity Mr. Hill gives us the following reasons:—"The Groper, though plentiful, is not a common market fish, neither is it much sought after by professional fishermen for various reasons, among which may be mentioned that it is out of the lay for their general fishing grounds, as it is essentially a dweller among the caves and rocks of the coast, and the rocky points within the harbor, where their operations rarely extend, and also that the Groper may not be, from its coarse appearance, a favorite with the general public." Notwithstanding its appearance, it is not difficult to persuade anyone, who has once been tempted to make a meal off Groper, to do so again; in fact a Blue Groper's head and shoulders boiled with egg sauce, is equally as good as, and in the estimation of many infinitely better than, the same portions of a Cod (*Gadus morrhua*), and, if the fish were more easily obtainable, would worthily hold a similar position on colonial dinner tables.

Blue Gropers are sometimes taken in the trammel set close along the rocks (*see p.* 41), but the greater number sent to the market are caught by hook and line, crab, squid, and cuttle being the best baits. Mr. Hill says that these fishes are caught with hook and line along the rocks of our sea coast, but the bait should be crabs; it is usual to wrench off the legs and shell, and having broken them up throw them out as berley along with comminuted oysters and oyster shells, by which means they are often decoyed from their hiding places; "the body of the crab is then secured to the hook with a piece of thread or flax and thrown out; if a Groper should be at home that is the surest way to entice it."

As an instance of the extraordinary patience, cunning, and dexterity of the Aboriginals when in pursuit of so shy a fish as the Groper, and armed with spear only, the same writer continues:—"The Aboriginal when seeking this fish, armed with a couple of spears, prosecutes his search with cat-like caution, and when in view is as motionless as a statue, keeping, if necessary, that position for a considerable time till a chance offers, when he darts one of his spears with an unerring and powerful plunge into the fish, and fixes it firmly to the rock or ground."

The Blue Groper is found abundantly in suitable localities along the whole coastline of the Colony, and according to Mr. Thomas Stewart "there is not a more prolific fishing ground on the east coast than the Bellinger Bight for Snapper, Groper, and Rock Cod."

Though first described from King George's Sound—where it is presumably common, since Richardson, on the authority of Neill, states that it is known to the Aborigines of that district by no less than three distinct names, Koojenuck, Quejuinuck, and Knowl—it has not as yet been recorded from any intermediate point on the Australian coast, though Johnston catalogues it as common in Tasmania, nor is it mentioned by Saville Kent as occurring in Queensland waters.

The Blue Groper attains to a maximum weight of forty pounds, with a length of three and a half feet.

PLATYCHŒROPS BADIUS.

Red Groper.

B. vi. D. 11/10. A. 3/11. V. 1/5. P. 17. C. 14. L. lat. 45. L. tr. 8/14.

Length of head 3·80, of caudal fin 6·60, height of body 3·50 in the total length. Eye rather small, its diameter 5·33 in the length of the head, 2·50 in the elongate rounded snout, and 2·00 in the broad, slightly convex interorbital space. Nostrils small, the anterior opening at the extremity of a low tube; the posterior a little larger, oval, subhorizontal, midway between the eye and the anterior nostril. Jaws equal: lips fleshy. Cleft of mouth short and horizontal, the maxilla not expanded behind, and not extending beyond the anterior nostril: intermaxillary processes reaching to about the same distance, their length one third of that of the head. Length of preorbital greater than its depth. Upper profile of snout slightly concave; of occiput slightly convex; a moderate protuberance in front of and between the anterior margins of the eyes. Two pairs of strong canines in front of each jaw: a lateral row of conical teeth, connected together by an osseous ridge beyond which the teeth slightly protrude, and inside of which are a number of irregular series of minute granular teeth: a strong posterior canine curving inwards. The dorsal fin commences above the anterior angle of the base of the pectoral, and terminates above the eighth anal ray; the spines are stout, strongly compressed, especially on their upper half, and increase in length to the sixth, which is subequal to those which follow, one fourth of the length of the head, and four sevenths of the longest (seventh) ray: the anal commences beneath the first dorsal ray; its spines are similar to, but much longer and stronger than, those of the dorsal, the third the longest, not so strong or so compressed as the second, four fifths of the longest (seventh) ray, and 2·75 in the length of the head; the rays longer than those of the dorsal: ventral short and rounded, its length three fifths of the distance between its origin and the vent, equal to the distance between the tip of the snout and the anterior margin of the eye, or 2·20 in the length of the head; its spine broad and strongly compressed, acute anteriorly, equal in length to the third anal spine: pectoral rather large, rounded posteriorly, 1·40 in the length of the head: caudal truncate, the pedicle strong and but little compressed, its least height two fifths of the height of the body. Snout, preorbital, interorbital space, and preopercle scaleless; anterior rays of the vertical fins enclosed in a basal scaly sheath, which is more developed in the anal than in the dorsal, and almost disappears on the posterior half of the rayed dorsal and the last three rays of the anal. Lateral line gently curved up to the caudal pedicle, on which it is straight; the tubes branched.

Colors.—Uniform dull brick red, a little lighter on the abdomen; cheeks, opercles, and lower surface of the head washed with gold: the spinous dorsal and the anal with a basal white band sparsely blotched with orange; remainder of the web hyaline; spines and other fins dusky; the ventral pale red basally.

Though this fish is but rarely brought to the market, it is so well known to the professional fishermen under the vernacular name given above, and cannot, therefore, be considered rare, that we have decided to give it a place in the present limited work, the more so that it is a large and handsome species, and excellent for the table. The single specimen examined was caught by hook and line off Port Jackson, and measured twenty three inches; its stomach contained the triturated remains of crustaceans and molluscs.

It is hoped that this short notice will be the means of drawing attention to this fine species, and by inciting captors to forward examples to the Australian Museum, enable us ultimately to learn more concerning its habits and distribution.

As it does not appear to have been previously described, we are compelled to give it a specific name.

Genus III.—COSSYPHUS.

Cossyphus, Cuv. & Val. Hist. Nat. Poiss. xiii. p. 102, 1839.

Branchiostegals six: pseudobranchiæ present. Body oblong and compressed. Snout more or less pointed. Preopercle serrated or entire. The four anterior teeth in each jaw conical and free: lateral teeth free, in a single series: a posterior canine: hypopharyngeal teeth not confluent or pavement-like. One dorsal fin with twelve or thirteen spines and nine to eleven rays: the anal with three spines, and from ten to fourteen rays. Scales of moderate size, imbricate on the cheeks and opercles: bases of the vertical fins scaly. No enlarged row of scales at the base of the caudal fin. Lateral line continuous.

Geographical distribution—Nearly all tropical and subtropical seas.

COSSYPHUS UNIMACULATUS.

Cossyphus unimaculatus, Gnth. Catal. Fish. iv. p. 109, 1862; Casteln. Proc. Linn. Soc. N.S. Wales, iii. p. 389; Macleay, Catal. Austr. Fish. ii. p. 77; Woods, Fisher. N.S. Wales, p. 75, pl. xxxii.

Cossyphus oxycephalus, Bleek. Notices Ichthyol. Versl. en Mededeel. Ak. Wet. Amsterd. xiv. 1862.

Spotted Pigfish.

Plate XXXIV.

B. vi. D. 12/11. A. 3/12.V. 1/5. P. 17. C. 14. L. lat. 33–35. L. tr. 6/12. Vert. 11/16–17.

Length of head 3·40–3·60, of caudal fin 4·40–4·80, height of body 3·66–4·00 in the total length. Diameter of eye 4·60–5·50 in the length of the head, 1·90–2·40 in that of the pointed snout, and 1·00–1·30 in the slightly convex interorbital space. Nostrils but little separated, the anterior minute, and pierced in a low tube, the posterior larger, horizontal and oval, with a low overhanging flap. Upper profile of head straight. Jaws equal. Cleft of mouth moderate and horizontal, the maxilla, which is concealed by the preorbital, extending to beneath the anterior nostril, or even so far as the front margin of the eye. Intermaxillary processes extending backwards to between the middle of the orbits, their length one half of that of the head. Length of preorbital rather more than its depth: vertical limb of preopercle roughened. Both jaws with two pairs of anterior canines, those of the upper subequal, the middle pair of the lower small; sides of the jaws with a single series of conical teeth, seven or eight in each ramus of the upper, twelve to fifteen in each of the lower jaw; inside these there is a band of small granular teeth: one or two posterior canines. The dorsal fin commences above the upper angle of the pectoral, and terminates a little in front of the last anal ray; the spines are strong, and the membrane extends beyond their tips so as to form a short flap; they increase in height gradually to the last, which is about one half of the first, 2·85–3·05 in the length of the head, and 1·33 in the sixth and seventh rays, which are equal and longest; the base of the spinous dorsal is rather more than twice the length of the rayed portion, the outer margin of which is pointed: the anal commences beneath the eleventh dorsal spine; the spines are much stronger and more compressed than those of the dorsal, the third the longest, equal to the last dorsal spine, and very little less than the rays, whose outer margin is slightly convex: ventral fin reaching to the vent, or even to the origin of the anal fin, its length 1·33–1·66 in that of the head; the spine is strong, equal to the last dorsal spine, and 1·66 in the outer ray, which is slightly produced: pectoral rounded behind, reaching to beneath the twelfth scale of the lateral line, its length 1·70–1·85 in that of the head: caudal emarginate, with the lobes produced, the least height of the pedicle 2·50 in the height of the body. Snout, preorbital, interorbital space, and preopercle scaleless; vertical fins with a basal scaly sheath, whose greatest development is about the middle. Lateral line with a gentle curvature to the caudal pedicle, the tubes curved, but unbranched.

Colors.—Deep scarlet above, gradually changing into pink or saffron yellow below; each scale on the sides has a narrow median reddish streak, thus giving the fish a longitudinally banded appearance; a large pinkish patch below the origin of the rayed dorsal, and some small spots of a similar color in front of it on or near the lateral line; dorsal and caudal fins scarlet, with a more or less broad lighter margin; the former with a large dark blue spot between the sixth and eighth or seventh and ninth spines, surrounded, except at its base, by a pearly white band; similar, but small, spots generally present on the adjoining spines; anal scarlet anteriorly, yellowish posteriorly; ventrals hyaline, with the outer ray golden; pectorals reddish, with a small dark blue axillary spot: irides orange.

The Pigfish, so called on account of its elongate, conical snout, and thick fleshy lips, is, for the reasons adduced under the heading of Blue Groper, not often obtainable in the Sydney markets; nevertheless, it occurs more commonly than either of the Gropers, or than the succeeding species.

Nothing has been recorded as to the season of spawning, nor the places selected for depositing the ova, nor whether any special precautions are taken to ensure the safety thereof after its extrusion and fertilisation. From personal observation, however, we are inclined to fix the early spring months—such as September and the first half of October—as the period at which this important function takes place, several specimens which have passed through our hands within the specified time having been found distended with spawn, which could with but slight pressure be made to ooze from the fish; individually the ova are very minute.

In the quality of its flesh the Pigfish is as excellent as in appearance it is handsome, and it is, therefore, the more regretable that the market is not more bountifully supplied with them, since there can be no doubt that they are common in all suitable localities in the Port Jackson district; beyond the metropolitan district, however, we have no record of its occurrence on any part of the Australian coast, and the specimen which formed Günther's type, and which is merely labelled "Australia," probably came from Sydney; it is, however, included by Johnston in his supplementary list of Tasmanian fishes, and by Sherrin in his list of New Zealand fishes.

The common Pigfish attains to a length of eighteen inches, and the author does not remember to have ever seen one measuring less than twelve.

COSSYPHUS BELLIS.

Cossyphus bellis, Rms. & Ogl. Proc. Linn. Soc. N. S. Wales (2) 1887, ii. p. 561.

Banded Pigfish.

B. vi. D. 12/11. A. 3/12. V. 1/5. P. 17. C. 14. L. lat. 32. L. tr. 6/13. Vert. 11/17.

Length of head 3·33–3·60, of caudal fin, 5·00–5·25, height of body 3·50–3·70 in the total length. Eye rather small, its diameter 4·50–5·50 in the length of the head, 1·60–2·10 in that of the conically pointed snout, and 1·10–1·20 in that of the slightly convex interorbital space. Nostrils small, the anterior opening at the extremity of a low tube, the posterior a little larger, oval, and almost horizontal. Jaws equal. Lips fleshy. Cleft of mouth of moderate size, horizontal, the maxilla, which is almost concealed by the preorbital, club-shaped, and extending to beneath the posterior nostril or the anterior margin of the eye: intermaxillary processes extending backwards to between the anterior margins of the eyes, their length one third of that of the head. Length of preorbital rather more than its depth: posterior margin of preopercle feebly serrated. Upper profile of snout flat, of occiput convex. Two pairs of canines anteriorly in each jaw, those of the upper jaw subequal; the symphyseal pair in the lower jaw much smaller than the outer pair: sides of the jaws with a single series of conical teeth, six or seven in number in the upper, twelve to fourteen in the lower jaw; inside these are several irregular series of small granular teeth: a posterior canine tooth curving outwards. The dorsal fin commences above the opercular flap, and terminates a little in front of the last anal ray; the spines are strong, and each is furnished with a skinny terminal filament; they increase in length to the last, which is from 2·50–3·20 in the length of the head, and about five sevenths of the longest (sixth to eighth) rays: the anal commences beneath the eleventh dorsal spine; its spines are longer and stronger than those of the dorsal, subequal to the longest rays, but not so high as the dorsal rays, and 2·33–2·85 in the length of the head: ventral fins reaching the vent, or not quite so far, equal in length to the distance between the tip of the snout and the posterior margin of the eye, or from 1·70–1·90 in the length of the head: pectoral rounded posteriorly 1·50–1·80 in the same length: caudal slightly emarginate, without produced lobes, the pedicle deep and strongly compressed, its least height 2·50–3·00 in the height of the body. Snout, preorbital, interorbital space and preopercle scaleless; base of the vertical fins enclosed in a scaly sheath. Lateral line with a gentle curvature as far as the caudal pedicle, on which it is straight; the tubes crooked, but without branches.

Colors.—Red above, the upper surface of the head brightest, gradually passing into pale saffron below; each series of scales with a narrow, dull, reddish-brown longitudinal streak; three rows of oblong crimson spots on the back and sides, the upper one just below the base of the dorsal fin; the median and lower rows commencing close together at the posterior margin of the eye, the former following the curvature of the lateral line, the latter straight: spinous dorsal, pectorals, and ventrals pink; rayed dorsal, anal, and caudal yellow: irides silvery, with three orange spots round the pupil.

The Spotted Pigfish is even more rarely seen in the market than is *Cossyphus unimaculatus,* the same causes operating to produce the same result.

In habits and mode of life it presents no difference to its congener, but the spawning season appears to commence rather earlier in the year, as we have examined specimens in which the ova were fully developed during the latter half of July. Its flesh is equally nutritious and well flavored as that of the last species.

For some time we inclined to the opinion that the differences between *Cossyphus bellis* and *C. unimaculatus* were merely sexual, but the examination of specimens of both sexes belonging to either form has induced us to so far recede from that position as to present full descriptions of the two fishes to our readers, in the hope of eliciting further information on so interesting a subject; it must, however, be borne in mind that, notwithstanding the fact that the difference in the coloration is not always concurrent with the difference in the sexes, yet we may have here two distinct varietal races living under similar conditions and inhabiting the same waters, but which, nevertheless, preserve intact their color variations.

Broken Bay and Shoalhaven are at present the outside limits from which this form has been received. It does not appear to grow so large as the blue-spotted form, the largest examined, a female with ripe ova, measuring less than fifteen inches, while several have been observed which did not measure ten.

Genus IV.—PSEUDOLABRUS.

Pseudolabrus, Bleeker, Proc. Zool. Soc. 1861, p. 415; Gill, Proc. U.S. Nat. Mus. 1891, xiv. p. 395.
Labrichthys, Günther, Catal. Fish. iv. p. 112, 1862 (*not Bleeker.*)

Branchiostegals six: pseudobranchiæ present. Body oblong-ovate, compressed. Snout rather pointed. None of the opercular bones serrated: opercle and subopercle without a backward expansion. Jaws with a pair of canine teeth anteriorly, those of the mandible fitting in between the maxillary ones; and a lateral series of conical teeth, with an interior series of smaller teeth, destined to replace those in function when lost: posterior canines present. Dorsal fin with nine spines and eleven rays: anal with three spines and ten rays: second ventral ray the longest. Scales large: present on the opercle, and in a greater or less degree on the cheeks: forehead naked: bases of the vertical fins inconspicuously squamose. Lateral line continuous, each scale more or less branched.

Geographical distribution.—Coasts of Australia, Tasmania, New Zealand, and the adjacent islands; Chinese and Japanese Seas.

There can be no doubt that, as contended by Gill, the union by Günther of the Bleekerian genera *Labrichthys* and *Pseudolabrus* is indefensible; even, therefore, though it necessitates the renomination of all the Australasian species which we have been afforded an opportunity of examining, we are compelled to reject the generic title *Labrichthys*, now in common use, for that adopted above.

The genus *Pseudolabrus* is abundantly represented in Australian seas, and probably on no section of our coastline are they more numerous than on that of New South Wales; the great differences in coloration observable in the same species, individually, seasonally, and sexually, have, however, led to a deplorable multiplication of species by amateur ichthyologists, and a thorough revision of this genus and *Labrichthys* is urgently required.

PSEUDOLABRUS GYMNOGENIS.

Labrichthys gymnogenis, Gnth. Catal. Fish. iv. p. 117, 1862, and Ann. Nat. Hist. (3) 1867, xx. p. 66. 1867; Steindachn. SB. Ak. Wien. lvi. p. 342; Klunzing. SB. Ak. Wien, 1879, lxxx. p. 403; Casteln. Proc. Linn. Soc. N. S. Wales, iii. p. 389; Macleay, Catal. Austr. Fish. ii. p. 82.

White-spotted Parrotfish.

B. vi. D. 9/11. A 3/10. V. 1/5. P. 13. C. 12. L. lat. 25-26. L. tr. 3/8-10.

Length of head 3·60-3·66, of caudal fin 5·50-5·66, height of body 3·00-3·50 in the total length. Eye small, its diameter 4·33-5·25 in the length of the head, and 1·25-1·60 in the moderately pointed snout: interorbital space flat or very slightly convex, 1·00-1·25 in the diameter of the eye. Nostrils small, the anterior preceded by a low flap, the posterior simple. Upper profile of head almost flat, with a slight median concavity between the front margins of the eyes. Upper jaw the longer. Cleft of mouth small and almost horizontal, the maxilla reaching to beneath the posterior nostril or, in small examples, the anterior margin of the eye. A pair of anterior canines in either jaw, those of the lower subhorizontal and fitting in between the upper pair when the mouth is closed; lateral teeth gradually decreasing in size backwards, the outer series numbering eight to ten in the upper, and ten to twelve in the lower jaw; an inner series of small blunt teeth inside the laterals, probably designed to replace those, which by the nature of their food, and the means employed for obtaining it, are liable to be broken off or worn away; a few small pavement-like teeth behind the canines in both jaws: one or two posterior canines. The dorsal fin commences above the margin of the bony opercle; its spines are rather weak, but acute, and gradually increase in height to the last, which is from 2·85-3·15 in the length of the head, and 1·25 in that of the first ray; the posterior rays of both dorsal and anal are elongated, the last being the longest: the anal commences beneath the second dorsal ray; its third spine is the longest, not quite so long as the last dorsal spine ; ventral pointed, not quite reaching to the vent, the second ray the longest, from 1·90-2·10 in the length of the head ; hind margin of pectoral pointed above, cuneiform in the middle, and rounded below, the second and third rays the longest, reaching to the tenth scale of the lateral line, and from 1·25-1·33 in the length of the head : caudal emarginate, the least height of the pedicle 2·25 in the height of the body. Head naked, with the exception of the posterior half of the opercle, a series of about ten small scales on the cheek behind, and below the infero-posterior margin of the orbit, and a single large isolated scale on the temporal region ; dorsal and anal fins with a low scaly sheath. Lateral line scales profusely branched.

Colors.—Brick red, the upper surfaces washed with olive green ; body ornamented with more or less numerous round cream-colored spots ; soft dorsal and anal with a dark blue median longitudinal band, and a similar marginal one, between which are a series of spots ; posterior half of caudal and pectorals yellow, the latter with a dark blue basal band.

This is by far the least variable in coloration of all our *Pseudolabri*, the only noticeable differences being in the greater or less depth of the olive green tinting on the upper surface, the number of the spots, and the amount of rose-color with which their whiteness is suffused.

Nothing has hitherto been published regarding the breeding habits of the members of this genus, notwithstanding their abundance on our coast, and we are pleased, therefore, to be in a position to record the fact that this species deposits its ova among weed-covered rocks about midwinter, that is, the latter part of June and July.

Opinions vary as to the merits of the *Pseudolabri* from an edible standpoint, many people rejecting them, seemingly for no better reason than that, as " Parrot-fishes," they have gained a bad name, while others go to the opposite extreme, and are enthusiastic in their praise. The flesh is firm, flaky, and coarse in the fibre, with a peculiar flavor, which may or may not be appreciated, and which probably constitutes the reason why it is held in such different estimation. Described by Günther from specimens labelled "Australia," it was long known from the neighborhood of Port Jackson alone ; it has, however, been recorded since by Klunzinger from King George's Sound, the two districts being at present the only localities from whence it is known.

The White-spotted Parrotfish grows to a length of twelve inches, but is rarely seen of that size, seven to nine inches being about the average.

PSEUDOLABRUS NIGROMARGINATUS.

Labrichthys nigromarginata, Macleay, Proc. Linn. Soc. N. S. Wales, iii. p. 35, pl. iii. fig. 3, 1879.

Crimson-banded Parrotfish.

B. vi. D. 9/11. A. 3/10. V. 1/5. P. 13. C. 13. L. lat. 25-27. L. tr. 3/8. Vert. 9/16.

Length of head 3·50-3·80, of caudal fin 5·00-5·50, height of body 3·40-3·60 in the total length. Diameter of eye 5·00-5·75 in the length of the head, 1·50-1·80 in that of the moderately pointed snout, and 1·00-1·33 in the convex interorbital space. Nostrils small and slightly tubular, the anterior with a low skinny flap behind, the posterior oval and horizontal. Upper profile of head with a distinct concavity between the anterior margins of the eyes. Jaws equal. Cleft of mouth small and but little oblique, the maxilla reaching to beneath the posterior nostril, or between it and the front margin of the orbit. Opercular bones with a broad skinny flap. Both jaws with a pair of canine teeth in front, those of the mandible fitting in between the maxillary teeth when the mouth is closed, and with from eight to twelve lateral teeth on each ramus of the upper jaw, and eight to ten on each of the lower jaw, these teeth successively decreasing in size from the front: one or two posterior canines. The dorsal fin commences a little in front of the margin of the bony opercle; its spines are rather weak but acute, and gradually increase in height to the last, which is from 3·33–3·75 in the length of the head, and 1·33–1·50 in that of the first ray; the last ray is the longest: the anal commences beneath the first or second dorsal ray; its third spine is the longest, equal in length to the last or penultimate dorsal spine: ventral pointed, reaching to, or not quite so far as, the vent, the second ray the longest; its length from 1·60–2·00 in that of the head: hinder margin of the pectorals pointed above and rounded below, the intervening space concave; the second ray the longest, reaching as far as the tenth or eleventh lateral line scale, and from 1·25–1·40 in the length of the head: caudal slightly rounded, with the upper rays produced; the least height of the pedicle 2·40–2·66 in the height of the body. Posterior half of the bony opercle scaly; a single series of seven to nine small scales on the cheeks, and a single isolated scale on the temporal region; a moderate scaly sheath at the base of the dorsal fin, none on the anal; skin of the head pierced by large open pores in close proximity. Lateral line abruptly curved downwards beneath and behind the last dorsal ray; each tube with from five to seven branches before and two or three behind the curve.

Colors.—Head purple, darkest above; body purplish-green, gradually assuming a yellowish tint posteriorly; a broad crimson band generally present between the rayed dorsal and the anal; free portion of the tail dull yellow or pale olive green: spinous portion of the dorsal yellow, either blotched with red or with the base and two anterior rays purple; rayed dorsal and anal crimson with a narrow purple marginal band; the anal sometimes yellow, with a crimson blotch on the three last rays, and olive green spots inside the marginal line; outer rays of the ventrals black; pectorals yellow with a purplish blotch posteriorly, broad above and gradually narrowing below, and the upper ray dark; caudal orange.

In habits, food, &c., the Crimson-banded Parrotfish agrees in all respects with the preceding species, but we are unable to record the breeding season, no example with developed ova having as yet fallen into our hands.

Its range, so far as is known, is similarly restricted, examples having so far been known from Port Jackson, Broken Bay, and the outer reefs in the neighborhood only, in all of which it is common. It grows to a larger size than *Pseudolabrus gymnogenis*, twelve inches being a not uncommon length for the species to attain, while the largest hitherto examined measured a trifle over fifteen inches. Possibly for this reason it is held in somewhat higher estimation for the table than the other Parrotfishes.

Genus V.—CORIS.

Coris, Lacépède, Hist. Nat. Poiss. ii. p. 96, 1800.
Ophthalmolepis, Bleeker, Proc. Zool. Soc. 1861, p. 413.

Branchiostegals six: pseudobranchiæ present. Body oblong and compressed. Canine teeth anteriorly in the jaws: lateral teeth in two or more series, those of the outer row being much the larger: posterior canines present or absent.

A single dorsal fin with eight or nine spines: the anal with three. Scales small, in fifty or more transverse series; head entirely naked except in *C. lineolata*. Lateral line continuous.

Geographical distribution.—Tropical and subtropical zones of the Indian and Pacific Oceans; Mediterranean and the Atlantic seaboard from the south coast of England to Sierra Leone.

CORIS LINEOLATA.

Julis lineolata, Cuv. & Val. Hist. Nat. Poiss. xiii. p. 436, 1839.
Julis cyanogramma, Richards. Ann. Nat. Hist. (2) 1851, vii. p. 289, *and* Proc. Zool. Soc. 1850, p. 73.
Ophthalmolepis lineolata, Bleek. Proc. Zool. Soc. 1861, p. 413; Kner, Voy. Novara, Fisch. p. 258, pl. xi. fig. 1.
Coris lineolata, Gnth. Catal. Fish. iv. p. 206; Casteln. Proc. Linn. Soc. N.S.Wales, iii. p. 390.
Julis adelaidensis, Casteln. Res. Fish. Austr. p. 35, 1875.

Maori.

B. vi. D. 9/13. A. 3/13. V. 1/5. P. 13. C. 12. L. lat. 52-56. L. tr. 6/20. Vert. 10/17.

Length of head 4·10-4·25, of caudal fin 4·90-6·00, height of body 4·00-4·40 in the total length. Diameter of eye 6·00 in the length of the head 2·15 in that of the pointed snout, and 1·00-1·15 in the slightly convex interorbital space. Nostrils moderately approximate, small, rounded, and simple, directed forwards. Upper profile of head rounded. Jaws equal. Cleft of mouth small and but little oblique, the maxilla reaching to between the nostrils. A pair of strong anterior canines in each jaw, those of the mandible fitting between the maxillary pair when the mouth is closed; upper jaw with an outer row of eight or nine strong conical teeth on each ramus, inside of which are from one to three series of smaller granular teeth; lower jaw similarly armed, but with nine or ten enlarged conical teeth, and the inner teeth fewer in number; one or two posterior canines on each side. The dorsal fin commences above the middle of the opercle, and its outer margin forms a gentle curve along its entire length; the spines are slender and flexible, increasing in height to the last, which is one half longer than the first, 2·75 in the length of the head, and 1·33 in the height of the last ray, which is slightly elongated: the anal commences beneath the anterior dorsal ray; its first spine is short, the third and longest equal to the fifth dorsal spine; its rayed portion is similar to that of the dorsal: ventral fin pointed, reaching to the vent; the two outer rays are elongate, 1·70 in the length of the head; the spine is equal in length to the last dorsal spine, and five eighths of the outer ray: upper pectoral rays the longest, 1·50 in the length of the head: caudal rounded, the least height of its pedicle 2·10 in the height of the body. A few small scales behind the eye, and on the extreme upper angle of the opercle. Lateral line tubes branched.

Colors.—General colors red above, yellowish below, separated by a more or less conspicuous pink longitudinal band, which is generally bordered above and below by purplish bands; all the lower scales with a violet bar forming together more or less regular vertical streaks; upper and lower surfaces of head olive green, the sides golden, the whole traversed by blue bands which are broadest below: dorsal with four narrow longitudinal violet bands and small spots of the same color between them; an olive green blotch between the second and third spines; anal with irregular rows of violet spots separated by golden bands; caudal with violet bars between the rays; pectorals and ventrals immaculate: irides crimson.

How or why this fish obtained its vernacular name it would be difficult to say, since it is not a native of New Zealand, nor indeed is the genus represented there, so far as our present knowledge goes.

Though obtainable in the market in considerable quantities and at all seasons of the year, nothing appears to be known definitely as to time or place of its spawning. They frequent rocky shores, and are partial to sheltered spots where patches of sand are interspersed among the weed-covered rocks; in such places on a calm day they may be observed swimming slowly to and fro, and may be caught with the greatest ease by dropping a hook baited with crab or yellowtail in front of them.

Their food consists of small crustaceans, molluscs, and such other organisms as they can pick up among the rocks which they frequent. As food it is superior to the Parrotfishes.

As is the case with so many of our Labrid Fishes, the Maori, which is abundant on the coast of New South Wales—where, however, its range northwards is as yet undetermined—has not so far been included in the later lists of Victorian or Tasmanian Fishes, but reappears at Adelaide according to Castelnau (*Julis adelaidensis*), and at King George's Sound, whence it was received by Richardson and Klunzinger, while the British Museum contains examples from Swan River, West Australia; the type specimens are, however, said to have been obtained by Quoy and Gaimard at Western Port, Victoria.

The Maori grows to a length of sixteen inches.

Genus VI.—ODAX.

Odax, sp. Cuv. & Val. Hist. Nat. Poiss. xiv. p. 298, 1839.

Branchiostegals five: pseudobranchiæ present. Body elongate and moderately compressed. Snout well developed, conical. Jaws composed of numerous teeth firmly ankylosed together, and with the edge sharp: dentigerous plate of the hypopharyngeal triangular, much broader than long. One dorsal fin with sixteen to eighteen flexible spines: the anal with two or three. Scales moderate or rather small: cheeks and opercles scaly. Lateral line continuous. Airbladder of moderate size.

Geographical distribution.—Coasts of temperate Australia, Tasmania, and New Zealand.

ODAX RICHARDSONI.

Odax pullus, Cuv. & Val. Hist. Nat. Poiss. xiv. pl. ccccviii. (*not descr.*; *not Sparus pullus, Forst.*)

Odax richardsoni, Gnth. Catal. Fish. iv. p. 241, *and* Ann. Nat. Hist. 1867 (3) xx. p. 66; Casteln. Proc. Zool. Soc. Vict. i. p. 155; Klunzing. SB. Ak. Wien, 1879, lxx. p. 404; Macleay, Catal. Austr. Fish. ii. p. 107.

? *Odax hyrtlii*, Steindachn. SB. Ak. Wien, 1866, liii. p. 464; Klunzing. SB. Ak. Wien, 1879, lxxx. p. 405.

Rock Whiting.

Plate XXXVI.

B. v. D. 17-16 13-14 A. 3/11-12. V. 1/4. P. 14. C. 12. L. lat. 55-58. L. tr. 7/20.

Length of head 3·75-4·00, of caudal fin 6·00-6·80, height of body 5·50-6·20 in the total length. Diameter of eye 5·30-5·70 in the length of the head, 2·25-2·50 in that of the pointed snout, and 0·85-1·10 in the slightly convex interorbital space. Nasal apertures widely separated, the anterior circular, and protected by a low superior valve; the posterior oval, simple, pierced on a slightly higher plane than the anterior, and raised above the surrounding epiderm. Upper surface of head almost flat. Upper jaw the longer: lips fleshy. Cleft of mouth small and horizontal, the maxilla reaching midway to the eye, or a little further. Vertical limb of preopercle finely serrated. The dorsal fin commences above the base of the pectoral; the spines are flexible, and the outer margin of the spinous portion gradually increases in height, the anterior spine being four sevenths of the last, which is 2·80 in the length of the head; the tenth or eleventh rays are the longest, about one seventh longer than the longest spine, and equal to the postorbital portion of the head: the anal commences beneath the second or third dorsal ray; the third spine is the longest and equal to the second dorsal spine; the outer margin of the rayed fin is convex, the last six rays being slightly elongated, and much less branched than those preceding them: ventral short and rounded, its length 2·33-2·50 in that of the head: pectoral rounded, 2·10-2·33 in the same: caudal rounded, its pedicle 1·30-1·40 in its length behind the dorsal fin, and 2·00-2·10 in the height of the body. Scales on the cheeks in three series. Lateral line gently curved to behind the pectoral fin. Rows of distinct pores surrounding the eyes, and a series from the chin along the edge of the preopercle to its upper angle.

Colors.—Above purple or reddish-brown, deepest on the head; sides bright greenish-blue, lower surfaces bluish-white, the whole profusely spotted with orange, and sometimes with indistinct, transverse, darker bands; cheeks greenish-blue vermiculated with orange: spinous dorsal pale green, the basal half immaculate, the marginal crossed by narrow, oblique, orange or lilac bars; soft dorsal with a large black spot, often broken up into several smaller spots, occupying the greater part of the base, and with a broad purple marginal band spotted or streaked with orange; anal violet with purple and orange spots; the greater part of the ventral rays white, the membrane and tips purplish with a few large orange spots near the base; pectorals gray; caudal greenish-blue with orange spots.

This species is very similar in appearance to *Odax semifasciatus* C. & V. from which it is easily distinguished by the presence of small but constant denticulations on the preopercle; the two species are confounded by the fishermen under the common name of Rock Whiting.

It is but rarely seen in the market, its habits being similar to those of the Drummer and Kelpfish (*see p.* 41); being, therefore, free from the operations of the seine fisher, and preferring the shallow waters of sheltered bays and inlets to the outside reefs, they are but little liable to fall victims to aught but the rod and line of the amateur angler.

Their food consists of small molluscs, crustaceans, and zoophytes, and is often intermixed with small pieces of fuci, which are perhaps excised while attempting to disengage the animal attached thereto.

The Rock Whiting is common in the Port Jackson District, but from the want of local observers we are unable to say how far its range extends up the coast beyond Port Stephens, from the neighborhood of which we have received one example; to the southward it increases in numbers, and is, remarks Castelnau, "very common all the year round in the Melbourne market, and is moderately-esteemed as food." In Tasmania, as in Victoria, it is known as the "Stranger," but this name does not necessarily signify that it is a rare fish, but more probably that, as elsewhere, it is rarely caught; Johnston, writing of it, remarks ;—"The Stranger is caught occasionally in the upper waters of the estuaries of the Derwent, and is in fair estimation for the market."

Günther considers that Steindachner's *Odax hyrtlii* is the same as the present species, and, if this view be correct, which Klunzinger (*loc. cit. p.* 405) denies, its western range must be extended to King George's Sound.

Our Rock Whiting attains to a length of sixteen inches, and individuals measuring over twelve inches are of common occurrence.

Genus VII.—OLISTHEROPS.

Olisthops, Richards. Ann. Nat. Hist. (2) 1851, vii. p. 290, *and* Proc. Zool. Soc. 1850, p. 74.
Olistherops, Günther, Catal. Fish. iv. p. 243, 1862.

Branchiostegals five: pseudobranchiæ present. Body oblong and compressed. Snout of moderate extent. Jaws composed of numerous teeth firmly anchylosed together, the extreme tip only being free; no distinct teeth anteriorly: dentigerous plate of the hypopharyngeal triangular, much broader than long, with a narrow anterior process, bearing about four strongly compressed conical teeth on its anterior half; body of the bone with a median transverse band of minute pavement-like teeth, and an outer series of rudimentary teeth. One dorsal fin, with seventeen or eighteen flexible spines; the anal with two or three. Scales of moderate size; head with a few scales on and above the opercle. Lateral line continuous.

Geographical distribution.—Coasts of temperate Australia.

OLISTHEROPS CYANOMELAS.

Olisthops cyanomelas, Richards. Ann. Nat. Hist. (2) 1851, vii. p. 290, *and* Proc. Zool. Soc. 1850, p. 74 ; Macleay, Catal. Austr. Fish. ii. p. .
Olistherops brunneus, Macleay, Proc. Linn. Soc. N.S. Wales, iii. p. 36, pl. v. f. 1.

Herring Cale.

B. v. D. 17/10. A. 2/10. V. 1/4. P. 13. C. 13. L. lat. 50 L. tr. 7/15. Vert. 19/20.

Length of head 5·25, of caudal fin 5·40, height of body 4·75 in the total length. Eye small, its diameter 5·60 in the length of the head, 1·90 in that of the pointed snout, and 1·66 in the slightly convex interorbital space. Nasal apertures moderately close together, the anterior pierced in the centre of a circular depression, larger and on a slightly higher level than the posterior, which abuts upon the orbital ring ; the openings of both concealed by skin. Snout strongly convex in front, the upper surface of the head flat ; upper jaw the longer. Cleft of mouth small and horizontal, the maxilla reaching to beneath the anterior nostril. The dorsal fin commences above the base of

K

the pectoral; the spines are very flexible; the outer margin of the spinous portion is deeply concave, that of the rayed being convex; the first four spines are subequal in length. 2·40 in the length of the head; from thence they decrease to the eleventh or twelfth, which are 1·60 in the longest, the last spine being 1·10 in the same, and 1·30 in the anterior ray; the fifth, sixth, and seventh rays are the longest; the anal commences beneath the second dorsal ray; the second spine is the longest, equal to the sixth and the last dorsal spines: the outer margin is truncated, the height gradually decreasing from the first to the penultimate ray: ventral short and rounded, its length about one-half of that of the head: pectorals rounded, 1·50 in the same length: caudal emarginate, with the lobes produced considerably in male, less so in female examples; the pedicle long, its least weight 2·25 in its length behind the dorsal fin, and in the height of the body. A small patch of scales in two series on the upper margin of the opercle, and from one to three scales on the temporal region. Lateral line with a gentle curve to a little behind the pectoral fin, thence straight.

Colors.—♂ Uniform bluish-black above, lighter below: a bright blue band near the outer margin of each caudal lobe; a similar one near the upper margin of the pectoral, and a few spots of the same color sometimes present above the lateral line (*O. cyanomelas, Richards.*)   ♀ Rich brown, lighter below; all the body scales with a narrow orange margin, and generally with a dull blue central spot: head above blackish, the opercles and sides with orange and bluish vermiculated bands; below gray, with large orange spots: dorsal and anal fins reddish-brown, the former with faint olive green spots, the latter with zig-zag orange bands; ventrals and pectorals orange, with the rays blue, the latter with three blue cross bands; caudal reddish-brown with irregular blue cross bands (*O. brunneus, Mcl.*).

In habits, food, and all other characteristics this species differs in no wise from the preceding, but from examination of female specimens we are able to fix the date of the deposition of the ova approximately in August.

The type specimen was sent to Richardson from King George's Sound, where it is known to the natives by the name of "Toobitoet," or "Toobitooet," and is said to frequent rocky places and to be rarely captured. It is common on the New South Wales coast at least as far north as Broken Bay, beyond which we have no record of its occurrence, though it is doubtless found in suitable localities. Castelnau states that it is common in Victorian waters, but Johnston omits it from the Tasmanian list.

This species grows to a length of eighteen inches.

Family XX.—GERRIDÆ.

Branchiostegals six: pseudobranchiæ present. Body ovate or elevated, compressed. Eyes rather large, lateral. Opercle without spine: preopercle finely serrated or entire. Mouth in front of the snout, very protractile, directed downwards when extended. Villiform teeth in the jaws: vomer, palatines, and tongue edentulous: lower pharyngeal bones firmly united by a suture. Dorsal fin continuous: ventrals thoracic. Scales moderate, cycloid or minutely serrated, deciduous. Lateral line continuous. Airbladder present. Pyloric appendages in small numbers.

Geographical distribution.—Tropical and temperate seas of both hemispheres.

Genus.—GERRES.

Gerres, Cuvier, Règne Anim.; Cuv. & Val. Hist. Nat. Poiss. vi. p. 446, 1830.

Branchiostegals six: pseudobranchiæ present. Body oblong-ovate or elevated, compressed. Mouth very protractile, and descending when produced. Eyes rather large. Preopercle usually entire. Teeth in the jaws villiform: hypopharyngeal bones firmly united. One dorsal fin, subequally divided into nine or ten spines and ten or eleven rays, the anterior spines more or less elevated: anal with three spines and seven to nine rays: caudal forked. Scales of moderate size, cycloid or ciliated. Airbladder simple. Pyloric appendages few.

Geographical distribution.—Tropical and temperate seas, entering fresh waters.

GERRES OVATUS.

Gerres ovatus, Gnth. Catal. Fish. i. p. 343, 1859, *and* iv. p. 257; Casteln. Proc. Linn. Soc. N. S. Wales, iii. p. 391; Macleay, Catal. Austr. Fish. i. p. 76.

Silver Belly.

B. vi. D. 9/10-10/9. A. 3/7. V. 1/5. P. 15. C. 17. L. lat. 36-41. L. tr. 5/10. Cœc. pyl. 3. Vert. 10/13.

Length of head 4·60-4·90, of caudal fin 4·00-4·50, height of body 3·00-3·33 in the total length. Eye large, with an anterior adipose lid, its diameter 2·75-3·00 in the length of the head, and 1·10-1·20 in the interorbital space, which is convex: snout short, obtusely rounded, 1·10-1·20 in the diameter of the eye. Nostrils oval, approximate, pierced on a level with the upper fourth of the eye, the posterior a little the larger, and slightly higher up. Jaws, equal. Cleft of mouth, small; maxilla pyriform, extending to beneath the anterior fifth of the orbit: intermaxillary processes reaching backwards to between the middle of the orbits, their length being four ninths of that of the head. Breadth of preorbital two thirds of its depth: preopercle entire. A slight concavity on the snout; occiput convex. Jaws with a broad band of villiform teeth in front, the outer row being slightly enlarged; the band narrowing to a single row laterally: inferior pharyngeal teeth in the shape of an equilateral triangle, formed by the coalescence of the inferior pharyngeal bones; they consist of a central patch of granular teeth, broadly margined by a band of acute cardiform teeth. Dorsal fin slightly notched, the spines slender, flexible, and curved, the anterior one being strongly compressed; the second spine a little longer than the third, 1·40-1·70 in the length of the head; the remaining spines grow gradually shorter, the last being five ninths of the length of the second, and three fourths of that of the first ray; all the rays provided with a short filamentous appendage; the anal commences beneath the fifth dorsal ray; its spines are straight, stronger than those of the dorsal, the second the strongest and compressed, the third the longest, 2·33-2·75 in the length of the head: the length of the ventral is two thirds of the distance between its origin and the vent, and three fourths of the length of the head: pectoral elongate, sickle-shaped, not quite or only just reaching to the vertical from the vent, its length one third more than that of the head: caudal deeply forked, the least height of its pedicle two sevenths of the height of the body. Snout, preorbital, maxilla, and interorbital space scaleless; dorsal and anal fins without basal scaly sheath. Lateral line gently curved. Airbladder large, bifid posteriorly, and with two short horns anteriorly.

Colors.—Silvery, the back washed with bright green, which gradually dies away on the sides: fins opaline, the posterior third of the ventral golden. Irides brown.

Nothing is accurately known as to the places selected by these fishes for the deposition of their ova, but as it is well known that they are to be found only on shallow sandy flats or gently shelving shores we may conclude that it is in such localities that they spawn. This important function takes place twice in the year, the principal season being the months of December and January, this being supplemented by a winter season in July and August.

If obtained perfectly fresh they are delicious little fishes, but being very delicate they quickly deteriorate when kept, and become soft and flavorless. Their food consists of minute shellfishes, crustaceans, entomostraca, foraminifera, and the like.

They are not known to take a bait, but are sent to market in large numbers by the seine fishermen, especially during the breeding seasons; they are, however, to be found all the year round.

This species does not appear to run up estuaries to any great extent, as is said to be the case with certain of its congeners.

The range of the Silverbelly is limited to the south-eastern shores of Australia, and extends northwards at least as far as Moreton Bay, its place on the Queensland coast being taken by numerous other species; it has not been recorded from Victoria, being replaced on the southern coast by the allied *Chthamalopteryx melbournensis.* (See Proc. Zool. Soc. 1887, p. 616, fig.)

They attain to a length of eight inches.

Order II.—ANACANTHINI.

All the fin rays (except in *Gadopsis*) articulated: ventral fins, when present, jugular or thoracic. Airbladder, when present, without pneumatic duct.

Group I.—ANACANTHINI GADOIDEI.

Both sides of the head symmetrical.

Family I.—GADOPSIDÆ.

A portion of the dorsal and anal fins formed by true spines: ventrals jugular. Gill-openings wide.

Referring to the position of this unique Anacanth, Günther writes:—
"Before entering into an account of the true Gadid fishes we must intercalate the type of a separate family, which, although having every character of a Gadid, has true spines in the dorsal and anal fins, thus forming a connecting link between the Acanthopterygians and Malacopterygians. The structure of the dorsal fin, the presence of pyloric appendages, &c., prevent its being placed among the Blenniids."

One genus only.

Genus.—GADOPSIS.

Gadopsis, Richards. Voy. Erebus & Terror, Fish. p. 122, 1846.

Branchiostegals six: pseudobranchiæ present, glandular. Body moderately elongate, compressed. Snout of moderate extent, obtuse, with the upper jaw overlapping the lower. Cleft of mouth of moderate width. Gills four, with a narrow slit behind the fourth: gill-openings wide: gill-membranes not united. Both jaws with a band of small cardiform teeth, and an outer enlarged series of conical ones: small teeth on the vomer and palatine bones: tongue edentulous. One dorsal fin, the spinous portion not so long as the rayed: anal spines three: ventrals jugular, composed of a single bifid ray: caudal free. Scales very small, cyclid. Airbladder present. Pyloric appendages in moderate numbers.

Geographical distribution.—Temperate Australia and Tasmania; fresh waters only.

GADOPSIS MARMORATUS.

Gadopsis marmoratus. Richards. Voy. Erebus & Terror, Fish. p. 122, pl. lix. ff. 6–11, 1846; Gnth. Catal. Fish. iv. p. 318; Casteln. Proc. Zool. Soc. Vict. 1872, i. p. 160; Macleay, Catal. Austr. Fish. ii. p. 112; Johnston, Proc. Roy. Soc. Tas. 1882, pp. 60, 124; Woods, Fisher. N.S. Wales, p. 105.

Gadopsis gracilis, McCoy, Prodr. Zool. Vict. dec. iii. pl. 27, f. 2.

Gadopsis gibbosus, McCoy, Prodr. Zool. Vict. dec. iii.

Marbled River Cod.

B. vi. D. 10–13/ 28–25. A. 3/17–19. V. 1. P. 15. C. 16. Vert. 18/28.

Length of head 4·50–5·00, of caudal fin 6·10–6·60, height of body 5·50–6·25 in the total length. Diameter of eye 4·80–5·20 in the length of the head, and 1·33–1·50 in that of the snout: interorbital space slightly convex, 1·10–1·30 in the length of the head. Upper profile of head slightly concave before, convex behind, the eyes. Upper jaw the longer. Cleft of mouth oblique, the maxilla extending to the posterior fourth of the orbit, or between that and the hinder margin. A small, flattened, opercular spine. Both jaws with a band of small cardiform teeth and an outer series of much enlarged, widely set, conical ones; small teeth in a patch on the vomer, and in bands on the palatine bones. The dorsal fin commences above the anterior third of the pectoral; the spines increase in length to the last, which is one sixth shorter than the first ray, and 3·50–4·00 in the length of the head; the longest dorsal and anal rays are immediately in front of the last ray: the anal commences beneath the fourth dorsal ray; the spines are much stronger than those of the dorsal, the third the longest, equal in length to the last dorsal spine: ventral fin divided to the base, the inner lobe filamentous, 1·75–2·10 in the length of the head, and 2·75 in the distance between its origin and the vent, which is situated slightly in front of the middle of the total length: pectoral well developed, rounded, 1·85–2·10 in the length of the head: caudal rounded, the least height of the pedicle 2·75 in the height of the body. Scales concentrically sculptured. Lateral line following the curvature of the back, its tubes simple.

Colors.—Pale olive green or yellowish-brown on the back and sides, marbled with more or less numerous, irregular, dark brown blotches; abdominal region pale yellow, with or without blotches: vertical fins yellowish-brown blotched with darker brown; ventrals and pectorals immaculate, the latter with or without a basal yellow band: irides silvery.

This species is so variable, not only in its coloration, but also in its comparative measurements, and the number of spines and rays in the dorsal fin, that we consider the differences between the typical form and the two species described by McCoy, great as they may appear individually, to be only such as might be expected to occur in a freshwater species of wide range, and which exists under such varying conditions of life and diversities of climate. Referring to the same subject Johnston writes:—" Having closely studied the variability of the Tasmanian *G. marmoratus* I am unable to admit that the characters which distinguish *G. gracilis* and *G. gibbosus* are sufficient to separate them from Richardson's *G. marmoratus*, for the individual variations of the latter species in the North Esk and other rivers of Tasmania are greater than the differences which Prof. McCoy considers to form distinct specific characters." He then proceeds to enumerate the variations in seven individuals taken together from a spot near Corra Lynn on the North Esk; these are as follows:—Dorsal fin, 11–13/26–28; head to total length 4·0–4·9. From these data he concludes that neither of McCoy's species can be admitted, and goes on to say:—" It is very hazardous in this genus to create a new species based upon the examination of only two or three individuals"; with which remark we cordially agree.

No mention is made anywhere, so far as we have been able to ascertain, of the breeding season or the place of the deposition of the spawn of this fish, but the former doubtless differs considerably with the latitude; specimens, however, from the Bell River, Wellington, were shedding their spawn when obtained during the month of October. The ripe ova are few in number, of large size, and orange colored.

Their food consists of worms, small molluscs and crustaceans, insects, and entomostraca. They take a bait freely; but, according to Tenison Woods are " generally caught by emptying the waterholes, when the heat of summer has partially dried them up." They are said to be good eating, but, like all mud fishes, very rich and oily.

This curious fish is common in many of the rivers of the Colony, inhabiting both those of the eastern and western watersheds. It is generally known as the "Fresh-water Blackfish"; but this is so complete a misnomer that we have changed it to that given at the head of this article. At Guntawang, I am informed by Mr. Alexander G. Hamilton, it is known as the "Tailor." They are also abundant in all the streams of Victoria and South Australia, as far west as the Murray River, beyond which we have no record of their occurrence.

"In Tasmania," writes Johnston, "they are abundant in the Ringarooma, Forrester, Piper, and other rivers of the north-east, where they grow to a considerable size, and are highly esteemed as food. The species has been introduced from the north-east into the North and South Esk Rivers, and probably other streams, where they are now abundant, and afford ample sport to the angler, who cares to linger over a calm still waterhole during the hours of the night. The angler must be careful, however, to provide himself with a lantern, or his labors will be fruitless." Elsewhere the same author remarks:—"The Blackfish somewhat resembles a small Ling (*Genypterus australis*) in markings and general appearance. It is much esteemed as food, and is a welcome addition to the fare of bushmen and settlers who are far removed from the centres of population. The fishes are usually taken in considerable numbers by rod and line all the year round, the hook, baited often with the large white grub of a species of moth obtained from the 'wattle' or 'honeysuckle' (*Acacia dealbata*—*Banksia marginata*). A good take can always be relied upon in most of the northern streams, especially in the Ringarooma. * * * * The average weight runs from three to four pounds, except in the North Esk, where they run smaller than elsewhere." In connection with the natural distribution of this species in Tasmania, Johnston remarks:—"The Blackfish is found in nearly all the rivers of Tasmania which flow into Bass' Straits; their original absence in some northern streams, such as the South Esk is somewhat puzzling; but the total absence from all the other rivers and streams of Tasmania where conditions are identical, can only be explained on the principles of geographical distribution as illustrated by Darwin and Wallace." With the latter part of this quotation we cannot agree, and we think the solution of the "puzzle" will be found in the different character of the geological formations through which the stream flows, or the different composition of the water constituting such streams. As somewhat confirming this view Johnston's remark that in the North Esk, into which they were introduced, they do not grow to such a size as in their natural streams, may be quoted against him.

Discussing the sexual characters of *Gadopsis*, he tells us:—"Mr. Brown and others, who have observed our freshwater fishes closely, assert that they cannot distinguish the male from the female, although they have purposely opened hundreds of them. I have opened a good number myself, but at the time I did not know of the fact, and naturally supposed that they were ordinary females. I am inclined now to consider that they are bisexual." With this view we cannot coincide, since the specimens from Wellington mentioned were both normally developed, full-roed females.

These fishes are sometimes taken in the brackish water of tidal rivers.

The Marbled River Cod attains to a length of twenty five inches in the southern colony, but in New South Wales half that size would be considered very large.

Family II.—GADIDÆ.

Pseudobranchiæ, when present, glandular and rudimentary. Body more or less elongate. Gill-openings wide: gill-membranes generally not attached to the isthmus. One, two, or three dorsal fins, occupying as a rule the entire length of the back, the rays of the last fin well developed: one or two anal fins: caudal usually free: ventrals jugular, composed of several rays, or if reduced to a filament the dorsal is divided into two. Scales cycloid, of moderate or small size. Airbladder and pyloric appendages usually present.

Geographical distribution.—Cosmopolitan, but found in the greatest abundance in the northern temperate zone.

Günther writes:—"The family of 'Codfishes' consists partly of littoral and surface species (and they form the majority), partly of deep-sea forms. The former are almost entirely confined to the temperate zones, extending beyond the Arctic Circle; the latter have, as deep-sea fishes generally, a much wider range, and hitherto have been found chiefly at considerable depths of rather low latitudes. Only two or three species inhabit fresh waters."

Although the last sentence is undoubtedly true, it does not follow that many of the species most valuable to man do not exist in purely fresh water, and could not be artificially bred and retained therein. Day gives instances, on the authority of Lord Ducie, of Cod, Coalfish, and Pollack residing from choice in freshwater lakes fed by snow streams; while, on account of the want of ossicles connecting the airbladder with the internal ear, he advances the theory of a probable marine ancestry for the well known and highly esteemed Burbot (*Lota vulgaris*), which is now a native of the fresh waters of the temperate parts of the northern hemisphere, and never descends to the sea.

This is one of the most important families to the human race.

Genus.—LOTELLA.

Lotella, Kaup, in Wiegm. Arch. 1858, p. 88.

Branchiostegals seven (or six): pseudobranchiæ absent. Body of moderate length. Chin with a barbel. Both jaws with a series of widely set conical teeth: the upper with an inner band of villiform teeth: none on the vomer or palatine bones. Two dorsal fins, the anterior with from four to nine rays: one anal fin: ventral fins with a flat base, and composed of several rays: caudal free. Scales small. Pyloric appendages in moderate numbers.

Geographical distribution.—Coasts of south-eastern Australia and Tasmania; New Zealand and Japan.

LOTELLA CALLARIAS.

Lotella callarias, Gnth. Ann. Nat. Hist. (3) 1863. xi. p. 16; Casteln. Proc. Linn. Soc. N.S. Wales, iii. p. 391; McCoy, Prodr. Zool. Vict. dec. ii. pl. 19; Macleay, Catal. Austr. Fish. ii. p. 114.
Lotella schuettii, Steindachn. SB. Ak. Wien, 1866, liii. p. 456.
Lotella marginata, Macleay, Catal. Austr. Fish. ii. p. 114, 1881; Woods, Fisher. N.S. Wales, p. 76, pl. xxiii (*lower figure*).
? *Lotella swanii*, Johnston, Proc. Roy. Soc. Tas. 1882, p. 126.
Lotella limbata, Ogilby, Catal. N.S. Wales Fish. p. 47, 1886.

Beardie: Ling.

Plate XXXVII.

B. vii. D. 5. 60-65. A. 56-59. V. 7. P. 23. C. 23. Cœc. pyl. 16. Vert. 14/34.

Length of head 4·40, of caudal fin 10·00, height of body 4·40-4·55 in the total length : breadth of head 1·55 in its length. Eye moderate and sunken, its diameter 4·75 in the length of the head, and 1·10-1·25 in that of the snout, which is broad, very obtusely rounded, and vertically truncated in front: interorbital space flat, 1·15-1·25 in the length of the head. Nostrils pierced in a nasal fossa, approximate, the anterior circular and slightly tubular, the posterior longitudinally oval and simple. Upper profile of head slightly concave in front. Upper jaw the longer. Cleft of mouth large, the maxilla extending to or a short distance beyond the orbit : mandibular barbel half the length of the pectoral. Upper jaw with a narrow band of villiform teeth, and an outer enlarged series of rather widely set incurved conical ones ; lower jaw with a similar enlarged series, but with no villiform band, that being replaced by a limited number of small sharp teeth interspersed between the larger teeth, and forming a patch at the symphysis. The first dorsal commences midway between the origin of the pectoral and the opercle ; the middle ray is the longest, 2·40-2·66 in the length of the head : the two outer ventral rays are filamentous, the second the longer, not quite reaching to the vent, and from 1·50-1·60 in the length of the head : pectoral rounded, most of the rays terminating in hair-like filaments, its length 1·40-1·55 in that of the head : caudal rounded, the pedicle strongly compressed and attenuated, its height nowhere so great as the diameter of the eye. Fins scaly.

Colors.—Rich chestnut brown above, paler below, especially on the thoracic region : fins darker, with a narrow white marginal band ; the two outer ventral rays white.

Nothing is known as to the breeding of this species, but as in an example obtained during the first week in August the lobes of ova were only just becoming apparent we may conclude that the spawn is deposited during the summer months.

The Beardie, though common enough, is not often brought to market, since from its frequenting weedy and rocky localities, it never or very rarely comes within the scope of the operations of the seine fishers, and it is, therefore, only the few specimens which fall to the lot of the hook and line men which ever appear there.

Their food consists of small fishes, crustaceans, molluscs, and such like, and its flesh is white, flaky, and of moderate flavor, but being rather soft it is preferable, when baked, to any other mode of cooking.

It is common along the New South Wales coast south of Broken Bay, but we have no certain knowledge of the distance to which it pushes in a northerly direction, more than that it has not been recorded from the coast of Queensland. The Beardie frequents our harbors and inlets as well as the coastal reefs and bomboras, and is readily taken with a fish, crab, or prawn bait. It is " rather rare" says McCoy " in Victorian waters, but is caught with hook and line during the colder months in Port Phillip on rocky reefs in five or six fathoms water; it is sold in the markets commonly for the table, but the flesh is soft and not very good. The fishermen report the spawning time to be in April." If we are right in considering that Johnston's *L. swanii* is not specifically distinguishable from *L. callarias*, the range of that fish extends to Tasmania, where, however, it is not common.

The Beardie grows to a length of sixteen inches.

Group II.—ANACANTHINI PLEURONECTOIDEI.

Sides of the head asymmetrical.

Family II.—PLEURONECTIDÆ.

Branchiostegals six to eight: pseudobranchiæ well developed. Gills four. Body strongly compressed and flattened, with one of the sides, which is always turned upwards, colored, while the other is colorless, or at the most spotted. Both eyes (except in the very young) situated on the upper surface: sometimes they are rudimentary. The bones of the two sides of the head, though present, are not equally developed or symmetrical. The jaws and dentition may be nearly equally developed on both sides, or more so on the blind side. Dorsal and anal fins very long, undivided: pectorals present, rudimentary, or absent: caudal free, or confluent with the dorsal and anal fins. Scales present or absent. Lateral line on the colored side single, double, or triple. No airbladder.

Geographical distribution.—All temperate and tropical seas.

The "Flatfishes," as the members of this family are generally termed on account of their greatly compressed bodies, undergo remarkable changes during the earlier stages of their existence; when born they swim on edge, with the dorsal fin above and the anal below, in the same way as do most other fishes, and have then an eye on each side of the head. In a short time, however, one of the eyes makes its way round to the other side, which then becomes the upper, and subsequently the colored side, but how this transmigration is effected, whether by passing beneath the integument or by forcing its way through the intervening cartilage, is not yet clearly known.

Almost all the Pleuronectidæ are littoral fishes, very few species being found at any considerable depth; they are inhabitants of sandy shores or sandy and muddy estuaries, and though as a rule strictly marine, many species penetrate rivers far beyond the influence of the tide, while some have permanently established themselves in fresh water, and others have been acclimatized therein through human agency.

Like the preceding this family contains many species of great importance to mankind.

Genus I.—PSEUDORHOMBUS.

Pseudorhombus, Bleeker, Compt. Rend. Ac. Sc. Amsterd. 1862, xiii. Pleuronect. p. 5.
Teratorhombus, Macleay, Catal. Austr. Fish. ii. p. 126, 1881.

Branchiostegals seven: pseudobranchiæ present. Cleft of mouth wide. Gill-membranes united beneath the throat, but not attached to the isthmus. Eyes on the left side, without a free orbital edge: interorbital space not concave. Jaws and dentition nearly equally developed on both sides: teeth in both jaws of unequal sizes, and in a single row: vomer, palate, and tongue edentulous. The dorsal fin commences on the snout, its rays and those of the anal are simple. Scales of moderate size or rather small, extending on to the dorsal and anal fins. Lateral line with a strong curve anteriorly.

Geographical distribution.—Coasts of Australia, through Malaysia, to the seas of China and Japan, eastward through the Indian seas to the east coast of Africa, and westward to the Pacific coasts of Central and South America.

PSEUDORHOMBUS ARSIUS.

Pleuronectes arsius, Ham. Buch. Fish. Ganges, p. 128, 1822.
Platessa russellii, Gray. Illustr. Ind. Zool. pl.—f. 2; Cantor, Catal. Malac. Fish. p. 214.
Rhombus lentiginosus, Richards. Ann. Nat. Hist. 1843, xi. p. 495; Bleek. Pleuronect. p. 15.
Platessa chrysoptera, Richards. Ichthyol. China, p. 278.
Platessa balteata, Richards. Ichthyol. China, p. 278.
Rhombus arsius, Bleek. Beng. en Hind. p. 76.
? *Rhombus polyspilus*, Bleek. Batav. p. 203.
Pseudorhombus russellii, Gnth. Catal. Fish. iv. p. 424; Kner, Voy. Novara, Fisch. p. 283; Day, Fish. Malab. p. 172; Bleek. Atl. Ichthyol. Pleuronect. p. 6, pl. ccxxxiii. f. 2; Macleay, Proc. Linn. Soc. N. S. Wales, ii. p. 362, *and* Catal. Austr. Fish. ii. p. 124; Castelu. Proc. Linn. Soc. N. S. Wales, iii. p. 391; Woods, Fisher. N. S. Wales, p. 76, pl. xxxiii.
Pseudorhombus arsius, Gnth. Catal. Fish. iv. p. 426; Day. Fish. Ind. p. 423, pl. cxi. f. 5.
? *Pseudorhombus polyspilus*, Bleek. Atl. Ichthyol. Pleuronect. p. 7. pl. ccxxxvii. f. 3; Klunzing. SB. AK. Wien, 1879, p. 406.
Teratorhombus excisiceps, Macleay, Catal. Austr. Fish. ii. p. 126.

Large-toothed Flounder.

B. vii. D. 73-78. A. 55-60. V. 6. P. 11-12. C. 15. L. lat. 73-80. L. tr. 37/24-27. Cœc. pyl. 4. Vert. 9/28.

Length of head 4·33-4·50, height of body 2·33-2·50 in the total length. Eyes large, the upper slightly in advance of the lower, which is situated above the angle of the mouth, and whose diameter is 4·66-5·00 in the length of the head, and 1·00-1·20 in that of the snout: interorbital space reduced to a narrow elevated bony ridge. Nostrils simple; the anterior sinistral nostril small and oval, separated by a considerable space from the posterior, which is situated in front of the interorbital ridge, and on a lower level than the anterior; dextral orifice single, round. Jaws equal. Cleft of mouth oblique, the maxilla reaching to beneath the hind margin of the orbit or not quite so far, its length from 2·10-2·33 in that of the head. Upper jaw with from three to five strong conical pointed teeth anteriorly, and a single series of about twenty smaller teeth laterally; lower jaw with six strong teeth on the colored, and nine to eleven on the blind side, the two anterior pairs being the largest. The dorsal fin commences above the anterior margin of the upper eye; the longest rays are between the fiftieth and sixtieth, their length being from 2·25-2·50 in that of the head: ventral fins of equal size, separated from the anal by an interspace which almost equals their own length, which is from 2·66-3·00 in that of the head: the anal commences beneath the base of the pectoral: pectorals well developed, reaching to beyond the curve of the lateral line, the length of the left one 1·50-1·66 in that of the head: caudal cuneiform, the least height of its pedicle 4·50 in the height of the body. Scales on the colored side ctenoid, on the blind side cycloid: head scaly, with the exception of the snout, preorbital, maxilla, and interorbital space; a row of small scales between each pair of fin rays. Lateral line arched above the pectoral fins, the height of the arch 2·75 in its length; it is continued forwards by a double branch on to the front of the head, one branch passing above, the other below the eyes; a third branches upwards to about the base of the ninth dorsal ray. Gill-rakers rather short, placed at a moderate distance apart, one third of the diameter of the orbit in length.

Colors.—Yellowish-brown with or without darker blotches, which are most constant, and frequently edged with white, on the lateral line.

Although this is a common fish on our coasts, and occurs in the market at all seasons of the year, no reliable information in regard to its breeding, has hitherto been published. As, however, several specimens examined during the month of September were found to contain ova in a moderate state of development, it would appear that this is more or less a summer-breeding fish; nevertheless, it is worthy of remark that an equal number of fishes taken at the same time as those referred to above showed no trace whatever of breeding; all these examples were taken in Port Jackson by the trawl on the same day; it remains, therefore, for future investigation to decide whether these fishes are semi-annual or biennial breeders. Young flounders, up to two or three inches in length, are but rarely taken either by seine, dredge, or trawl, within Port Jackson, and it is, therefore, improbable that the spawn is deposited in shallow water near the shore; and this is borne out in some degree by the fact that but few of those sent to market contain ripe ova; from these negative data we may perhaps be allowed to draw the conclusion that, like many other Pleuronectids, the spawn is shed in the open sea, and the ova float.

These fishes show a decided preference for sandy ground at a small or moderate depth, whether on banks or on shelving shores, and although they are occasionally taken by the trawl on a muddy bottom, such an occurrence is the exception with this and the succeeding species, while it is the rule with the Black Sole (*see* p. 161). As might be expected, such a difference of feeding grounds induces a corresponding difference in flavor, those captured in pure sea water on a clean bottom being incomparably superior to those taken in muddy estuaries. In point of delicacy and sweetness we consider this fish far beyond the Sole, which has been so cried up by a very few writers that it now bears a ridiculously inflated value in the market. The food of those examined consisted solely of crustaceans and molluscs.

Like many other Flatfishes, such as the English Plaice (*Pleuronectes platessa*), our Flounders are at certain seasons gregarious and migratory; these periodical movements have, however, no connection with the functions of reproduction, but are merely caused by a common movement from deeper water shoreward and back again, and the schools consist principally of small-sized fishes.

The principal supply sent to market is taken locally with hook and line, the bait used being mackerel or yellowtail, crab, or prawn. They are not often captured by the seine, as they bury themselves so deeply in the sand that the ground rope passes over without disturbing them; with the otter trawl, however, many fine fish have frequently been caught by various scientific parties.

From the metropolitan district northward this Flounder is common in our waters, frequenting as well the harbors and estuaries, as the shelving shores of, and the sandbanks off, the coast; it is essentially a tropical species and becomes, therefore, more common as we proceed in a northerly direction. It is found along the coasts of Queensland and Northern Australia, through Malaysia to the Chinese and Japanese seas, and westward through India to the Red Sea and the east coast of Africa, at least as far south as Natal.

It attains a length of fifteen inches.

PSEUDORHOMBUS MULTIMACULATUS.

Pseudorhombus multimaculatus, Gnth. Catal. Fish. iv. p. 427, 1862; Macleay, Catal. Austr. Fish. ii. p. 125.

Small-toothed Flounder.
Plate XXXVIII.

B. vii. D 69. A. 52-55. V. 6. P. 12. C. 15.

Length of head 4·10-4·70, height of body 2·33-2·50 in the total length. Eyes prominent, the upper very slightly in advance of the lower, which is situated entirely behind the angle of the mouth, and whose diameter is 4·50-4·75 in the length of the head, and one tenth more than that of the snout: interorbital space reduced to a narrow bony ridge. Both sinistral nostrils with a low skinny margin, highest on the hinder edge of the anterior nostril, which is transversely oval, the posterior one being longitudinally oval; dextral nostrils simple, the anterior small and round, with a posterior bilobate tentacle, its lower lobe being half as long as the diameter of the orbit; the posterior much larger and cordiform. Upper jaw a little the longer. Cleft of mouth large and oblique, the maxilla reaching to beneath the posterior margin of the orbit, its length 2·50 in that of the head. Jaws with a single series of small conical teeth, a few on either side of the symphysis in the upper being the stronger, while in the lower none are enlarged; upper jaw with twenty five to twenty seven teeth in each ramus, the lower with from eighteen to twenty. The dorsal fin commences in front of the upper eye; the longest rays are between the thirty fifth and fiftieth, their height being from 2·15-2·40 in that of the head; all the rays have their tips produced, the anterior ones considerably so: ventral fins of almost equal size, that on the coloured side reaching backwards to the fourth anal ray, the second ray the longest, and more distinctly filamentous its length 2·33-2·50 in that of the head: the anal commences beneath the opercular flap: pectoral well developed, reaching to beyond the curve of the lateral line, its length from 1·50-1·80 in that of the head: caudal cuneiform, the least height of its pedicle 4·20 in the height of the body. Scales on the upper side ctenid, on the lower eyelid: head scaly, with the exception of the snout, preorbital, and interorbital space; left maxilla with several series of small scales on its postero-superior margin; a row of small scales on each of the dorsal and anal rays. Lateral line arched above the pectoral fins, the height of the arch 2·50 in its length; it is continued forwards to the upper eye, where it curves downwards to the lower one, ceasing at the junction of the maxilla and the suborbital ring; a short curved branch passes upwards from the opercle, but does not as a rule reach the dorsal fin. Gillrakers short, stout, and widely set, about one fifth of the diameter of the eye in length.

Colors.—Rich brown above, the edges of the scales with a rusty tinge, with numerous small, round, milk white spots, which are sometimes confluent, and with five dark spots on the lateral line, the second and fourth of which are the most conspicuous, each spot being closely dotted with yellow: the anterior portion of the dorsal faintly marbled, posterior with dark blotches, which are more pronounced on the outer two thirds of the fin; anal similar, but more richly colored; caudal clouded with light brown; lower surfaces white.

In several characters this species differs from the description given by Günther of his *P. multimaculatus*, to which it has been referred, and of which the habitat of the type specimens is unknown, the most important of these differences are,— the constantly larger eye, the greater number of the teeth in each ramus of the lower jaw, the character of the scales, and the different shape and length of the gillrakers; we are not, therefore, by any means satisfied that we are correct in continuing to assign to our species Günther's name.

In habits, &c., it is similar to *P. arsius*, but in the Port Jackson District it is individually more abundant, while the principal spawning season seems to be the earlier months, specimens with the ova half developed being common in the market during February and March, while an occasional example may be found in the market during May and June, in which the ova are ready for extrusion. Along with the usual molluscan and crustacean contents of the stomach we have frequently detected remains of fishes, among others *Sillago maculata* and *Hippocampus novæhollandiæ*, the presence of this latter proving that these Flounders sometimes seek their prey among weeds.

This species would appear to have but a limited range, the limits within which we can with any certainty record it being narrowed to the seaboard of New South Wales, between Botany Bay and Cape Hawke. It is true that Saville Kent records it from Queensland waters, but, if we turn to his figure, we find a fish without any resemblance to the species now under consideration; the initial point of the dorsal fin, the continuance of the membranes of the anterior rays to their tips, the shape of the ventral fin, and the small size of the pectoral fin, at once prove to anyone conversant with the fish in question, that whatever the illustration may really represent, it certainly bears little or no affinity to *P. multimaculatus*, and though our species doubtless ranges as far north as the coast of Queensland, the evidence which we have before us is not, we submit, sufficiently conclusive to warrant us in adding that colony to its habitat

The Small-toothed Flounder grows to a length of sixteen inches.

Genus II.—SOLEA.

Solea, Cuvier, Regne Anim.

Cleft of mouth narrow, twisted round to the left side. Nostrils variously formed. Eyes on the right side, the upper being partially or entirely in advance of the lower. Teeth on the blind side only, where they form villiform bands: no vomerine or palatine teeth The dorsal fin commences on the snout: pectorals present or absent: caudal free. Scales very small, ctenid. Lateral line straight.

Geographical distribution.—All temperate and tropical seas, except the southern portion of the south temperate zone; some specimens entering or permanently inhabiting fresh water.

In connection with this latter propensity Day remarks of the European Sole (*Solea vulgaris*) *—" On retaining some in fresh, and others of a like weight in saline water, the first at the end of a year were found to have increased at twice the rapidity of those which were kept in salt water." Experiments tending in this direction should be tried with all our Flatfishes.

---

* For a full account of this valuable fish, see Cunningham, " Treatise on the Common Sole."

The various members of the genus *Solea* differ greatly in the development of the pectoral fin, and the genus has been in consequence subdivided as follows:—
  A. Pectorals well developed, *Microbuglossus*.
    a. Nostrils on the blind side not dilated, *Solea*.
    b. One of the nostrils on the blind side dilated and broadly fringed, *Pegusa*.
  B. Pectorals on both sides rudimentary or small, *Buglossus*.
  C. Pectorals absent, *Aseraggodes*.
It is to the last of these sections that our species belongs.

On this subject Günther writes:—"Although the extreme forms of this genus show differences of apparently sufficient importance for generic distinction, the intermediate species are so numerous, and form so gradual a transition from the true Soles with the pectorals fully developed to the *Achiri* proper, that we prefer to consider them as one genus."

SOLEA MACLEAYANA.

Solea macleayana, Ramsay, Proc. Linn. Soc. N. S. Wales, v. p. 462, 1881.

Narrow-banded Sole.

D. 61. A. 49. V. 5. C. 18. L. lat. 102. L. tr. 36/46. & Vert. 9/27.

    Length of head 6·25, height of body 2·75 in the total length. Eyes small, the upper one half of its diameter in advance of the lower, which is situated above the angle of the mouth, and whose diameter is 2·50 in that of the snout, the length of which is one fourth of that of the head: interorbital space broad and slightly convex, about one tenth more than the diameter of the eye. Cleft of mouth crescentic. Lips naked. Dextral nostrils rising from the margin of the upper lip, the anterior one with a thick lip, the posterior opening from a tube whose length is fully two thirds of the diameter of the eye; they are situated close together, and a little nearer to the eye than to the end of the snout; sinistral nostril tubular. A few short filaments on the chin. Both jaws on the blind side with a band of minute teeth. The dorsal fin commences in front of the upper eye: two ventral fins, the right connected with the anal, the left free: the anal commences beneath the posterior margin of the gill-covers: caudal rounded, its length rather less than that of the head; the distance between the posterior dorsal, and anal rays three tenths of the height of the body. Head and body scaly, each scale strongly ctenid, bearing on both sides from six to eight strong, sharp, spinate points. Lateral line slightly arched behind the head.

    Colors.—Right side rich purplish-brown, with numerous narrow lighter bands, which frequently branch and connect with the neighboring bands, and are extended on to the margins of the fins; left side white.

    This Sole, which, for reasons previously given, does not appear in our market as regularly as its abundance warrants, is an excellent fish for the table, much preferable in our opinion to the next species. They are, however, occasionally found in considerable numbers, especially during the spring months, when they come in apparently from the open sea in shoals, all being of large size and about the same length; these school fish are very thick and firm, and of delicious flavor, but are without rudiments of spawn. Small examples measuring less than three inches are not infrequently taken in the harbor by trawl and dredge.

So far, this species has only been recorded from the limited district lying between Port Hacking and Lake Macquarie.

The Narrow-banded Sole attains to a length of eleven inches, but does not average more than eight or nine.

Genus III.—SYNAPTURA.

Synaptura, Cantor, Catal. Malay. Fish. p. 222, 1850.

Cleft of mouth narrow, twisted round to the left side. Nostrils variously formed. Eyes on the right side, the upper in advance of the lower. Teeth on the blind side only, villiform forming bands: no vomerine or palatine teeth. Vertical fins confluent, the dorsal commencing on the snout: pectorals present or absent. Scales small, ctenid. Lateral line straight.

Geographical distribution.—Indian Ocean and Archipelago; Chinese, Japanese, and Australian seas; Cape of Good Hope; Mediterranean, and the coast of Portugal. Though normally marine fishes, some species are permanantly resident in fresh water, and these forms are without pectoral fins.

The species have been subdivided thus :—
A. One of the nostrils on the blind side dilated.
B. No dilated nostril on the blind side.
   a. Pectoral fins well developed, the right being more or less the longer, *Synaptura*.
   b. Left pectoral fin rudimentary, *Æsopia*, pt.
   c. Left pectoral fin longer than the right, *Anisochirus*.
   d. Pectoral fins absent, *Achiroides*.

Our species belongs to section A.

SYNAPTURA NIGRA.

Synaptura nigra, Macleay, Proc. Linn. Soc. N. S. Wales, v. p. 49, 1881; Woods, Fisher. N. S. Wales, p. 77.

Black Sole.

Plate XXXIX.

B. vi. D. 57–62. A. 44–52. V. 4. P. d.7, s.5. C. 14. L. lat. 74–80. L. tr. 29–31/33–35. Cœc. pyl. Vert. 10/28.

Length of head 5·00–5·20, height of body 2·20–2·33 in the total length. Eyes small, the upper one half of its diameter in advance of the lower, which is situated above the angle of the mouth, and whose diameter is 2·00–2·50 in the length of the snout, which is about 3·40 in that of the head : interorbital space narrow, 1·60–2·00 in the diameter of the eye. Cleft of mouth crescentic. Lips of both sides fringed with simple papillæ of moderate length. Dextral nostrils simple and tubular, situated close together, immediately in front of the lower eye ; anterior sinistral nostril dilated, pierced in the centre of an isolated patch, which, except at the antero-superior angle, is entirely separated from the surrounding epiderm by a deep fossa, which is connected with the upper lip, and the margins of which are densely fringed with simple papillæ : posterior sinistral nostril situated in a depression which also enters the fossa, and is protected inferiorly by a densely papillose skinny flap. Inferior margin of head with numerous short simple papillæ, the posterior pair of which is much larger and more conspicuous than those preceding them. Both jaws on the blind side with a band of minute teeth. The dorsal fin commences in front of the upper eye : two ventral fins, separate from the anal, which commences beneath the middle of the gillcovers ; vent with a conspicuous papilla at its postero-superior angle : pectorals small and rounded, the right from one third to three sevenths, the left one fourth of the length of the head: caudal of moderate size and rounded, its length five sevenths of that of the head. Head, body, and fin rays scaly, each scale strongly ctenid, bearing on the right side from six to eight, on the left from three to five strong, sharp spinate points, which are much more conspicuous in young than in adult examples. Lateral line single, straight, along the middle of the body on both sides, duplicated above the middle of the gill-covers, the lower branch extending forwards a short distance along the sides of the head, the secondary branch directed upwards at right angles to the main branch, its upper half being gently arched forwards, but not quite reaching to the base of the dorsal fin.

Colors.—Right side rich dark olive brown with some large round darker blotches, and occasionally with small round yellowish or cream white spots; left side white, not unfrequently clouded with yellowish-brown or slate blue in irregular patches; vertical fins narrowly margined with white, or pale straw-color; posterior half of the dextral pectoral black.

Double examples are occasionally obtained; a beautiful example of such, having the left side equally richly colored as the right, passed through the writer's hands some years ago; it was taken in the Parramatta River by shrimpers.

This fish is the Sole of the Sydney market, and is one of the most highly priced fishes brought thither; it is tolerably common, though if the account published by the late Rev. J. E. Tenison Woods, on the authority of Mr. Edward Hill, be accurate, their numbers must have lamentably decreased within the last few years, since that gentleman mentions having taken "a hundred pairs in one morning at Woniora," up George's River, by spearing.

The Sole appears to be a purely estuary fish, never, so far as we can ascertain, having been recorded from the open sea, while Mr. Smithers, Travelling Inspector of Fisheries, states that he has on several occasions and in several localities obtained both Soles and Flounders (*Pseudorhombus*) in water, to use his own expression, "sufficiently fresh for the cattle to drink." The same gentleman specially mentions having caught them "in the Bega River well up to the Jellat-Jellat Flats," and refers to the frequent closure of the embouchure of that river, which, when lasting for any considerable time, necessarily causes the water in the upper reaches to become almost, if not absolutely, fresh, owing to the continued supply of water from the river and the shutting out of further supplies from the ocean. The Wonboyn River, which flows into Disaster Bay, is also mentioned as producing Soles, Flounders, and other marine fishes "right up to the falls"; and, refering to the freshness of the water, he further writes that "the same may be said of all the small lakes to the southward, whose outlets are nearly always closed," special reference being made to the Wallagoot and Curallo Lakes.

Returning to Port Jackson it is a somewhat significant fact that in no single instance was a Black Sole captured down the harbor on any one of the scores of trawling and dredging excursions undertaken by the authorities of the Australian Museum, though Flounders (*Pseudorhombus*), True Soles (*Solea*), Crested Flounders (*Lophonectes*), and less commonly Lemon and Marbled Soles (*Plagusia* and *Pardachirus*) were obtained; while on the other hand, when working riverwards the genera above mentioned were absent, but specimens of *S. nigra* were almost invariably captured. The Black Sole frequents localities where the bottom is formed of soft mud in preference to sandy, shelly, or mixed ground, and it is consequently a very local species, and not addicted to wandering away from its haunts.

* Erroneously "Wallanora" in Tenison Woods.

In three adult female specimens examined during the last week in May the ova were in an advanced stage of development, so that it may reasonably be concluded that the spawning season is about midwinter; in a paper, however, sent to the Royal Commission on the Fisheries of New South Wales, Mr. Lee Lord states that the best lot he ever procured were full of roe on the 21st of February; the truth of this I have verified, so that as with most, if not all, of our fishes there are two distinct breeding seasons annually, and, in the case of the Sole, the short space of time separating the two ascertained seasons points to the possibility of a third season about the end of spring. The ova are very small and numerous.

Their food principally consists of small crustaceans and molluscs, worms, and brittlestars.

As food they are undeniably good, but they do not by any means merit the high price which they always bring in the Sydney markets.

The greater number of Soles exposed for sale in Port Jackson come to hand, through the agency of the prawn fishers, from the estuaries of the rivers and creeks which fall into the headwaters of Port Jackson, Botany and Broken Bays; but there can be little doubt that if the otter trawl were in more general use in the estuaries of our rivers, the supply would be greatly augmented, and the present prohibitive price to the consumer proportionately lessened.

According to the author of the "Fish and Fisheries of New South Wales" the spear is the most prolific means of effecting its capture, but, of hundreds examined I have not noticed a single specimen in the market, which had been obtained by this means. Hill's remarks on this species, published in the above mentioned work must be received with grave suspicion, as he has evidently mixed up several species, and it is palpable that plate xxxiv of Woods' work, labelled "Sole" is a flounder (*Pseudorhombus arsius*) and plate xxxiii, labelled *Pseudorhombus russellii* is really *P. multimaculatus*. So far as I can ascertain this fish has never been known to take a bait.

The Black Sole has been recorded from the estuaries of the New South Wales coast, along the entire length of its coastline; to the northwards it occurs at least as far as Moreton Bay, according to Saville Kent, while we have Mr. Smithers' assurance of its presence in the Wonboyn river, close to the Victorian border. Mr. Lucas does not, however, include it in his "Census" of Victorian fishes; but a record of its occurrence in the Gippsland lakes is probably a mere question of time.

The ordinary marketable size of this species is from six to ten inches; but specimens of larger size are not of infrequent occurrence, especially during the summer of 1891-92, in the latter part of which Soles were more plentiful, and of a larger size than in any of the six preceding years; the largest specimen examined measured thirteen and a half inches.

Genus IV.—PLAGUSIA.

Plagusia, pt. Cuvier, Règne Anim.

Upper part of the snout produced backwards into a long hook, covering the mandible: cleft of mouth asymmetrical, rather narrow: lips of the colored side with tentacles. One nostril on the left side, before the angle of the lower orbit: none between the eyes, Eyes on the left side. Gill-opening very narrow. Teeth minute, on the blind side only : no vomerine or palatine teeth. Vertical fins confluent: pectorals absent. Scales small, ctenid. Lateral line on the colored side double or triple.

Geographical distribution.—Indian, Malayan, Australian, and Japanese seas

PLAGUSIA UNICOLOR.

Plagusia unicolor, Macleay, Catal. Austr. Fish. ii. p. 138, 1881.

Lemon Sole.

B. vi. D. 107–109. A. 81–85. V. 4. C. 8. L. lat. 102–105. L. tr. 22/23. Vert. 9/42.

Length of head 5·00–5·40, height of body 4·00–4·25 in the total length. Eyes small, the upper eye half of its diameter in advance of the lower, which is situated in front of the angle of the mouth, and whose diameter is from 3·50–3·80 in the length of the snout, which is 2·25–2·33 in that of the head: interorbital space narrow, about one third of the diameter of the orbit, slightly concave. A tubular nostril in front of the lower eye on the left side, and a similar one vertically above the anterior angle of the mouth on the right side. Rostral hook of moderate length, extending slightly beyond the lower eye. Cleft of mouth crescentic. Lower lip and anterior moiety of upper lip on the colored side fringed with stout papillæ. A distinct band of small teeth in the lower jaw on the blind side, and a few scattered minute teeth on the posterior half of the upper jaw of the same side. The dorsal fin commences in front of the upper eye; a single ventral fin confluent with the anal, which commences beneath the posterior margin of the gillcovers; caudal small and pointed, one third of the length of the head. Head and body scaly, the scales on the colored side uniformly and finely ctenid, those on the blind side with a semicircular ctenid patch on the middle of the posterior margin: fins scaleless. Two lateral lines on the left side, separated at their point of greatest distance by sixteen longitudinal series of scales, the lower one extending in an almost straight line from the tip of the snout to the base of the caudal fin, the upper from the posterior dorsal rays to the tip of the rostral hook following the curvature of the body, the two joined above the opercles by a short line traversing eleven scales; other more or less eccentric lines run from the median line downwards across the opercular region, from the chin to the inferior angle of the gill-opening, and from the base of the rostral hook to the interorbital space; right side without lateral line.

Colors—Upper side pale yellowish-brown, the body ornamented with round spots of an even lighter shade: fins profusely ornamented with brown and milk white spots, the latter disappearing in alcohol; below bluish-white.

We have included this species in the present work in the belief that with proper appliances it will be found to be common along the greater part of our seaboard, and because its flesh is firm and delicate. It is rarely taken by the seine, as it buries itself so deeply in the sand, and is so strongly compressed, that the ground rope of that net passes over it except in accidental cases; with the trawl, however, we have known it to be captured on several occasions, when the net was worked on shallow sandy flats, such being the only localities which they affect. Even if the small size of the mouth, and the shape of the elongated snout would allow of it, the nature of their food would prevent them taking any bait which would be likely to be offered to them; their stomachs generally contain a quantity of sand, among which are found numerous foraminifera, entomostraca, and such like minute organisms.

On our coast they inhabit sandy beaches and banks, on which there is but a moderate depth of water; they occur as far to the south as Wollongong, and doubtless become more plentiful as we proceed northwards. It is also included by Saville Kent in his list of the food fishes of Queensland, but he gives no information as to the extent of its range on that coast. We have also seen an example from Lord Howe Island.

The Lemon Sole grows to a length of twelve inches.

Order III.—*PHYSOSTOMI.*

All the fin rays articulated, with the exception of the first in the dorsal and pectoral fins, which are frequently more or less ossified (some genera, belonging to the *Sternoptychidæ*, have a rudimentary first dorsal): ventrals, when present, abdominal and spineless. Airbladder, when present, with a pneumatic duct (except in the Scombresociform Fishes).

Family I.—SILURIDÆ.

Margin of upper jaw formed mainly by the premaxillaries. Maxilla rudimentary, frequently constituting the base of a barbel. Barbels always present. No subopercle. Adipose fin present or absent. Skin scaleless, either smooth or covered with osseous plates, or with small tubercles. Airbladder, when present, either free in the abdominal cavity, or more or less enclosed in bone, and communicating with the organs of hearing through the medium of the auditory ossicles.

Geographical distribution.—Inhabitants of the fresh waters of the temperate and tropical regions, some species entering the sea, but not venturing far from land.

Group I.—PLOTOSINA.

Gill-membranes not confluent with the skin of the isthmus, or united to it by a narrow strip only, remaining more or less separate. Dorsal divided into two portions; a short anterior with a strong spine, and a long posterior which, like the anal, is confluent with the caudal: ventrals multiradiate. A dendritic postanal apparatus.

Genus.—CNIDOGLANIS.

Cnidoglanis, Günther, Catal. Fish. v. p. 27, 1864.

Branchiostegals eleven? Gill-openings wide, the membranes united below the throat, and attached to the isthmus along the entire median line; the second and third branchial arches with a series of long cartilaginous processes covering the base of the gill laminæ on the sides facing each other. Head depressed. Cleft of mouth transverse. Eyes small. Nostrils remote, the anterior tubular and on the front edge of the snout, the posterior simple. Barbels eight. Teeth conical in the upper jaw, molariform on the vomer, and mixed in the lower jaw. Two rayed dorsals, the first with one spine and four or five rays: a pectoral spine.

Geographical distribution.—Rivers and coasts of Australia.

CNIDOGLANIS MEGASTOMA.

Plotosus megastomus, Richards. Voy. Erebus & Terror, Fish. p. 31, pl. xxi, ff. 1-3.
Cnidoglanis megastoma, Gnth. Catal. Fish. v. p. 27, *and* Study of Fish. f. 258; Casteln. Proc. Linn. Soc. N. S. Wales, iii. p. 392; Macleay, Catal. Austr. Fish. ii. p. 144; Woods, Fisher. N. S. Wales, p. 81.
Chæroplotosus decemfilis, Kner, Voy. Novara, Fisch. p. 300, pl. xiii, f. 1. (*an Plotosus limbatus*, Cuv. & Val. Hist. Nat. Poiss. xv. p. 122.)

Estuary Catfish.

B. xi. 1 D. 1/4. 2 D. + C. + A. 222-234. V. 10. P. 1/9. Vert. 12/52.

Length of head 4·15, height of body beneath the origin of the second dorsal 8·00 in the total length. Head broad and depressed, its breadth 1·30 in its length. Eye small, entirely covered by the skin: interorbital space a little concave mesially. Nostrils widely separate, the anterior, which is pierced on the summit of a slight eminence, small, circular, and situated on the front of the snout; the posterior a narrow longitudinal slit pierced behind the base of the nasal barbels which reach to or slightly beyond the posterior margin of the orbit; all the barbels rather short, those of the maxilla reaching as far or not so far back as the nasal barbels; the outer mandibular barbels are the longest, and are compressed and broad basally, as also are the inner; their length is equal to the postorbital portion of the head. Lower lip broad and pendent, with a pair of lateral lobes on each side, the upper of which, situated at the angle of the mouth, frequently resembles a small barbel. Premaxillary teeth conical, forming two small circular patches; mandibular teeth molariform, with an outer conical series, in two much larger spatuliform patches; a large subcordate patch of molariform teeth on the vomer. The first dorsal fin when laid back reaches slightly beyond the origin of the second; its spine is moderately strong, feebly serrated in front, its length 2·00 in the postorbital portion of the head: ventral fin not quite reaching to the origin of the anal, its breadth at the base 1·60 in its length: pectoral spine feebly serrated, longer and stronger than that of the dorsal.

Colors.—Dark brown above shading into dirty white below, when frequenting muddy estuaries: stone gray or clouded yellow blotched and marbled with deep rich brown when on sandy ground.

The Estuary Catfish breeds during the spring months, and the ova are few in number and of large size. Hill's account of the breeding habits refers to the River Catfish. *Copidoglanis tandanus*, and is copied by Tenison Woods. It is common in our bays and estuaries, and, although a well flavored fish, is unsaleable except at a nominal price to foreign sailors or Chinese, owing to a prejudice caused by its appearance. Their food consists of small fishes, squid, cuttlefishes, and other molluscs, prawns, &c. It is taken by hook and line, seine, and trawl, and is nocturnal in its habits; care should be taken in handling these fishes, as they are both able and willing to inflict a severe wound by means of the serrated spines of both the first dorsal and the pectoral fins. Mr. Hill remarks, "Not only is the pain intense, but the after consequences are generally grave," and he gives an instance from personal knowledge, of an Aboriginal whose hand having been wounded by one of these fishes, had, through inflammation having set in, to have his arm amputated; that so extreme a case as this is very rare, is, however, undoubted, as we have ourselves on one occasion been rather badly cut, and have seen others of our party similarly injured, while incautiously searching among the *débris* of the trawl or dredge, and in no case were the after effects more unpleasant than might be conjectured when the saw-like nature of the weapon is taken into consideration; it is probable, however, that, should any of the mucus remain in the wound, it would produce considerable irritation in the part affected; immediate and careful washing would, however, obviate this.

This species is common in all the estuaries and bays of the metropolitan district, but, owing to its unsaleable qualities, it is difficult to trace the limits of its distribution. It has not, however, been recorded by the naturalists of

Queensland, Victoria, or Tasmania, nevertheless, an element of uncertainty on this subject is imparted by the fact that the British Museum possesses a specimen from Kangaroo Island, and the only recognised island of that name lies off the coast of South Australia.

This Catfish grows to a length of thirty inches.

Family II.—SCOPELIDÆ.

Branchiostegals generally numerous: pseudobranchiæ well developed. Margin of upper jaw formed by the premaxillaries. Opercular apparatus sometimes incomplete. Gill-openings very wide. Barbels absent. Two dorsal fins, the posterior adipose. Scales present or absent. Eggs enclosed in the sacs of the ovaries, and excluded by oviducts. Intestinal canal short. Airbladder present or absent. Pyloric appendages normally few.

Geographical distribution.—Pelagic or deep sea fishes, chiefly of the tropical and temperate zones.

Genus.—AULOPUS.

Aulopus, Cuvier, Règne Anim.

Branchiostegals numerous: pseudobranchiæ well developed. Gill-openings very wide. Head and body rather elongate, slightly compressed. Cleft of mouth very wide: maxilla well developed, dilated posteriorly. Eye of moderate size. Teeth small and cardiform, present on the jaws, vomer, palatine and pterygoid bones, and on the tongue. Dorsal fin situated midway along the body, rather elongate, with fifteen or more rays, some of the anterior being produced into a long filament in the male: a small adipose dorsal: anal of moderate length: ventral and pectoral fins well developed, the former with nine rays, and inserted close behind the pectorals, beneath the anterior dorsal rays: caudal forked. Scales of moderate size. Airbladder absent. Pyloric appendages in small numbers or numerous.

Geographical distribution.—Seas of temperate Australia; Mediterranean and the neighboring parts of the Atlantic.

AULOPUS PURPURISSATUS.

Aulopus purpurissatus, Richards. Icon. Pisc. p. 6, pl. ii. fig. 3, 1843; Guth. Catal. Fish. v. p. 403; Casteln. Proc. Zool. Soc. Vict. 1872, i. p. 172; McCoy. Prodr. Zool. Vict. dec. vi. pls. 54, 55; Macleay, Catal. Austr. Fish. ii. p. 157; Woods, Fisher. N. S. Wales, p. 82, pl. xxxv.
Aulopus milesii, Cuv. & Val. Hist. Nat. Poiss. xxii. p. 519, pl. DCL.

Sergeant Baker.
Plate XL.

B. xiv.–xv. D. 19–21. A. 12. V. 9. P. 11. C. 18. L. lat. 49. L. tr. 5/7–8. cœc. pyl. numerous. Vert. 32/16.

Length of head 3·75–4·10, of caudal fin 5·50–6·00, height of body 6·00–6·33 in the total length. Eye rising above the upper surface of the head, its diameter 5·20–5·50 in the length of the head, 1·60–1·80 in that of the moderately long and pointed snout, and 1·00–1·33 in the interorbital space, which is deeply concave. Nostrils large and approximate, the anterior circular and with a broad, skinny valve on its hinder margin; the posterior, oval, horizontal, and patent. Upper profile of head, along the median line, flat. Lower jaw very slightly projecting. Cleft of mouth large and oblique, the maxilla extending to beneath the posterior margin of the eye or a little beyond it. Both jaws with a band of cardiform teeth, the inner series being much the larger; vomer and palatines with similar teeth biserially arranged, those of the latter being the largest in the mouth, and with an anterior and lateral row of much smaller teeth; pterygoids with an oval, tongue with an elongate, patch of villiform teeth. The dorsal fin commences above the fifth scale of the lateral line, and ends above the twenty fifth; the length of its base is rather less than the distance between its origin and the tip of the snout; the first ray is short, two sevenths (*in the* ♀) of the second, which is the longest, 1·90–2·00 in the length of the head; the middle rays are the shortest, one or two of the posterior ones being as long as the third or fourth rays, the outer margin of the fin being thus concave; *in the* ♂ the second and third rays are produced into long filaments, the length of the second being equal to the distance between its base and the adipose fin or between that and the base of the last ray; the adipose fin is small and rounded, three times as high as long, and situated above the thirty sixth or thirty seventh scale of the lateral line: the anal commences slightly behind the termination of the dorsal, and the length of its base is equal to the space between its origin and the base of the last dorsal ray; the second ray is the longest, not equal in length to the middle dorsal rays; its outer margin is slightly convex: the ventral reaches to the vent; the four outer rays are simple, the fourth the longest, 1·20–1·33 in the length of the head: pectoral rather small, reaching to the twelfth or thirteenth lateral line scale, 1·75–1·90 in the same: caudal forked, the least height of its pedicle equal to its breadth immediately in front of the fin, and about one third of the height of the body. Scales moderate, cycloid, adherent; occiput, snout and preorbital scaleless: basal two thirds of adipose fin scaly, the other fins without scales. Lateral line straight, the tubes unbranched.

Colors.—Upper surfaces purple with a more or less prevailing tinge of red and with the edges of the scales crimson, and the top of the head sometimes spotted with the same color; back and sides with large irregular crimson spots or transverse bands covering two or three scales in width, not reaching across the abdomen; the sides are of a paler purplish-red than the back, and gradually merge into the pearly white of the abdominal region: dorsal and caudal fins pale yellowish-red obliquely banded with rows of crimson spots, which are frequently confluent on the caudal lobes; adipose fin basally purple, terminally crimson; anal white or pale straw-color with orange longitudinal bands; ventrals and pectorals yellow with crimson transverse bands.

The Sergeant Baker—so named probably from having been first obtained after the founding of the settlement by a sergeant of that name—frequents moderately deep water on the outside reefs, but is rarely taken inside Port Jackson. It is not an uncommon fish, but as those which find their way to the Sydney market are with rare exceptions taken by the Snapper fishers the supply is never equal to the demand. In examining a series of fresh specimens taken at all seasons of the year two points are likely to strike the observer, namely, that the stomach is almost invariably empty, and that it is exceedingly rare to find ova in any stage of development in the ovaries; in the few cases in which we have been able to detect such the ova were in a very early stage, and these occurred during the spring months. It is a good fish for the table, the flesh being white, firm, flaky, and well flavored.

The range of this beautiful fish is very imperfectly known; so far it has only been recorded from the coast line of New South Wales south of and including the metropolitan district, and it is omitted from the lists of Queensland and Tasmanian fishes, while McCoy states that it is rare in Hobson's Bay.

The Sergeant Baker attains to a length of twenty four inches.

Family III.—SCOMBRESOCIDÆ.

Branchiostegals variable : pseudobranchiæ glandular, concealed. Margin of upper jaw formed mesially by the intermaxillaries and laterally by the maxillaries. Barbels present or absent. Hypopharyngeals united into a single bone. Dorsal fin opposite to the anal, in the caudal section of the vertebral column, with or without posterior finlets : no adipose dorsal. Body scaly : a keeled row frequently present along each side of the free portion of the tail. Airbladder generally present, simple, sometimes cellular internally, without pneumatic duct. Stomach not distinct from the intestine, forming together a straight undivided tube with or without pyloric appendages.

Geographical distribution.—Carnivorous and herbivorous fishes, belonging to the tropical and temperate zones, for the most part marine, but with many species entering or even inhabiting fresh water.

Genus I.—BELONE.

Belone, Cuvier, Règne Anim.

Branchiostegals generally numerous. Gill openings wide. Body elongated, subcylindrical or compressed. Eyes lateral. Jaws prolonged into a slender beak, the upper of which is formed by the premaxillaries, which are united by a longitudinal suture. Both jaws with fine teeth or roughened, and with a single series of long, pointed, widely set teeth : vomer and palatines with or without teeth. The anterior dorsal rays may or may not be elevated, while the middle and posterior ones may be short or elongate : no finlets. Scales small. Lateral line on the free portion of the tail with or without a keel. Airbladder large. No pyloric appendages.

Geographical distribution.—Temperate and tropical seas of both hemispheres; many species entering and some resident in fresh waters.

As food the members of this genus which find their way to the Sydney market are excellent, but here, as elsewhere, a prejudice exists against them in many quarters on account of the green color of the bones, a character which appears to be constant in all the known species. They are exceedingly voracious, and being very swift in their movements are correspondingly destructive to all small fishes swimming high in the water.

Both of the species here described belong to the section in which the gill-rakers are wanting, and for which the name *Tylosurus* has been proposed.

BELONE FEROX.

Belone ferox, Gnth. Catal. Fish. vi. p. 242, 1866; Castelu. Proc. Linn. Soc. N.S. Wales, iii p. 239. *and* iii p. 394 ; Macleay, Catal. Austr. Fish. ii. p. 176 ; Woods, Fisher. N. S. Wales, p. 83, pl. xxxvi.

Slender Long Tom.

B. xi. D. 21-22. A. 25-26. V. 6. P. 12. C. 15. Vert. 57/32.

Length of head 3·33-3·75, of caudal fin 11·50-12·00, height of body 15·00-18·66 in the total length : breadth of body 1·20-1·40 in its height. Diameter of eye 2·75-3·00 in the postorbital portion of the head, 6·00-6·80 in the distance between its anterior margin and the tip of the upper jaw, and from 1·10-1·25 in the interorbital space, which is flat. Preorbital elongate, with the inferior margin straight, its height 4·00-4·40 in its length. Maxilla scarcely expanded behind, with an acutely rounded angle posteriorly, its hinder portion partially concealed by the preorbital, and reaching to beneath the anterior third of the orbit. Lower jaw the longer. Upper surface of head flat, with a median groove, broadest in front, between the base of the upper jaw and the occiput: supraciliary and occipital striæ feeble or obsolete: lateral margins of occiput sharply ridged. No well marked preorbital pores. Jaws with an outer band of minute teeth, and an inner band of strong conical teeth twenty-five to twenty-nine in number in the upper, twenty four or twenty five in the lower jaw. The distance between the origin of the dorsal and the base of the caudal is 4·60 in that between the same point and the tip of the upper jaw, or equal to that between the anterior margin of the eye and the same; the dorsal commences above the seventh or eighth anal ray; both fins are falciform, the second ray the longest, that of the dorsal 1·40 in the anal ray; the posterior dorsal rays are not elongate, the length of the last being about one third of the distance between its base and that of the caudal; the base of the dorsal is 1·30 in that of the anal, and the distance between the origin of the two fins is but a trifle less than the longest anal ray: the distance between the origin of the ventral and the base of the caudal is 1·50–1·75 in that between the same point and the tip of the lower jaw; its length is rather less than the height of the body, 2·25 in the distance between its origin and the vent, and 1·33 in the postorbital portion of the head: the pectoral is rounded behind, its length equal to the distance between its base and the posterior margin of the orbit, 3·33–3·80 in the length of the head, and one third longer than the height of the body: caudal truncated, the lower lobe the longer; its pedicle broad and depressed above and rather acutely rounded below, its height much less than its width immediately behind the dorsal fin, and without lateral keel. Scales small, thin, and adherent; cheeks and entire cephalic groove scaly. Gillrakers absent.

Colors.—Above bright green with violet reflections, below silvery; a broad well marked steel blue band from the axil of the pectoral to the base of the caudal, becoming fainter beyond the origin of the anal; a bright blue band in front of the vertical margin of the preopercle: dorsal, caudal, pectoral, and elongated rays of anal fins purplish; rest of anal and ventrals gray.

Both species of Long Tom are common on our coast, and are to be found in the Sydney market during every month of the year, coming in to the bays and harbors at irregular intervals in shoals of greater or less magnitude; they are, however, always present during the spring and early summer months, at which time they are engaged in spawning, and for this purpose they apparently frequent the shallower parts of harbors, while the ova are of large size, and consequently few in number. During the months of September and October we examined four specimens of this fish, from each of which the ova were exuding, and in each case the right ovary was found to be fully developed, while that on the left side was empty. Nothing is known about the deposition of the spawn in our species: but it is doubtless similar to that of the common European Garfish*, of which Day gives the following account:—"The eggs of many have filaments springing from their outer covering, which enable numerous ova either to adhere together in a mass or attach themselves to contiguous objects, preventing thus their subsidence into the mud." And again:—"These eggs when extruded must float in the

---

* This name properly belongs to *Belone*, but with the usual perversity of the fishing community they persist in according it to the *Hemirhamphus*, which should more correctly and naturally be termed the Halfbeak.

sea with their long filaments waving about until they meet with some object to which they can attach themselves; or they may serve to bind together large numbers of eggs into one mass and fix such to some suitable substance."

Like all predacious forms, which swim high in the water with great velocity, necessitating great muscular exertion, these fishes are very voracious, and their digestion being equally rapid they are among the worst enemies of all such species as they are able to swallow; nor, according to reliable authorities do they hesitate to attack much larger fishes than they could by any means make a meal of, since the conformation of their jaws would prevent them tearing the body of their victim to pieces; as an instance Day relates, *fide* Clogg, Zoologist, June 1874, p. 4160, how a Salmon, Peal was entirely transfixed by a Garfish (*Belone vulgaris*) through the thickest part of the body. As a rule the specimens which we have examined have the stomach empty, but in some cases small fishes were found.

In the report of the Royal Commission the statement is made, and subsequently reiterated by Tenison Woods and others that the Long Tom will not take a bait; this may be the case, but such abnegation would be entirely subversive of the nature and known habits of the genus, and there can be little doubt that if whiffing—as practiced for Mackerel, Yellowtail, and the Tasmanian Barracouta, and Kingfish (*Thyrsites*)—were indulged in when Long Toms were about, many would be caught and good sport would result to the amateur fishermen, with the addition to the *menu* of a firm and well flavored, though rather dry fish; it is hardly necessary to say that the color of the backbone, which is bright green both before and after cooking, does not in any way affect the wholesomeness of the flesh. This peculiarity is apparently common to most of, if not all, the species of *Belone*.

The slender Long Tom has not been recorded as yet beyond the limits of New South Wales, for though Saville Kent states that eight species occur on the Queensland coast, he considers that *Belone depressa*, Poey, is the common Moreton Bay form, the "remaining species being most abundantly represented in the intertropical zone," which could hardly be the case with so common a New South Wales fish.

They attain to a length of three feet.

BELONE MACLEAYANA.

Belone gracilis, Macleay, Catal. Austr. Fish. ii. p. 179, 1881 (*not Lowe nor Schlegel*).
Belone macleayana, Ogilby, Catal. N. S. Wales Fish. p. 53, 1886.

Stout Long Tom.
Plate XLI.

B. xiii. D. 20–21. A. 19–21. V. 6 P. 13–14. C. 15. Vert. 52/28.

Length of head 3·33–3·50, of caudal fin 10·00–10·50, height of body 13·00–15·75 in the total length: breadth of body 1·00–1·33 in its height. Eye rather small, its diameter one third of the postorbital portion of the head, from 6·50–6·90 in the distance between its anterior margin and the extremity of the upper jaw, and from 1·33–1·66 in the interorbital space, which is flat. Preorbital elongate and curved, its height 2·00–2·60 in its length. Maxilla expanded behind but with an acute postero-inferior angle, its posterior two thirds completely concealed by the preorbital, and reaching to beneath the anterior two thirds of the orbit. Lower jaw the longer. Upper surface of head with a shallow median groove between the occiput and the upper jaw: occiput moderately striated, the striæ diverging from a pair of lateral centres: posterior half of occiput deeply grooved laterally. A series of large pores near the hinder margin of the preorbital. Jaws with an outer band of fine teeth and an inner series of moderately stout conical ones. The distance between the origins of the dorsal and the caudal is 3·30–3·75 in that between the same point and the tip of the snout, and equal to or less than that between the posterior margin of the eye and the tip of the lower jaw; the anal commences in front of the dorsal; both fins are falciform, and the anterior rays of the former are one sixth higher than those of the latter; the posterior dorsal rays are elongate, and extend backwards to the base of the caudal; the bases of the two fins are subequal, and the distance between their origins is 1·33–1·66 in the height of the longest anal rays: the distance between the origin of the ventral and the base of the caudal is 1·40–1·66 in that between the same point and the tip of the lower jaw; its length is rather more than the height of the body, from 1·75–2·20 in the distance between its origin and the vent, and five sixths of the postorbital portion of the head: the pectoral is rounded behind; its length is equal to or not quite so much as the distance between its base and the posterior margin of the orbit, 3·25–3·50 in the length of the head, and from one eighth to two fifths longer than the height of the body: caudal emarginate, with the lower lobe produced: its pedicle much depressed, about as high as wide, one third of the height of the body, and without, or with hardly recognisable lateral keel. Scales small, thin, and deciduous; cheeks and anterior half of cephalic groove scaly.

Colors.—Dark green above, silvery below, the snout blackish: dorsal and caudal fins yellowish-green more or less distinctly tipped with black, the pectoral yellow with the outer third distinctly black; elongate anal rays and ventrals pale yellow, the latter more or less clouded.

This species differs in no wise in its habits, breeding, &c, from *Belone ferox*, and is equally common and equally irregular in its appearance, while the ova are shed during the same months.

Their distribution, so far as is known, and the size to which they grow is also similar.

Genus II.—HEMIRHAMPHUS.

Hemirhamphus, Cuvier, Règne Anim.
Arrhamphus, Gunther, Catal. Fish. vi. p. 276, 1866.

Branchiostegals numerous. Gill-openings wide. Body elongate, slender, and slightly compressed. Eyes lateral. Lower jaw more or less produced beyond the upper, which is short, the premaxillaries forming a triangular plate. Both jaws with a narrow band of minute teeth: no vomerine or palatine teeth. All the dorsal and anal rays connected by a membrane. Scales large or of moderate size. Intestinal tract simple. Airbladder large. No pyloric appendages.

Geographical distribution.—Tropical and temperate seas, many species entering fresh waters.

We do not think that the single unimportant character of a less produced lower jaw in *Arrhamphus sclerolepis* is sufficient to separate that species generically from *Hemirhamphus*, the transition from the long and slender-beaked forms to the short-beaked being gradual. Young *Hemirhamphi* have both jaws short.

HEMIRHAMPHUS INTERMEDIUS.

Hemirhamphus intermedius, Cantor, Ann. Nat. Hist. 1842, ix. p. 485; Richards. Ichthyol. China, p. 264; Gnth. Catal. Fish. vi. p. 260; Macleay, Catal. Austr. Fish. ii. p. 181; Johnston, Proc. Roy. Soc. Tas. 1882, pp. 91, 132; McCoy, Prodr. Zool. Vict. dec. xiv. pl. 135; Sherrin, Handb. N.Z. Fish. p. 33; Woods, Fisher. N. S. Wales, p. 84, pl. xxxvii. (*upper figure.*)

Hemirhamphus melanochir, Cuv. & Val. Hist. Nat. Poiss. xix. p. 41 (18); Casteln. Proc. Zool. Soc. Vict. i. p. 179, 1872, *and* Proc. Linn. Soc. N. S. Wales, iii. p. 391.

Sea Garfish.

Plate XLII.

B. xiv. D. 15-16. A. 18. V. 6. P. 12. C. 15. Vert. 36/20.

Length of head 3·20-3·40, of caudal fin 8·50-9·00, height of body 11·50-12·33 in the total length: breadth of body 1·15-1·25 in its height: length of lower jaw beyond the extremity of the upper one half or more than one half of the length of the head, and 6·10-6·40 in the total length: the length of the upper jaw measured along the median line, is from 1·00-1·20 in its breadth at the base. Eye moderate, its diameter 1·66-1·90 in the postorbital portion of the head, from 1·60-2·00 in the distance between its anterior margin and the tip of the upper jaw, and from 1·10-1·25 in the flattened interorbital space. Height of preorbital equal to, or but little less, than its length. Maxilla expanded behind, completely concealed posteriorly by the preorbital when the mouth is closed, and extending to beneath the middle or the posterior margin of the nasal fossa, which is pyriform in shape, with a rounded posterior angle, which does not extend beyond the anterior margin of the orbit. Both jaws with a broad band of small tricuspid teeth, the median cusp being the longest. The distance between the origin of the dorsal fin and the base of the caudal is 3·90 in that between the same point and the tip of the upper jaw, or equal to the length of the head without the lower jaw; the anterior dorsal rays are not quite so high as those of the anal, and are about three fourths of the distance between the origins of the two fins: the anal commences a little behind the origin of the dorsal, and the bases of the two fins are of equal length: ventral small, the distance between its origin and the base of the caudal equal to that between the same point and the posterior angle of the base of the pectoral; its length less than that of the postorbital portion of the head: pectoral pointed, its length equal to the height of the body, and 3·25-3·60 in the length of the head: caudal fin moderately forked, the lower lobe the longer; the least height of the pedicle 3·33 in the height of the body. All the scales very deciduous, except those posterior to the origins of the vertical fins, which are more or less persistent. Lateral line with sixty perforated scales, which are profusely branched inferiorly.

Colors.—Back bright green, with three narrow dark brown streaks from the occiput to the origin of the dorsal, immediately in front of which the three meet; a silvery lateral band, broadest posteriorly, and margined above by a narrower lead-colored band; lower surfaces pale greenish-silvery: posterior part of the ventrals and the pectorals dusky.

In the Report of the Royal Commission we find the following statement:—"The ordinary Sydney Garfish (*H. regularis*) comes in from the sea in the latter end of summer to deposit its spawn in suitable spots in the harbor." As we have pointed out in our account of the River Garfish (*see* p. 174), the authors of the above report have apparently confused the two species, and the season given as that in which the ova are shed is too late, for these fishes may be found distended with ripe ova at any date between the latter half of September and midsummer. The ova are very large, globular, and of a pale yellow colour.

These fishes are greatly and deservedly esteemed as one of the most delicious forms belonging to the Colony; the flesh is white, flaky, and delicate. Their food, so far as can be ascertained from the many hundreds examined by us consists almost entirely of a small green weed, among which, however, minute crustaceans and molluscs are frequently to be found, but whether these latter are taken in accidentally along with the weed, or that the latter is swallowed for the sake of the animal life is not quite apparent; Australian writers, however, seem to prefer the former theory; be this as it may, it will be seen below that the Sea Garfish can be caught with fish bait.

In this Colony we are indebted for our supplies entirely to the seine net, and so important is the fishery that special provision is made to allow of a small-meshed net for the capture of these fishes during the winter months; they are abundant along our coasts throughout the year, but are in best condition and most plentiful from January or February to about October, at which time they for the most part retire to the open sea. Hill states that this species is known to the professional fishermen as "Ballahoo."

It is found in large quantities along our whole seaboard, and is always in demand at remunerative prices. Its range is very wide, comprising the whole coast line of Australia, Tasmania, and New Zealand; it is abundant at certain seasons round Lord Howe Island, where they are taken in vast numbers, and are greatly esteemed; they are also found throughout the Malay Archipelago, northward to the Chinese seas. Castelnau states that it is "one of the commonest fishes in the Melbourne market, during all seasons of the year," and he also records that young specimens are often found in the brackish waters of the lower Yarra. Johnston says of its presence in Tasmanian waters:—"It is found in great abundance in the shallow waters of estuaries during the summer months, and is most highly esteemed in the market. It does not ascend within the influence of the fresh water so freely as the other migratory fishes, and its capture by the seine is not affected by the closing of the upper waters of the estuaries. * * * The fish may be captured at any time between April and October."

Among the Maories this Garfish is known as the "Ihi" or "Heihe," while in Auckland it goes by the name of Piper. Sherrin, quoting from a writer in the *Field*, tells us how angling for Garfish is carried on there :—"In many parts of New Zealand they swarm in the estuaries at certain seasons of the year, and may be caught three and four at a time with a light, stiffish rod and fine tackle. I look on the Piper as *the* float fish of New Zealand, for, though you may have plenty of fun with others here and there, it is the only one which really requires a float to keep the bait in proper position. The bait to begin with is a tiny bit of beef or mutton, wherewith you catch, most probably, a so-called "herring," which is not a herring at all, but which serves your purpose. Scaling it and cutting a wee triangular bit out of its side, and hooking it so as to make it play nicely, you fish till you catch a Piper, and then you cut little triangular bits out of *his* side to entrap his brethren." He further remarks :—" In Dunedin they are most plentiful during the months of October and November according to Mr. Thompson's records; and in some years are remarkably abundant, large shoals being in the lower harbor for several days together, when they are caught in nets." He also notices their gradual diminution in Auckland Harbor of late years.

The Sea Garfish attains a length of eighteen inches.

HEMIRHAMPHUS REGULARIS.

Hemirhamphus regularis, Gnth. Catal. Fish. vi. p. 261, 1866; Casteln. Proc. Linn. Soc. N. S. Wales, iii. p. 394; Macleay, Catal. Austr. Fish. ii. p. 181; Woods, Fisher. N. S. Wales, p. 84, pls. xxxvii. (*lower figure*) and xxxviii.

River Garfish.
Plate XLIII.

B. xi. D. 15. A. 17. V. 6. P. 11–12. C. 15. L. lat. 58. L. tr. 8. Vert. 34/19.

Length of head 3·20–3·33, of caudal fin 7·00, height of body 10·00–10·66 in the total length: breadth of body 1·33–1·50 in its height: length of lower jaw beyond the extremity of the upper one half of the length of the head: the length of the upper jaw, measured along the median line is from 1·40–1·60 in its breadth at the base. Eye large, its diameter 1·40 to 1·60 in the postorbital portion of the head, and from 1·25–1·50 in the distance between its anterior margin and the tip of the upper jaw: interorbital space flat, equal to or very little less than the diameter of the orbit. Height of preorbital about four fifths of its length. Maxilla broadly expanded behind, the expanded portion entirely concealed by the preorbital when the mouth is closed, and extending to beneath the anterior margin of the nasal fossa, which is cordiform, with the posterior angle acute, and reaching to above the anterior margin of the pupil. Both jaws with a broad band of small tricuspid teeth, the median cusp being much the longest. The distance between the origin of the dorsal and the base of the caudal fins is from 3·50 in the distance between the same point and the tip of the upper jaw, or equal to the length of the head without the lower jaw; the anterior dorsal rays are equal in length to those of the anal, and eight ninths of the distance between the origins of the two fins: the anal commences on the same vertical plane as the dorsal: ventral small, the distance between its origin and the base of the caudal equal to that between the same point and the posterior margin of the eye; its length equal to that of the postorbital portion of the head: pectorals pointed, from 2·66–3·00 in the length of the head, and equal to the distance between the anterior margin of the eye and the hinder margin of the opercle: caudal fin moderately forked, the lower lobe a little the longer; the least height of the pedicle three eighths of the height of the body. Scales on the anterior two thirds of the body deciduous, on the last third persistent.

Colors.—Back pale green, the upper surface of the head darker with golden reflections; three narrow black vertebral streaks not extending backwards to the dorsal; two similar but irregular and broader streaks between these and the broad lateral silvery band, which is bordered above by a narrow orange streak; a faint black spot at the base of the pectoral.

The River Garfish is said to deposit its ova in still lagunes or the brackish water near the mouths of rivers among thick weeds to which the ova probably adhere by means of filamentous appendages; as with its congener the ova are of large size and consequently few in number.

This species, probably through the uncertainty caused by the lax way in which the trivial name is used in the Royal Commission Report, and which laxity and its concomitant error has been perpetuated to the present day, is frequently said to be a better flavored fish than *H. intermedius*; this is not the case, the flavor of the ocean species being undoubtedly much more delicate than that of the present species which being a permanent resident in muddy estuaries and lagunes retains a flavor of its surroundings.

In habits, food, &c., this Garfish differs in no way from the preceding, but it has not so extensive a range, the tropical and subtropical parts of Australia being so far the only recorded habitat of the species. On our own coast it is abundant at least as far south as Illawarra, but beyond that place the limit of its range is undefined. It is not recorded from Victoria or Tasmania; there is a specimen from West Australia in the British Museum.

The River Garfish rarely exceeds twelve inches in length.

HEMIRHAMPHUS SCLEROLEPIS.

Arrhamphus sclerolepis, Gnth. Catal. Fish. vi. p. 260, 1866; Macleay, Proc. Linn. Soc. N. S. Wales, ii. p. 364, *and* Catal. Austr. Fish. ii. p. 184.

Hemirhamphus krefftii, Steindachn. SB. Ak. Wien, 1867, lvi. p. 332, pl. i.

Short-beaked Garfish.

Plate XLIV.

B. xi. D. 13–15. A. 15–17. V. 6. P. 13–14. C. 15. L. lat. 48–53. L. tr. 9. Vert. 31/17.

Length of head 4·66–4·85, of caudal fin 5·40–5·80, height of body 7·00 to 7·50 in the total length: breadth of body 1·33–1·50 in its height: the length of the lower jaw beyond the extremity of the upper is equal to that of the latter measured along the median line, which is 1·66 in its breadth at the base. Diameter of eye 1·66 in the postorbital portion of the head, 1·50–1·66 in the distance between its anterior margin and the tip of the upper jaw, and 1·25–1·50 in the interorbital space, which is very slightly convex. Height of preorbital equal to its length. Maxilla expanded behind, completely concealed posteriorly by the preorbital when the mouth is closed, not extending to the vertical from the middle of the nasal fossa, which is subcircular in shape and broadly enters the eye. Both jaws with a broad band of small tricuspid teeth. The distance between the origin of the dorsal fin and the base of the caudal is 3·45–3·60 in that between the same point and the tip of the upper jaw, and a little less than the length of the head without the lower jaw: the anterior dorsal rays are equal in length to those of the anal, and are five sixths of the distance between the origins of the two fins: the anal commences slightly in front of the origin of the dorsal, and the bases of the two fins are of equal length: ventral moderate, the distance between its origin and the base of the caudal but a fraction less than that between the same point and the tip of the lower jaw; its length equal to that between the orbit and the upper angle of the base of the pectoral: pectoral pointed, its length equal to the height of the body, and 1·50–1·66 in the length of the head: caudal fin moderately forked, the lower lobe the longer; the least height of the pedicle 2·25 in the height of the body. Scales everywhere persistent. Lateral line tubes with small branches inferiorly.

Colors.—Bright green above, the head darkest, pale green below; sides with a broad well defined silvery band.

The Short-beaked Garfish occurs occasionally in large numbers during the winter months among consignments sent to market from our northern rivers. Those which we have examined in August had the roe very slightly developed, and we may therefore conclude that the deposition of the spawn takes place during the early summer months.

It is a much stouter and more fleshy fish than either of its congeners, and is quite as delicious for the table as *H. intermedius*. The contents of the stomach were similar to that of the others.

This species was first described by Günther from examples supposed to have come from New Zealand, but it is doubtful if that locality is correct. On our coast odd examples are occasionally taken in Port Jackson and Botany Bay in company with the Sea Garfish, but they are not found in any numbers south of the Richmond and Clarence Rivers district. In Moreton Bay, Saville Kent says " that it is taken, but that it is more plentiful further north." The collectors to the Challenger Expedition obtained this species in fresh water in the Mary River.

The Short-beaked Garfish attains a length of fourteen and a half inches.

Family IV.—GALAXIIDÆ.

Branchiostegals in varying numbers: pseudobranchiæ absent. Margin of the upper jaw formed chiefly by the premaxillaries, which are short and continued by a thick lip, behind which are the maxillaries. Barbels absent. Belly rounded. No adipose fin: dorsal fin opposite to the anal, in the caudal section of the vertebral column. Body naked. Airbladder large and simple. Pyloric appendages in small numbers. The ova fall into the cavity of the abdomen before extrusion.

Geographical distribution.—Freshwater fishes of small size, belonging to the southern hemisphere.

Genus.—GALAXIAS.

Galaxias, Cuvier, Règne. Anim.
Mesites, Jenyns, Voy. Beagle, Fish. p. 118, 1842.

A series of conical teeth in the jaws, on the palatine bones, and along each side of the tongue: teeth on the tongue hook-like.

Geographical distribution.—Southern half of Australia, Tasmania, New Zealand, southern portion of south America, and the Falkland Islands.

GALAXIAS COXI.

Galaxias coxii, Macleay, Proc. Linn. Soc. N. S. Wales, v. p. 15, 1880.

Cox's Mountain Trout.

B. vi. D. 11. A. 13. V. 7. P. 13. C. 16. Vert. 35/24.

Length of head 5·25-5·33, of caudal fin 6·33-6·75, height of body 5·40-6·33 in the total length: greatest breadth of body 1·50 in its height. Eye small, its diameter 5·00-5·50 in the length of the head, 1·60-1·75 in that of the obtusely rounded and depressed snout, and 1·80-2·00 in the interorbital space, which is flat. Lower jaw a little shorter than the upper: cleft of mouth deep and oblique, the maxilla reaching to the vertical from the middle of the eye, or rather beyond. Body stout. The dorsal fin is rather pointed, its height being 1·33-1·50 in the length of the head, and slightly less than the distance between its origin and that of the anal: the latter fin commences beneath the middle of the dorsal, and is a little higher and has a more rounded margin than that fin, and when laid back reaches to or beyond the origin of the caudal: the base of the ventral fin is rather nearer to the origin of the middle caudal rays, than to the tip of the snout, and its length is 1·75 in the distance between its base and the vent, and 1·40-1·50 in the length of the head: the length of the pectoral is equal to or a trifle more than the distance between its origin than that of the ventral: caudal emarginate in half grown, truncated in adult, examples; the least height of the pedicle 1·60 in the distance between the dorsal and caudal fins.

Colors.—Upper surfaces yellowish-brown the head darkest, with the operculum dusky, and an inconspicuous, oblique, dark bar below the eye; sides pale greenish-yellow, with numerous, narrow, irregular, vertical stripes, which are frequently broken up into spots especially on the caudal region; abdominal region pinkish-white; a conspicuous black spot above the base of the pectoral, and a dusky blotch in front of the caudal; under the lens the entire body, head, and fins appears to be powdered with dusky dots: fins orange, the dorsal, caudal, and pectorals more or less dusky basally: irides orange.

During the latter part of March and the beginning of April the ova, which are small and exist in very large numbers, are ready for extrusion; at this season they conceal themselves and refuse to take a bait, though during the summer months they greedily snap at any flesh bait offered, and are even said to rise at any small substances floating on the surface; it is probable, therefore, that they would rise to a small trout fly. As the waters in the deep gullies which they frequent is very cold during the spawning season, it is probable that the ova do not mature until the succeeding spring.

Their food consists principally of small water insects, but portions of worms, grasshoppers, crickets, and such-like are eagerly seized when used as bait. They are excellent little fish for the table.

Cox's Mountain Trout was originally described from examples taken in the streams flowing from Mount Wilson and emptying into the Grose River; we have since received it from streams in the neighborhood of Springwood, and since these empty into the Nepean, Macleay's conjecture that it does not occur in the tributaries of that river is not borne out; it is more probable that this species is common to all suitable streams in that section of the Blue Mountains. Their favorite haunts are the cool, shady pools, margined by overhanging rocks, in the clear streams flowing down the deep and secluded gullies of that district. At Springwood it is known as the Mud Gudgeon, a most inappropriate name.

This species attains to a length of eight inches, and finds its nearest allies in the Tasmanian *G. truttaceus* and the New Zealand *G. fasciatus*.

Family V.—CLUPEIDÆ.

Clupeidæ, pt. Cuvier, Règne Anim.
Clupeoidei, Müller, Arch. f. Natur. 1843, p. 324.

Gill-openings usually very wide: pseudobranchiæ, when present, well developed. Abdomen generally compressed into a sharp edge, which is usually serrated. Opercular apparatus complete. Eyes lateral, with or without an adipose lid. Margin of the upper jaw formed mesially by the premaxillaries, and laterally by the maxillaries, which are composed of three pieces not ossified together. The mouth may have a deep cleft, with small premaxillaries, an elongated maxilla, and either the upper or the lower jaw projecting; or it may be transverse. Fin rays articulated. A single dorsal with a moderate or small number of weak rays: anal sometimes many-rayed. Body covered with scales: head generally naked. Lateral line usually absent. Stomach with a blind sac. Airbladder more or less simple. Pyloric appendages, when present, numerous.

Geographical distribution.—Almost all seas, many species periodically ascending rivers, and some permanently resident in fresh water.

M

Group I.—CHATOËSSINA.

Mouth transverse, inferior or subinferior, narrow, and toothless; upper jaw overlapping the lower. Abdomen serrated.

Genus I.—CHATOËSSUS.

Chatoëssus, sp. Cuvier, Règne Anim.
Chatoëssus, Cuv. & Val. Hist. Nat. Poiss. xxxi. p. 94.

Branchiostegals five or six: pseudobranchiæ present. Body compressed, oblong-ovate, with the abdominal serrature extending forward into the thoracic region. Mouth anterior, the cleft small and more or less transverse: snout obtuse or obtusely conical, more or less projecting beyond the jaw: maxillary coalescent with the ethmoid, its upper portion being behind the premaxillary. Teeth none. Eyes with free adipose lids. Dorsal fin situated opposite to the ventrals: anal of moderate length, or rather long. Scales of moderate size.

Geographical distribution.—Coasts and fresh waters from Australia, through Malaysia, eastward to India, and northward to China and Japan; North and Central America.

CHATOËSSUS RICHARDSONI.

Chatoëssus erebi, Casteln. Proc. Zool. Soc. Vict. i. p. 184 (*not Gunther*).
Chatoëssus richardsonii, Casteln. Proc. Zool. Soc. Vict. ii. p. 144; Macleay, Proc. Linn. Soc. N. S. Wales, iv. p. 369; Woods, Fisher. N. S. Wales, p. 106.

Bony Bream.

B. vi. D. 15. A. 20. V. 7. P. 15. C. 17. L. lat. 45. L. tr. 17.

Length of head 5·10, of caudal fin 4·75, height of body 3·00 in the total length. Eye rather small, with the adipose lid moderately developed, though not reaching the pupil, in front, rudimentary behind; its diameter 4·50 in the length of the head, a little longer than the rather obtuse snout, and 1·25 in the convex interorbital space. Nostrils approximate, pierced in a lateral groove midway between the tip of the snout and the orbit; the anterior small, elliptical, and vertical; the posterior large and subcircular. Upper profile of head flat, bordered by an elevated hexagonal ridge, which commences on the snout, and touching the supraciliary ridge, passes on to the extremity of the occiput, where it forms an obtuse angle with its fellow. Upper jaw the longer. Cleft of mouth small and transverse, the maxilla reaching to beneath the anterior third of the orbit. Opercle feebly striated. The distance between the origin of the dorsal and the tip of the snout is 1·15 in that between the same point and the base of the caudal; the first dorsal ray is minute, the second short; thence they increase in length to the fifth, which is but little longer than the fourth and sixth, and 1·25 in the length of the head; the last ray is divided to the base, the anterior portion being short and branched, the posterior filiform, expanded at the base, and extending back to above the termination of the anal fin: the anal is falciform, the third ray the longest, 2·00 in the length of the head; the last ray is similarly constructed to that of the dorsal, but the filiform portion is short, barely half as long as the longest ray: the ventrals are inserted beneath the anterior dorsal rays; the upper rays are the longest, 1·80 in the length of the head: pectoral pointed, its length equal to that of the longest branched dorsal ray: caudal forked, the least height of the pedicle 3·60 in the height of the body. Scales pitted and feebly carinated, each with a low vertical basal ridge: a triangular scale, about equal in length to the diameter of the orbit, above the insertion of the ventral; abdominal scutes well developed, seventeen in front and thirteen behind the origin of the ventral. Gillrakers short, fine, and closely set, eighty five on the lower limb of the outer branchial arch, the longest one third of the diameter of the eye.

Colors.—Silvery, the back with a bluish tinge; head with a golden gloss tip of the ventrals dusky.

Except that in the only fresh specimen which we have been able to obtain while engaged on this work, there are six branchiostegal rays, and that the ventral fins are situated beneath, not in front of the anterior dorsal rays, we should have unhesitatingly placed Castelnau's species as synonymous with *C. erebi*, but until we have the opportunity of examining a series of authenticated examples from the rivers of New South Wales we conceive it to be in the best interests of the science to keep them provisionally distinct.

None of the authors who have written of this species make any mention of its breeding habits, and we are, therefore, left entirely in the dark as to this important function. These fishes are only taken by net, and, though well flavored, are but little used by the white population on account of the excessive number of bones contained by them. Castelnau, however, remarks that it is much esteemed in the Melbourne market, where it sells at a high price, but is very scarce. Blandowski states that the Murray River Aborigines call it "Mamur"; and adds that it "leaps frequently out of the water, and is easily caught by its elongated ray in thin, fine nets laid by the natives horizontally on the water. * * * In June and July it is considered a delicacy by the natives and forms their principal food during these two months." Macleay says:—"The name in the Wooradjerie language" (that of the Murrumbidgee Aboriginals) "is 'Ka-ee-ra'; it is not common, and is considered too bony to be an article of food. I never tasted it but once, and then I found that, though the flavor was delicate enough, it was such a mass of bones as to make it useless as an article of food."

This species, in the restricted sense in which we are here keeping it, is a native of the Murray River and its tributaries.

It grows to a length of sixteen inches.

Group II.—CLUPEINA.

Upper jaw not overlapping the lower. Abdomen serrated.

Genus II.—CLUPEA.

Clupea, sp. Artedi, Gen. Pisc. 1738.
Clupea, Cuvier, Règne Anim.

Branchiostegals five to ten: pseudobranchiæ well developed. Body compressed, oblong or somewhat elongated, with the abdominal serrature extending forward into the thoracic region. Mouth anterior or antero-superior, the cleft small or of moderate width; upper jaw not projecting beyond the lower. Eyes with free adipose lids. Teeth, when present, rudimentary or deciduous. Dorsal fin situated opposite to the ventrals: anal of moderate extent, with less than thirty rays: caudal forked. Scales of large, moderate, or rarely of small size. Pyloric appendages in large, moderate, or small numbers.

Geographical distribution.—Cosmopolitan; many species entering, and some residing in, fresh water.

CLUPEA SAGAX.

Clupea sagax, Jenyns, Voy. Beagle, Fish. p. 134, 1842; Gnth. Catal. Fish. vii, p. 443; Casteln. Proc. Zool. Soc. Vict. 1872, i. p. 187; Macleay, Proc. Linn. Soc. N. S. Wales, iv., p. 371; Woods, Fisher. N. S. Wales, p. 86; Sherrin, Handb. N.Z. Fish. p. 71.
Alosa melanosticta, Cuv. & Val. Hist. Nat. Poiss. xx. p. 444 (*not Schlegel*).
Meletta cærulea, Girard, Proc. Acad. Nat. Sc. Philad. 1854, p. 138, *and* U.S. Pacif. R.R. Exped. Fish. p. 330, pl. lxxv. ff. 5–7.
Alosa musica, Girard, Proc. Acad. Nat. Sc. Philad. 1854, p. 199, *and* U.S. Nav. Astron. Exped. Zool. p. 246, pl. xxxi. ff. 1–4.
Harengula punctata, Bleek. Verh. Bat. Gen. xxv. Japan, p. 49 (*not Cuv. & Val.*)
Alausa californica, Gill, Proc. Acad. Nat. Sc. Philad. 1862, p. 281.
Alosa fimbriata, Kner. & Steindachn. SB. Ak. Wien, 1867, liv. p. 386, pl. xv. (*not Spratella fimbriata, Cuv. & Val.*)

Pilchard.

Plate XLV.

B. vii. D. 18–20. A. 18–20. V. 8. P. 15. C. 17. L lat. 50–55. L. tr. 12–13. Vert 19/31.

Length of head 4·33–4·75. of caudal fin 5·50–6·00, height of body 5·75–6·75 in the total length. Eye moderate, with well developed adipose lid reaching to the pupil both in front and behind, its diameter 3·66–4·00 in the length of the head, and 1·10–1·25 in that of the snout, which is compressed and moderately pointed: interorbital space flat, 1·50–1·80 in the diameter of the eye. Nostrils with a single orifice only, which is situated a little nearer to the tip of the snout than to the orbit. Upper surface of head flat, with a median longitudinal groove and lateral ridges, which form two groups of striæ on the occiput. Lower jaw very slightly projecting. Cleft of mouth moderate and oblique, the maxilla reaching to the vertical from the anterior third of the eye. Opercle with very distinct radiating striæ, descending towards the subopercle. Teeth none. The distance between the origin of the dorsal and the snout is from 1·05–1·15 in that between the same point and the base of the caudal; fifth and sixth dorsal rays the longest, 1·75–2·00 in the length of the head; outer edge of the fin slightly emarginate; its basal length not so long as the longest rays: anal fin low, with the anterior rays the longest, and the last two slightly produced; its basal length rather more than that of the dorsal: ventral inserted slightly behind the middle of the base of the dorsal, its length 2·75–3·00 in that of the head: pectoral pointed, truncate posteriorly, 1·60–1·75 in the same length: caudal deeply forked, the least height of its pedicle 2·50–2·75 in the height of the body. Scales deciduous, finely striated: abdominal scutes not much developed, about seventeen in front of, and eleven behind the origin of the ventrals. Gillrakers fine, long, and closely set, equal in length to the diameter of the eye.

Colors.—Dark blue above, changing rather abruptly into the silvery of the sides; a series of round blackish spots along the middle of the sides.

Though in all probability but few of the inhabitants of New South Wales are aware of the fact, we have off our coast two species of Clupeid fishes, the Southern Pilchard and the Maray (*see* p. 186) which annually pass northwards along our shores in what is described as incredible multitudes; these are allowed to go absolutely free, and thus a valuable source of national wealth, and an almost exhaustless supply of excellent food is allowed to escape without an effort to utilise it, nor need we hope to see any improvement on the present deplorable state of affairs until we import a race of fishermen who will not be afraid of venturing to sea to reap the abounding harvest there awaiting them.

Though the great abundance of this species has been known for many years, it will probably astonish and perplex the members of less sleepy communities—we are referring to matters connected with our fisheries only—to hear that during a constant attendance on our market for a space of eight years we could count on the fingers of one hand the number of Pilchards which have found their way thither.

Günther states that "this species is so closely allied to the European Pilchard that it might be more properly described as a climatal variety," and this error is copied again and again by subsequent writers on Australian fishes; as, however, there are not more than thirty series of body scales in *C. pilchardus*, nor less than fifty in *C. sagax* it is manifest that there can be no possible resemblance between the two species. Day also points out that whereas Günther gives seven as the number of pyloric appendages in the Pilchard that species possesses them in large numbers, and deduces therefrom that the example from which Günther took his description was a Sprat, that being the only British species of *Clupea* in which so small a number is found.

Macleay remarks:—"The usual time, so far as I can ascertain from the fishermen, of its annual visit to the coast of New South Wales is in June and July, but it is not easy to fix the time within a few weeks. . . . The shoals are described as enormous, covering miles of sea and accompanied by flights of birds and numbers of large fishes. These shoals are generally observed from one to three miles from the land, and are always proceeding in a *northerly* direction." Tenison Woods, alluding to their scarcity in our market, says:—"Herrings are rarely seen in our markets, but this is due to the fact that the shoals do not, as a rule, enter our harbors, and to fish for them in the open sea requires appliances not at present in the possession of our fishermen."

On the Victorian coast, McCoy and Castelnau notice the occurrence of this fish at various dates between August and January, and the former, in the International Exhibition Essays, 1866-67, gives an account of an extraordinary visitation which took place in Hobson's Bay during August of the former year; he writes:—"They arrived in such countless thousands that carts were filled with them by simply dipping them out of the sea with large baskets. Hundreds of tons of them were sent up the country to the inland markets, and through the city for several weeks, they were sold for a few pence the bucketful, while the captains of the ships entering the bay reported having passed through closely packed shoals of them for miles. As to how far west of Victoria it extends its wanderings we have no means of ascertaining, but it is common on the coast of Tasmania, but not so much so as the Sprat."

Speaking of its abundance in New Zealand waters, Hector remarks:—"This is a true representative of the Herring kind in these seas, and it visits the east coast of Otago every year in February and March, and when the schools migrate they extend as far as the eye can reach, followed by a multitude of gulls, mutton birds, barracouta, and porpoises. So densely packed are they in some years, that by dipping a pitcher in the sea, it would contain half fish; so that if large boats and suitable nets were employed, thousands of tons could be caught. In the beginning of April they appear in Queen

Charlotte Sound, and are caught in large numbers, and converted into the highly esteemed Picton Herring." Mr. Fell is quoted by Sherrin as saying:—"The fish is found all round Queen Charlotte Sound, and also the adjoining Pelorus, but is only caught here (Picton). Generally it is believed that they do not breed outside, but my half-caste fisherman maintains that, if sought for properly, they would be found all round Blind Bay, and in the Strait. They are not easy fish to find unless they are rushing to the surface, which is not often, and is a most peculiar sight. These Herrings are in Queen Charlotte Sound during the whole year, but only come into shallow bays during the winter. At that time of year they keep together in large shoals, but in summer time they keep more apart, and are sometimes caught then, though rather hard to find. No systematic fishing goes on during the summer; the fish prefer colder water, and thus leave the shallow bays when spring sets in. They spawn during summer, and are always full of roe about Christmas time, and then keep in small shoals. As to the probable numbers visiting the Sound it is difficult to say, but four smoke-houses were kept going all last winter (1882). The hauls made average from one and a half to two tons, but at times ten tons have been landed." Sherrin remarks:—"They appear only occasionally in the Dunedin market. They are very abundant in the Auckland waters, and especially so at the Thames, which Mr. Wilson considers to be one of the best fishing stations in the Colony. They come in large shoals, but no attempts have been made to catch them." Mr. Donald Sutherland states that "there are large shoals of Pilchards at the head of Milford Sound. They are from six to ten inches long, and finished spawning on the second or third of December. Tons of them are on the beach in Freshwater Basin."

The above is practically all we know of a species which, with little expenditure of energy and capital, might be made a source of almost incalculable wealth to those Colonies on whose shores it occurs in such prodigious numbers.

Beyond the limits of the Australasian Colonies this species has still a wide range, being found in the seas of Japan, and along the Pacific coast of America, from the shores of California to those of Chile.

They attain a length of at least ten inches.

CLUPEA SUNDAICA.

Clupea sundaica, Bleek. Atl. Ichthyol. Clup. p. 105, pl. cclxxi. f. 5; Macleay, Proc. Linn. Soc. N. S. Wales, iv. p. 373; Woods, Fisher. N. S. Wales, p. 86.

Herring.

Plate XLVI.

B. vi. D. 18. A. 20–21. V. 8. P. 15. C. 19. L. lat. 44–45. L. tr. 12.

Length of head 4·90–5·25, of caudal fin 3·66–4·25, height of body 3·60–4·00 in the total length. Eye rather large, with the adipose lid equally developed before and behind, just or not quite reaching to the pupil, its diameter from 2·90–3·10 in the length of the head: snout obtuse, 1·30–1·40 in the diameter of the eye: interorbital space flat, 1·20–1·40 in the same. Nostrils approximate, situated nearer to the tip of the snout than to the orbit, the anterior minute and circular, the posterior large and subcrescentic. Upper surface of head flat, bordered by a raised ridge, which is split up into numerous striæ on the outer margins of the opercles. Chin prominent. Cleft of mouth small and transverse, the maxilla reaching to beneath the middle of the orbit. Opercle and preopercle feebly striated inferiorly. A single series of minute teeth on either side of the symphysis in both jaws; a few small teeth anteriorly on the palatines; tongue with a median toothed ridge. The distance between the origin of the dorsal and the tip of the snout is 1·20 in that between the same point and the base of the caudal; the fourth dorsal ray is the longest, 1·25–1·40 in the length of the head; the outer margin of the fin is subtruncate, the posterior rays being the shortest; the basal length of the fin is a little less than the longest ray: the anal is low, the anterior rays the longest, the posterior ray thickened; its basal length 1·20–1·33 in that of the dorsal: the ventrals are inserted beneath the middle of the dorsal fin, the outer ray is the longest, 2·00–2·15 in the length of the head: pectoral pointed, its length 1·25 in the same: caudal deeply forked, the least height of the pedicle 2·75–3·00 in the height of the body. Scales deciduous, each with four or five irregular vertical striæ: a triangular scale, about four sevenths of the diameter of the orbit in length, above the insertion of the ventral: abdominal scutes strongly developed, seventeen or eighteen in front of and twelve or eleven behind the insertion of the ventrals. Gillrakers moderately stout and closely set, about half the diameter of the eye in length. Airbladder large and simple.

Colors.—Upper surface blue, the head brownish-yellow, sides and lower surfaces silvery, from one to three more or less distinct golden bands along the upper half of the sides: fins hyaline, the tip of the dorsal and of the caudal lobes blackish: irides golden.

The Herring, though passing northwards in enormous shoals during the mid-winter months, but rarely enters our harbors and inlets in any numbers, and though a few may be seen in the market during any month of the year, generally associated with *Gerres ovatus*, no attempt is made to obtain a regular supply, and these vast communities, from whence come and whither bound we know not, pass on their way untithed. At this season they are in fine condition and full of roe, and are delicious for the table, its flesh being beautifully white and delicate.

In his paper on the *Clupeidæ* of Australia Macleay says:—" Like *Clupea sagax* this species visits our coasts in winter in enormous shoals, which are also always travelling in a northerly direction. It seems probable, however, from what the fishermen tell me, that its breeding grounds are not far distant, as some of them are to be found in the Hawkesbury, about Mullet Island, at all seasons of the year, and the young fry of apparently the same species are sometimes very abundant there." Alluding to the subject of the latter part of this quotation, Tenison Woods adds:—" The same Herring is rather common in the Upper Hunter at all seasons, but it is small. At West Maitland the anglers value the fish for sport, though it very seldom exceeds seven inches in length; but it is delicious eating. It is best caught with the common house-fly dropped gently upon the water and moved along the surface with caution." We have never seen the species here referred to, and are sceptical as to its being *C. sundaica*, while the fry, mentioned by Macleay are possibly *Diplomystus sprattellides*[*] or young *D. novæhollandiæ*, the former of which is sometimes very abundant in the Hunter River.

This species, which was originally described from the Celebes and Java by Bleeker, is found along the northern and eastern seaboard of Australia, and grows to a maximum length of nine inches.

---

[*] See Records of the Australian Museum, ii. p. 24.

Genus III.—DIPLOMYSTUS.

Diplomystus, Cope, Bull. U. S. Geol. Surv. Terrs. 1877, p. 808.

Branchiostegals eight: pseudobranchiæ present. Body elongate and compressed, with the abdominal serrature extending forward into the thoracic region, and with a corresponding dorsal serrature between the occiput and the origin of the dorsal fin: the dorsal scutes with a single median tooth. Jaws equal, or the lower slightly projecting. Cleft of mouth moderate. Adipose lid not much developed. Teeth present on the jaws, palate, and tongue, or absent. Ventrals inserted in front of, or beneath the anterior fourth of the dorsal: anal of moderate length: caudal forked. Scales of moderate size. Pyloric appendages in moderate numbers.

Geographical distribution.—Rivers and estuaries of south-eastern Australia and Chile.

The above diagnosis is taken from the species now existing in Australia, without regard to the fossil forms for which Cope established the genus.

The genus *Diplomystus* was originally separated from *Clupea* by Cope for the inclusion of six species of Tertiary Clupeids from the Green River portion of the Wasatch Beds situated in the central region of the United States.

He points out that the genus is divisible into two sections, characterised by the form of the dorsal scutes. "In section i," says he, "these shields are transverse, and their posterior borders are pectinate, a median tooth being especially prominent. In section ii, the scuta are not wider than long, and have but one, a median, tooth, which is the extremity of a median longitudinal carina. * * * The species of section i display a longer anal fin than those of section ii. The species of this genus were more numerous than all others combined during the period of the Green River Lake."

DIPLOMYSTUS NOVÆHOLLANDIÆ.

Meletta novæ-hollandiæ, Cuv. & Val. Hist. Nat. Poiss. xx. p. 376.
Clupea novæ-hollandiæ, Gnth. Catal. Fish. vii. p. 431; Macleay, Proc. Linn. Soc. N. S. Wales, iv. p. 378.
Meletta novæ-hollandiæ, Casteln. Proc. Zool. Soc. Vict. 1872, i. p. 189 (*not Cuv. & Val.*)
Meletta vittata, Casteln. Res. Fish. Austr. p. 16, 1875.
Clupea vittata, Macleay. Proc. Linn. Soc. N. S. Wales, iv. p. 379 (*not Mitchell*).
Clupea richmondia, Macleay, Proc. Linn. Soc. N. S. Wales, iv. p. 380.

Freshwater Herring.
Plate XLVII.

B. viii. D. 16–17. A. 16–17. V. S. P. 15. C. 19. L. lat. 45–48. L. tr. 11–12. Cæc. pyl. 14. Vert. 46.

Length of head 5·20–5·33, of caudal fin 5·33–5·66, height of body 4·66–4·80 in the total length. Eye moderate, the adipose lid about equally developed in front and behind, not reaching to the pupil; its diameter, 2·90–3·10 in the length of the head: snout short and moderately pointed, 1·20–1·40 in the diameter of the eye: interorbital space nearly flat, 1·33–1·50 in the same. Nostrils small and approximate, equidistant from the eye and the tip of the snout, the anterior circular, the posterior crescentic. Upper profile of head flat. Jaws equal. Cleft of mouth moderate, the maxilla reaching to beneath the anterior fourth of the orbit. Opercles smooth; subopercle narrow, tapering behind. Lower jaw with a band of small teeth anteriorly; a small anterior patch on the palate; and a series along the median ridge of the tongue. The distance between the origin of the dorsal and the tip of the snout is four fifths of that between the same point and the base of the caudal; the third and fourth rays are the longest, from 1·20–1·33 in the length of the head, and much higher than the base of the fin; the outer margin of the fin is truncate, or but slightly concave: anal low, the longest rays subequal to the diameter of the eye: ventrals inserted on a line with the anterior fourth of the dorsal, their posterior margin rounded, and their length equal to the distance between the tip of the snout and the posterior margin of the orbit: pectorals rounded behind, their length three fourths of that of the head: caudal deeply forked, the least height of the pedicle 2·66–2·90 in the height of the body. Scales thin, smooth, and firmly adherent: a triangular scale rather more than half the diameter of the orbit in length, above the insertion of the ventral: abdominal scutes well developed, sixteen to eighteen in front, and fifteen behind the origin of the ventrals; well developed scutes along the median line of the back between the occiput and the dorsal fin. Gillrakers fine and closely set, half as long as the diameter of the eye.

Colors.—Back and sides straw-color or olive green, belly silvery; a broad silvery dark-edged longitudinal band down the middle of the sides: fins hyaline: irides silvery.

Though abundant in many of the coastal rivers of New South Wales and Victoria, nothing whatever appears to be known concerning the breeding habits of this species, nor have we succeeded in eliciting any information on the subject from our correspondents. With regard to the supposed differences in color and size between specimens from the Hawkesbury and its tributaries and those from the Richmond River, we may mention that the Freshwater Herrings from the former drainage area have the silvery lateral band quite as well developed as those from the latter, and that we have seen numbers from both localities which exceeded seven inches in length. We have not seen specimens of Castelnau's *C. vittata*, but the description is not sufficiently full to enable us with any certainty to establish its identity or otherwise with *C. novæhollandiæ*; nevertheless the position of the ventral, if correctly stated, the increased number of rays in the anal fin, and the small size, suggest a close alliance with *D. sprattellides.**

Macleay tells us that angling for this fish is a favorite sport in some of the upper waters of the Nepean, and that it is of no great value as a food fish.

Castelnau writing of the Melbourne market says:—"This little fish is very abundant at times; its length is about four inches. It is known in Melbourne as the Smelt. This species is never found in the Sydney market."

The Freshwater Herring grows to a length of nine inches, and the largest examples seen as yet were forwarded from the Richmond River.

---

* See foot-note p. 183. Should *Meletta vittata* and *Diplomystus sprattellides* prove identical, the latter name must stand, since that of Castelnau has been previously utilised by both Mitchell and Valenciennes.

Group III.—DUSSUMIERIINA.

Mouth anterior and lateral: upper jaw not overlapping the lower: abdomen neither keeled nor serrated: no osseous gular plate.

Genus IV.—ETRUMEUS.

Etrumeus, Bleeker, Verh. Bat. Gen. xxv. Japan, p. 48.

Branchiostegals numerous: pseudobranchiæ well developed. Gill-membranes entirely separated. Body elongate and subcylindrical: abdomen not compressed or serrated. Snout pointed: supplementary bones of the maxilla very narrow. Eyes with adipose lids. Jaws with small, fixed teeth, which are not deciduous: patches of villiform teeth on the vomer present or absent, on the palatine and pterygoid bones and on the tongue. Dorsal fin situated entirely in advance of the ventrals: anal fin short. Pyloric appendages in large numbers.

Geographical distribution.—Seas of eastern Australia and Japan; Atlantic coasts of the United States.

ETRUMEUS JACKSONENSIS.

Etrumeus jacksoniensis, Macleay, Proc. Linn. Soc. N. S. Wales, iii. p. 36 pl. iv. fig. 1, *and* iv. p. 382.

Maray.

B. xv. D. 19. A. 11. V. 10. P. 16. C. 17.

Length of head 4·75, of caudal fin 6·40, height of body 6·75 in the total length. Eye very large, entirely covered by adipose tissue, its length 2·75 in that of the head: snout compressed and moderately pointed, its length 1·50 in the diameter of the eye, and equal to the interorbital space. Nasal openings inconspicuous, pierced at the opposite ends of a low, rounded, skinny prominence. Upper surface of head very slightly convex, with a median longitudinal ridge and lateral grooves, which latter joining on the occiput where the ridge disappears, form an acutely triangular space, the sides of which are scalloped. Lower jaw very slightly projecting. Cleft of mouth moderate, clupeiform, and a little oblique, the scimitar-shaped maxilla just reaching beyond the anterior margin of the eye. Preopercle with four branched poriferous tubes passing backwards and downwards from the angle. Teeth in the jaws in a single series; those in the upper jaw exceedingly minute; on the sides of the lower jaw much larger, conical, and compressed; a pyriform patch on the vomer; palatine bones and tongue rough. The distance between the origin of the dorsal and the tip of the snout is 1·15 in that between the same point and the base of the caudal; fifth dorsal ray the longest, 1·75 in the length of the head; outer edge of the fin emarginate; its basal length longer than its height: anal fin short and low, the last ray produced and equal in height to the long anterior rays, leaving the outer margin deeply indented; its basal length 2·75 in that of the dorsal: ventrals small, equal in length to the diameter of the eye; they are inserted entirely behind the dorsal fin, the distance between their origin and that of the anal being 1·15 in that between the same point and the origin of the dorsal, which latter distance is equal to the length of the head: pectoral pointed, concave posteriorly, 1·66 in the same length: caudal forked, the least height of its pedicle 2·50 in the height of the body. Scales very deciduous, obscurely carinated: a lanceolate axillary scale, almost as long as the pectoral fin. Gillrakers fine and closely set, one third of the diameter of the eye.

Colors.— Dark blue above, silvery on the sides and below.

We have included this species on the strength of Macleay's statement that it is one of those known to the fishermen as 'Marny,' and that it passes northwards every winter in enormous shoals; he concludes:—" It is said also to be very much appreciated as food by the few who have had the opportunity of tasting it." Specimens of this fish are unknown, with the exception of the one mentioned by Macleay and taken in Port Jackson, and two or three others in the Australian Museum, the largest of which measures seven and two thirds inches.

They are very closely allied to the *Clupea micropus*, Schlegel, of the Japanese Seas.

Family.—MURÆNIDÆ.

Murænoidei, Müller, Abhandl. Ak. Wiss. Berl. 1845, p. 193.

Body elongate, cylindrical, or band-shaped. Humeral arch not attached to the skull. The branchial openings in the pharynx may be wide or narrow slits. Margin of upper jaw formed anteriorly by the premaxillaries, which are more or less coalescent with the vomer and ethmoid; laterally by the tooth bearing maxillaries. Vertical fins, when present, confluent or separated by the projecting tip of the tail: ventrals absent: pectorals present or absent. Scales, when present, rudimentary. Vent situated at a great distance from the head or near to the base of the pectoral fins. The heart may be approximate to or remote from the gills. Stomach with a blind sac. No pyloric appendages. Ovaries destitute of oviducts.

Geographical distribution.—Seas and fresh waters of all temperate and tropical regions.

Genus I.—ANGUILLA.

Anguilla (Thunberg), Cuvier, Règne Anim.

Body moderately elongated. Gill-openings of moderate extent, situated near the base of the pectoral fins. Upper jaw not projecting beyond the lower. Teeth small, forming bands. Dorsal fin commencing at some distance behind the occiput: pectorals present. Small scales imbedded in the skin.

Geographical distribution.—The genus *Anguilla* appears to be resident in the fresh waters and estuaries of the habitable globe, the circumpolar regions, and certain localities lying at so high an altitude as to be subject to intense cold, being the only exceptions.

ANGUILLA REINHARDTI.

Anguilla reinhardtii, Steindachn. SB. Ak. Wien, 1867, lv. p. 15; Guth. Catal. Fish. viii. p. 27; Macleay, Catal. Austr. Fish. ii. p. 203, *and* Proc. Linn. Soc. N. S. Wales, viii. p. 210.

Long-finned Eel.

B. xi. D. C. & A. 488. P. 17. Vert. 43/63.

Length of head 2·30–2·50 in the distance between the extremity of the snout and the origin of the dorsal fin, 3·20 between the chin and the origin of the anal, and a trifle more than that between the origins of the two fins. Eye small. Snout depressed and spatulate, its breadth immediately in front of the eyes rather more than its length. Nostrils remote, the anterior situated on the outer angle of the snout, tubular; the posterior in front of the middle of the orbit, oval and longitudinal. Lips moderately fleshy. Lower jaw a little the longer. The angle of the mouth situated a short distance behind the posterior margin of the orbit. Teeth cardiform on the jaws and vomer; the maxillary bands are nowhere so broad as the anterior three fifths of the vomerine band, but extend considerably further back than does that band; the mandibular bands are equal in length to the maxillary, and are divided into an outer and an inner series by a narrow longitudinal groove. Pectoral small and rounded, its length 3·25–3·60 in that of the head: the length of head and body is 1·10 in that of the tail.

Colors.—Above dark olive, more or less spotted and streaked with black; below white: fins rather darker: irides orange: teeth purple.

The breeding habits of Eels is a subject as yet so imperfectly understood that it is needless to say more here than that it is known that they are obliged to descend from the fresh water to the brackish or pure sea water in order to develop their spawn; that the young migrate to the upper waters of rivers and creeks in countless thousands, overcoming in their course obstacles seemingly insurmountable; that they increase in such places in size, but not in numbers; that the adults, after spawning, either become permanently resident in the tidal waters to which they have descended, or return to their freshwater haunts irregularly and individually; and that they are unisexual and not, as was long supposed, hermaphrodite.

This is the common Eel of the Sydney markets, and is the species figured as *Anguilla australis* by Tenison Woods. They occur in greater or less numbers at all seasons of the year, and should be present much more abundantly but that, strange as it may appear when we take into consideration the very high price which they can always command in the market, there is no regular fishery for them, such as are offered for sale being the produce of the seine and prawn net, taken accidentally when seeking other prey, in much the same way that the markets are supplied with that other abnormally high-priced fish, the Black Sole, *Synaptura nigra* (see p. 160).

In addition to the above mentioned method, it may be easily taken with hook and line, for, being exceedingly voracious, it will greedily snatch at almost any bait, provided always that it shall be fresh, or better still, living; tainted meat they will avoid unless pressed by hunger. They take the bait best during the night time, and a live frog, worm, or singing locust (*Cyclochila australasiæ*),* a piece of fresh fish or meat, and the entrails of fowls or fishes, will all be found excellent baits. Eels are also taken in wicker or wire fish creels, the former for preference, baited with fish or any fresh offal, and by spearing.

It is almost needless to mention that as a food fish the Freshwater Eel has few rivals, being rich, wholesome, and nutritious; though of excellent flavor, by whatever method it may have been cooked, it is perhaps best when stewed.

---

* The scientific name has been given to me by Mr. Skuse, of the Australian Museum.

Eels are very tenacious of life, and given favorable circumstance, can remain for a long time out of their natural element without inconvenience; and the fact is well attested that should they for any reason take a dislike to their surroundings, such, for instance, as from the pollution of the water, or the imminence of a prolonged drought, they will leave any such localities as isolated ponds, and migrate overland to the nearest pure water; while it has also been asserted that they voluntarily leave the water on damp cool nights and traverse the surrounding pastures in search of frogs, snails, worms, and similar food. When on migration they are not easily turned from their path, crossing even ploughed fields in their effort to reach more suitable quarters.

Eels are very susceptible of cold, and in localities subject to a low winter temperature are accustomed to bury themselves deeply in the mud during the continuance of the cold season; nevertheless, that they can bear great cold without life becoming extinct is evident from the following extract, quoted by Day, from "Chamber's Edinburgh Journal," for November 29th, 1851: "Dr. Kirkland, of Cleveland, states that last winter as the frost set in, a number of eels in a millpond, incommoded by the subsidence of the ice, migrated to other ponds, from which he obtained eight or ten bushels half frozen. Having been placed in a cold, exposed room, they were as stiff and almost as brittle as icicles in the morning. A tub was filled with them, and water from a well added; then they were placed in a warm storeroom for the purpose of thawing. In the course of an hour or two they were resuscitated and as active as if just taken during the summer."

In the streams which rise in the Blue Mountains, and flow into the Nepean, Eels are in some places common in summer, but they totally disappear about the month of March, probably making their way down stream to the deeper and warmer waters of the parent river, though it is possible that some may remain concealed during the winter months under rocks or among driftwood and other *débris*; the water of these streams is clear and intensely cold.

The Long-finned Eel is common in all the rivers and estuaries which drain the eastern watershed of New South Wales, but whether this or any other species of Eel inhabits the rivers and lagunes of the vast territory lying to the westward of the mountains is still an open question. They have on many occasions been reported from thence; nor is there any reason why they should not be plentiful, nor any obstruction in the main river system of the Murray, which could effectually bar their passage from its embouchure to the interior, since we have received from Bourke a species of Toadfish (*Tetrodon inermis*). When on a visit to the Cooma district, the author was informed that Eels were plentiful in the Umaralla River, which empties into the Murrumbidgee, but no specimens were obtained, nor have examples ever been sent to either the Australian or the University Museum, the preponderance of evidence is, therefore, against any Eel being a resident of our western waters. It has been suggested that many of these reports arise through the ignorance of their captors causing them to mistake the common Freshwater Catfish (*Copidoglanis tandanus*)—not, as erroneously asserted by Tenison Woods, *Plotosus anguillaris* Lacép., which is a marine littoral species for an Eel, though this suggestion is apparently supported by the name "Eelfish," applied to *C. tandanus* by Sir Thomas Mitchell.

Though not alluded to by Saville Kent, this species is found along the entire Queensland coast, north to Cape York, from whence were obtained several specimens now in the British Museum collection, while Macleay records it from the Mary River, and the Lillesmere Lagunes. By Castelnau it is noticed as from Western Port and the Mordialloc River.

These Eels attain to a length of at least three feet, with a weight of twelve or even more pounds.

This species should be carefully compared with typical specimens of *A. aucklandii*, *A. amboinensis*, and *A. fidjiensis*, and, in the event of these proving to be but varietal forms, *A. aucklandi* would be the oldest name.

Genus II.—MURÆNA.

Muræna, sp. Artedi, Gen. Pisc. 1738.

Body moderately or greatly elongated. Gill-openings reduced to narrow slits. Two nostrils on each side of the upper surface of the snout, the anterior tubular, the posterior a round orifice with or without a tube. Teeth well developed, either acute or molariform: maxillary teeth in one or two rows. Dorsal and anal fins elevated or low: pectorals absent. Scales none.

Geographical distribution.—Seas of the temperate and tropical regions, some species ascending tidal rivers.

According to Günther the "number of species known exceeds eighty. The majority are armed with formidable pointed teeth, well suited for seizing other fish on which they prey. Large specimens thus armed readily attack persons in and out of the water; and as some species attain a length of six or eight feet, they are justly feared by fishermen. The minority of species have obtuse and molar-like teeth, their food consisting chiefly of crustaceans and other hard-shelled animals. Most of the Murænas are beautifully colored and spotted, some in a regular and constant manner, whilst in others the pattern varies in a most irregular fashion; they have quite the appearance of snakes."

In connection with the subdivision of the genus *Muræna* the same author remarks:—"Sir John Richardson has divided the species of this genus into smaller groups, distinguished by the dentition. Dr. Kaup has done nothing beyond adopting these groups and attaching generic names to them. However, only in a comparatively small part of the species is the arrangement of the teeth of systematic value, as the dentition changes to a considerable extent with age. Young examples have generally more series of teeth than mature or old individuals. Especially with regard to the one, two, or three large teeth, forming an inner maxillary series, it appears that normally these teeth enter the outer series as the age of the individual advances. This change is by no means regular, and one or two inner teeth are sometimes found in examples of considerable size. Further, in some species the biserial arrangement appears to be persistent through life; in other species, which are known from a few examples only, we have no means of judging of the extent of change. The uni- or biserial arrangement of the vomerine teeth is also subject to much variation."

Carrington in the *Zoologist*, commenting on their reputed savage disposition, expresses the opinion that they do not deserve the character; our Green Eel, however, richly deserves it, as they will without hesitation attack a foot or hand incautiously placed in the water in the neighborhood of their haunts.

MURÆNA AFRA.

Gymnothorax afer, Bloch, Ausl. Fisch. ix. p. 85, pl. ccccxvii; Bl. Schn. p. 526.

Muræophis afra, Lacép. Hist. Nat. Poiss. v. p. 642.

Gymnothorax funebris, Ranz. Nov. Comm. Ac. Sc. Inst. Bonon. iv. 1840, p. 76.

Murœna lineopinnis, Richards. Voy. Erebus & Terror, Fish. p. 89.
Murœna prasina, Richards. Voy. Erebus & Terror, Fish. p. 93.
Murœna boschii, Bleek. Mur. p. 52, *and* Sumatra, p. 103.
Murœna monochrous, Bleek. Ternate, p. 384.
Murœna tristis, Kaup, Catal. Apod. p. 62.
Thyrsoidea lineopinnis, Kaup, Catal. Apod. p. 82.
Thyrsoidea boschii, Kaup, Arch. Natur. xxii. i. p. 82, *and* Catal. Apod. p. 87.
Murœna infernalis, Pocy, Mem. Cuba, ii. pp. 347, 354.
Tœniophis westphali, Kaup. Aale Hamb. Mus. Nacht. p. 1.
Gymnothorax boschi, Bleek. Atl. Ichthyol. Mur. p. 105, pl. xlvi. f. 3.
Gymnothorax monochrous, Bleek. Atl. Ichthyol. Mur. p. 106, pl. xlvii. f. 2.
Gymnothorax jacksoniensis, Bleek. Verst. en Meded. Ak. Wet. Amsterd. 1863, xv. p. 450.
Gymnothorax infernalis, Pocy, Fis.-nat. Cuba, ii. p. 258.
Murœna afra, Gnth. Catal. Fish. p. viii, p. 123; Day, Fish. Ind. p. 671; Steindachn. Denk. Ak. Wien, xliv. p. 59; Macleay, Catal. Austr. Fish. ii. p. 217.

Green Eel.

Vert. 59/66.

The distance between the tip of the lower jaw and the anterior margin of the gill-opening 7·90 in the total length, and 4·30 between the same and the origin of the anal: height of body 14·00 in the total length. Eye small, its diameter 14·75 in the length of the head, and 2·50 in that of the snout, which is narrow, pointed, and but moderately produced. Both nostrils tubular, that of the anterior the longer, two fifths of the diameter of the eye. A series of large pores along each jaw. Upper profile of head gibbous. Lower jaw much the longer. Cleft of mouth wide, 2·85 in the length of the head. Angle of the mouth about two diameters of the eye behind its posterior margin. The diameter of the eye is 1·50 in that of the gill-opening, which forms a horizontal slit. Teeth in both jaws biserial, the inner series much the larger, compressed, pointed, and curving inwards and backwards, each with a shallow notch in front and a deep one behind, twenty one or twenty two on each ramus of the maxilla, and twenty five on each mandibular ramus, the three or four anterior ones the largest; a triangular patch of three strong teeth on the head of the vomer and a double row posteriorly. Fins low. Length of tail 1·20 in that of the trunk.

Colors.—Ground color yellowish-brown, almost hidden by purplish-brown spots. When first taken from the water bright green.

Though the Green Eel is very common along the New South Wales coast, frequenting the crannies and crevices among the rocks, and the larger rock pools on the shore reefs, it is not often brought to market, its habits and the peculiar localities which it frequents not leading the professional fisherman to seek for it. It is an excellent food fish, its flesh being white, delicate, and of good flavor. They are said to be easily taken in the rock pools with a prawn or fish bait, by the use of a short, stout rod, and short line, but the moment they are hooked they must be jerked out of the water, for if once allowed to retreat into their crevice great difficulty is experienced in inducing them to come out again.

As an instance of the ferocity of this species, we may quote Macgillivray (*see Richardson, Voy. Erebus & Terror, Fish. p. 93, as M. prasina*), who speaks of it as follows :—" It frequents weedy pools among the rocks on the north side of Bondi Bay, near Sydney. It is very savage when irritated, and once, when I was collecting corallines in that locality, a large individual made a dart at my arm, and returned repeatedly to the attack, swimming slowly about, winding among the seaweeds, and raising its snout to the surface."

These Eels are common on the east coast of Australia, as far south as the metropolitan district, beyond which their range has not been accurately defined. They occur all along the north coast, and doubtless are found to about the same latitude south of the tropics on the west as on the east coast. From the southern Colonies it has not been recorded.

At Lord Howe Island this is the most common Eel on the shore, and is easily obtained under stones between tidemarks, up to a length of two feet. *

Beyond the limits of these colonies it has been recorded from many parts of the Indian and Atlantic Oceans, within the tropics, while the British Museum contains specimens from such widely-separated localities as Sumatra, Jamaica, and the Niger.

The Green Eel grows to a length of thirty three inches.

---

* Zoology, &c., of Lord Howe Island Austr. Mus. Mem. No. 2, 1889.

Order IV.—*PLECTOGNATHI.*

Skeleton incompletely ossified with the vertebræ in small numbers. Gill-openings narrow, situated in front of the pectoral fins: gills pectinate. Mouth narrow: the bones of the upper jaw usually firmly united, and sometimes produced into the form of a beak. Teeth in the jaws may be distinct or absent. A soft dorsal fin, situated opposite to the anal, and belonging to the caudal portion of the vertebral column : elements of a spinous dorsal also present in some genera: ventral fins none or reduced to spines. Skin smooth, or with rough scales, or ossified in the form of plates or spines. Airbladder without pneumatic duct.

Geographical distribution.—Mostly pelagic, but some inhabit large rivers, while many are resident in the estuaries and tidal waters of the tropical and temperate zones.

Family.—BALISTIDÆ.

Body compressed: snout somewhat produced. Jaws armed with distinct teeth in small numbers. Spinous dorsal reduced to one, two, or three spines: ventral to a single pelvic prominence or entirely absent. One genus with a barbel. Skin covered with scutes, or rough, or spinate.

In the genus *Balistes* the consumption of the flesh is at times attended with symptoms of acute poisoning; this, according to Dr. Meunier, is caused by the action of the poison on the nervous tissue of the stomach, which occasions virulent spasms of that organ, and shortly afterwards of all the muscles of the body; the usual symptoms of poisoning soon follow, and the patient frequently expires in a paroxysm of suffering. No attempt appears to have been made to locate the seat or distribution of the poison in *Balistes*; this, however, has been successfully demonstrated, in the case of another Plectognathous genus, *Tetrodon*, by a series of experiments conducted in Japan by Drs. D. Takahashi and Y. Inoko, whose researches conclusively prove that the chief seat of the toxic power lies in the ovaries and liver. The Leatherjackets (*Monacanthus*) are, however, free from all poisonous properties and are excellent as food.

Genus.—MONACANTHUS.

Monacanthus, Cuvier, Règne Anim.

Body compressed. Barbel absent. Upper jaw with a double series of incisiform teeth, six in the outer and four in the inner series; lower jaw with a single series of six similar teeth. The first dorsal reduced to a spine, which may be strong or feeble, barbed or merely rough; behind this a second rudimentary spine is generally present: ventral reduced to a fixed or movable osseous process, which may be rudimentary or even entirely absent. Scales minute and rough : some species with cutaneous filaments: adult males of some species with a peculiar armature of the sides of the tail, which in females is much less developed or entirely absent. Vertebræ 7/11-14.

Geographical distribution.—Tropical and temperate seas.

Alluding to the edible qualities of the Leatherjackets—by which name the *Monacanthi* are universally known in the Colonies—Saville Kent, in his Preliminary Report on the Food Fishes of Queensland, writes :—" Although not incorporated among the ordinary food fishes, it is worthy of mention here that many of the species of the Leatherjackets (*Monacanthus*), which abound in the Queensland and other Australian seas, are in many instances most excellent eating, their flesh when cooked—the skin being previously removed—having been compared to that of the Sole and Flounder." On the same subject Castelnau remarks:—"Those of the Victorian waters are not generally used as food, although the fishermen say that when their thick skin has been removed they are not to be despised." Johnston, too, referring to its estimation in Tasmania, says:—"Some of them are said to be very good for the table when skinned ; but they are not held in esteem in the market, and consequently are seldom seen there."

MONACANTHUS HIPPOCREPIS.

Balistes hippocrepis, Quoy & Gaim. Voy. Uranie, Zool. p. 212.
Aleuterius variabilis, Richards. Voy. Erebus & Terror, Fish. p. 67, pl. lii. ff. 1–7.
Monacanthus hippocrepis, Holland, Ann. Sc. Nat. 1854, ii. p. 338 ; Steindachn. SB. Ak. Wien, 1868. lvii. p. 1002 ; Gnth. Catal. Fish. viii. p. 246 ; Castelu. Proc. Linn. Soc. N. S. Wales, iii. p. 399 ; McCoy, Prodr. Zool. Vict. dec. xiii. pl. 125.

Variable Leatherjacket.
Plate XLVIII.

D. 39. A. 37. P. 13. C. 12.

Length of head 3·80, of caudal fin 6·33, height of body 3·25 in the total length. Eye moderate, its diameter 4·20 in the length of the snout, and 1·20 in the interorbital space, which is convex. Nostrils small, approximate, oval, subequal. Snout long, obtusely rounded, its upper surface slightly convex. Gill-opening situated beneath the posterior half of the orbit, its length 2·85 in that of the snout. Dorsal spine strong and straight, its length 1·40 in the same ; it is situated above the posterior half of the orbit, and is compressed and transversely expanded ; anteriorly it is rounded, and bears a double row of small spinate points, with a narrow, mostly naked, space between them ; the hinder lateral margins are armed with much stronger spines pointing outwards and downwards, and the space intervening between the two sets of spines is covered by minute conical points. Soft dorsal and anal fins rather low, with the outer margins convex, and the middle rays the longest, those of the anal being a little longer than the dorsal rays, 2·60 in the length of the snout : the anal commences beneath the sixth dorsal ray, and ends a little behind that fin ; its basal length is 1·20 in that of the dorsal: ventral spine small, immovable, its tip encircled by small spines : pectoral small, rounded posteriorly, situated behind the vertical from the orbit, its length 2·66 in that of the snout : caudal subtruncate, with the angles slightly produced in old examples ; the pedicle with three pairs of strong spines directed forwards, its least height 3·66 in the height of the body. Scales well marked, rough, and velvety.

Colors.—Upper surfaces olive green darkest on the head, shading into lighter below ; middle of the sides with an oval orange blotch, within which a horseshoe-shaped band is present or absent ; lips surrounded by two or three dull blue yellow-edged bands ; sides of the abdomen with narrow, sinuous, blue bands : fins pale yellow, immaculate ; caudal with a broad sublunate band, convex anteriorly, near its outer margin.

This large and handsome species is not so often to be found in the market as are the two which follow, and appears to be of a more solitary disposition than they. The flesh of the Variable Leatherjacket is beautifully white and flaky, and of excellent flavor. It is more of an ocean fish than the majority of its congeners ; and the few that find their way to market are taken on the outside reefs by hook and line, and is not *exigeant* as to the character of the bait used, but in a natural state its principal food consists of molluscs and crustaceans, the hard shells of which are easily crushed by its strong incisor teeth.

Alluding to a closely allied species (*M. convexirostris*), which is found both on our coast and that of New Zealand—where it is said to be the sole representative of the genus—Sherrin writes: "Though usually cast aside as worthless, it has really palatable flesh, when the tough skin, from which it receives its trivial name, is removed. The Maori name for this fish is 'Kiriri'."

The Variable or Orange-spotted Leatherjacket is found along our coast at least as far north as the Port Jackson District, but to what extent it ranges from thence we are unable to say, since, from the fact that they do not pay for their carriage when sent from a distance, we have no means of ascertaining their true distribution. They are also found in the seas of Victoria, Tasmania, and South Australia, and are, according to McCoy, not uncommon in the former Colony. Klunzinger has also recorded it from King George's Sound.

They attain a length of eighteen inches.

MONACANTHUS TRACHYLEPIS.

Monacanthus trachylepis, Guth. Catal. Fish. viii. p. 248 ; Klunzing. SB. Ak. Wien, 1879, lxxx. Abth. i. p. 422 ; Macleay, Catal. Austr. Fish. ii. p. 249.
Monacanthus rudis, Klunzing. SB. Ak. Wien, 1872, p. 43 (*not Richardson*).
Monacanthus convexirostris, Klunzing. SB. Ak. Wien, 1872, p. 43 (*not Günther*).
? *Monacanthus baudini*, Casteln. Proc. Zool. Soc. Vict. ii. p. 55.

Yellow-finned Leatherjacket.

D. 36–39. A. 33–35. P. 12–13. C. 12.

Length of head 3·75, of caudal fin 5·50–6·00, height of body 2·90–3·00 in the total length. Eye small, its diameter 3·75 in the length of the snout, and 1·25 in the interorbital space, which is strongly convex. Nostrils approximate, situated a little below the plane of the upper margin of the eye, the anterior minute and circular, furnished with a small posterior flap ; the posterior patent and horizontally oval. Snout produced, with the profile slightly concave. Gill-opening advanced and very oblique situated beneath the anterior two thirds of the orbit, its length 3·00–3·25 in that of the snout. Dorsal spine strong and straight, equal in length to the snout, and situated above the middle of the orbit ; its latero-posterior margins armed with a series of small barbs pointing backwards and downwards, and with a double series of minute, closely set barbs anteriorly ; the remaining surface of the spine rough in front, smooth behind : soft dorsal and anal fins rather low, subequal in height, the longest rays in front of the middle of the fins, and three sevenths of the height of the dorsal spine : the anal commences beneath the fifth or sixth dorsal ray, and ends but little beyond that fin : ventral spine minute, immovable, with very short teeth radiating from its centre : pectoral small, placed beneath the hinder margin of the orbit, its length 2·25–2·40 in that of the snout : caudal rounded ; the pedicle with two pairs of strong compressed spines curved forwards on each side, and occasionally a supplementary spine on one or both sides, its least height 3·40–3·55 in the height of the body, and its length between the end of the dorsal and the base of the caudal equal to its height. Scales indistinct, replaced by vertical prominences, each of which bears from three to five spinelets ; a small patch of longer bristles immediately in front of the pedicular spines.

Colors.—Head, back, and abdominal region either dark greenish-brown, or olive green with three darker longitudinal bands; above the anal fin paler yellowish-brown; middle of the sides with several narrow undulated and branched black lines; two narrow purple bands, with a yellow streak between them round the lips, two broader purple bands, which quickly disappear after death, inside the bases of the soft dorsal and anal, which, with the pectorals and pedicular spines, are yellow, the latter having their tips blackish: membrane of dorsal spine black, with large pale blue spots; caudal rays pale brown, with the connecting membrane orange in large examples, in the young with a basal and submarginal olive band: teeth white, with yellow tips.

The habits of this species apparently differ in some respects from the two other Leatherjackets described in this work, inasmuch as it is never caught on the outside reefs by the line fishers, but occasionally visits the sheltered harbors and inlets of the metropolitan district in large shoals, whence it is sent in considerable numbers to the market, where they find a ready sale at moderate prices. Such a visitation took place during the summer of 1892, when they were sent to the market in large numbers from all the inlets lying between Port Hacking and Broken Bay, while their occurrence among other fishes from Port Stephens and Shoalhaven—localities from which Leatherjackets are not forwarded to the market as a general rule—proves that shoals of these fish were prevalent upon a considerable portion of our coastline at that time, since which none have appeared.

That these were true "school" fishes, even though they showed no signs of spawning, was evident from the fact that they were all of much the same size,—from twelve to fourteen inches; they were readily, even eagerly bought as long as the supply lasted, and we, among others, took the opportunity of testing their edible qualities, with the gratifying result that we found them, if anything, superior to the other Leatherjackets previously experimented on, and quite equal to any fish of these seas.

The Yellow-finned—or, as Johnston calls it, Lozenge-scaled—Leatherjacket is found in the seas of New South Wales, Victoria, and Tasmania, and very probably, since it is recorded from Port Darwin by Klunzinger, round the entire seaboard of Australia.

They attain to a length of sixteen inches.

MONACANTHUS AYRAUDI.

Balistes ayraudi, Quoy & Gaim. Voy. Uranie, Poiss. p. 216, pl. xlvii, fig. 2.
Aluteres velutinus, Jenyns, Voy. Beagle, Fish. p. 157.
Monacanthus vittatus (Solander), Richards. Voy. Erebus & Terror, Fish. p. 66; Steindachn. SB. Ak. Wien, 1866, liii. p. 476, *and* 1867, lvi. p. 335.
Monacanthus frauenfeldii, Kner, Voy. Novara, Fisch. p. 397.
Monacanthus ayraudi, Guth. Catal. Fish. viii. p. 244; Casteln. Proc. Linn. Soc. N. S. Wales, iii. p. 397; Macleay, Catal. Austr. Fish. ii. p. 262; Woods, Fisher. N. S. Wales, p. 89, pl. xlix.

Ayraud's Leatherjacket.

D. 32. A. 31. P. 13. C. 12.

Length of head 3·25, of caudal fin 6·75, height of body 3·50 in the total length. Eye moderate, its diameter 4·50 in the length of the snout, and 1·15 in the interorbital space, which is almost flat. Nostrils approximate, rounded, the anterior much the smaller. Snout much produced, with its upper profile slightly convex. Gill-opening situated beneath the middle of the orbit, its length 3·90 in that of the snout. Dorsal spine moderate and slightly curved backwards, its length two fifths of that of the snout; it is situated above the posterior margin of the orbit, and is strongly compressed and expanded laterally, the anterior facies being flat and feebly granulose, the posterior rounded and smooth; each sharp lateral edge armed with a series of small barbs, which point outwards and downwards: soft dorsal and anal fins falcate, the seventh to ninth rays the longest, subequal in length, and 1·40 in the basal length of the anal, which commences beneath the twelfth dorsal ray and terminates a short distance behind that fin: ventral spine small, immovable, and roughened, without distinct teeth: pectoral small, situated beneath the hind margin of the orbit, its length 3·25 in that of the snout: caudal subtruncate, the pedicle long, shallow, and spineless, its least height 4·50 in the height of the body, and its length between the end of the dorsal and the base of the caudal but little less than the base of the anal. Skin rough and pilose.

Colors.—Pale yellow or yellowish-brown, uniform or with two to four indistinct lighter longitudinal body bands in the adults, these bands being always present and well marked in small specimens: all the fins bright yellow.

Like *Monacanthus hippocrepis*, Ayraud's Leatherjacket is principally taken by hook and line on the ocean reefs by the boats engaged in fishing for Snapper. In such places it is unfortunately plentiful, and is a source of great annoyance to the fishermen, as, when hooked, it cuts the line with ease, its strong sharp teeth forming admirable nippers, and if present in any numbers the loss sustained from this cause is frequently very great, not so much from the actual loss of gear, as from the waste of time necessitated by remounting the lines making the capture of the more valuable fishes almost an impracticability.

Alluding to this subject, the Report of the Royal Commission says:—" It is a most serious annoyance to the fishermen, infesting their favorite fishing-grounds and cutting their lines. The plague of these fishes seems to be on the increase, and unless some means can be found of getting rid of the pest, Snapper fishing will have to be conducted with wire lines." We are not by any means sure that the proposed remedy would be as efficacious as the Commissioners appear to have thought. The same Report, with a slight touch of humor, refers to the Leatherjackets as being " numerously represented in the Australian seas, but out of the entire number one only can be cited as being in the least degree *useful, and that one is productive of more harm than good.*"

It is not, however, on the outer reefs alone that this species occurs, for it is at times plentiful in our bays and estuaries in its young or half grown state, when measuring up to ten inches in length, and is then taken in numbers by the seine, and when so captured is left to rot on the beach, or be washed away by the next tide, being objects of abhorrence to fishermen of all grades.

This species, in common with many other Leatherjackets—notably *M. chinensis*—forms the host of one, or more, species of isopodous crustacean (*Anilocra* ?) which burrows into the side of the abdomen immediately beneath the outer skin. These do not appear to cause any inconvenience to their hosts, specimens of which, when so attacked, are to all appearance equally healthy and in equally good condition as those which are exempt from attack.

The only localities from which this species can be recorded with certainty, are the metropolitan district of New South Wales, and King George's Sound, whence Klunzinger received it.

They attain a length of at least eighteen inches.

Class.—CRUSTACEA.*

Invertebrate animals, distinguished by the possession of a more or less hard, jointed, external crust, or exoskeleton, nearly all living habitually in water, and breathing by means of gills.

Of the Crustacea the large group of the Malacostraca are distinguished from the rest (the Entomostraca) by the number of the segments of the body, of which there are always twenty, except in certain cases in which amalgamation or abortion of one or more of the segments has taken place.

Tribe I.—BRACHYURA.

Abdomen short, inflexed beneath the thorax, without swimmerets, and with no appendages on the penultimate segment. Carapace greatly developed, forming wide branchial chambers above the bases of the legs. Sternum never linear; vulvæ situated on the sternum. Antennæ with the flagella usually very short, especially those of the inner pair, which are lodged in distinct cavities. External maxillipedes operculiform. Buccal cavity distinctly defined in front.

Subtribe.—Cyclometopa.

Carapace usually transverse, wide in front, regularly arcuate anteriorly (sometimes quadrate or suborbicular), never acuminate or rostrate. Epistome short, transverse. Internal antennæ usually transversely plicate.

Family I.—PORTUNIDÆ.

Carapace depressed, usually more or less hexagonal in shape, never very convex. Antero-lateral margins with well defined acute teeth. Inner ramus of the first (innermost) pair of maxillipedes with an internal lobe. Margin of the efferent branchial channel usually defined by a longitudinal ridge on each side of the prelabial plate or palate. Fifth pair of ambulatory legs natatorial, their terminal joint oval, expanded, and lamellate.

Genus I.—NEPTUNUS.

Neptunus, De Haan, Faun. Japon. Crust. p. 7, 1835.

Carapace very wide, with transverse granulous lines. Latero-anterior margins with nine or more teeth (including the external orbital angle), the last tooth much the longest. Front wide and divided into five or six teeth. Flagellum of external antennæ placed in the internal orbital hiatus. External maxillipedes short. Anterior legs long: arm with acute tubercles upon the anterior margin: hand nearly prismatic, with longitudinal ridges giving rise above to spiniform tubercles. Thigh of the swimming legs with the lower margin usually destitute of spines.

---

* All the technical diagnoses are taken from Dr. Haswell's "Catalogue of Australian Crustacea," the species selected being those most commonly found in the Sydney market.

NEPTUNUS PELAGICUS.

Cancer pelagicus, Linn. Syst. Nat. p. 1042, 1766.
Lupea pelagica, Milne-Edw. Hist. Nat. Crust. i. p. 450, 1834.
Neptunus pelagicus, part. A. Milne-Edw. Arch. Mus. Hist. Nat. x. p. 320 1861; Miers, Ann. Nat. Hist. (4) xvii. 1866, p. 221, *and* Catal. Crust. N. Zeal. p. 25, 1876; Haswell, Austr. Malacostr. p. 77, 1882.

Common Swimming Crab.
Plate L.

Carapace wide, with very coarse granulations, without tubercles on the gastric and cardiac regions. Teeth of the lateral margins short, wide at the base; ninth epibranchial spine long, acute. Front six-toothed, the median teeth smaller but never obsolete. Orbits divided above into three lobes by two deep fissures, the middle lobe with a small spine at its external angle. Anterior legs very long and slender. Anterior margin of the arm with three, four, or even five spines; there is also a single spine at the extremity of the posterior margin. Wrist with an acute spine upon its inner and a similar smaller spine upon its outer surface. Hand usually very long and slender, with three spines, two placed above the base of the mobile finger, and one over the articulation of the hand with the wrist.

This is the most common species of crab sent to the Sydney market, and is very widely distributed throughout the Oriental region. It occurs at all seasons, and is both used as food and as bait; it is principally taken by the seine, and weighs as much as a pound to a pound and a half.

Genus II.—SCYLLA.

Scylla, De Haan, Faun. Japon. Crust. p. 11, 1835.

Carapace very wide and rather convex. Latero-anterior margins with nine teeth, the ninth similar to the preceding. Basal joint of the external antennæ large, the flagellum inserted in the internal orbital hiatus. Epistome well developed; anterior margin of the buccal cavity separated by a transverse groove from the posterior margin of the antennary region. Anterior legs short and robust: hand without longitudinal ridges.

SCYLLA SERRATA.

Cancer serratus, Forskål.
Cancer olivaceus, Herbst, Krabben u. Krebse, ii. p, 157, pl. xxxviii. fig. 3, 1796.
Portunus tranquebaricus, Fabr. Ent. Syst. p. 366, 1798.
Lupea tranquebarica, Milne-Edw. Hist. Nat. Crust. i. p. 448, 1834.
Lupea lobifrons, Milne-Edw. Hist. Nat. Crust. i. p. 453.
Scylla serrata, De Haan, Faun. Japon. Crust. p. 44, 1834; A. Milne-Edw. Ann. Sci. Nat. (4) 'xiv. p. 252, pls. i, ii. 1860, *and* Nouv. Arch. Mus. x. p. 349, 1861; Miers, Catal. Crust. N. Zeal. p. 27, 1876; Haswell, Austr. Malacostr. p. 78, 1882.
Scylla tranquebarica, Dana, U. S. Expl. Exped. xiii. Crust. part i. p. 270, 1852.

Mangrove Crab.

Carapace convex, nearly smooth, very finely granulated; the lines on the gastric and branchial regions distinct. Latero-anterior margins very long. Front with six large flat teeth. Anterior legs very robust, arm trigonous, with three spines upon the anterior, and two upon the posterior margin. Wrist with an acute spine at its antero-internal angle, and two small spines upon its external surface. Hand very large, with three spines above, two above the base of the mobile finger, and one over the articulation with the wrist.

Color.—Olive brown.

Occurs at all seasons in small numbers, and is a large and well flavored crab, growing to a weight of three pounds; during May 1893, they were exceptionally common, as many as a dozen being in the market on some mornings.

Tribe II.—MACRURA.

Abdomen elongate, extended backward, with lamellar appendages beneath. Appendages to the penultimate segment large, laterally expanded and constituting, with the terminal segment, a fan-like swimming apparatus. Sternum usually linear throughout its length. Antennæ very greatly developed, inner without fossettes. External maxillipedes nearly always pediform. Buccal cavity not distinctly defined in front.

Family I.—PALINURIDÆ.

Carapace subcylindrical, broadly rounded laterally. External antennæ without a basal scale, the basal joints long, subcylindrical. Anterior legs monodactyle. Sternum trigonous.

Genus.—PALINURUS.

Palinurus, Fabr. Suppl. Ent. Syst. 1798.

Carapace with a small rostrum. Antennary segment very narrow above. External antennæ nearly in contact with one another at their bases, and concealing the bases of the internal antennæ, the flagella of which are very short.

PALINURUS HUEGELI.

Palinurus hügelii, Heller, Voy. Novara, Crust. p. 96, 1872; Haswell, Austr. Malacostr. p. 172, 1882.

? *Palinurus tumidus,* Kirk, Trans. N. Z. Inst. 1879, xii. p. 314.

Sydney Crawfish.

Plate XLIX.

Carapace a little narrowed anteriorly, convex and spinose above, the spines prominent, acute, and directed forwards and upwards. Rostrum acute, spiniform, directed almost straight forwards; the lateral cornua a little smaller, smooth above and below; anterior margin of the carapace near the orbit with a single spine. Spaces between the spines smooth. Carapace with a deep transverse sulcus in front of the posterior margin. Abdomen punctate, covered with small, miliary granules, not sulcate in the middle, the lateral cornua armed behind with several acute teeth.

This is the common Sydney Crayfish. Mr. T. W. Kirk has described and figured, in the Transactions of the New Zealand Institute for 1879, under the name of *P. tumidus,* a species of Rock-Lobster obtained in the North Island,

and mentions that Dr. Hector had told him that it is the same species as the common Crayfish of the Sydney market. The difference between *P. tumidus* and *P. hügelii* he states to be, (1) the greater size of the former, (2) the upward curvature of the beak, supraorbital, and antennary spines, and (3) the telson in the former being less triangular, and rounded instead of scarped. Leaving size out of consideration, the upward (and forward) direction of the spines mentioned is, so far as can be seen, present in *P. hügelii* as described and figured by Heller; and there is such a close agreement in all other points between that species and the common Sydney Crayfish that I am inclined to regard the concave posterior border of the telson shown in the figure (but not mentioned in the description) to be either an artist's slip, or the result of the wearing of the posterior thin edge of the telson in the specimen figured.

In young specimens of the Sydney Crayfish the spines on the carapace are very prominent, and all, without exception, pointed as represented in the "Reise der Novara," but in large specimens many of them become blunt, and reduced to the appearance of tubercles, as described by Mr. Kirk in the large New Zealand specimen. (*Haswell*.)

This large and valuable crustacean exists in countless numbers along our rocky shores, notwithstanding which the Sydney market is as a rule but poorly supplied, and that from only a few localities, the principal of which are Port Stephens, Cape Hawke, and sometimes Shoalhaven. Broken Bay, which used to be the main source of the metropolitan supply, now furnishes but few, this decadence being the result of the reckless destruction of the breeding females. So abundant is this Crayfish, and, with proper legislative precautions, so apparently inexhaustible the supply, that at but little expense a great and profitable canning industry might with ease be established in our various centres of distribution.

This fine species grows to a weight of six pounds or even more.

Family II.—ASTACIDÆ.

Carapace oblong, subcylindrical, rostrate, scarcely narrower than the abdomen. External antennæ provided with a basal scale. First three pairs of ambulatory legs chelate. Sternum narrow.

Genus.—ASTACOPSIS.

Astacopsis, Huxley, 1878.

Epistome long and flattened: basal joint of the antennæ fixed by the overlapping edge of the cephalostegite: squame short: posterior thoracic sterna narrow: coxopodites of the hinder thoracic limbs large and approximated in the middle line. Rostrum straight; podobranchiæ not alate.

ASTACOPSIS SERRATUS.

Cancer serratus, Shaw, Zool. N. Holland, pl. viii.
Astacus armatus, E. von Martens, Ann. Nat. Hist. (3) xvii. p. 359.
Astacoides spinifer, Heller, Voy. Novara, Crust. p. 102, pl. ix.
Potamobius serratus, White, Proc. Zool. Soc. 1850, p. 95, pl. xv; McCoy, Ann. Nat. Hist. (3) xx. 1867, p. 189.
Astacoides serratus, E. von Martens, MB. Ak. Wiss. Berl. 1868, p. 615.
Astacopsis serratus, Haswell, Austr. Malacostr. p. 174.
? *Astacopsis parramattensis*, Spence Bate, Voy. Challenger, xxiv. p. 202, pl. xxvii. f. 1, 18.
? *Astacopsis sydneyensis*, Spence Bate, Voy. Challenger, xxiv. p. 204, pl. xxii. f. 2, 18.

River Crayfish.

Plate LI.

Sides of the carapace on the hepatic and branchial regions furnished with scattered conical spines, each enlarged at its base. Rostrum about as long as the peduncles of the outer antennæ, pointed and furnished on each side with four teeth; its borders continued backwards for a short distance on the carapace in the form of a ridge. A spine placed behind the middle of the orbit, continued backwards into a similar shorter ridge. Scales of the outer antennæ pointed. Merus of chelipedes with a row of sharp spines on its inner border, two or three spines on its upper surface, and a row of small irregular teeth on its upper border; carpus with two or three prominent spines on its inner surface—the first the longest—and one or two on the outer surface. Hand with both borders armed with a row of short spines bent forwards, and forming a double row on the external edge, and a single one on the internal. Following pairs of thoracic limbs with scattered spines. Segments of the abdomen with four to ten large conical acute spines, except the sixth, which usually has about a dozen smaller spines. Telson usually with about eighteen small spines. Appendages of sixth segment usually armed with about a dozen small spines.

Mr. Whitelegge considers that *A. parramattensis* and *A. sydneyensis* are only the young of *A. serratus*, which is a very variable species.

The River Crayfish is but rarely seen in the Sydney market, but is largely used as food by the residents on the banks of the rivers, in which it abounds, during the winter months, when they are in their best condition and most readily caught; they are excellent eating and grow to about a foot in length.

Family III.—PENÆIDÆ.

Three anterior pairs of legs chelate, longer than the rest, and more or less stronger.

Genus—PENÆUS.

Penæus, Fabr. Suppl. Ent. Syst. 1798.

Three anterior pairs of feet linear: two posterior pairs not annulated. Carapace with a long ensiform rostrum. Abdominal feet with two laminæ. External maxillipedes palpigerous.

PENÆUS CANALICULATUS.

Palæmon canaliculatus, Olivier, Encycl. viii. p. 660, 1811.
Penæus canaliculatus, Milne-Edw. Hist. Nat. Crust. ii. p. 414, 1837; De Haan, Faun. Japon. Crust. p. 190, 1849; Miers, Proc. Zool. Soc. 1878, p. 298; Haswell, Proc. Linn. Soc. N. S. Wales, iv. 1879, p. 38; and Aust. Malacostr. p. 198, 1882.
Penæus plebejus, Hess, Arch. f. Nat. xxxi. p. 168, pl. vii. fig. 19.

Sand Prawn.

A median crest, mesially grooved behind, and with a deep longitudinal groove on either side of it continued from the base of the rostrum to the posterior border of the carapace. Rostrum as long as the peduncles of the antennules, curved slightly upwards towards the acute extremity armed with 10–12 teeth above and one below. A very strong tooth on the anterior border of the carapace above the insertion of the antennæ; a second, much smaller between that and the rostrum ; and a third behind the rudimentary cervical suture at the base of the first. Base of the legs of the two first pairs armed with strong spines. Telson with three spines on each side.

This Prawn is taken in large numbers by small-meshed nets on the sandy beaches near the mouths of our rivers, the principal supply coming from George's and Cook's Rivers.

They are delicious food, and grow to five inches in length.

PENÆUS MONODON.

Penæus monodon, Fabr. Supp. p. 408 ; Latr. Hist. Nat. des An. et Ins. vi. p. 249 ; Lam. Hist. des An. sans Vert. v. p. 205 ; Desm. Consid. p. 225 ; M.-Edw. Hist. Nat. Crust. ii. p. 416 ; Miers, Proc. Zool. Soc. 1878, p. 307 ; Haswell, Austr. Malacostr. p. 199.

Penæus semisulcatus, De Haan, Faun. Japon. Crust. p. 191, pl. xlvi. f. 1, 1849 ; Miers. Proc. Zool. Soc. 1878, p. 299 ; Haswell, Austr. Malacostr. p. 199.

Penæus esculentus, Haswell, Proc. Linn. Soc. N. S. Wales, 1879, iv. p. 38, *and* Austr. Malacostr. p. 200.

Tiger Prawn.

A dorsal carina, not or obsoletely sulcated, generally not reaching to the posterior extremity of the carapace. Gastro-hepatic sulcus deep. Rostrum with six to eight teeth above, of which the most posterior is separated from the next by a distance greater than the intervals between the others; its lower border armed with three or four teeth. First pair of legs with a long acute spine on the under surface of the second joint, and another on the under surface of the third joint ; the second pair with a single spine on the second joint. Telson acute.

Mr. Whitelegge, in his "Marine and Freshwater Invertebrate Fauna of Port Jackson," writes of this species :—" *P. monodon*, Fabr. = *P. semisulcatus*, De Haan = *P. esculentus*, Hasw." This is the " Tiger Prawn " of the Sydney fishermen. Spence Bate in the Challenger Report, vol. xxiv. p. 250, says that the females alone have a groove on the dorsal carina ; in Dr. Haswell's specimen from Port Darwin, there is a well marked groove ; the specimen is a male."

This species is at times common in the Sydney market, but is irregular in its appearance ; during the summer and autumn of 1891-92 it was exceptionately plentiful, since which time but few specimens have been observed ; Dr. Haswell is mistaken in saying that this species is " the common edible Prawn of Sydney, Newcastle, &c."

This is a marine species and is taken principally, if not entirely, on clean sandy beaches. It does not mix much with other Prawns, but from its preference for the same class of ground sometimes occurs in company with *P. canaliculatus*.

PENÆUS, SP.

Mr. Whitelegge says : " This is probably an undescribed form. The carapace is hairy, sculptured, and each of the first three pairs of legs bears a spine near the base.

This is by far the most common species offered for sale, *P. canaliculatus* and *P. macleayi* are often seen intermixed with it, the lastnamed being the rarest of the two."

Abundant at certain seasons in the Sydney market and much valued as food.

Attains a length of three inches.

PENÆUS MACLEAYI.

Penæus macleayi, Haswell, Proc. Linn. Soc. N. S. Wales, iv. 1879, p. 40, *and* Austr. Malacostr. p. 201.

Mud or River Prawn.

Rostrum extending nearly as far forward as the end of the antennary scale, very slender and styliform near the apex, which is recurved; armed with five or six teeth above, of which the fifth is separated from the fourth by an interval greater than that separating the others; unarmed below; produced behind into a low carina, which broadens out and becomes lost before attaining the posterior third of the carapace; a lateral groove at the side of the rostrum and the anterior part of the carapace. Gastro-hepatic sulcus deep. Supraorbital spine absent; antennary and hepatic spines present. Filaments of antennules subequal, scarcely equal in length to the two last joints of the peduncle. External maxillipedes slender, hairy; palp extending as far as the middle of the third articulation of the endopodite. First pair of ambulatory legs as long as the antennary scale, very hairy internally; second and third progressively longer; fourth shorter than third; fifth the longest of all and very slender. First and second and sometimes third pairs each with a spine at the base of the second joint. Abdomen having the fourth, fifth, and sixth segments dorsally carinated; carina ending in a small spine at the posterior border of the sixth segment. Terminal segment longitudinally grooved in the middle dorsal line, ending in a spiniform apex, ciliated laterally, and armed on each side near the extremity with a strong spine, with two or three weaker spines immediately anterior to it (*Haswell*).

The remarks on the last species apply equally well to this.

The four following species often occur in the market and are used as food:—

Ibacus peroni; a few may be picked up in the market during any month in the year, but they are never common; we have seen them taken both by trawl and dredge in Ball's Head Bay, Port Jackson.

They are used as food and are said to be of good quality; they grow to a length of seven inches.

Goniosoma crucifera sometimes occurs in the market in considerable numbers, and is a large and handsome species, generally eaten, and attaining to a weight of at least one pound.

Platyonychus bipustulatus occasionally appears in numbers in the market, and we have seen the shore at Lady Robinson's Beach, Botany Bay, covered with them after a southerly gale.

Squilla lævis; this crustacean is always obtainable among prawns (*Penæus canaliculatus*) in the market, but is sometimes much more abundant than at others, in fact we have known them to form about one third of the total supply. They reach a length of about six inches.

APPENDIX.

LUTIANUS FULVIFLAMMA.
(Page 15.)

We have lately received a fine specimen from Cape Hawke, which measured sixteen and three-fourths inches.

SCATOPHAGUS MULTIFASCIATUS.
(Page 36.)

From an examination of several specimens obtained in the Sydney market since our description was written, we are now convinced that our *Scatophagus* differs specifically from that figured by Richardson and Günther. The name will, so far as we are at present able to decide, have to stand as *Scatophagus ætatevarians*, De Vis; we, however, take this opportunity of recording our protest against the practice of manufacturing specific names so utterly unmeaning as this.

CARANX TRACHURUS.
(Page 77.)

On page 78 we quote a passage from the Report of the Royal Commission, for the accuracy of which we were unable to vouch; we are, therefore, happy to be able to state that the authority therefor is Dr. Günther, who says :—
" The large Medusæ on our" *i.e.*, the British, " coast are almost always accompanied by young fishes. On the south coast I found them to be Scad, one large Medusa offering a temporary home to more than fifty of these young fishes, which were from two to three inches long." (*Voy. Challenger*, XX , *p.*   ).

SCOMBER PNEUMATOPHORUS.
(Page 93.)

In the description of this Mackerel, the following sentence occurs ;—
" Diameter of eye .... 1·40–1·60 in the interorbital space, which is flat"; it should be " interorbital space flat, 1·33–1·60 in the interorbital space."

During the months of May and June, 1893, large shoals of fine adult Mackerel appeared in the various indentations of our coast in the metropolitan and neighboring districts; these fishes were entirely devoid of ova, but were in magnificent condition, and were, we consider, quite equal in flavor to any British-caught Mackerel (*S. scomber*) ; in these examples the great thickness, rotundity, and fleshiness of the Australian Mackerel, as compared with that of *S. scomber*, were extremely noticeable. The average size of the individuals composing these shoals was between twelve and thirteen inches, but some examples were quite an inch larger. It is also to be remarked that these shoals are on the coast at midwinter, not midsummer as usually reported.

On page 96 we quote Castlenau as stating that in his *S. antarcticus* the air-bladder is absent, and make some remarks thereon; these remarks are justified by the publication in the following year (1873) of an essay by Castlenau—which we had previously overlooked—entitled "Notes on the Edible Fishes of Victoria," in which he states, as dogmatically as he in his former paper denied it, that *S. antarcticus* "has an air-bladder," without, however, making any reference to or correction of his former error; he does not, nevertheless, relinquish his opinion as to the specific value of his *S. antarcticus*, but as, the absence of an air-bladder having perforce to be given up as a means of discrimination, he relies mainly on the difference in coloration, a very unstable character in this genus. We still prefer to consider it as synonymous with *S. pneumatophorus*.

In his British Fishes, i, p. 91, Day, writing of *S. colias*—of which he and others consider *S. pneumatophorus* to be a mere variety—says:—"The posterior adipose lid . . . . crossing over the lower edge of the anterior lid, is inserted into the suborbital ring of bones." A reference to our description (p. 94) will show that the reverse is the case in our fish; presuming, therefore, that Day's account is correct, it would be interesting to know whether the same difference occurs between the Atlantic and Mediterranean forms of *S. colias* and *S. pneumatophorus*, or whether this character is confined to the Pacific form.

This species occurs on the coast of the Western States of America, the North Atlantic, and the Mediterranean.

PELAMYS CHILENSIS.
(Page 97.)

During the early part of May, 1893, numbers of these fishes were brought to market from Port Jackson and the neighbouring bays; these were of much larger size than is usual with us, some individuals measuring as much as twenty four inches; since then small examples of twelve inches and even less in length have been abundant.

The generic name *Pelamis* having been formed for a genus of Sea Snakes by Daudin many years previously to that on which the authors of the Histoire Naturelle des Poissons used it, it becomes necessary to look for another name applicable to this species, and we, therefore, follow Jordan and Gilbert in calling our Horse Mackerel *Sarda chilensis*. The generic quotation is:—*Sarda*, Cuvier, Règne Anim. 2nd. Ed. ii. 1829.

INDEX.

	PAGE.
Acanthopterygii	1
æquipinnis (Scorpis)	38
atatevarians (Scatophagus)	205
affinis (Beryxe)	69
afra (Murœna)	190
ambiguus (Ctenolates)	22
Anacanthini	149
Anguilla	187
annulatum (Plectropoma)	10
Apperdix	205
aquila (Sciœna)	72
argenteus (Psettus)	91
armatus (Enoplosus)	6
Arripis	20
arsius (Pseudorhombus)	155
Astacidæ	201
Astacopsis	201
ateladus (Otolithus)	75
Aulopus	166
australasica (Macquaria)	24
australis (Pagrus)	51
ayraudi (Monacanthus)	196
Ayraud's Leatherjacket	197
badius (Platychœrops)	134
Balistidæ	193
Banded Pigfish	137
Banded Sea-Perch	10
Batfish	91
Beardie	153
bellis (Cossyphus)	137
Belone	168
benmebari (Priacanthus)	31
Berycidæ	69
Beryx	69
bipustulatus (Platyonychus)	204
Black Bream	51
Blackfish	42
Black Rock-Cod	9
Black Sole	160
Black-spotted Red Rock-Cod	63
Black-spotted Sea-Perch	14
Bluefish	45
Blue Groper	132
Blue-spotted Groper	130
Blue-striped Red Mullet	33
Boarfish	29
Bony Bream	178
Brachyura	198
Bullrout	67
Bullseye	32
Butterfish	37
bynoënsis (Scorpæna)	65
Bynoe's Rock-Cod	65

	PAGE.
callarias (Lotella)	152
canaliculatus (Penæus)	202
Carangidæ	76
Caranx	77
Carp	59
carponemus (Chilodactylus)	55
Centropogon	66
Chætodontidæ	36
Chatoëssina	178
Chatoëssus	178
chilensis (Pelamys)	97, 206
Chilodactylus	55
Chironemus	54
Chœrops	130
ciliata (Sillago)	102
Cirrhitidæ	53
Clupea	179
Clupeidæ	177
Clupeina	179
Cnidoglanis	164
colonorum (Percalates)	2
Common Flathead	105
Common Swimming-Crab	199
Coris	141
Cossyphus	135
Cottidæ	104
coxi (Galaxias)	176
Cox's Mountain Trout	176
Crimson-banded Parrotfish	140
crucifera (Goniosoma)	204
cruenta (Scorpæna)	63
Crustacea	198
Ctenolates	22
Cuvier's Sea-Perch	12
cyanea (Girella)	45
cyanomelas (Olistherops)	145
Cyclometopa	198
dæmeli (Serranus)	8
Dart	90
Dinolestes	115
Diplomystus	184
dobula (Mugil)	118
Drummer	40
Dussumieriina	186
ellipticus (Therapon)	28
elongatus (Myxus)	128
Enoplosus	6
Estuary Catfish	165
Etrumeus	186
ferox (Belone)	168
Flat-tailed Mullet	126
Freshwater Herring	184
fulviflamma (Lutianus)	14, 205
fuscus (Chilodactylus)	59
fuscus (Platycephalus)	105
Gadidæ	152
Gadoidei	149
Gadopsidæ	149
Gadopsis	149
Galaxias	176

INDEX.

	PAGE.
Galaxiidæ ...	176
georgianus (Caranx)	80
Gerres ...	147
Gerridæ ...	146
Girella ...	41
Glaucosoma ...	15
Golden Perch ...	23
gouldi (Platychœrops)	132
Green Eel ...	191
Grystidæ ...	17
gymnogenis (Pseudolabrus)	139
Hard-gut Mullet ...	119
Hemirhamphus ...	171
Herring ...	182
Herring-Cale ...	145
hippocrepis (Monacanthus)	194
hippos (Seriola) ...	85
Histiopterus ...	29
Horse Mackerel ...	97
huegeli (Palinurus)	200
intermedius (Hemirhamphus)	172
Jackassfish ...	57
jacksonensis (Etrumeus) ...	186
Jewfish ...	72
Kelpfish ...	54
Kingfish ...	82
kumu (Trigla)	109
labiosus (Histiopterus)	29
Labridæ ...	129
lævis (Squilla)	204
lalandii (Seriola) ...	82
Large-toothed Flounder ...	155
Lemon Sole ...	163
lineolata (Coris) ...	142
Ling ...	153
Long-finned Eel ...	188
Long-finned Sea-pike ...	116
Lotella ...	152
Ludrick ...	44
Lutianus ...	14
Mackerel ...	94
macleayana (Belone)	170
macleayana (Solea)	159
macleayi (Penæus)	204
Macquaria ...	24
macquariensis (Oligorus)	17
Macquarie's Perch	24
macropterus (Chilodactylus)	57
Macrura ...	200
maculata (Sillago)	100
Mangrove Crab ...	200
Maori ...	142
Maray ...	186
Marbled River Cod	149
marmoratus (Chironemus)	54
marmoratus (Gadopsis)	149
megastoma (Cnidoglanis)	164
Monacanthus ...	193

o

monodon (Penæus)
Morwong
Mud Prawn
muelleri (Dinolestes)
Mugil
Mugilidæ
Mullidæ
Mullus
multifasciatus (Scatophagus)
multimaculatus (Pseudorhombus)
Muræna
Murænidæ
Murray Cod
Myxus

Nannygai
Narrow-banded Sole
Neptunus
nigra (Synaptura)
nigromarginatus (Pseudo-rhombus)
nigrorubrum (Plectropoma)
novæhollandiæ (Diplomystus)
novæhollandiæ (Sphyræna)

ocellatum (Plectropoma)
Odax
Old Wife
Oligorus
Olisthcrops
omnopterus (Chœrops)
Otolithus
ovatus (Gerres)

Pagrus
Palinuridæ
Palinurus
Pearl Perch
pelagicus (Neptunus)
Pelamys
Penæidæ
Penæus
Percalates
Perch
Percidæ
percoides (Sebastes)
peroni (Ibacus)
peroni (Mugil)
Physostomi
Pilchard
Pimelepterus
Pisces
Plagusia
Platycephalus
Platychœrops
Plectognathi
Plectropoma
Pleuronectidæ
Pleuronectoidei
Plotosina
pneumatophorus (Scomber)
polyommata (Trigla)
porosus (Mullus)
Portunidæ
Priacanthidæ

Priacanthus	31
Pristipomatidæ	22
Psettus	91
Pseudolabrus	138
Pseudorhombus	154
purpurissatus (Aulopus)	166
quadrilineatus (Therapon)	26
Red Groper	134
Red Gurnard	109
Red Gurnard Perch	62
regularis (Hemirhamphus)	174
reinhardti (Anguilla)	187
richardsoni (Clupeoïdes)...	178
richardsoni (Odax)	143
River Crayfish	202
River Garfish	174
River Prawn	204
robustus (Centropogon)	67
Rock Whiting	144
russelli (Trachynotus)	89
sagax (Clupea)	180
salar (Arripis)	20
Salmon	20
saltator (Temnodon)	86
Samsonfish	85
Sand Mullet	128
Sand Prawn	202
Sand Whiting	102
sarba (Pagrus)	50
Sarda	206
Scad	77
scapulare (Glaucosoma)	15
Scatophagus	36
Sciæna	72
sclerolepis (Hemirhamphus)	175
Scomber	93
Scombresocidæ	168
Scombridæ	92
Scopelidæ	166
Scorpæna	63
Scorpænidæ	61
Scorpis	38
Scylla	199
Sea Garfish	172
Sea Mullet	119
Sebastes	61
Seriola	82
Sergeant Baker	166
Serranidæ	8
Serranus	8
serrata (Scylla)	199
serratus (Astacopsis)	201
Sharp-beaked Gurnard	111
Short-beaked Garfish	175
Short-finned Sea-Pike	114
signatus (Mullus)	35
Sillago	91
Siluridæ	164
Silverbelly	147
Silver Perch	28
simplex (Girella)	44

	PAGE.
Slender Long Tom	168
Small-toothed Flounder	157
Snapper	47
Solea	158
Sparidæ	40
Sphyræna	113
Sphyrænidæ	113
sp. (Penæus)	203
Spotted Pigfish	136
Spotted Red Mullet	35
Stout Long Tom	170
sundaica (Clupea)	182
Sweep	38
sydneyanus (Pimelepterus)	40
Sydney Crayfish	200
Synaptura	160
Tailor	87
Tallegalane	128
Tarwhine	50
Teleostei	1
Temnodon	86
Teraglin	75
Therapon	26
Tiger Prawn	203
Trachinidæ	98
trachurus (Caranx)	77, 205
trachylepis (Monacanthus)	195
Trachynotus	89
tricuspidata (Girella)	42
Trigla	108
Trumpeter Perch	27
Trumpeter Whiting	100
unicolor (Pagrus)	47
unicolor (Plagusia)	163
unimaculatus (Cossyphus)	135
Variable Leatherjacket	194
White-spotted Parrotfish	139
White Trevally	80
Wirrah	13
Yellow-finned Leatherjacket	195
Yellowtail	77

[Illustrations.]

Plate I.

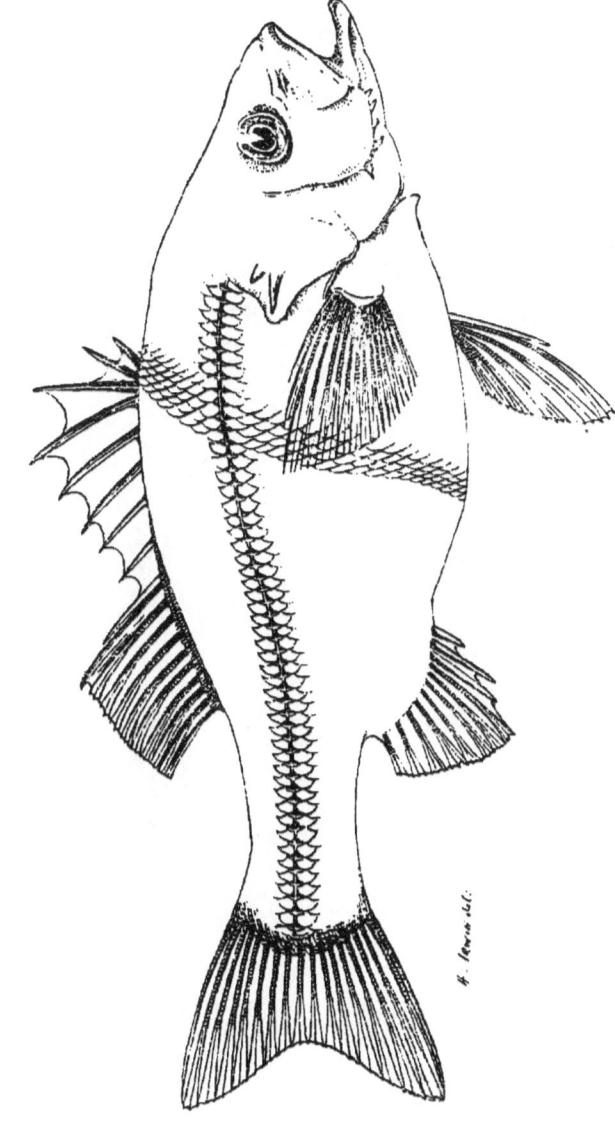

AUSTRALIAN PERCH. *Percalates colonorum.*

Plate II.

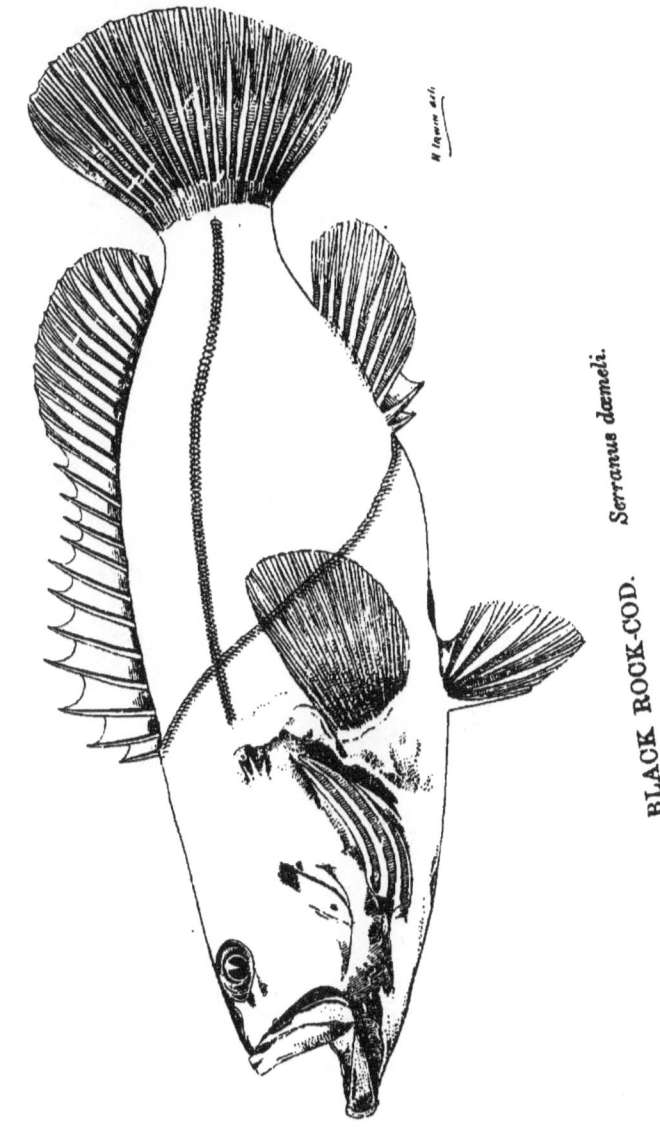

BLACK ROCK-COD. *Serranus daemeli.*

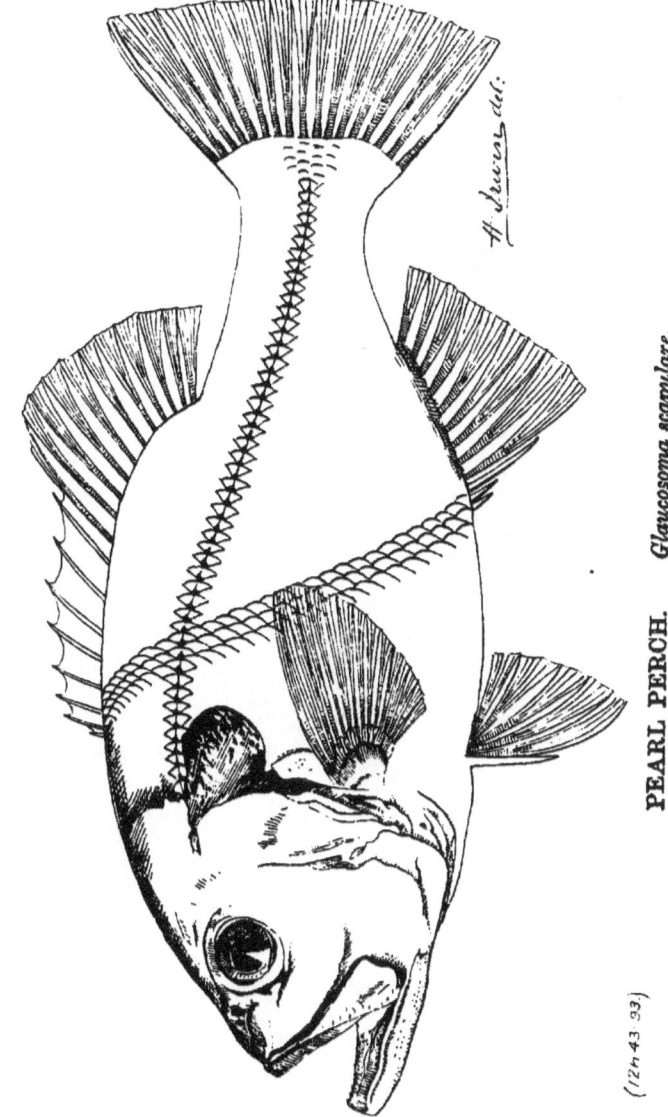

Plate III.

PEARL PERCH. *Glaucosoma scapulare.*

Plate IV.

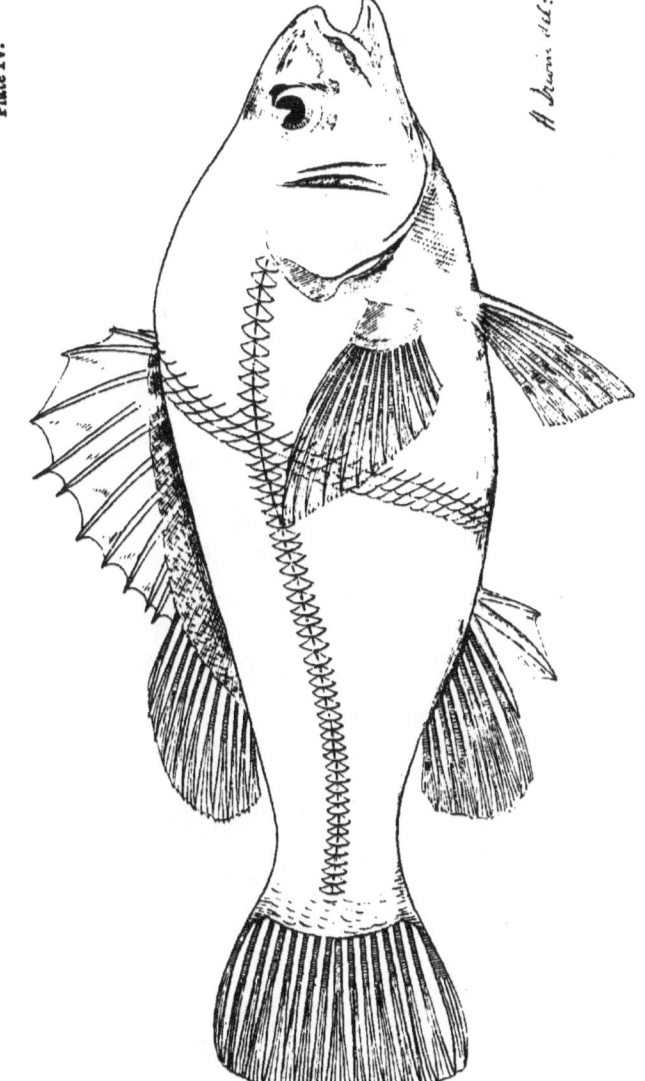

MACQUARIE'S PERCH. *Macquaria australasica.*

Plate V.

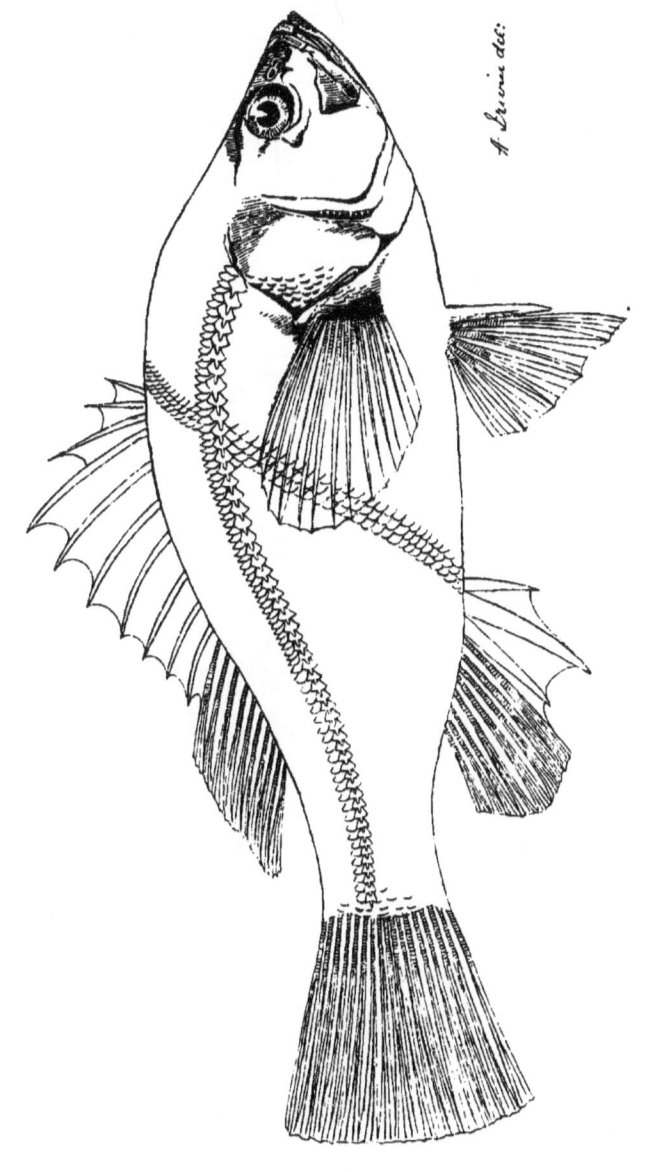

GOLDEN PERCH. *Ctenolates ambiguus.*

Plate VI.

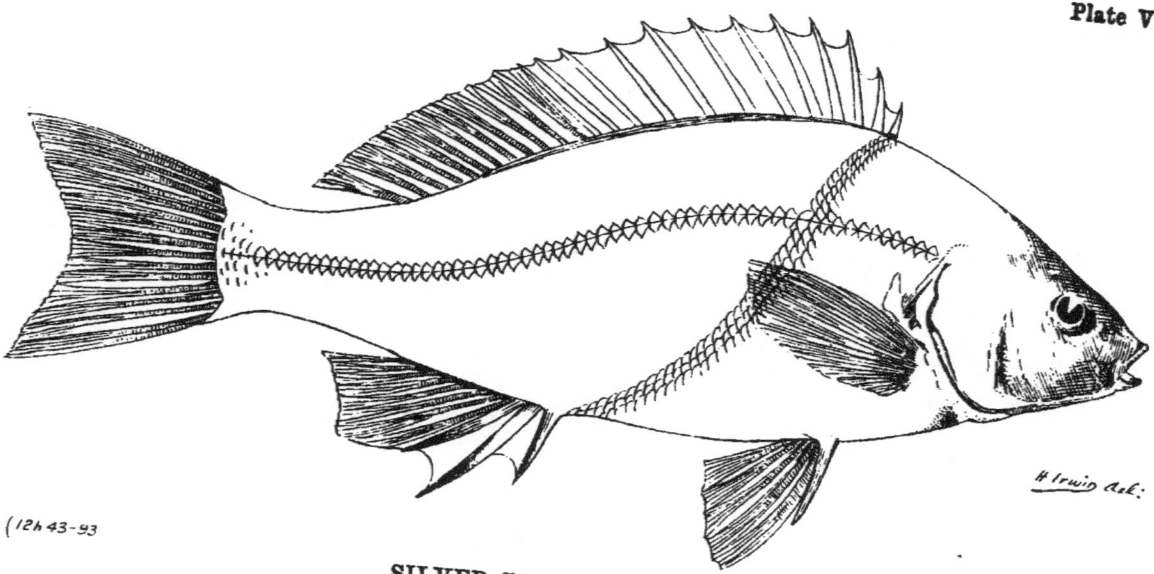

(12h 43-93

SILVER PERCH. *Therapon ellipticus.*

Plate VII.

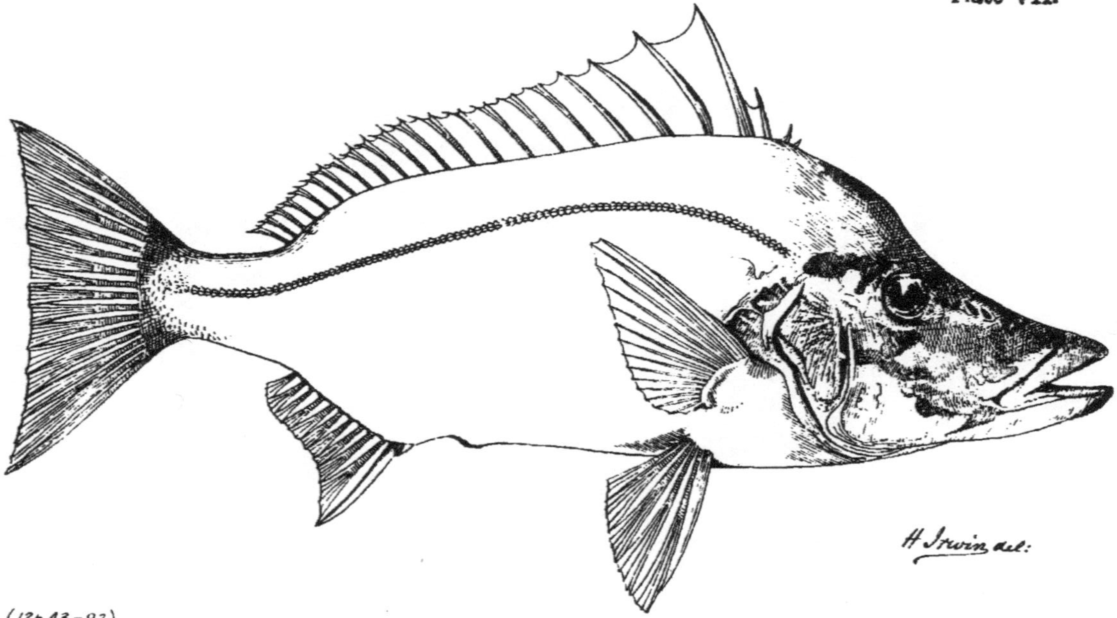

H Irwin del:

(12h 43-93.)

BOAR FISH. *Histiopterus labiosus.*

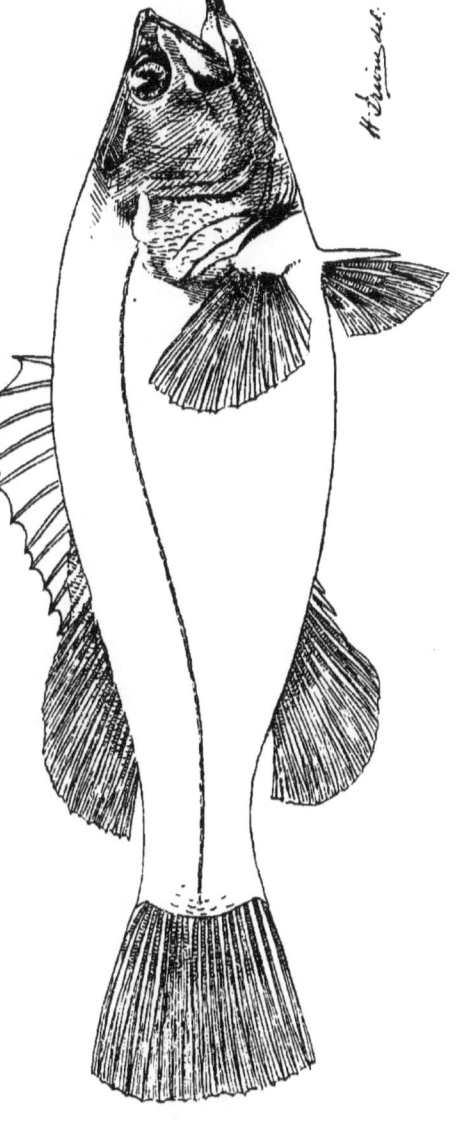

Plate VIII.

MURRAY COD.   *Oligorus macquariensis.*

Plate IX.

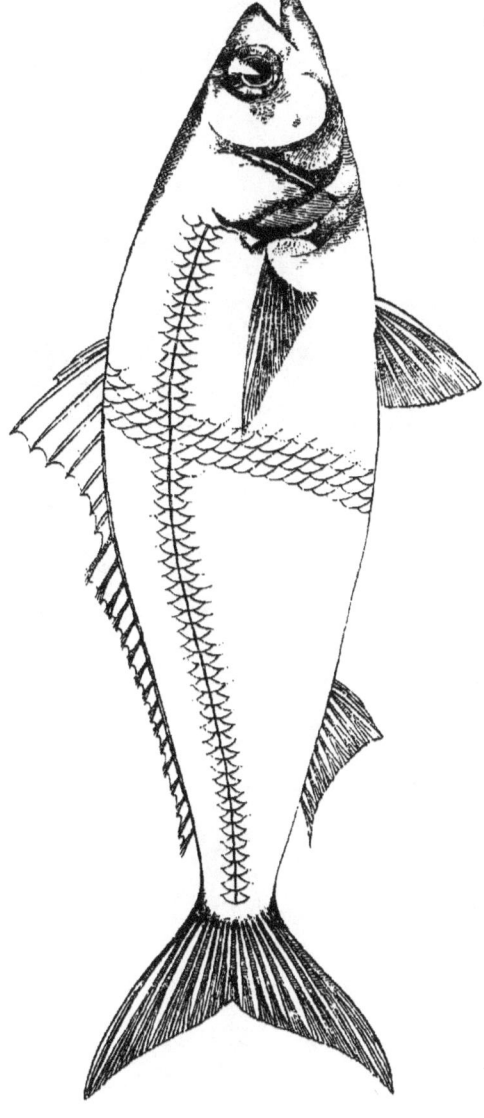

AUSTRALIAN SALMON. *Arripis salar.*

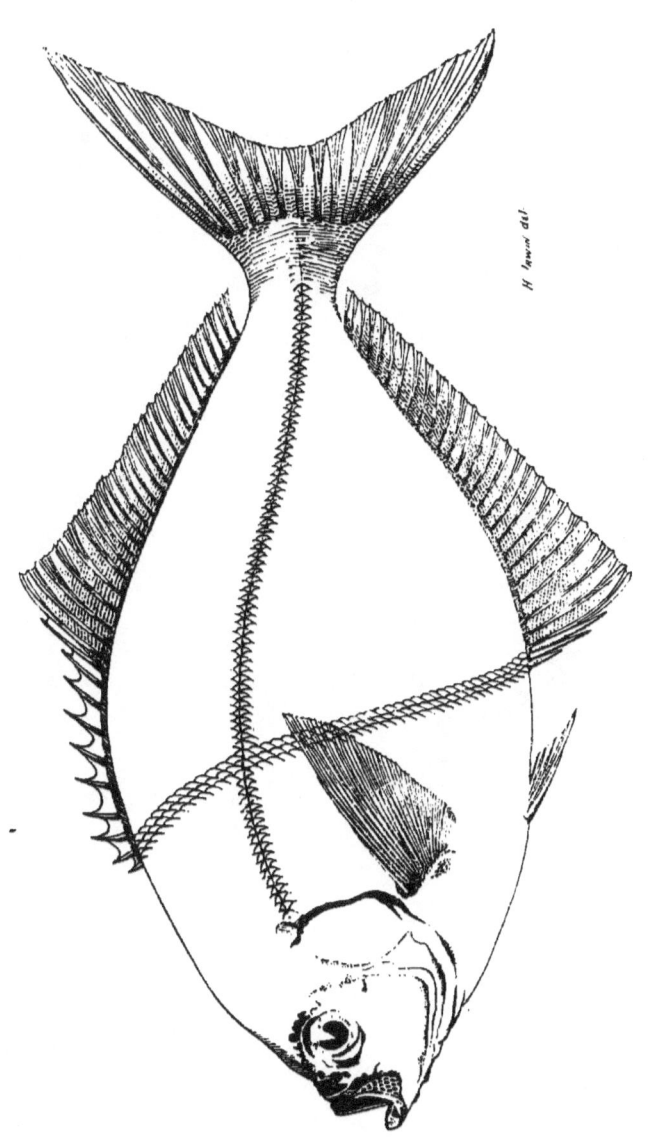

Plate XI.

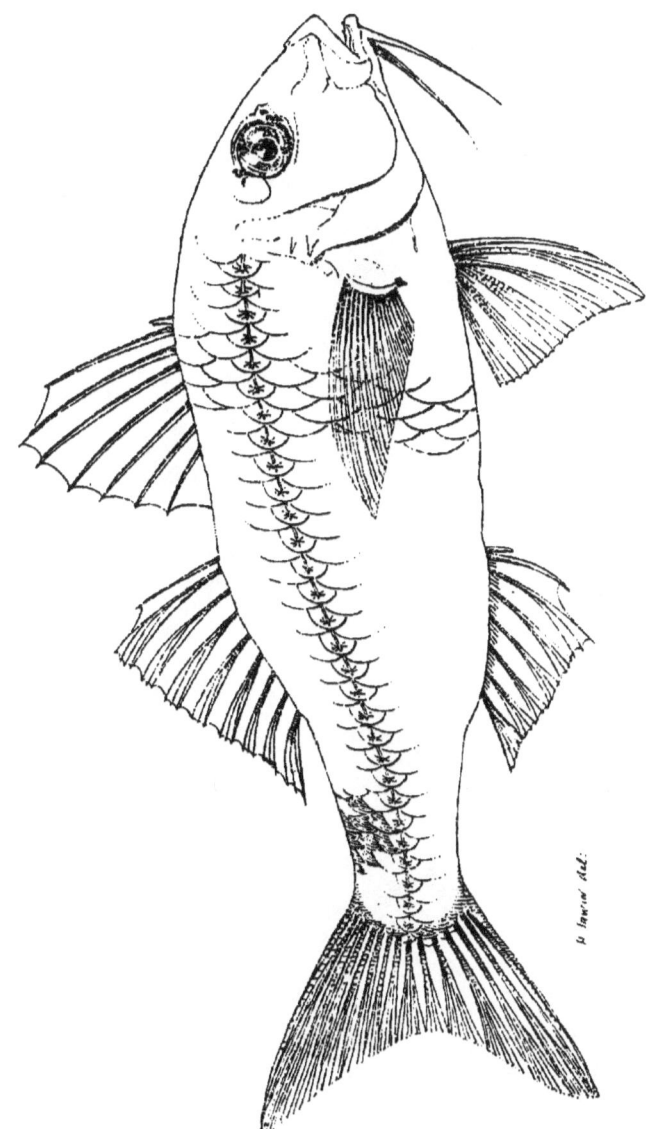

SPOTTED RED MULLET. *Mullus signatus.*

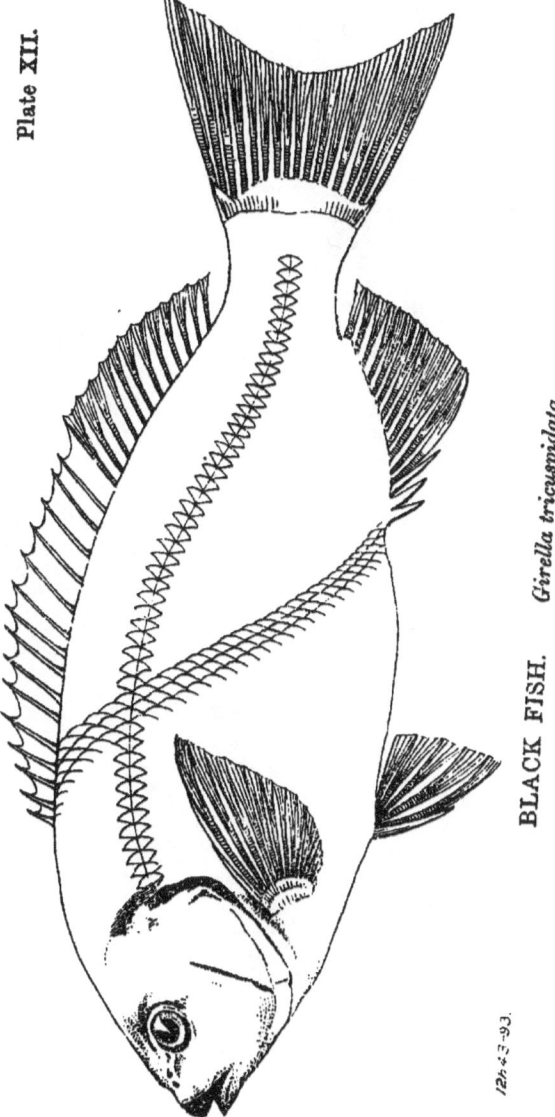

Plate XII.

BLACK FISH. *Girella tricuspidata.*

Plate XIII.

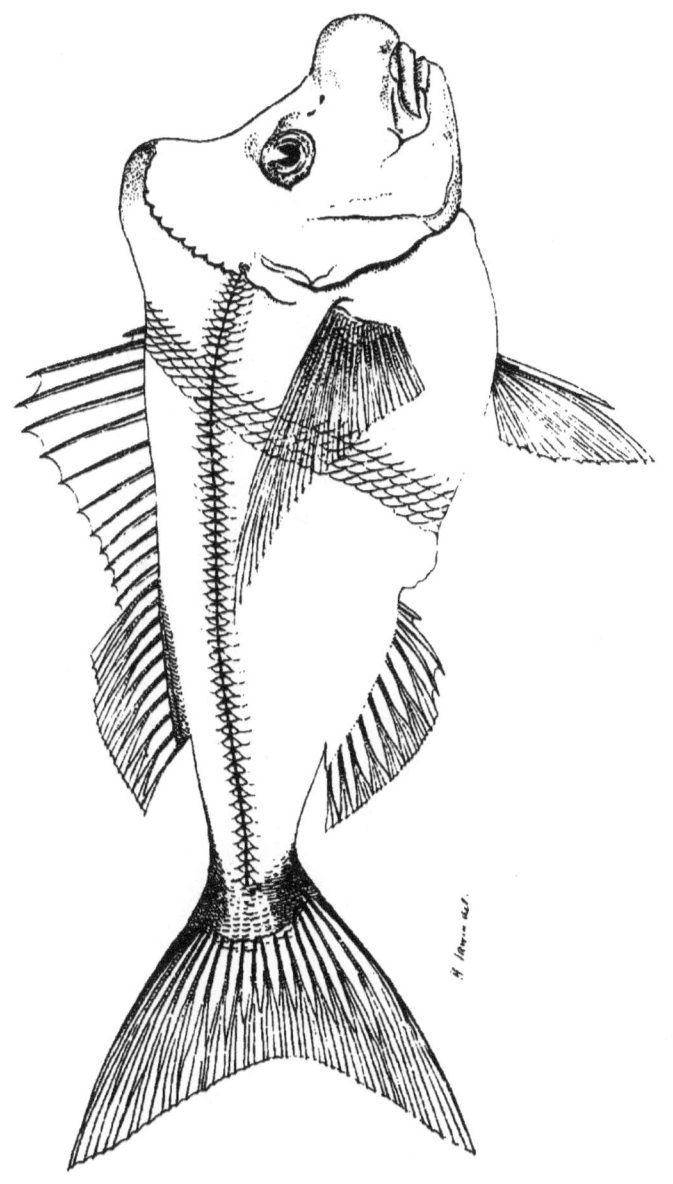

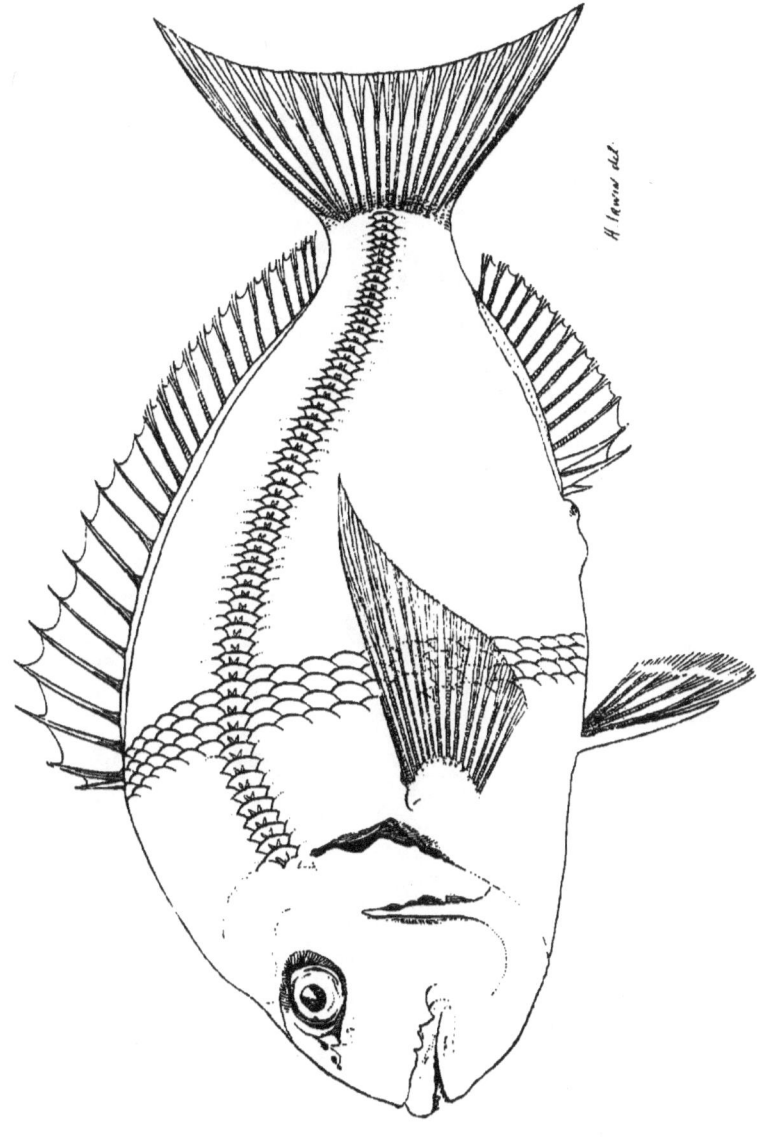

TARWHINE. *Pagrus surba.*

Plate XV.

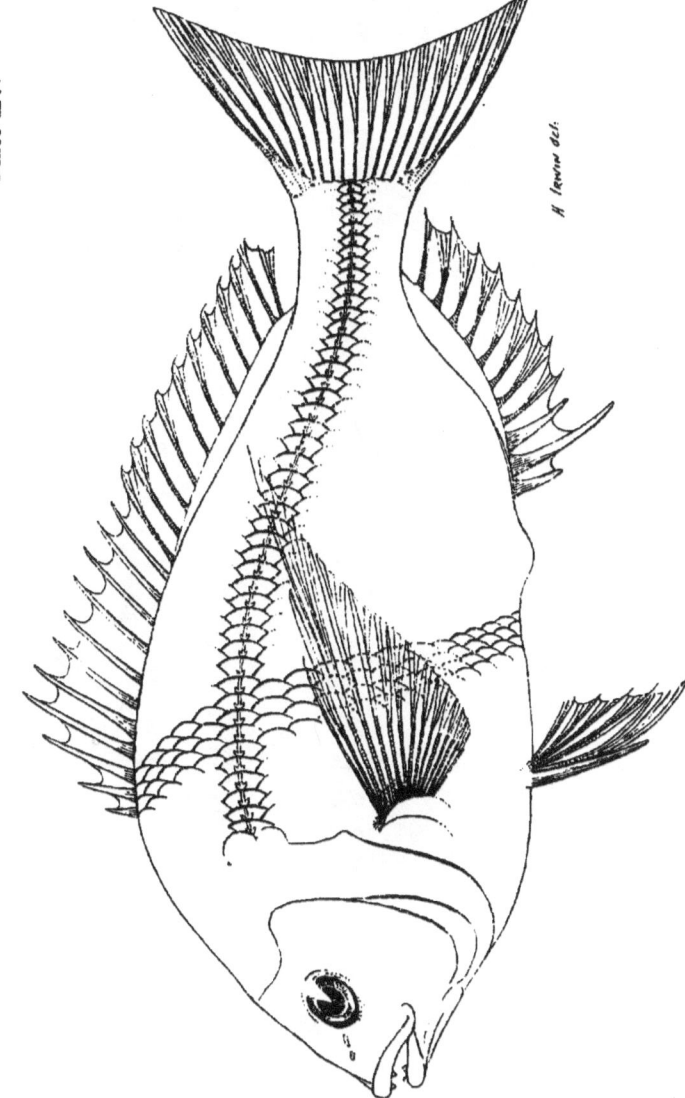

BLACK BREAM.   *Pagrus australis.*

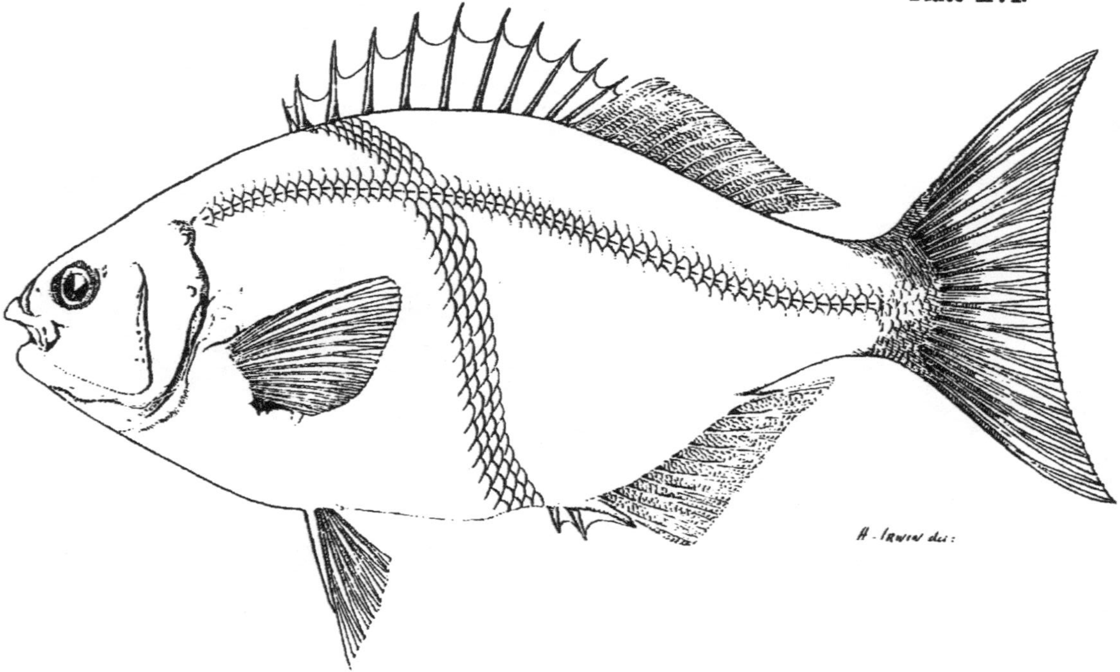

Plate XVI.

DRUMMER.   *Pimelepterus sydneyanus.*

Plate XVII.

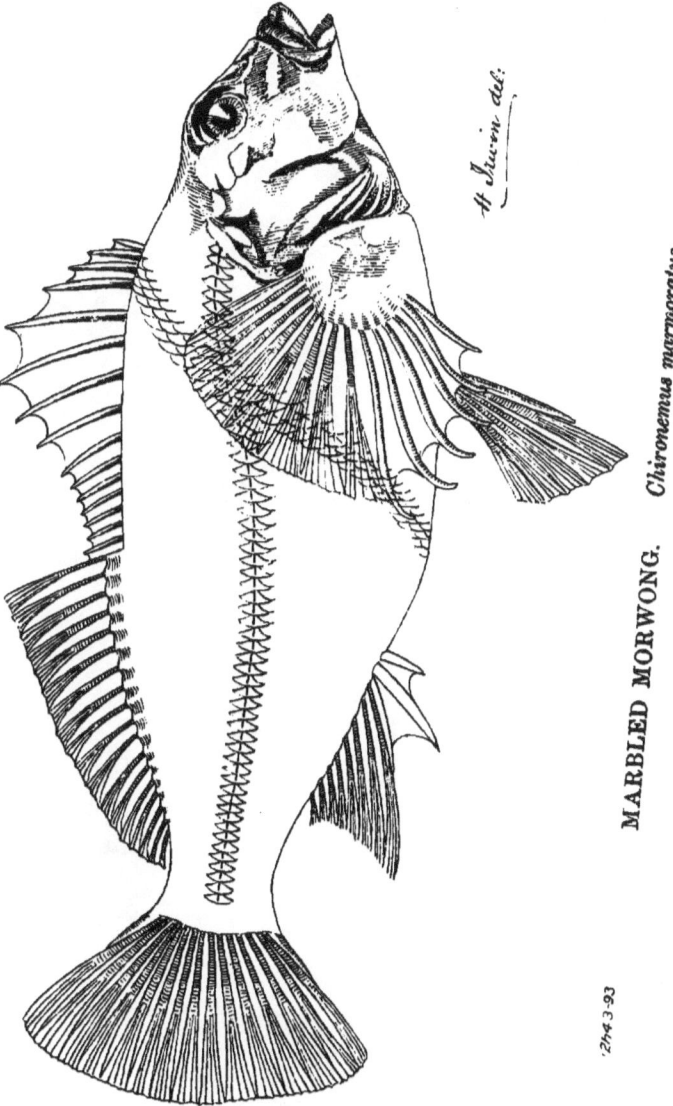

MARBLED MORWONG. *Chironemus marmoratus.*

Plate XVIII.

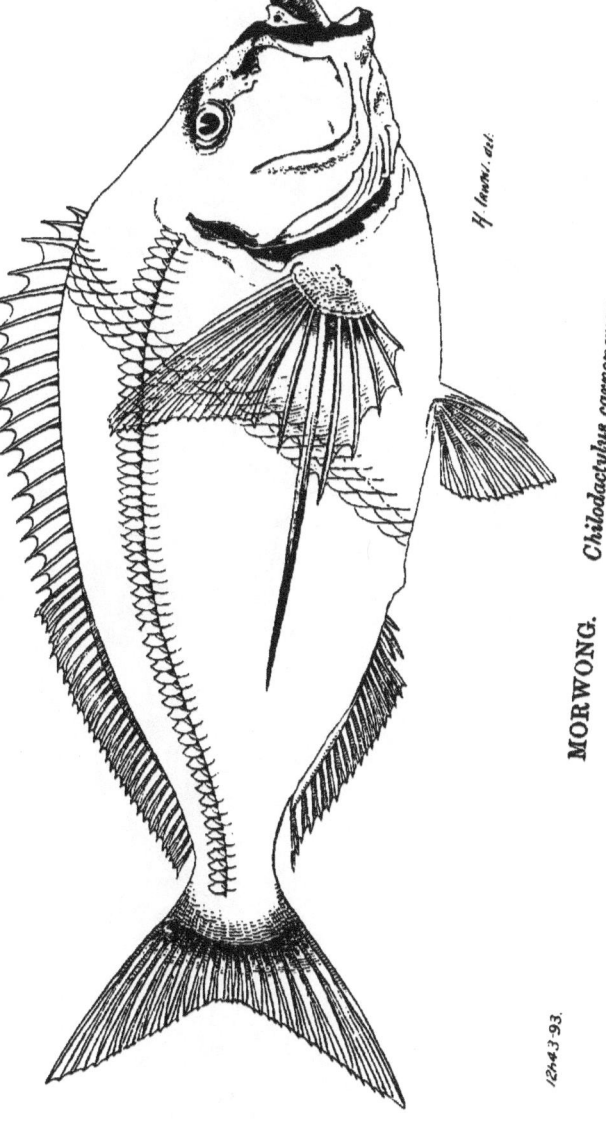

MORWONG. *Chilodactylus carponemus.*

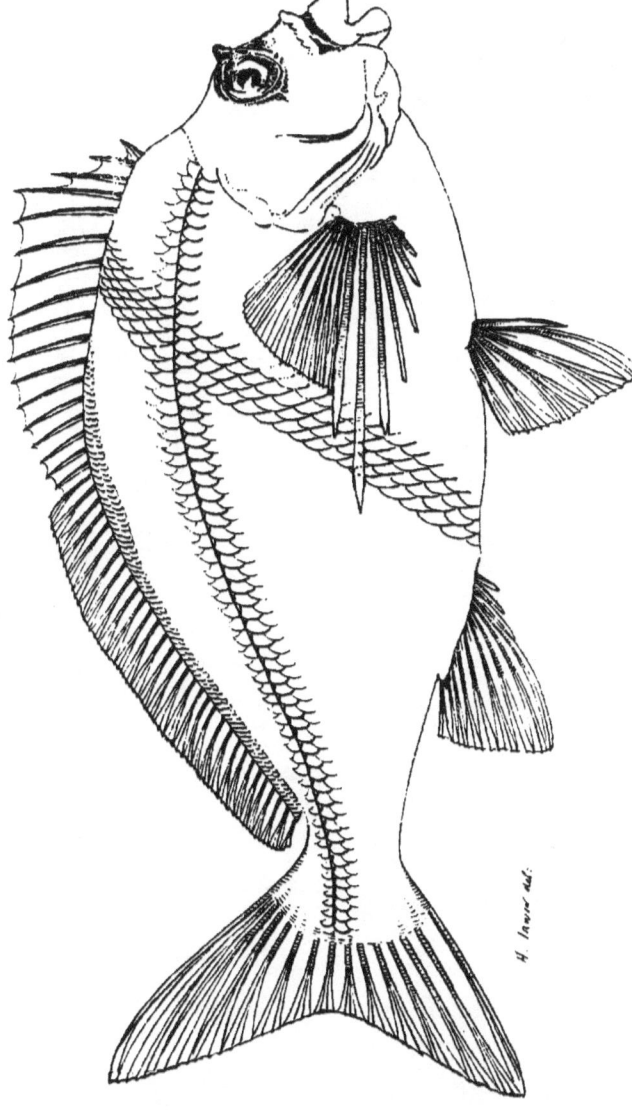

AUSTRALIAN CARP. *Chilodactylus fuscus.*

Plate XX.

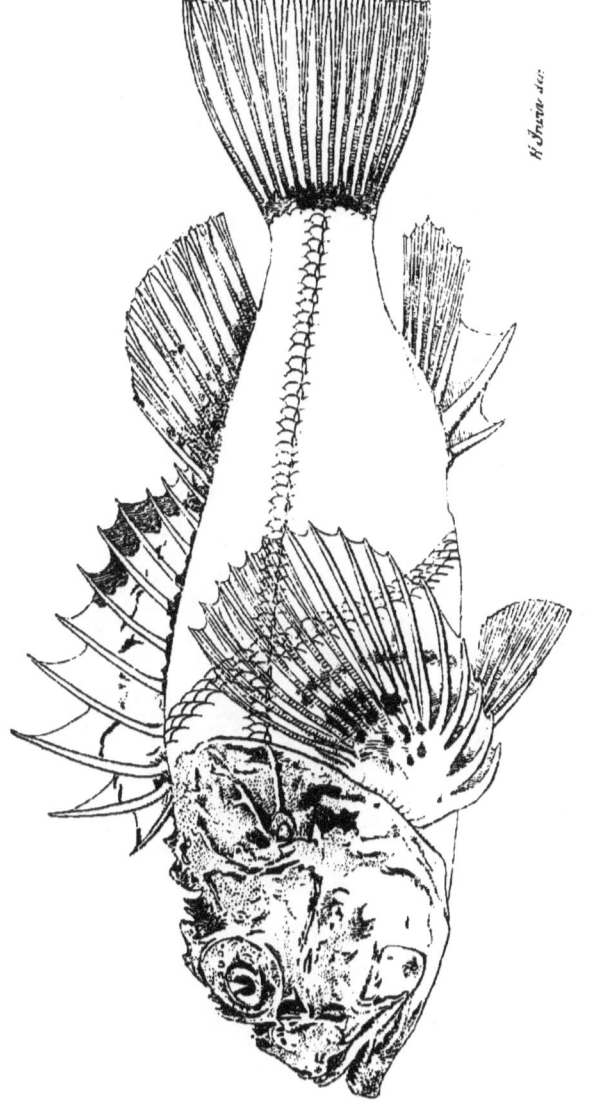

RED ROCK-COD. *Scorpæna cruenta.*

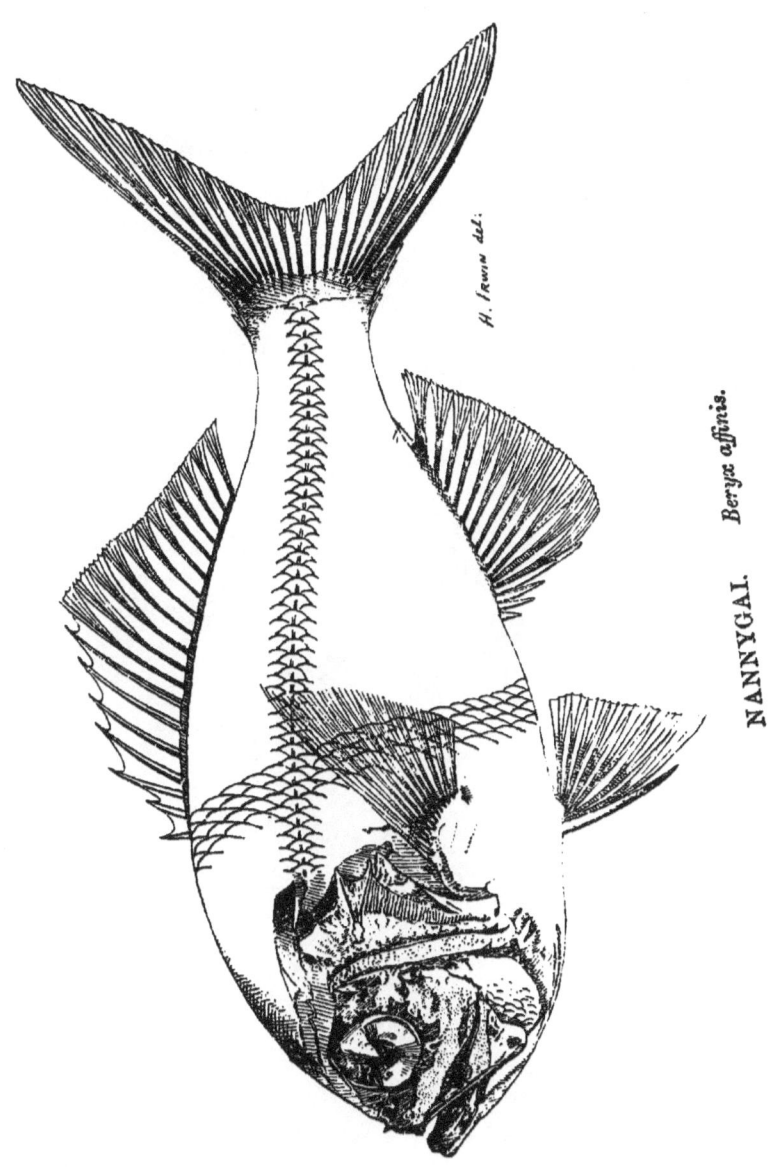

NANNYGAI. *Beryx affinis.*

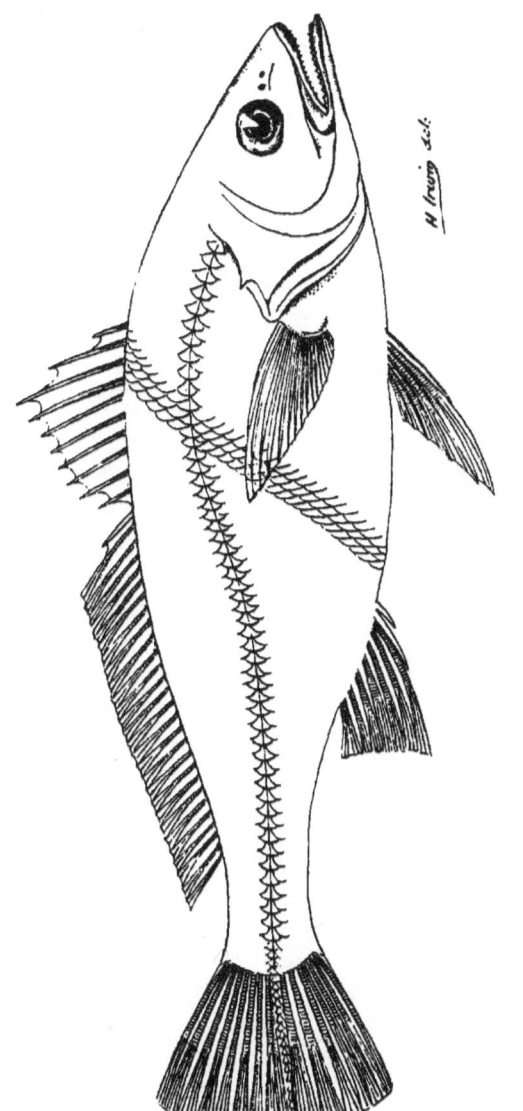

Plate XXII.

JEW FISH. *Sciæna aquila.*

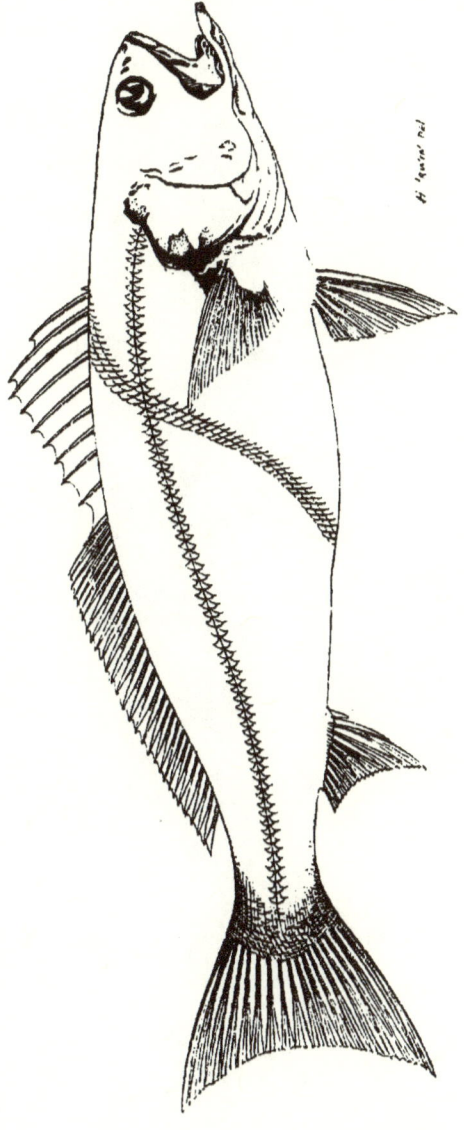

TERAGLIN. *Otolithus atelodus.*

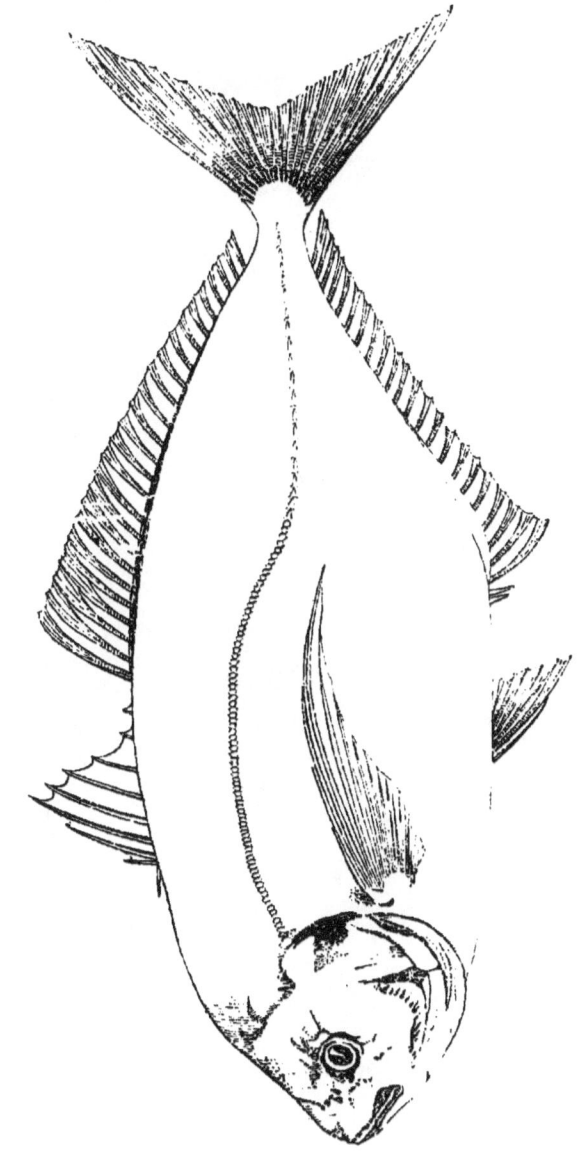

Plate XXIV.

TREVALLY. *Caranx georgianus.*

Plate XXV.

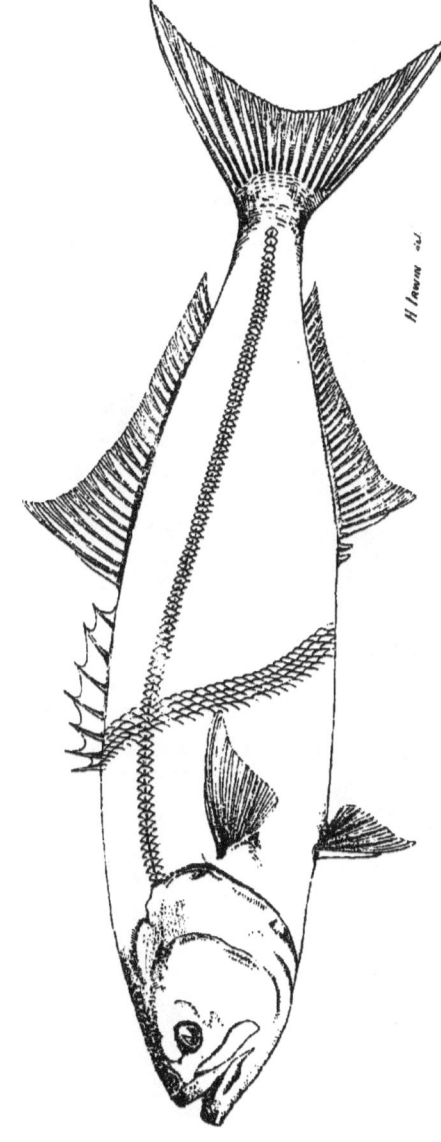

TAILOR.   *Temnodon saltator.*

Plate XXVI.

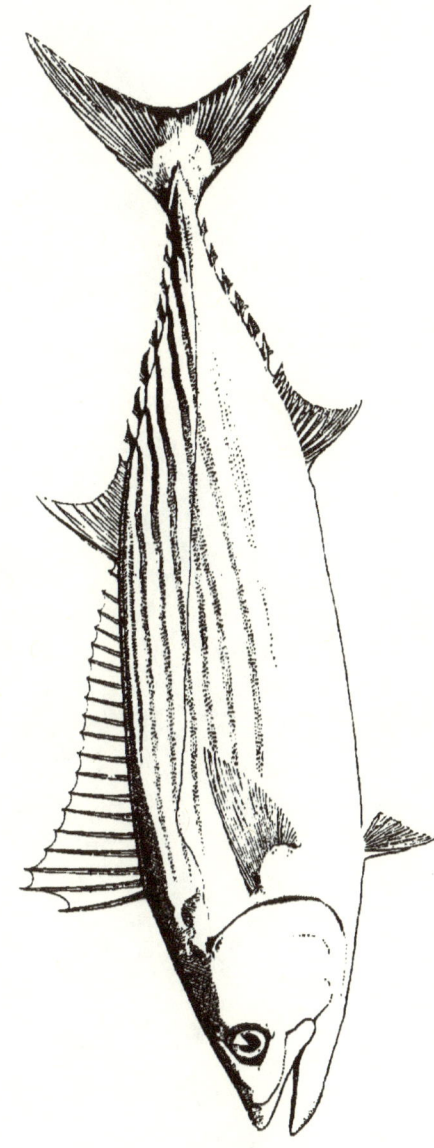

HORSE MACKEREL. *Pelamys australis.*

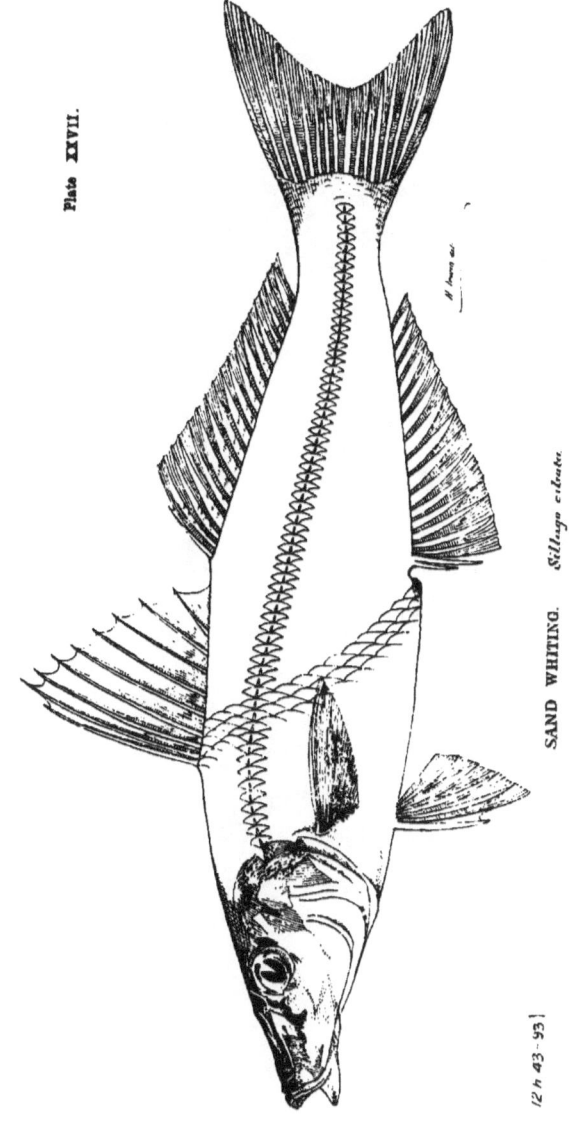

Plate XXVII.

SAND WHITING. *Sillago ciliata.*

Plate XXVIII.

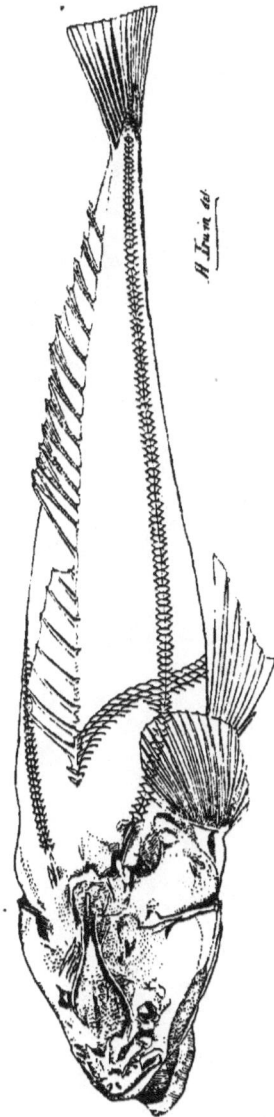

FLATHEAD. *Platycephalus fuscus.*

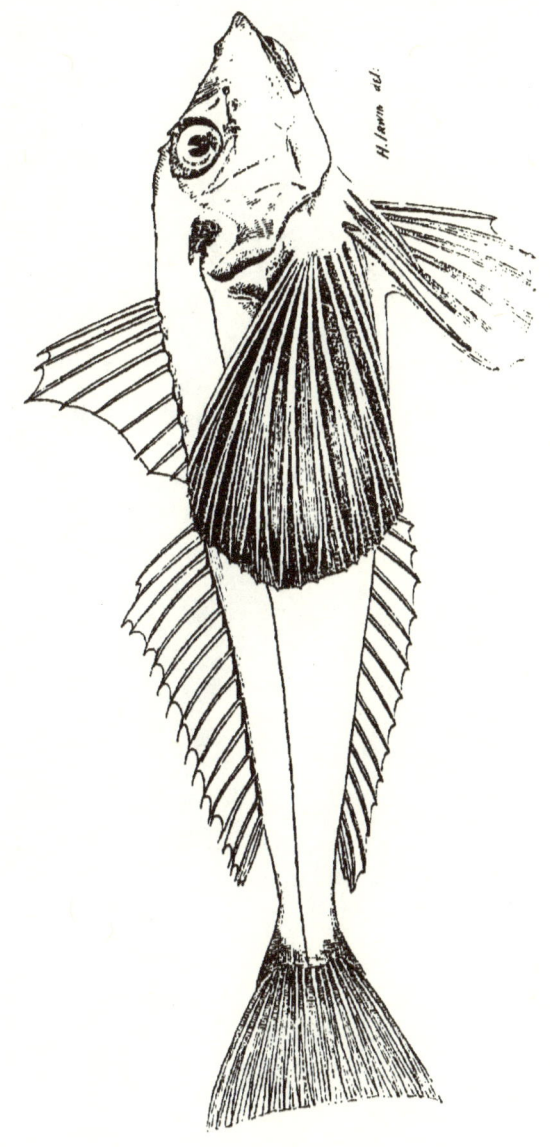

Plate XXIX.

RED GURNARD. *Trigla kumu.*

Plate XXX.

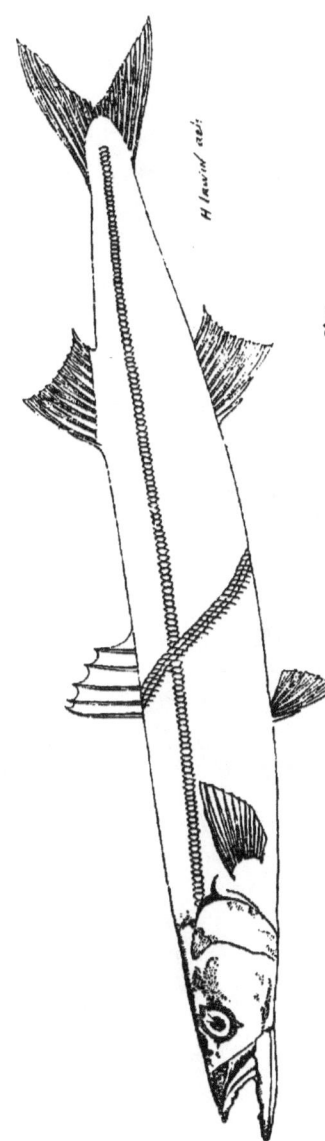

COMMON SEA-PIKE. *Sphyræna novæ-hollandiæ.*

Plate XXXI.

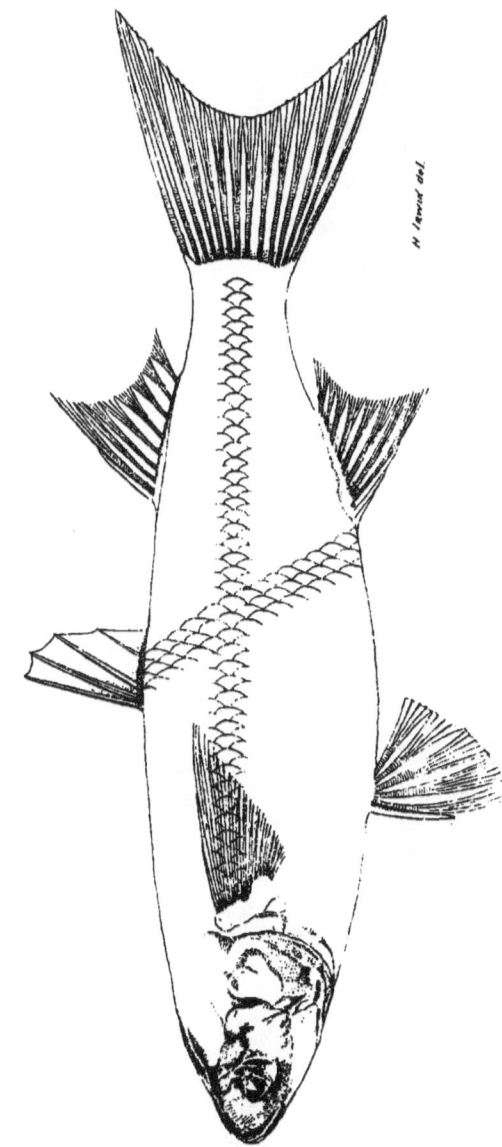

SEA MULLET.   *Mugil dobula.*

Plate XXXII.

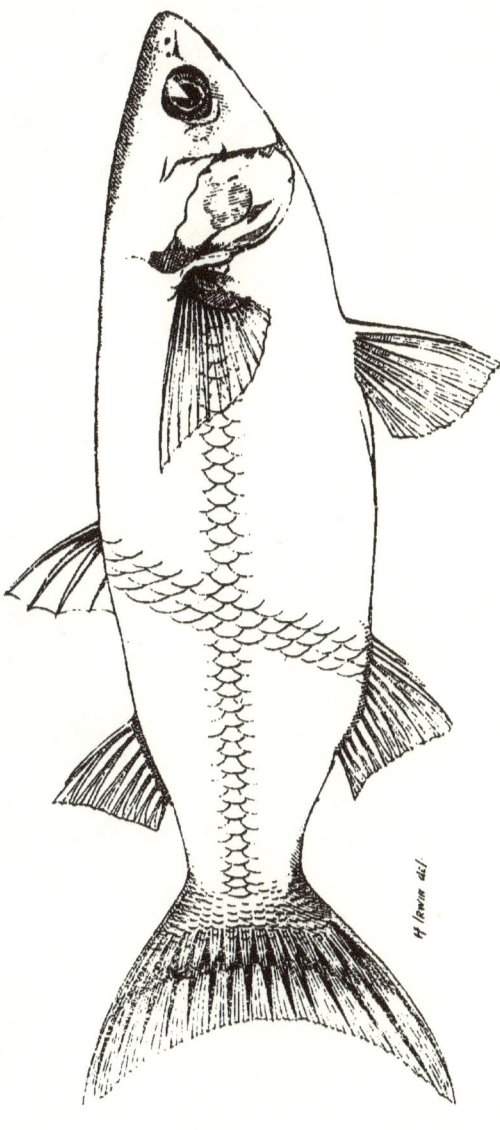

FLAT-TAILED MULLET.　*Mugil peroni.*

Plate XXXIII.

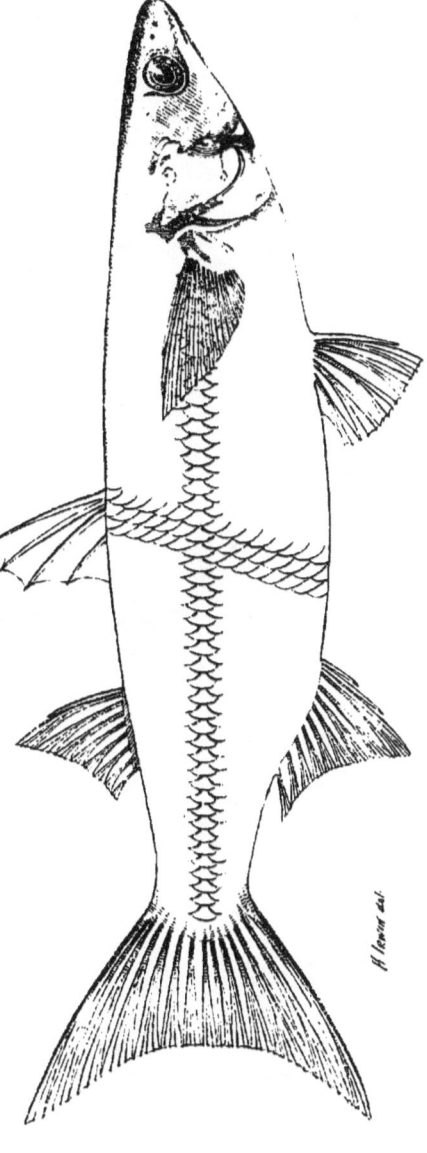

TALLEGALANE.   *Myxus elongatus.*

Plate XXXIV.

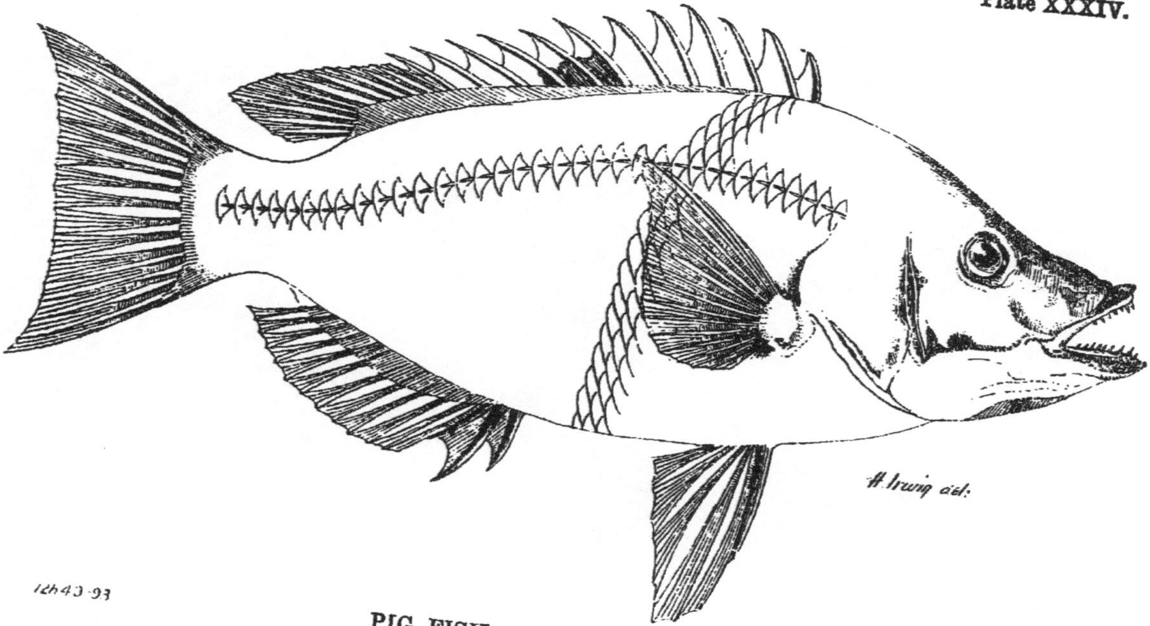

H. Irwin del.

12643·93

PIG FISH. *Cossyphus unimaculatus.*

Plate XXXV.

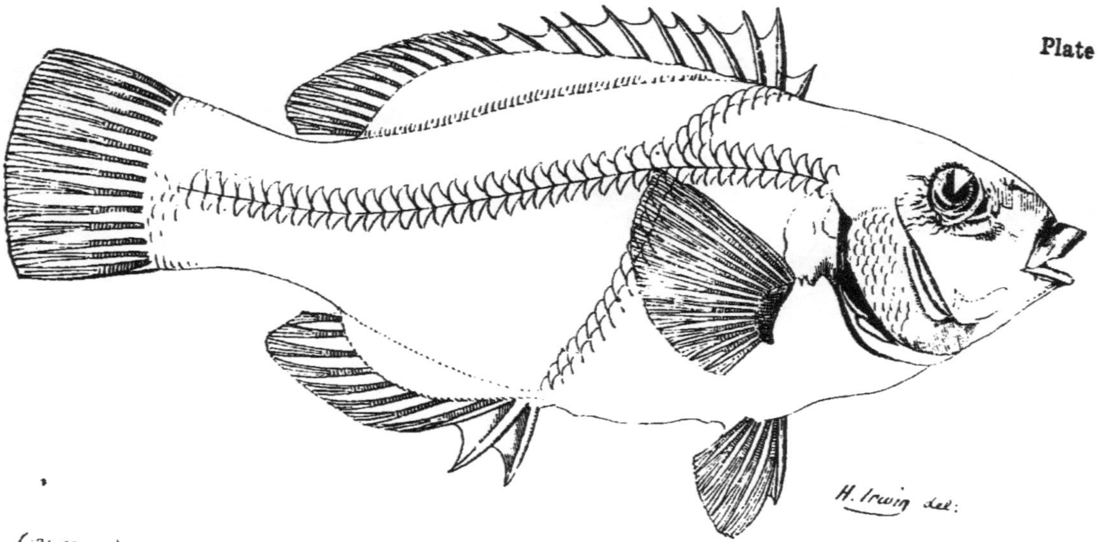

(2543-93)

BLUE GROPER. *Platychærops gouldi.*

Plate XXXVI.

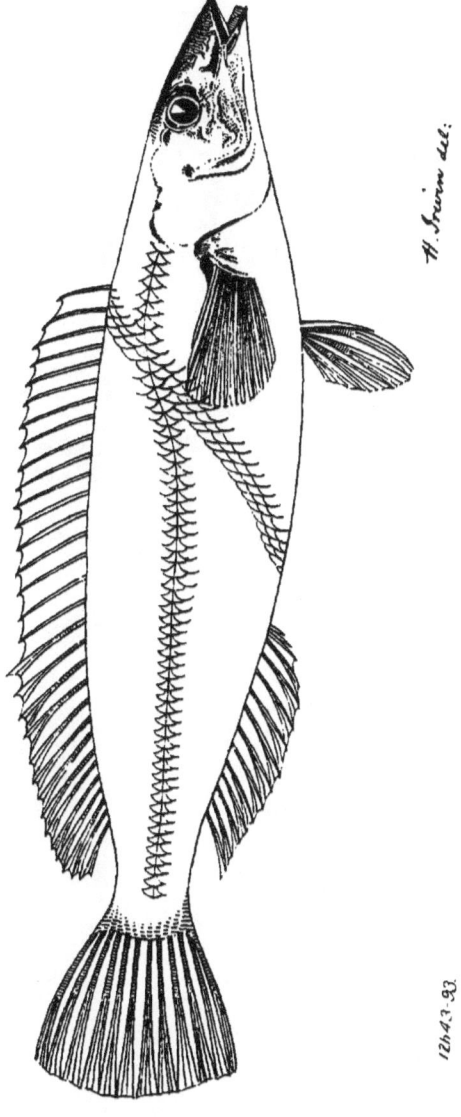

ROCK WHITING. *Odax richardsoni.*

Plate XXXVII.

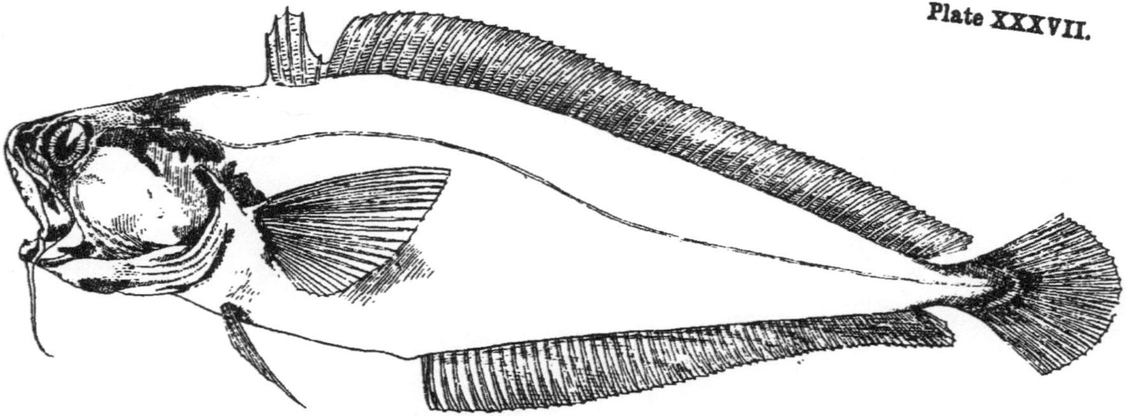

(12h 43-93)

H Irwin del:

LING. *Lotella limbata.*

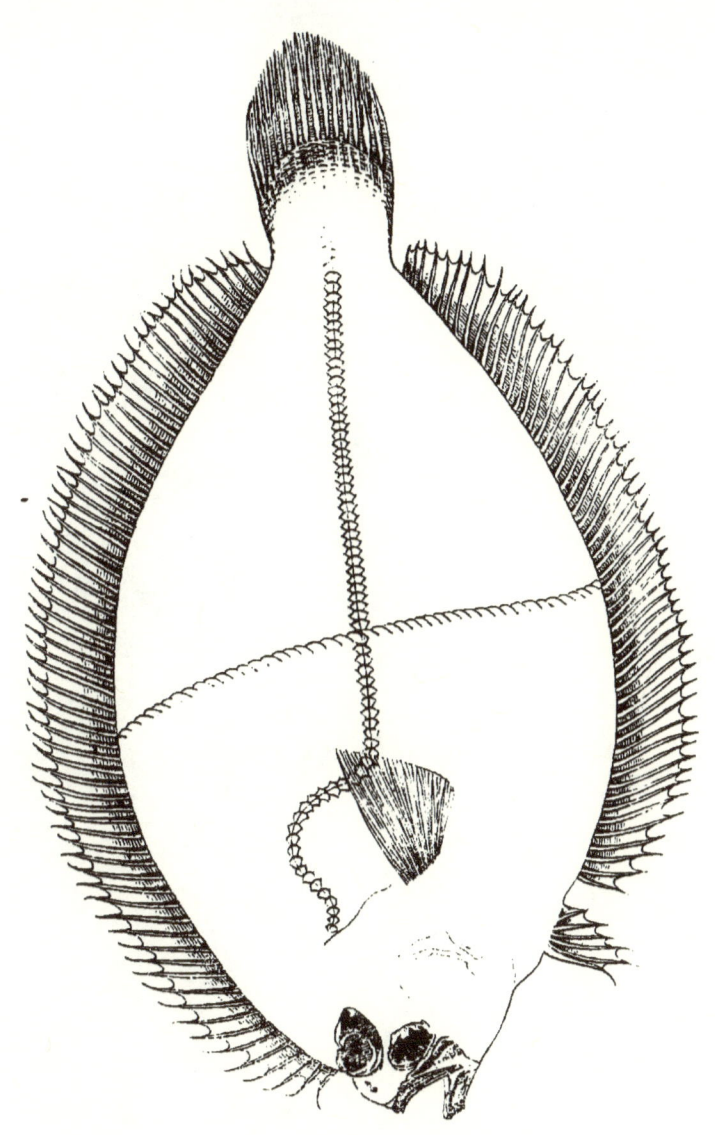

Plate XXXIX.

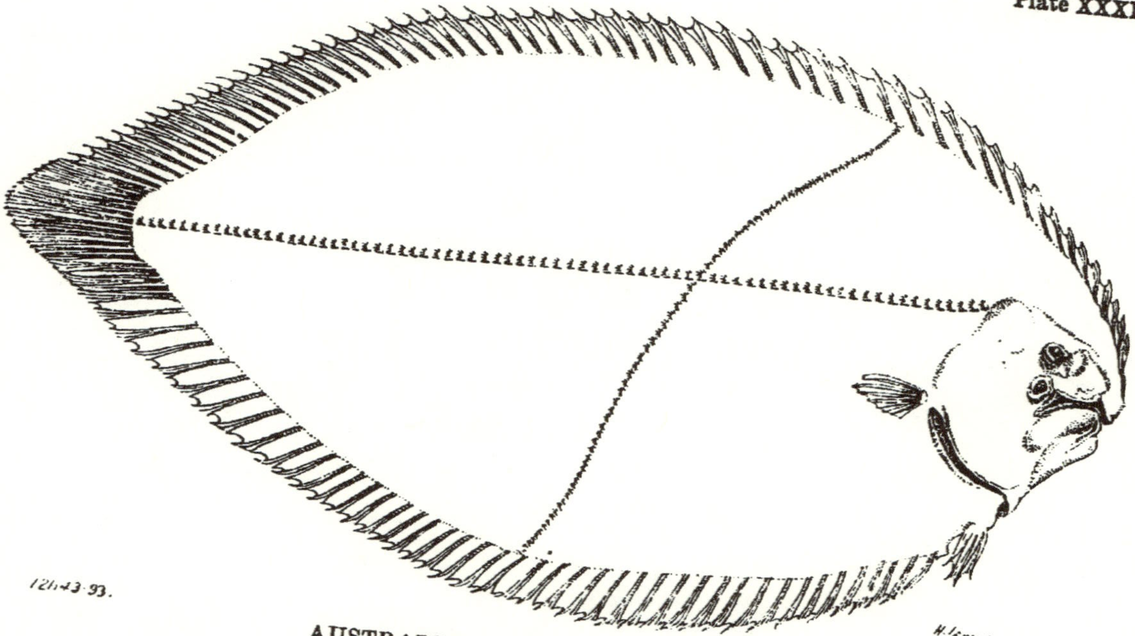

12643-93.

H. Irwin del.

AUSTRALIAN SOLE. *Synaptura nigra.*

Plate XL.

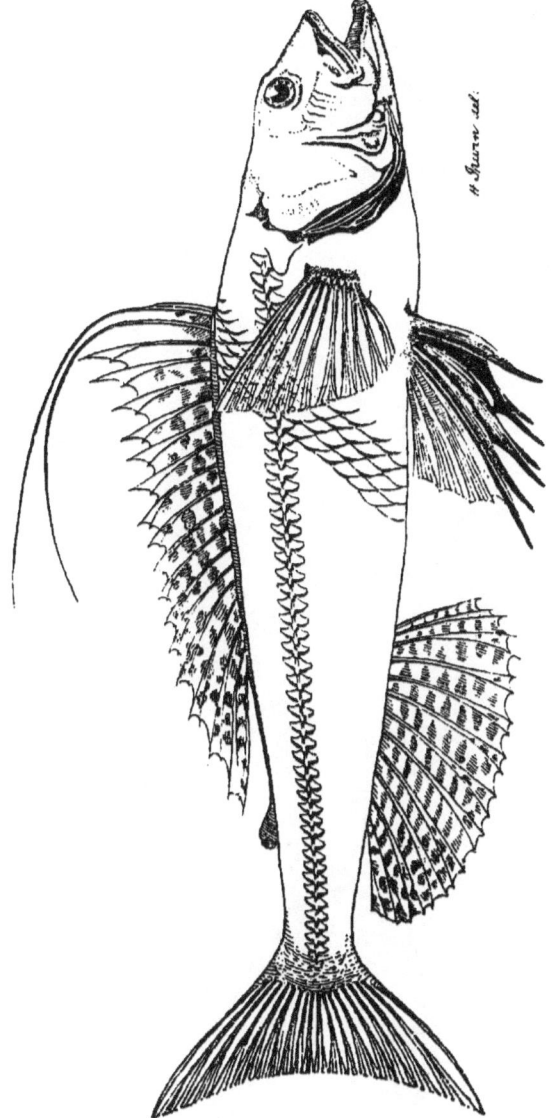

SERGEANT BAKER.   *Aulopus pupurissatus.*

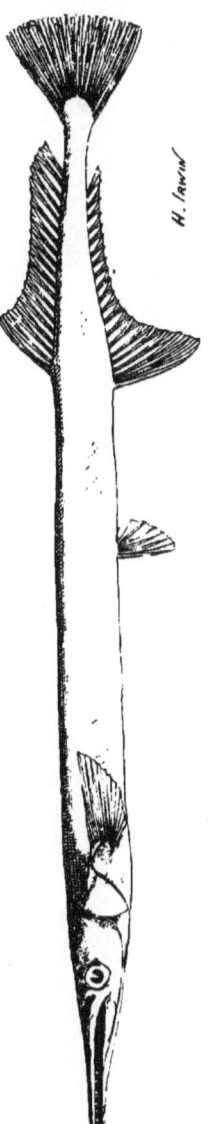

Plate XLI.

STOUT LONG TOM. *Belone macleayana.*

Plate XLII.

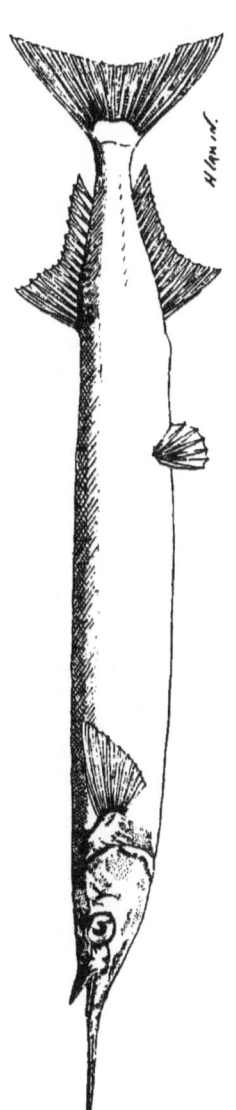

SEA GARFISH.   *Hemirhamphus intermedius.*

Plate XLIII.

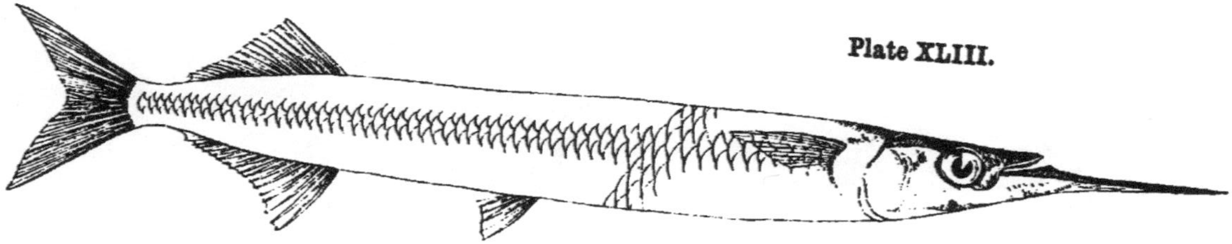

13h43-93.

RIVER GARFISH. *Hemirhamphus regularis.*

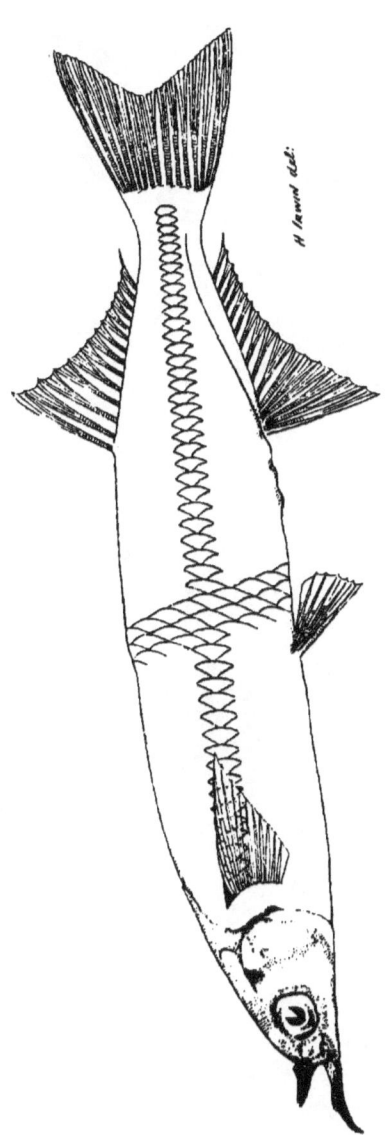

Plate XLIV.

SHORT-BEAKED GARFISH. *Arrhamphus sclerolepis.*

Plate XLV.

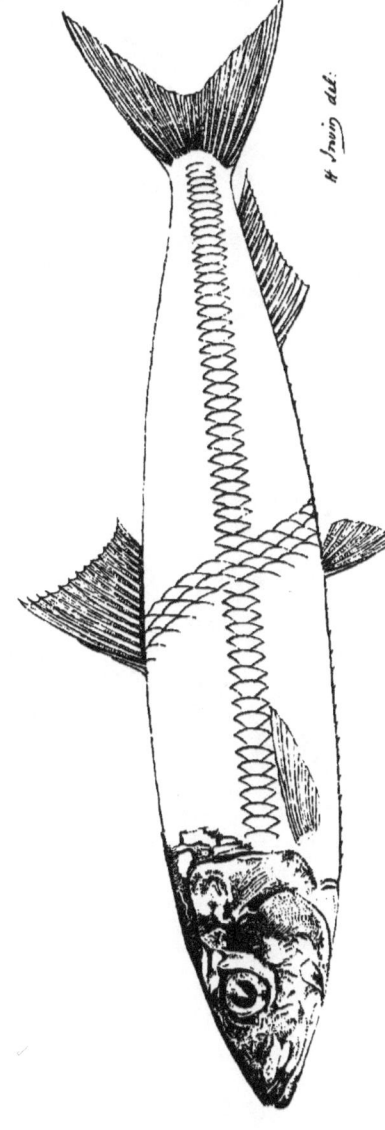

MARAY. *Clupea sagax.*

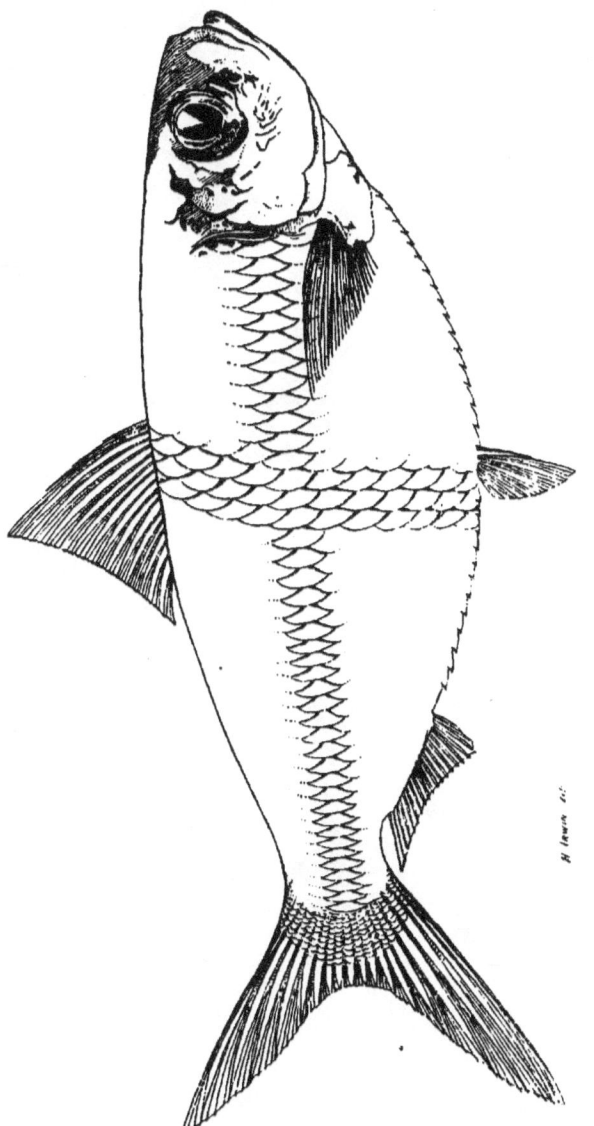

HERRING. *Clupea hypselosoma.*

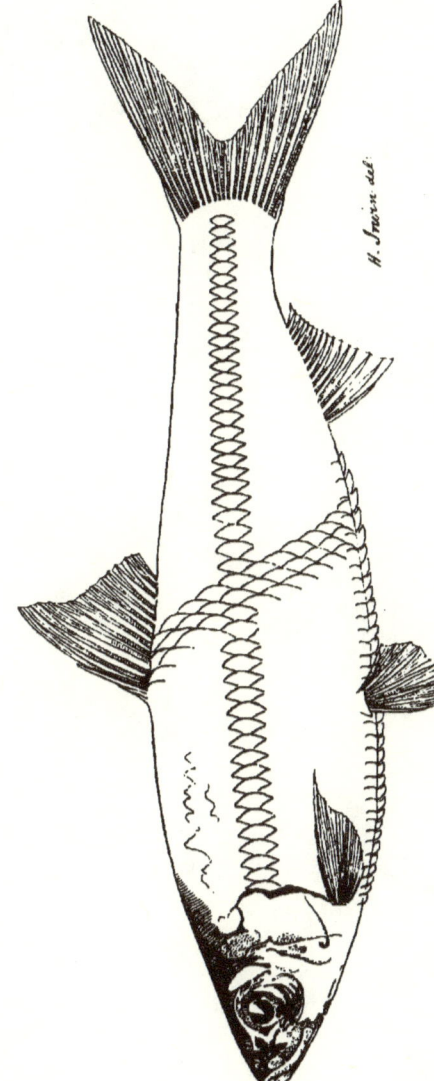

Plate XLVII.

NEPEAN HERRING. *Clupea novæ-hollandiæ.*

Plate XLVIII.

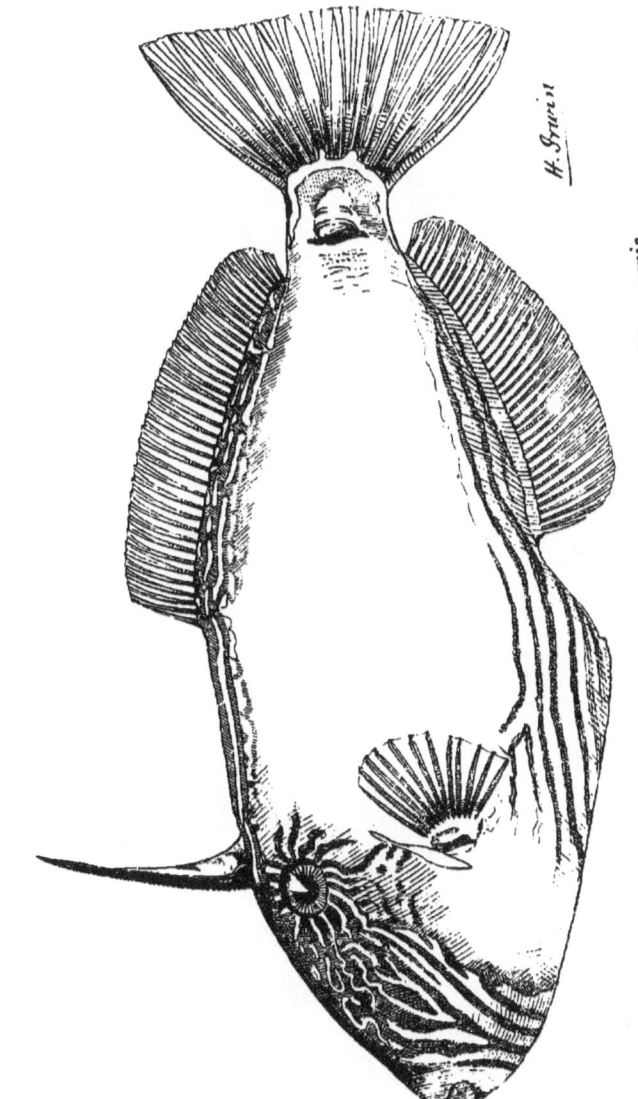

LEATHER JACKET. *Monacanthus hippocrepis.*

Plate XLIX.

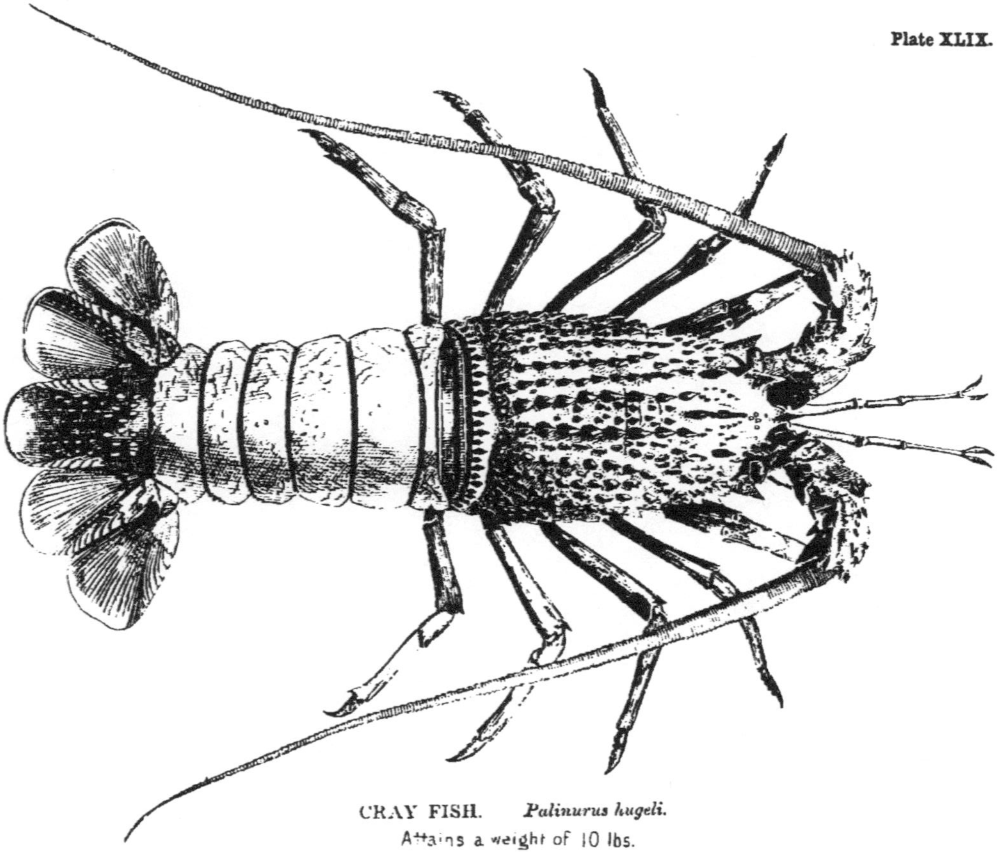

H. IRWIN DEL.

CRAY FISH. *Palinurus hugeli.*

Attains a weight of 10 lbs.

12h 43-93.

Plate L.

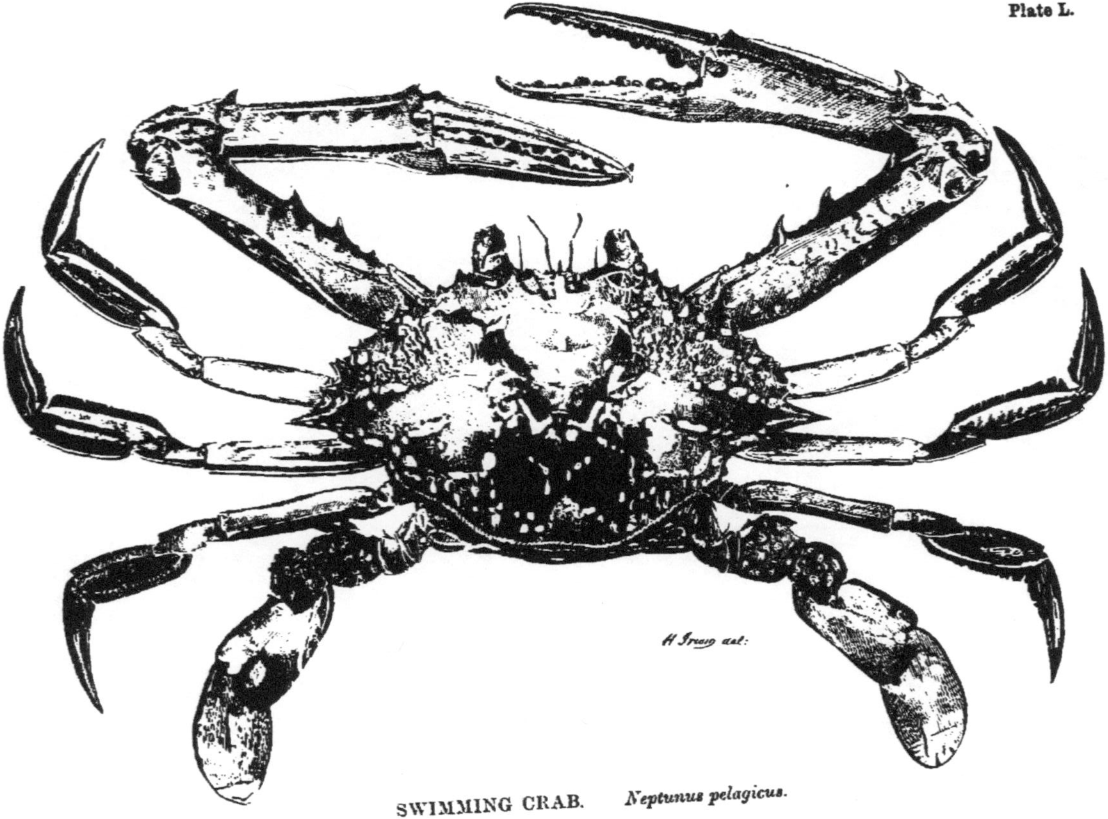

SWIMMING CRAB. *Neptunus pelagicus.*

Attains a weight of 3 lbs.

Plate LI.

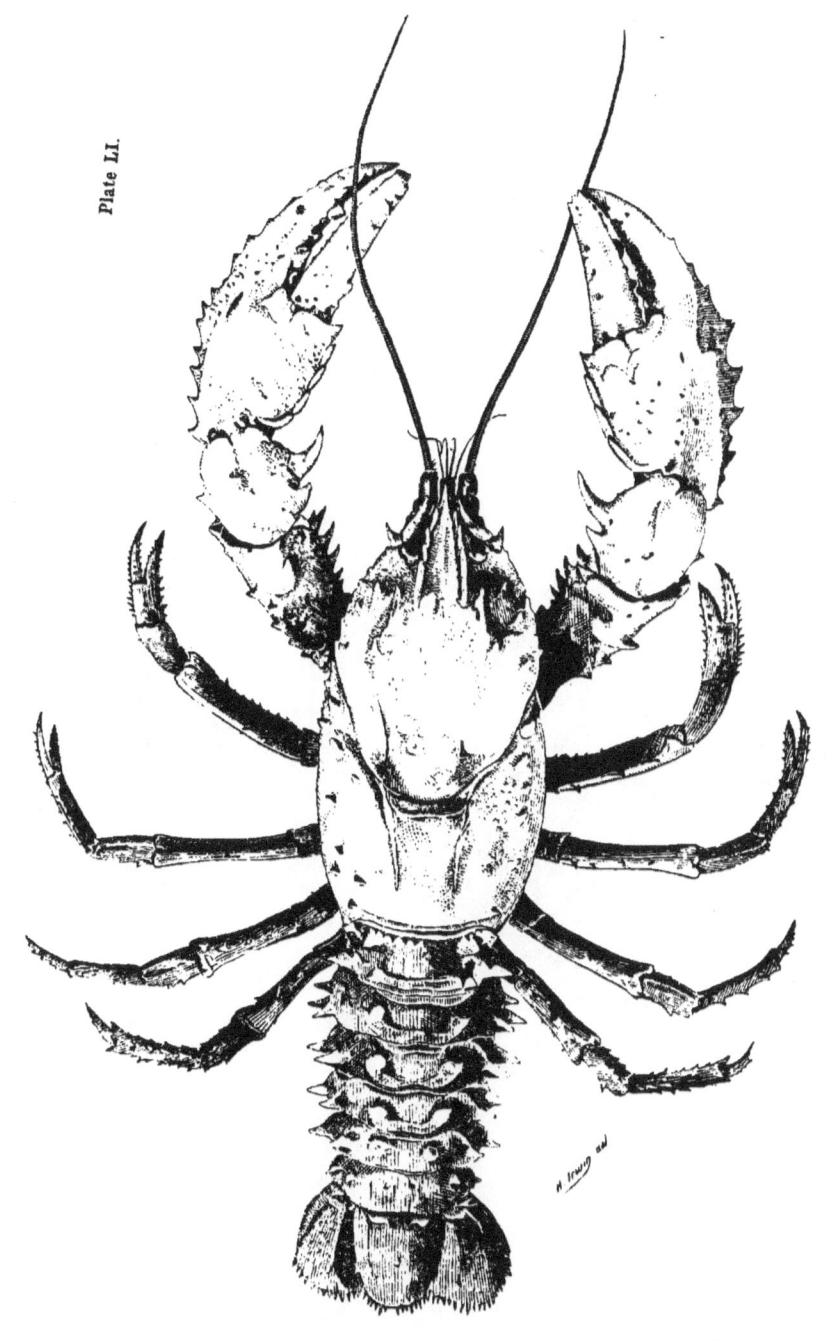